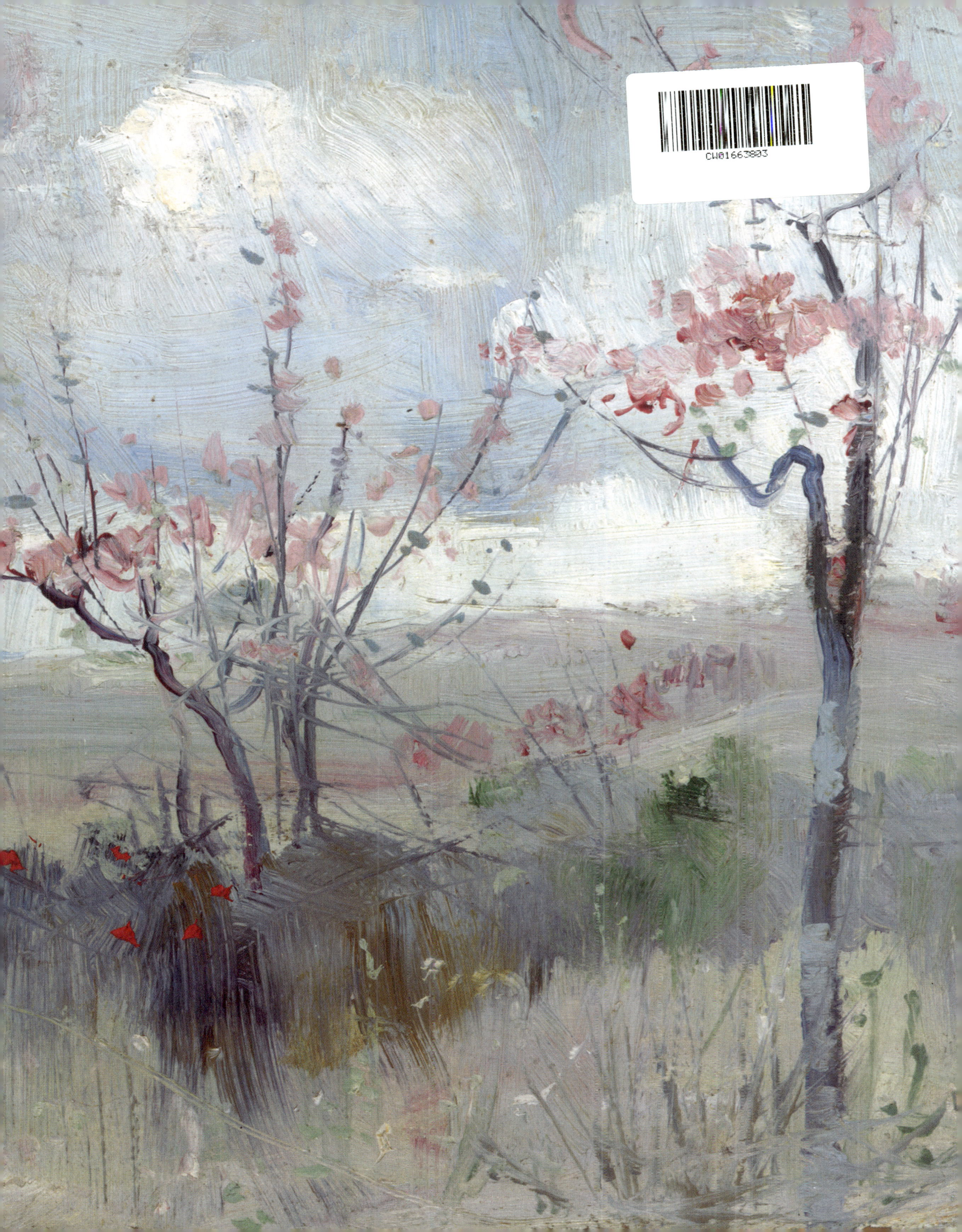

Impressionists
in their Gardens

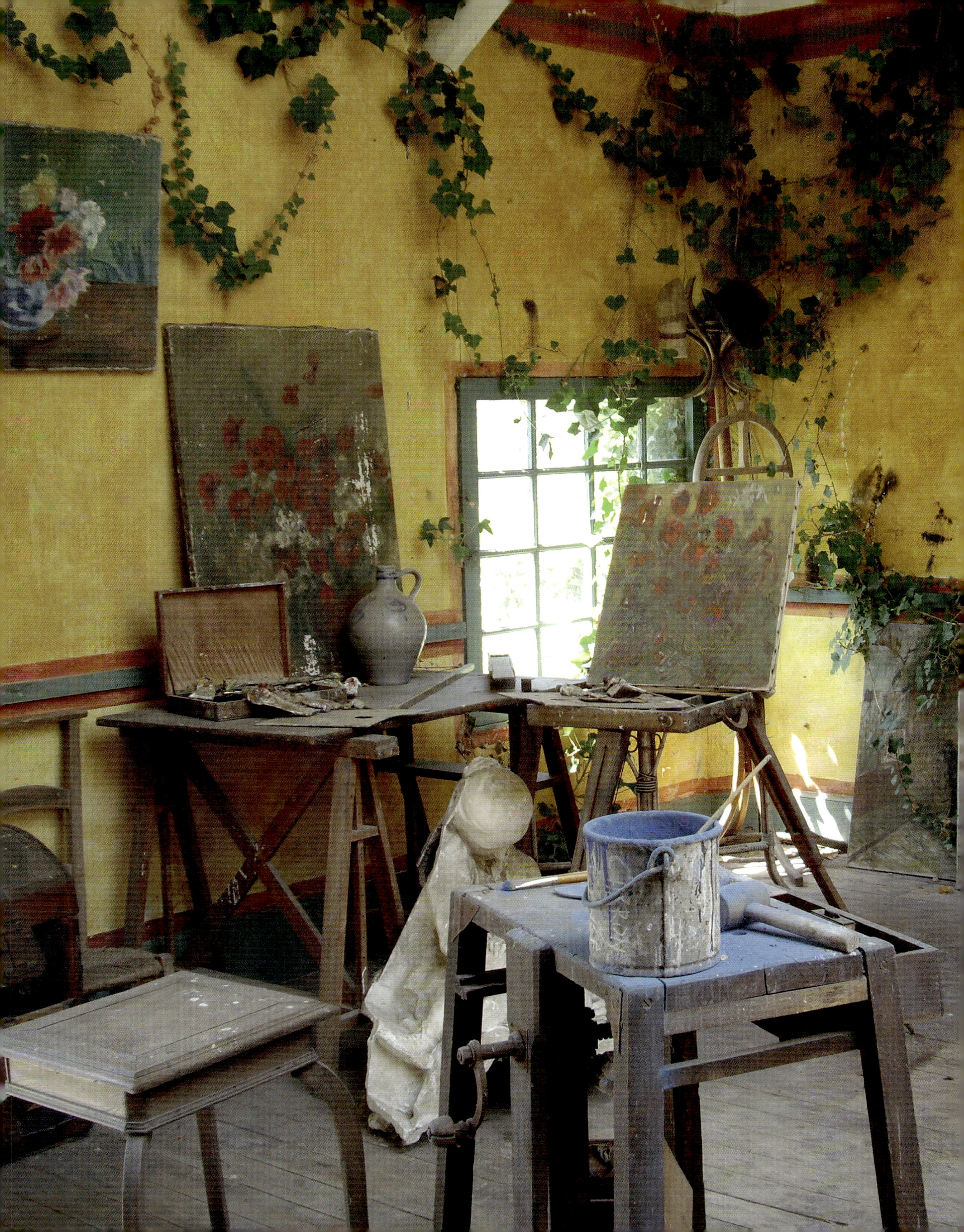

Impressionists *in their* Gardens

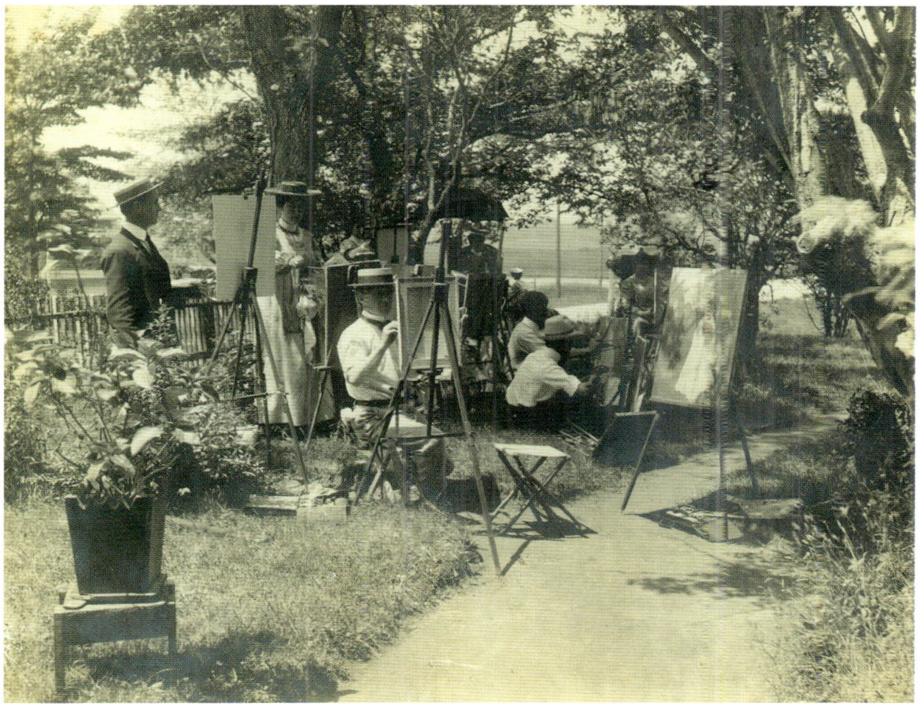

Caroline Holmes

Antique Collectors' Club

To
Craig Thomas and Rosalie
for inspiration

ACKNOWLEDGMENTS

This has been a wonderful book to write and research, enhanced by all the people who have helped me along the way. In Australia: good friends Craig Thomas and Betty Bracy, Chloe Bennett for the friends of friends link to Elena Harris and John Jones; Nick Nicholson of the National Gallery of Australia, Jennie Maloney of the National Gallery of Victoria, Mew Leng Mouy of the State Library of Victoria. Here in England Jennifer Francis of the Royal Academy, Lynda Clarke at the Fitzwilliam Museum, Cambridge and Tom Sloan at Getty Images. In America: Judith Felz of Glebe House Gertrude Jekyll Garden; Ron Sher of the Shoals Marine Laboratory and Tammi Flynn and Nichole Wholean of the Florence Griswold Museum. Last but not least, in France Rob Sheldon of SARL Latour-Marliac.

It has also been the first book that I have written since being able to access broadband in the wilds of Suffolk, and what treasures awaited me in museums and galleries around the world. What a box of delights is available, a combination of world class artists and modern designers.

Huge thanks to the wonderful team at ACC, not least Diana Steel for inviting me to write the book, Catherine Britton for stellar, astute and cheerful editing and Lynn Taylor for her excellent work on the book design. Eternal gratitude to David for loving support, copy reading and keeping the home fires burning during one of the coldest winters. And, as promised, thank you Harry for the comma.

In summer visits can be made to the Isle of Shoals from Portsmouth, Maine, details are available on:
https://www.sml.cornell.edu/sml_reservation.php

PICTURE CREDITS

Art Institute of Chicago 15, 89, 110-1, 133, 138, 170-1; Bowes Museum 167; Bridgeman Art/Getty Images 19, 49, 61, 71, 73, 75, 79, 84-5, 86-7, 92-3, 98/99, 131, 147, 148, 177; Carnegie Museum of Art, Pittsburgh 27, 59; Fitzwilliam Museum Cambridge 52-3, 90; Pat Crocker 35, 39, 109; Florence Griswold Museum, Connecticut 22, 102-3, 109; Steve Kemp 34, 41, 78, 81, 82, 83; Musee d Orsay, Paris 158-9; National Gallery of Australia 24-5, 36-7, 94-5, 174-5; National Gallery of New South Wales 143; National Gallery of Victoria 64/65, 140-1, 152-3, 155, 158-9, 164-5; Royal Academy courtesy Thomas Gibson Fine Arts 70; Scala Archives for Metropolitan Museum of Art, New York 67/68, 132; Scala Archives for Smithsonian American Art Museum 101, 106, 113, 134-5, 139, 150-1, 185; Shoals Marine Laboratory, New Hampshire 11, 108, 115, 172, 180; Surrey History Centre/Gertrude Jekyll Estate www.gertrudejekyll.co.uk 17, 20-1, 119; Elena Taylor 160, 161; Terra Museum of Art, Chicago 9, 30-1, 54-5, 76-7; David Austin Roses 29. All other photographs Caroline Holmes.

Every effort has been made to secure permission to reproduce the images contained within this book, and we are grateful to the individuals and institutions who have assisted in this task. Any errors or omissions are entirely unintentional, and the details should be addressed to the publisher.

ISBN 978 185149 653 2

British Library CIP Data
A catalogue record for this book
is available from the British Library

Printed in China
for the Antique Collectors' Club Ltd., Woodbridge, Suffolk IP12 4SD

CONTENTS

Through the Garden Gate

Gardeners cannot escape the natural vagaries of a late frost, autumn tempest or summer drought but the play of light, dancing breezes and visiting birds can be shaped by human husbandry. The enclosure of the garden acts like a picture frame showcasing a living canvas that exudes the individuality, vision and taste of its tenants, their family, friends, lifestyles and, in the simple words of the greatest Impressionist gardener Monet, providing motifs to paint. Going further into the canvas, in 1895 he explained to a Norwegian journalist: "To me the motif itself is an insignificant factor; what I want to reproduce is what lies between the motif and me …"

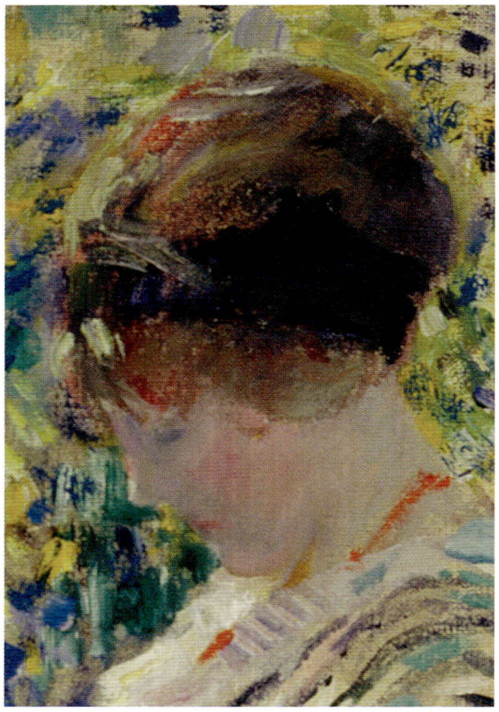

Frederick Frieseke, **Lady in a Garden***. Oil on canvas, 81 x 65.4cm (31⅞ x 25¾ in.), c.1912*

Monet's was not the only artist's garden in Giverny. The green shutters glimpsed in the top right hand corner of this painting identify the setting as Le Hameau which was occupied by Frederick and Sarah Frieseke between 1906 and 1919. The whole painting shimmers in vertical accents – the gladioli adding flashes of red around the lady's fashionable striped dress. She poses in a cloud of what appear to be hydrangea blooms, an equally fashionable and symbolic plant that threads a narrative through this book. The painting pervades an overwhelming sense of peace, scent and privacy.

The comforts of domestic life have become so advanced that we can now magic heating or air conditioning at the flick of a switch. In contrast, the artists and gardeners working in the open air are as much at one with the elements as our earliest ancestors. This artistic connection with nature is never more evident than in the work of the Impressionists, many of whose gardens are in rural regions such as Normandy, Brittany, Provence, Maine, Connecticut, and Victoria. In Australia, Impressionism shelters under its own unique umbrella: its artists took their academic influences equally from the Royal Academy School in London and the French Impressionists. However, unlike Europe or America, the centre of their continent was barely mapped, so they attempted to capture the life and spirit of that dawn before it was put to purpose.

Monet, Caillebotte, Manet and Renoir were all gardening before 1874 when a dismissive critic wrote that Monet's *Impression: Soleil Levant* was just that – a mere impression – and so the name was adopted. They recognised that the fecundity and fruits of the soil were sensuous treats within their power (albeit there are anguished records of horticultural disasters around the great gardens of Monet at Giverny and Gertrude Jekyll at Munstead Wood). In fact Monet and Jekyll used the same nurseries and gardened many similar trees and flowers but, as far as we know, the great Impressionist and the English Impressionist gardener were unknown to each other. They planted their flowers in drifts with careful attention to the harmony of colours created and shared a zeal for perfection, despite both suffering increasingly poor eyesight at the end of their lives. Curiously the discordant notes of dead flowerheads were easier for them to spot with their unfocussed sight, than for their fully sighted gardeners. Failure to adequately deadhead their floral displays was a flaw they would spot at a considerable distance.

In the mid 1830s, artists of the Ecole 1830 (also known as the Barbizon School), based themselves in and around Barbizon, south-east of Paris, where they rediscovered nature's wild and rugged form in the

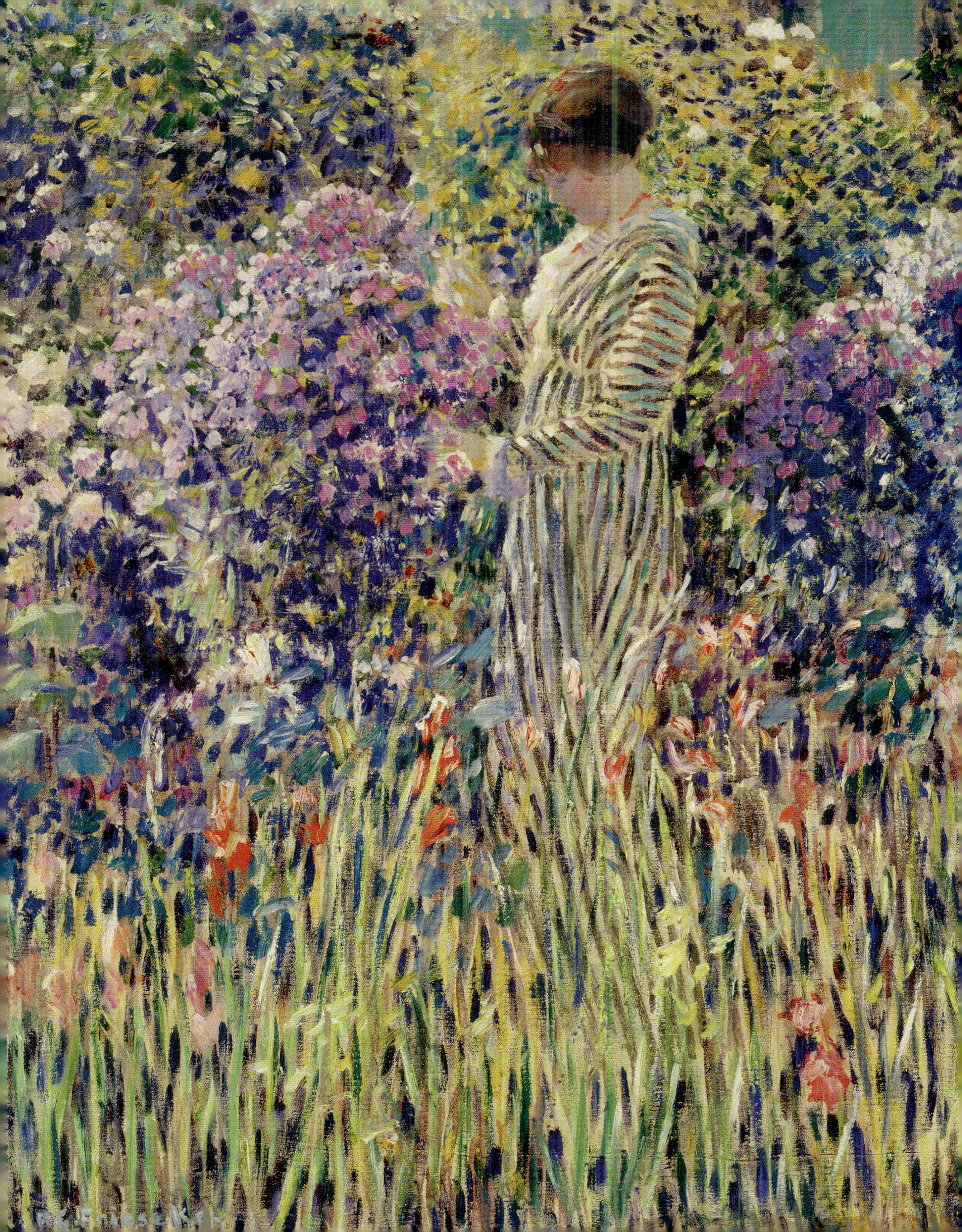

forests of Fontainebleau; meanwhile, thousands of miles away on New Year's Day 1837 the plant collector Sir Robert Schomburgk was paddling through titanic foliage on the River Berbere in Demerara, Guyana. He had rediscovered the vast round leaves and luxuriant highly scented flowers of the Great Water Lily. It would be another three years before he successfully dispatched seeds, and another six before William Hooker of Kew had 30-40 seedlings to give away, one went to Joseph Paxton, Head Gardener to the Duke of Devonshire at Chatsworth. In a tale of horticultural derring-do the race was on to successfully bring the first Great Water Lily into flower and Paxton won. He presented the first flower to the Queen for whom it had been named *Victoria regia*, demonstrating the plant's strength by standing his seven-year-old daughter Annie on one of the leaves. This media scoop was recreated in an engraving, which appeared in the *Illustrated London News*, but the story did not stop there.

The strength of the leaves lies in the underlying network of thick bracing ribs, which create a network of air pockets that ensure their buoyancy. Inspired by the lily's foliar engineering Paxton magnified its design into a glass building 1,848 feet long by 456 feet wide at its broadest point and 108 feet tall into its transept. It was a building to house 'The Great Exhibition of the Works of Industry of all Nations' which

Renoir spent the last years of his life at Les Collettes (below) in the south of France. The Roses 'Painter Renoir' are still flowering in late September, planted around the orange trees below the house. You can just see the tops of the trimmed agapanthus, in season their flowers provide a haze of blue flowers to edge the view up the garden from the lower path.

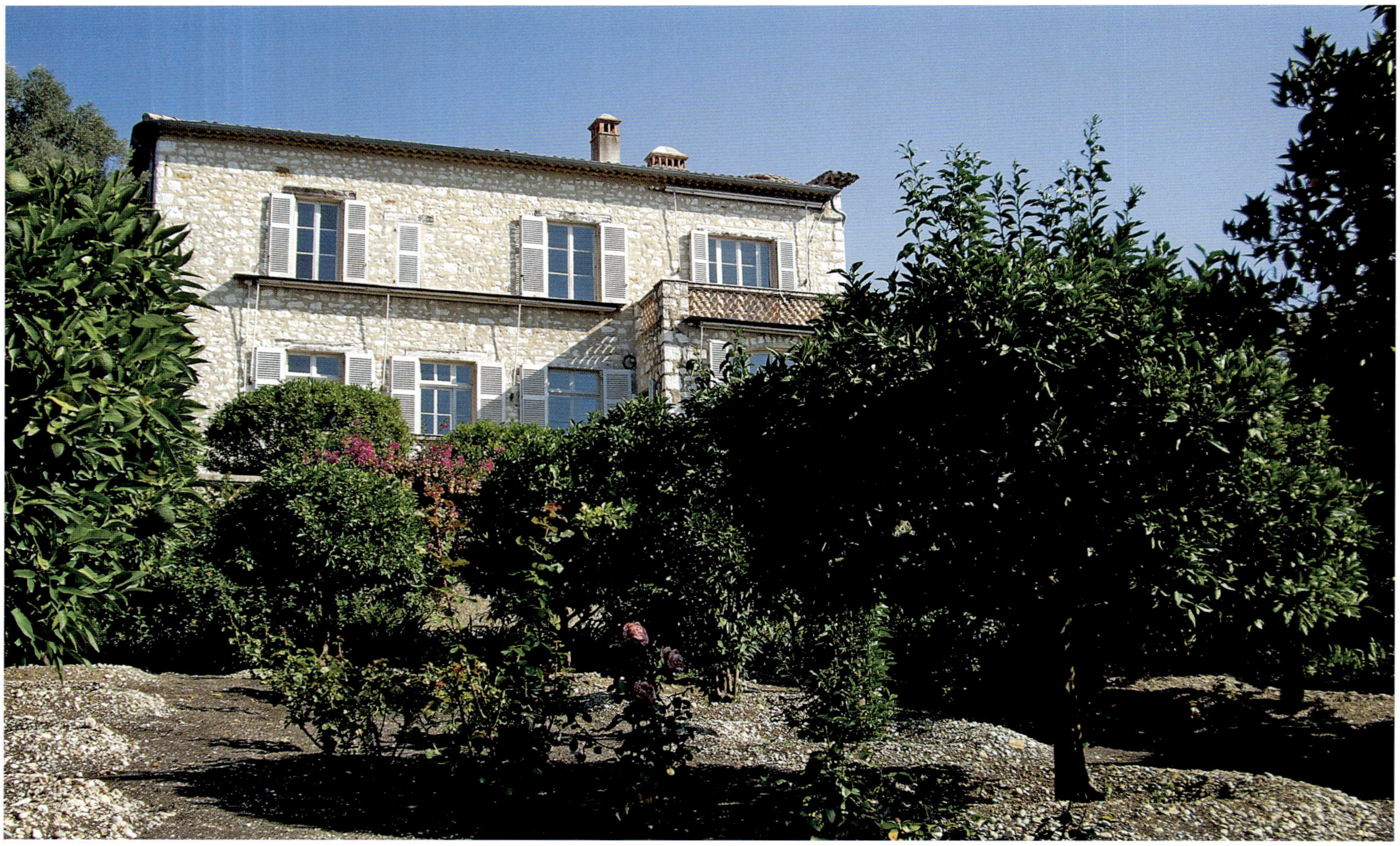

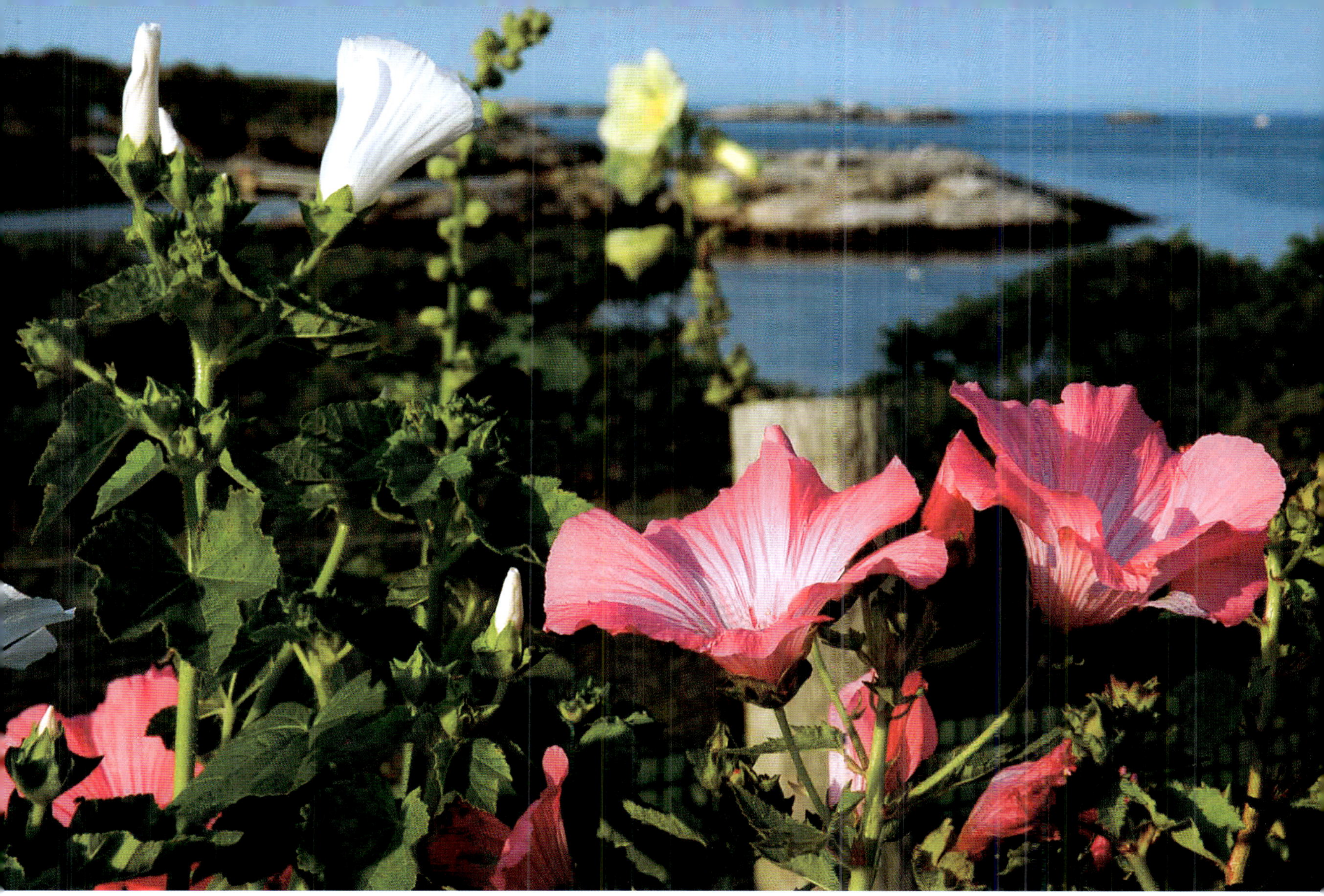

opened in Hyde Park on 1 May in 1851, and *Punch* christened it 'The Crystal Palace'. Although not the first great national exhibition in the world (Napoleon Bonaparte had already created an area on the Champs de Mars in Paris), it was the first on an international scale. At the same time, many of the Impressionists were still in school, but the series of exhibitions celebrating revolutions and empire over the following decades would all be of significance.

The World's Fair Centennial International Exhibition of 1876 celebrating the 100th anniversary of the signing of the American Declaration of Independence, was held in Philadelphia's Fairmont Park, billed as 'an International Exhibition of Arts, Manufactures and Products of the Soil and Mine'. It also kindled a sense of colonial heritage: this took the form of a revival of cottage gardens filled with 'olden tyme' nostalgic plants, to be perfected from the early 1880s by the poet Celia Thaxter at Appledore, Maine, a flowery setting with wafts of scent, music and the spoken word. Although cottage garden artists sought to instill the notion of the cottage idyll as an exemplar for 'olden tyme' morality and homely values, the Impressionists did not. Their expressive brushwork of nodding violets, blowsy poppies and tall hollyhocks were vehicles to capture light and evoke emotions. The writings of Celia Thaxter and the paintings of Childe Hassam inspired by the gardens around Appledore, became a serendipitous mixture.

Hardy and handsome hollyhocks, their flowers cupping the sun, creating a colour sensation of pink, white and blue. A cottage favourite, these tall floriferous biennials decorate many of the Impressionist gardens and are captured here with the ocean that surrounds the Isles of Shoals off the New England coast, in the poet Celia Thaxter's restored gardens of Appledore.

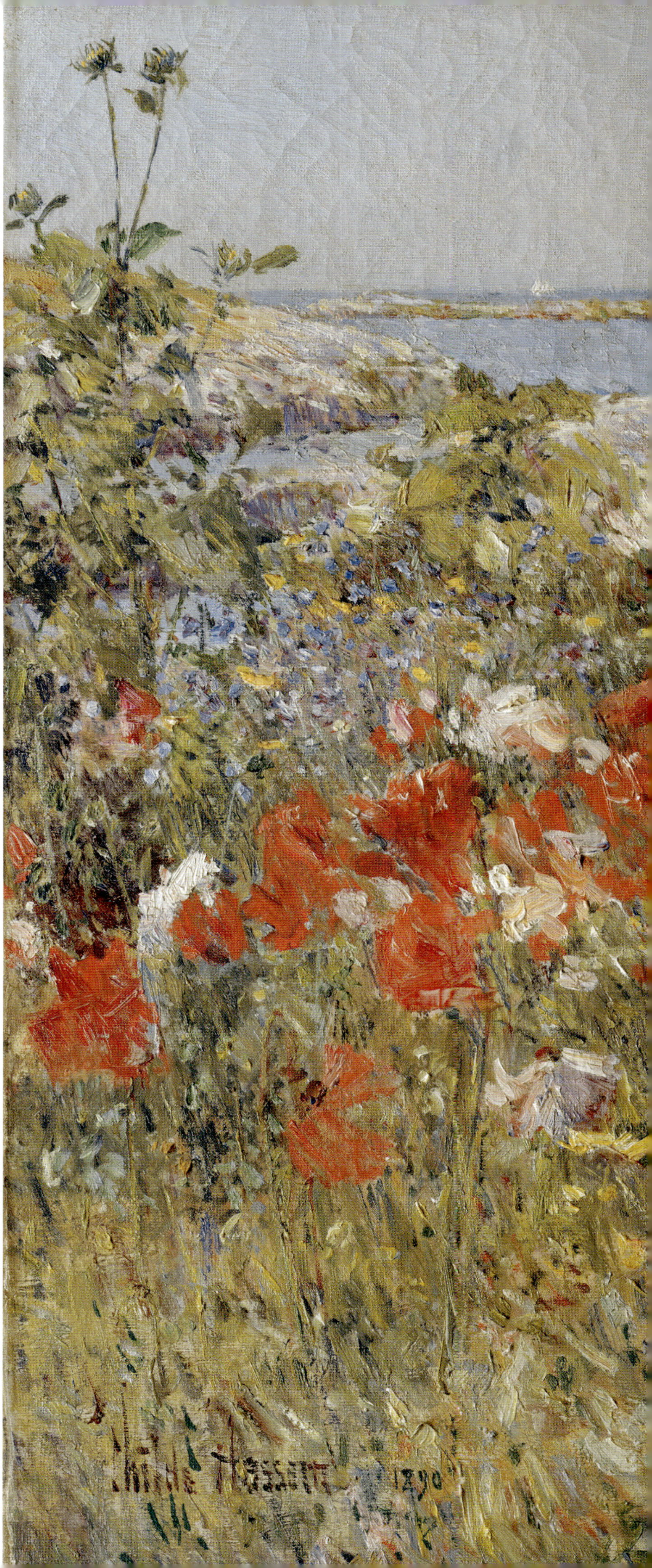

Childe Hassam, **Celia Thaxter's Garden, Isles of Shoals, Maine**. *Oil on canvas, 45 x 54cm (17 x 21in.), 1890*

Oceans and seas are relentlessly powerful, whether it is the silky smoothness of calm mill pond conditions or the adrenalin rush of breakers, they leave their impressions on mind and body. The water is in charge, it seems also to dictate the light, and it is no wonder that its magnificence features in the vast majority of Impressionist works. In contrast to the almighty power of the water, the control of the human hand is beautifully displayed in the colourful waves of flowers in Thaxter's lush gardens. They lap around the ocean view to the sun-bleached Babb's Rock.

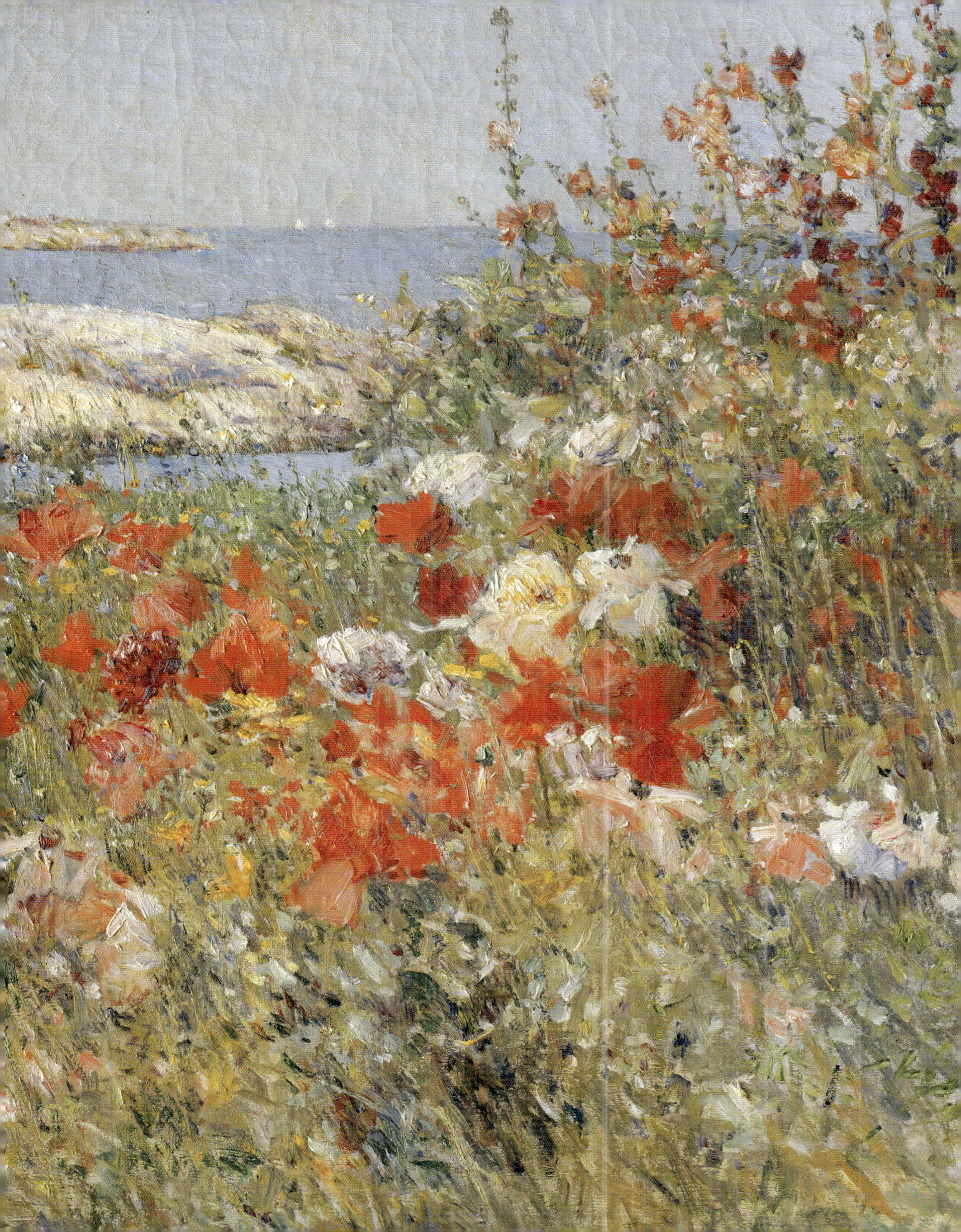

With a decidedly imperial focus 'Marvellous Melbourne' staged the Centennial International Exhibition to celebrate the centenary of European settlement in Australia which opened on 1 August 1888 in The Royal Exhibition Building. The Fine Arts Courts displayed over 3,000 paintings from Great Britain (including those of J.M.W. Turner), Germany, France and Italy. The wife of the Governor, Lady Loch, claimed that the display of the British Loan pictures were the saving of the exhibition financially – they attracted such continuous crowds of visitors.

A year later France hosted the Exposition Universelle, an exhibition of fine, decorative and industrial arts designed to celebrate the centenary of the French Revolution; the 'temporary' structure of the Eiffel Tower set in the Champs de Mars was 'softened' with the planting of over 100,000 tulips. Undeniably the world leader in the history of art and its latest development, Impressionism, France had, however, been lagging behind industrially and technologically. The Eiffel Tower now gave the world both something to look up to, and something to look down into, in the form of Latour-Marliac's tanks of water lilies which showcased innovative hybridisction.

Four hundred years after Columbus 'sailed the ocean blue', Chicago hosted the World's Columbian Exposition during 1892-3 which featured Impressionist paintings and extensive plantings of water lilies. Murals (now lost) included Mary Fairchild MacMonnies' *Primitive Woman*, which was displayed facing Mary Cassatt's *Modern Woman*. Cassatt's murals used symbolic imagery such as *Young Woman Plucking the Fruits of Knowledge* and *Young Woman Pursuing Fame*, a sense of which can be gained from her 1891 painting *Young Women Picking Fruit*. J. Carroll Beckwith also painted murals for the Liberal Arts Building in which he displayed his conviction that art should embody the technical refinement of form, colour, and expression. Water lilies were dispatched from France to the States for the exhibition and Lincoln Park in Chicago was transformed by its superintendent J.S. Pettigrew with 'every kind he could obtain' including heating one basin with pipes for an exotic display. Just five years later when William Tricker published *The Water Garden*, in which he praised the parks of Chicago for being leaders in the fashion for aquatic gardening with an illustration of the pool in Union Park.

The American market was the first to actively collect Impressionist paintings, which in turn inspired their own young painters, tired of narrow artistic traditions at home, to seek the greater freedom of France. They set up colonies in and around Giverny, many staying at the Hotel Baudy where their *atelier* still survives. Later in 1912 Frederick Frieseke wrote of his years in Giverny, 'It is sunshine, flowers in sunshine, girls in sunshine, the nude in sunshine which I have been principally interested in for eight years'.

Of Irish extraction, the English gardener and journalist William Robinson was vitriolic in his criticism of formality in gardens quoting William Morris' ability to blush 'when quite alone' at the thought of bedding plants. Robinson sought to get the British nation, if not the Empire, to create 'gardens of lovely colour and form, free from the pastry cook gardener'. Amongst many plants he popularised through his writings in

John Henry Twachtman, **The White Bridge**. *Oil on canvas, 77 x 77cm (30¼ x 30¼ in.), after 1895*

Described as the most poetic and abstract of the American Impressionists, John Henry Twachtman was part of the Cos Cob Colony who painted in and around Greenwich, Connecticut. He bought land to create a house and garden for his family using traditional methods and materials. The swiftly flowing Horseneck Brook provided the perfect division between the flower gardens near the house and the naturalistic wild gardens. The white bridge that spanned the two gardens was painted around 1895, before Monet's first depiction of his Japanese Bridge.

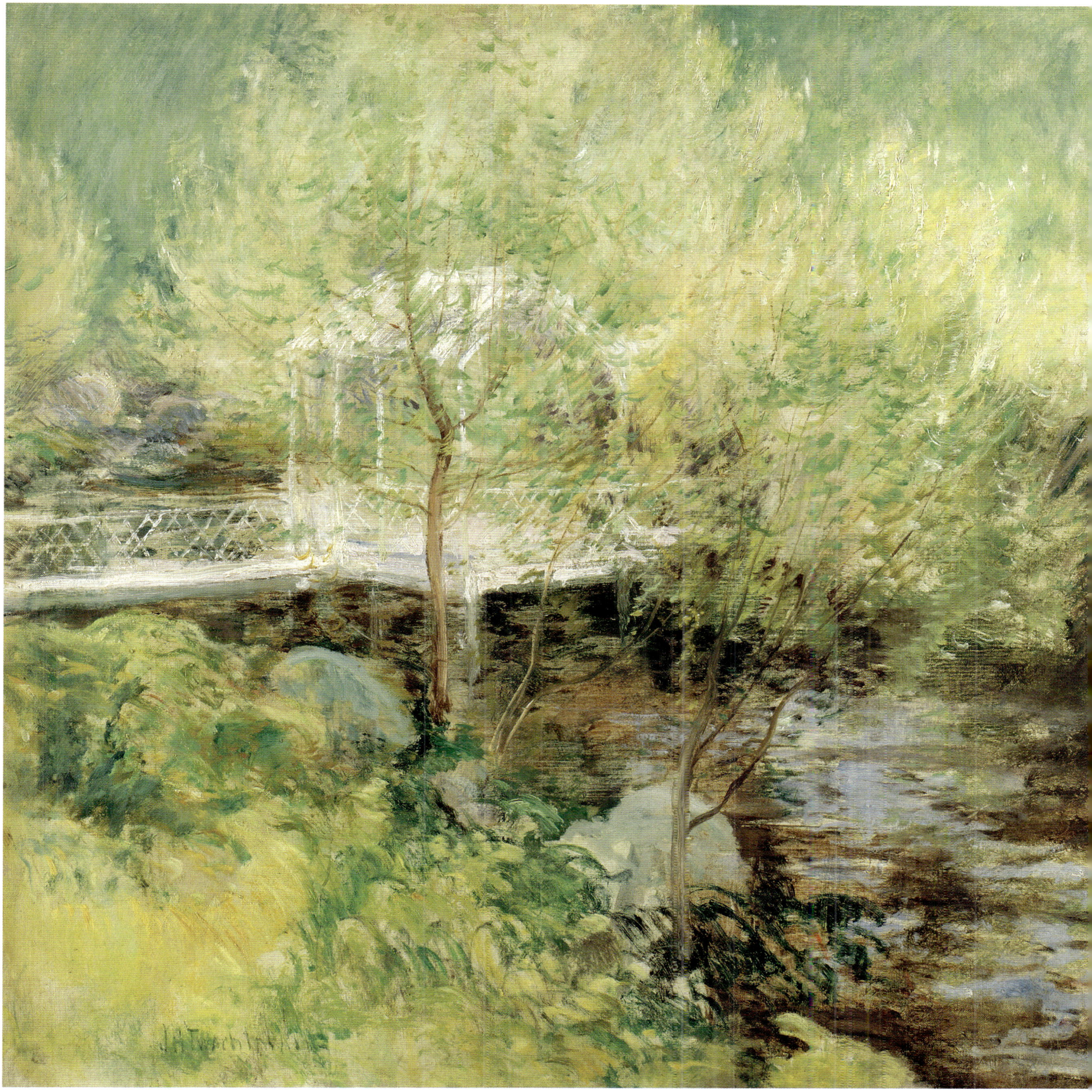

Gertrude Jekyll, **Campagne Maheiddin – Bougainvillaea**. *Watercolour, 27.6 x 37cm (11 x 14¾in.), c.1873-4*

Jekyll spent the winter of 1873-4 in Algiers with her good friend Madame Bodichon, studying arabic decoration and design. Her attention was drawn beyond the craze for Arab horses and sheiks to the bougainvillaea, pomegranates and asphodels that were used to soften the edges of gardens and buildings. Both Renoir and Monet were sent to Algeria during their national service, and both claimed that the glaring intense sunlight, radiant blue skies and seas seared into their collective memories. Renoir said that he had discovered the value of white in Algeria adding: 'And against it, the green of the orange trees and the grey of the fig trees'. When he returned from a second trip in 1881, his paintings included harsh rocks and drought resistant plants such as palms and agaves that in turn inspired his later use of them at Les Collettes. In April wisteria flowers seem to festoon themselves across the entire French and Italian Riviera, followed by the rather longer-lasting bougainvillea whose display continues to the end of October. Incidentally it is not the bougainvillea flowers but its bracts that radiate the colours.

both Britain and America, were those Impressionist stalwarts, the water lily and clematis. Gertrude Jekyll was a good friend of Robinson and shared his sentiments if not his vitriol. She had been gardening at Munstead Wood for sixteen years when her first book, *Wood and Garden*, was published in 1899; its arts and crafts sentiments regarding gardening were already popular in America and she soon found an enthusiastic readership there. Jekyll was also an excellent photographer, thus enabling her to illustrate all her books copiously, capturing the characteristics that matched her words.

The hand of the so-called 'pastry cook gardener' so despised by Robinson could be easily seen in most municipal parks in Europe, north America and Australia. No matter how far flung a colony of the British Empire, and regardless of weather, the colonial administration would create parks and especially rose gardens that offered a breath of home. However, Australians were waking up to a sense of nationhood, one in proud possession of an extensive flora that was avidly collected by Kew and plant hunters but had not been the subject of centuries of formal landscape painting, and was artistically, and in reality, still virgin ground. Gardening with native trees and shrubs that were adapted to heat and drought was visually and decoratively appealing, and helped to create a natural expression of Australian individuality.

There are surviving photographs of every artist mentioned in this book and, if they had one, of their gardens, but there is one major exception: Vincent Van Gogh who after the age of nineteen avoided the camera. During the major 2010 Royal Academy Exhibition 'The Real Van Gogh' David Hockney commented that 'Van Gogh was looking at the world in a different way. He makes us see a great deal more than the camera could. Most people who actually saw his subjects – the flat landscape around Arles, for instance – would have found them incredibly uninteresting. But if you had locked him in the dullest motel room in the world for a week, with some paints and canvases, he would have come up with astonishing paintings and drawings of a run-down bathroom or a frayed cardboard box. I think Van Gogh could draw anything and make it enthralling.'

Happily you, the reader, will not be locked in a motel room, but are invited here to explore gardens through the senses of artists from three continents – Europe, North America and Australia – who enjoyed the gardens' essentially similar pleasures but engaged with the light from their particular skies in order to create very different sensations. 'The Garden as Canvas' opens the gates to six contrasting and surviving Impressionist gardens: the water lily nursery of Joseph Bory Latour-Marliac, Monet at Giverny, Childe Hassam on Appledore, Gertrude Jekyll at Munstead Wood, Frederick McCubbin at Fontainebleau and Renoir at Les Collettes. These domains are interleaved with photographs and paintings that delve into the outdoor activities of the Impressionists. They are shown in their gardens, expressing themselves through eating, drinking, reading, sewing, singing and making merry. Finally, 'In Memoriam' takes the artists, their families and gardens from the Eurocentric Franco-Prussian war to the global battlegrounds of World War One.

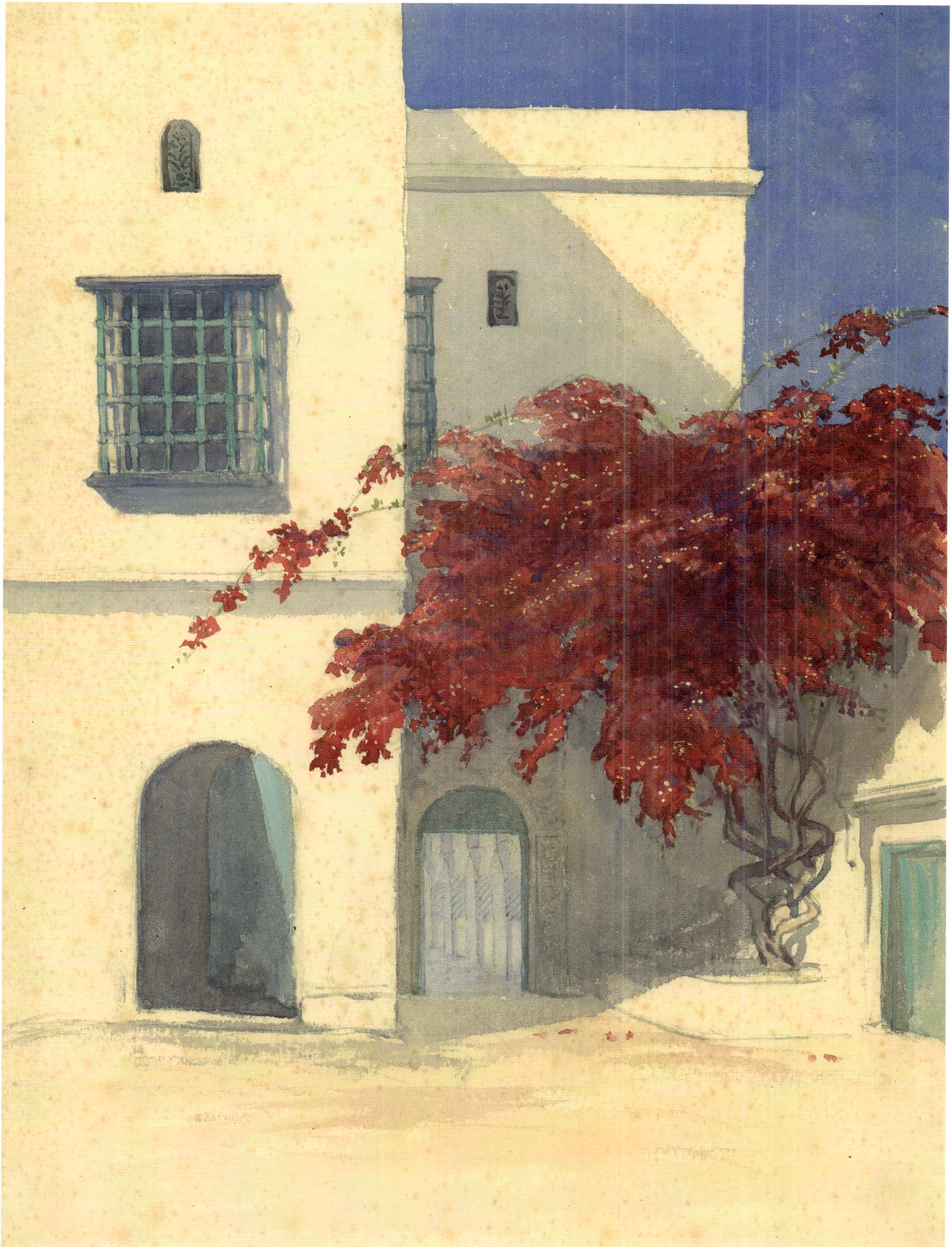

Chapter One

The Garden as Canvas

When the eye is trained to perceive pictorial effect, it is frequently struck by something – some combination of grouping, lighting and colour – that is seen to have that complete aspect of unity and beauty that to the artist's eye forms a picture. Such are the impressions that the artist-gardener endeavours to produce in every portion of the garden. …Then there are some days during the summer when the quality of light seems to tend to an extraordinary beauty of effect.

Gertrude Jekyll Colour Schemes for the Flower Garden, *1914*

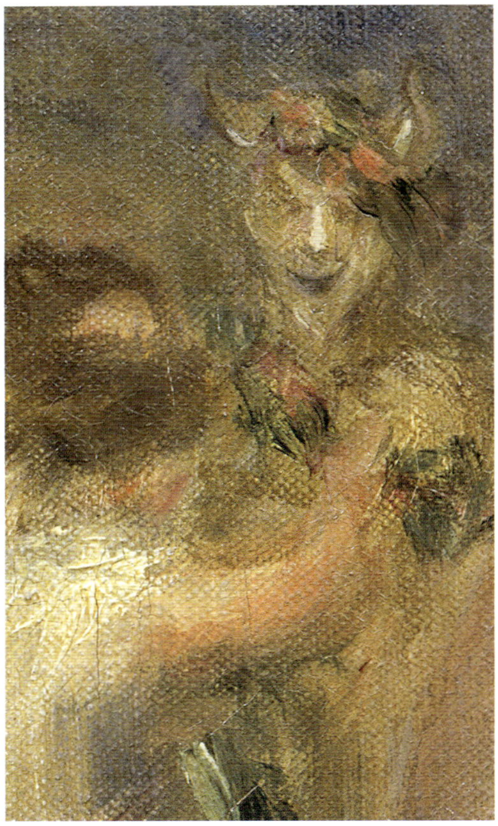

Pierre-Auguste Renoir, **Ode to Flowers**. *Oil on canvas, 46 x 36cm (18 x 14in.) 1903-09*

Renoir studied the soft colours of rose petals to help him capture flesh tones; the white tinged with pale pink medieval rose known in English as Maiden's Blush is called 'Cuisse de Nymphe' (nymph's thighs) in French. Models were more important in the garden than flowers for Renoir, this Callipygean Venus evokes just that.

As the nineteenth century drew to a close, a little light lawn tennis had become an increasingly fashionable activity with grass courts as an integral part of garden design. Many of the plans illustrated in Gertrude Jekyll's *Gardens for Small Country Houses* include both a bowling green and a tennis court. They created geometric blocks of smooth clipped green between the framed borders of drifting flowers and architectural spikes that celebrated spring, high summer or early autumn, before dissolving into areas of naturalistic woodland. Visiting American Impressionists wooed Monet's four stepdaughters on the two tennis courts at the Hotel Baudy, built by the artist and keen player Stanton Young, and in Australia, in December 1889 sixty members of The Victorian Artists' Society made an excursion to Eaglemont near the small Australian town of Heidelberg for a picnic, at which many of them played tennis and rounders. The beautiful ruined Eaglemont garden where the Heidelberg School camped and painted, was fondly remembered by Arthur Streeton in a letter to fellow artist Tom Roberts on 7th August 1908: "The brilliant blue mornings with the faint Dandenongs and the round she-oaks all the way down to the Station … and Oleander and Japonica and pinecones scattering on the dewy grass … And the thick small cypress trees near the Tennis Court where the balls used to hide, and the Fair Open Hilltop where K. did his 'Evening Star' and the row of Hazel and Pear trees and Pines round the well and the indigestible short cut to Ivanhoe; and the long warm afternoons of coppery light.' 'K' is Charles Conder who was renowned for spending more time chasing girls than painting. In Australia the stands of eucalyptus create a blue haze over their mountains, not least the Dandenong Ranges above the River Yarra.

I have selected half a dozen 'Centre Courts' that share the pleasures of living light and colour that flourished under very different skies and gardeners. None of them stands alone, the journey to each involves admiring borders, exchanging ideas and taking time to stand and stare. They have all survived the unrelenting spread of housing, some meticulously restored and maintained whilst others are flourishing in new hands. These primed canvases all fulfil the function of scene and setting, the sunny and stormy moods inextricably associated with artists flashed across the gardens but to a man (and woman) they were all consummate hosts to family and friends.

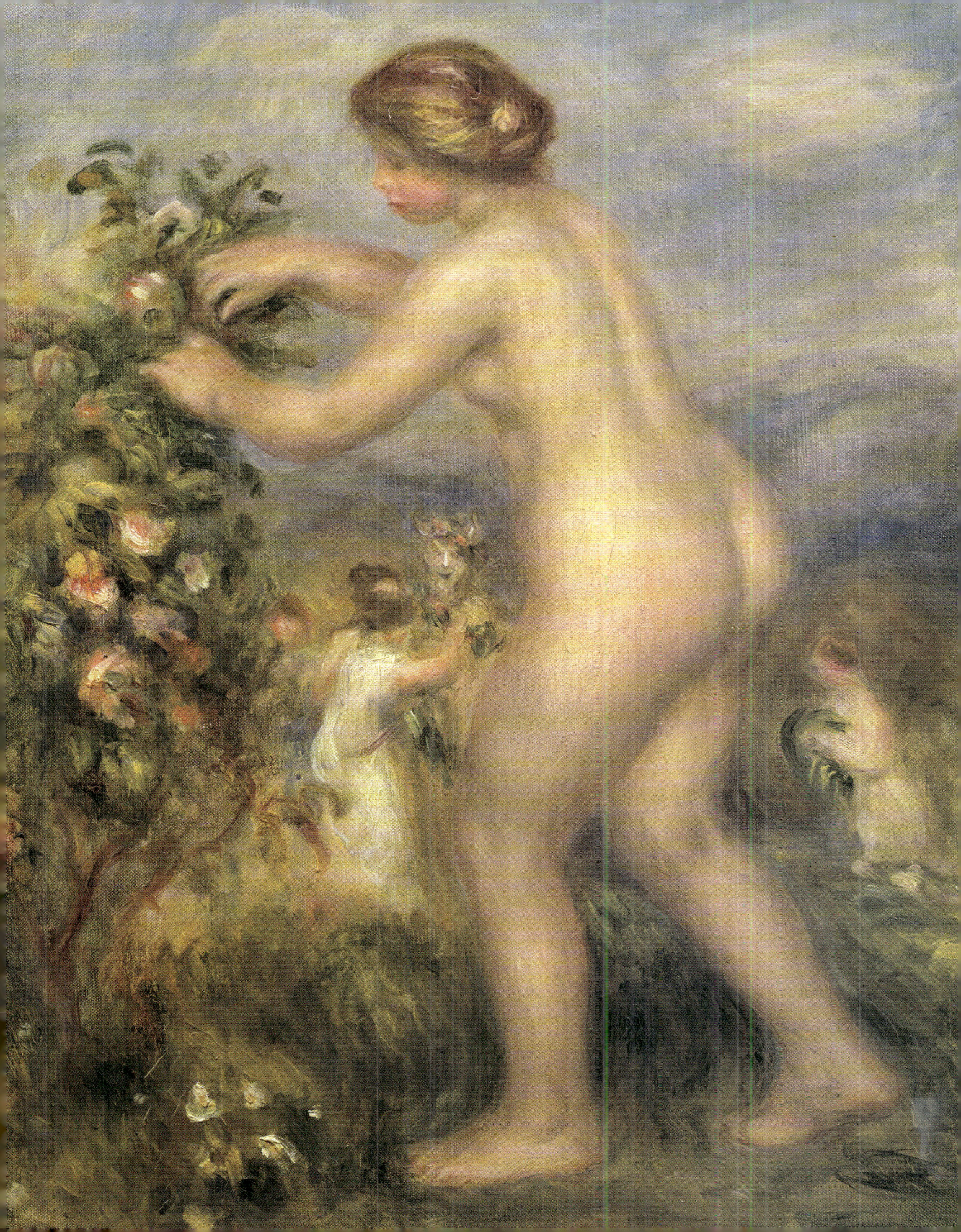

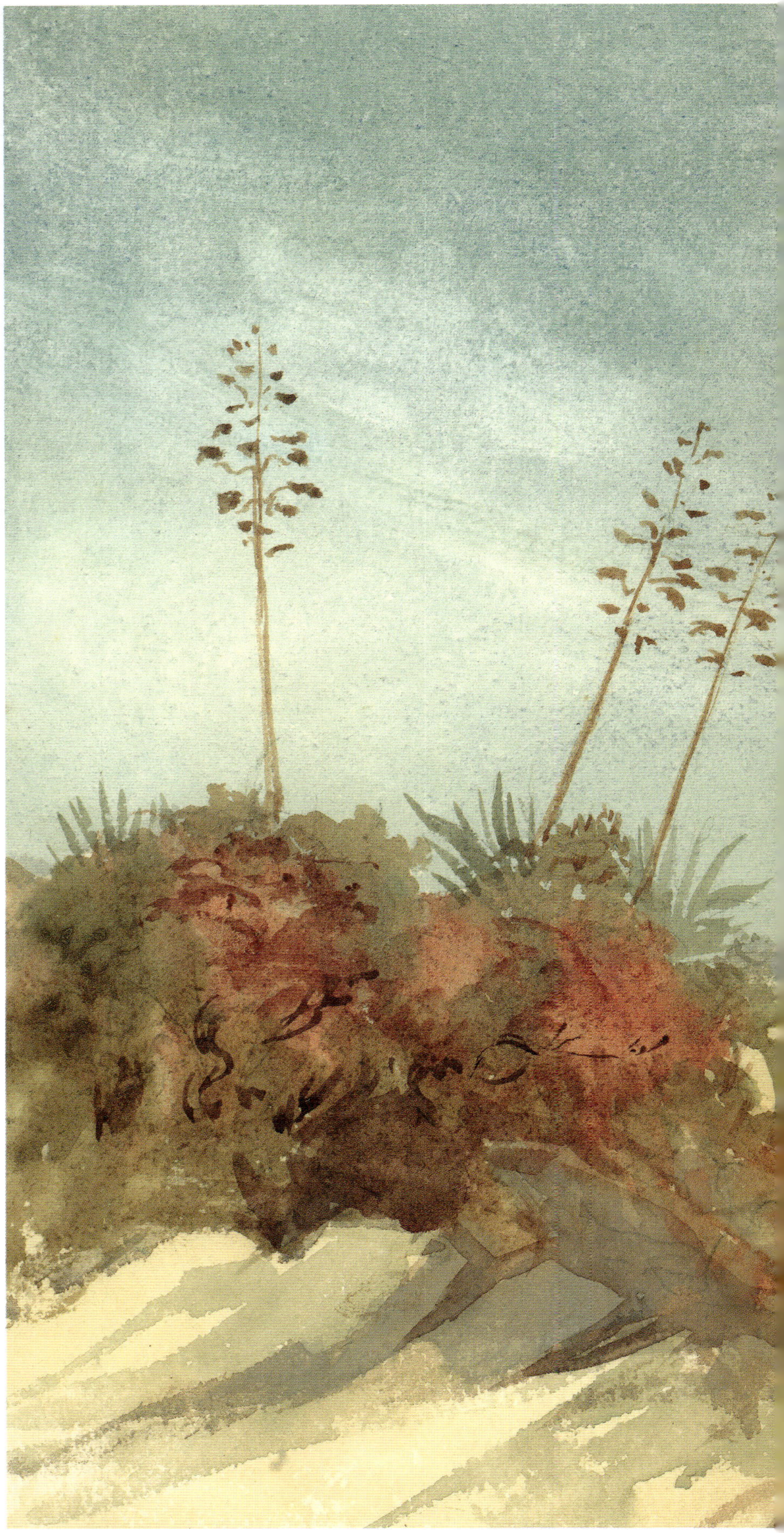

Gertrude Jekyll, **Arab house in the country**.
Watercolour, 38 x 27cm (15 x 10½ in.), 1873-74

Did the rocky foreground inspire Jekyll's later rockery designs? There are agaves and irises amongst the rocks, in a later hand she annotated this watercolour in pencil with 'Iris scorpiones'. Probably Iris Scorpioides, now known as Iris Planiflolia, a winter flowering native of North Africa, the Iberian Peninsula, Crete, Sardinia and Sicily. Like so many of the Impressionists, Jekyll found irises endlessly beautiful. The vivid oranges and blues that Monet used to paint the agaves at Bordighera seem muted here, dwarfing the Arab house and the umbrella pine in the background.

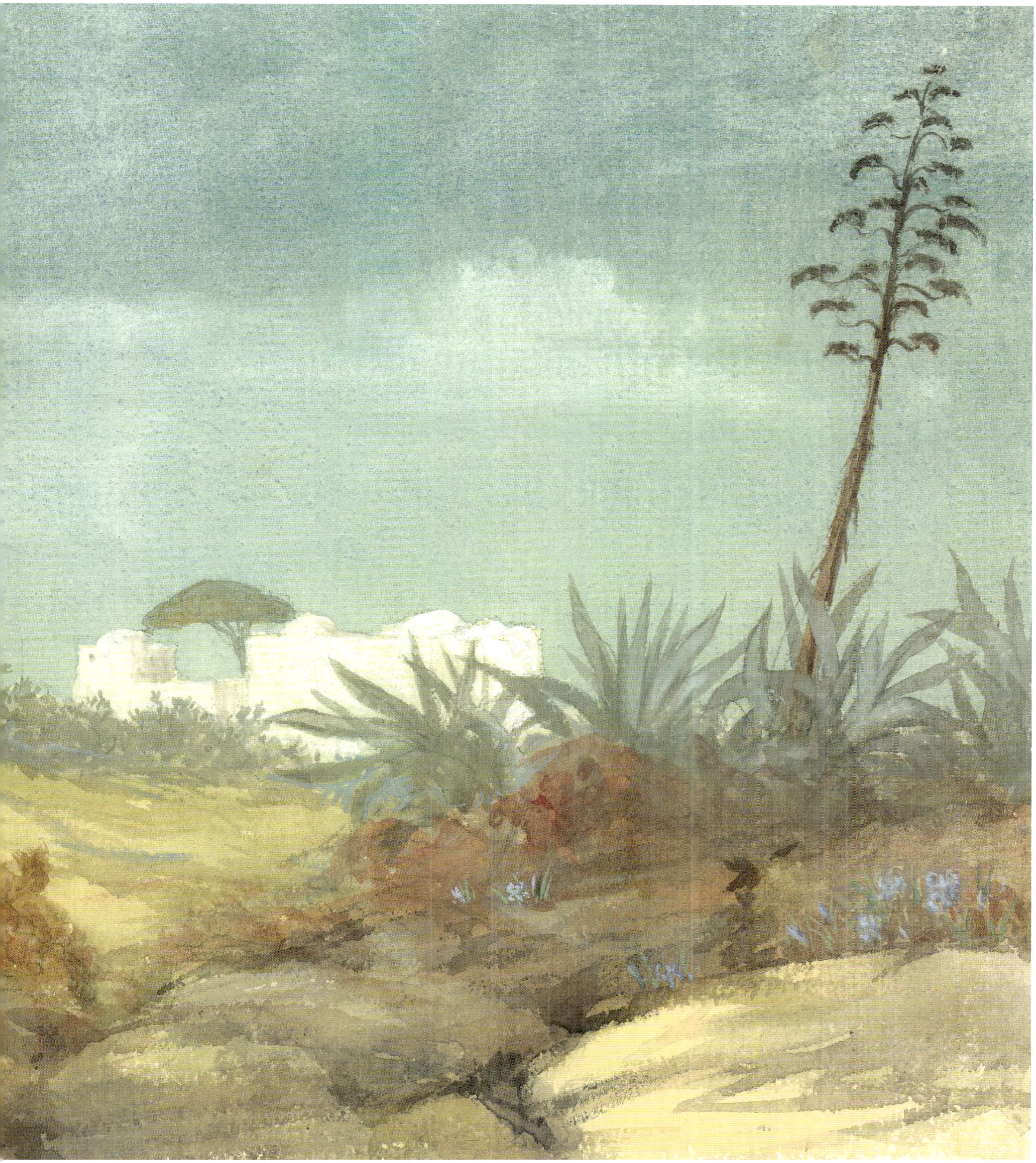

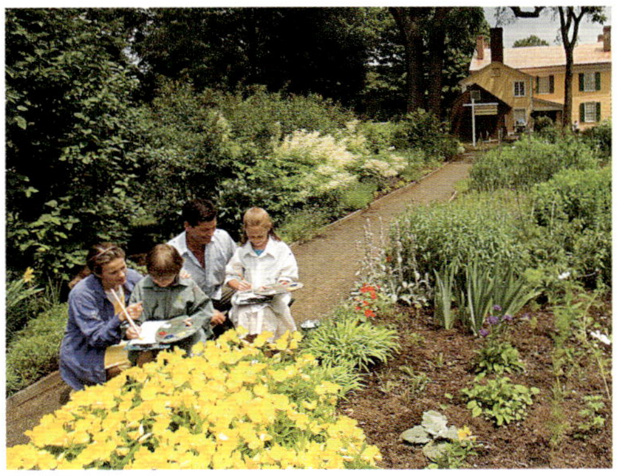

The ethos of the artist's colony continues at the Florence Griswold Museum, Old Lyme, Connecticut – how to catch that sensational yellow will be challenging. In her preface to Colour Schemes for Flower Gardens, *Jekyll wrote 'Merely having them [plants] … is only like having a box of paints from the best colourman, or, to go one step further, it is like having portions of these paints set out upon a palette. This does not constitute a picture; … our duty … is to use the plants that they shall form beautiful pictures.'*

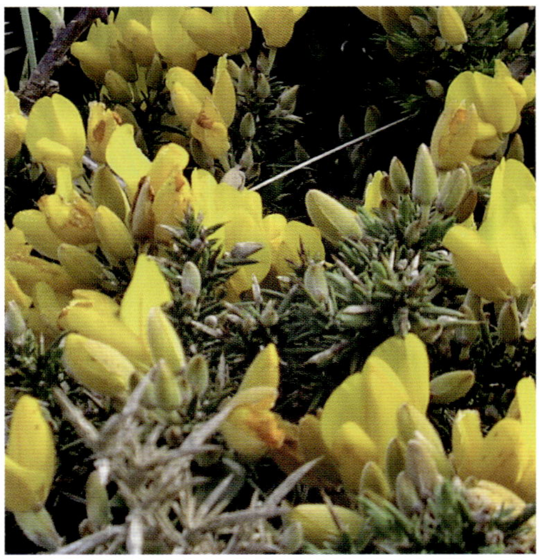

Ajoncs d'or *in full flower on the Port Goulphar headland on Belle Ile, Brittany, former site of Australian Impressionist Peter John Russell's* Chateau Anglais. *These golden gorse flowers could be used to fulfil Gertrude Jekyll's advice in* Colour Schemes for the Flower Garden: *'The Gold garden is chosen … because it contains the greater number of permanent shrubs and is bright and cheerful all the year round, and partly it is the best preparation, according to natural colour law, for the compartments on either side. … entering the Gold garden on even the dullest day, will be like coming into sunshine.*

As the twentieth century dawned Jekyll included tennis courts in her designs for her clients, and others appear in her photographs for her books. The courts were landscaped in symmetry with garden houses, long herbaceous borders, pergolas and the equally fashionable new stone-edged lily pool. Gardens such as this rely on good nurserymen such as Joseph Bory Latour-Marliac to whom the world owes its choice of colourful water lilies, as Jekyll wrote in *Home and Garden* 'Water-Lilies … the beautiful garden kinds that have been raised by the eminent French horticulturist, M. Latour-Marliac. To this gentleman's labours we owe a whole new range of lovely varieties of the highest garden value. Throughout the country our best amateurs are making ponds and tanks on purpose for their culture, and some day I shall endeavour to point out how their use might be adapted to some of the most highly refined developments of formal or architectural gardening.'

Monet had started his water garden in 1893 and Jekyll did indeed go on to publish *Wall and Water Gardens* in 1901. Monet's garden at Giverny is the masterpiece of Impressionist gardening but is it the template? During their lifetimes both Jekyll and Monet attracted many column inches on their gardens – did they ever read about each other? Today hundreds of thousands of visitors have made the pilgrimage to Giverny where the immaculate re-creation captures the course of the day's light and the green spirit of the man.

Across the Atlantic it is a hard choice to decide which should represent the Centre Court for this enquiry: Old Lyme versus Cos Cob, Connecticut or Appledore. So many of the American Impressionists who had painted (and played tennis) at Giverny and in its surroundings continued to meet and work during summers hosted by Florence Griswold at Old Lyme, where the gardens still survive. Of all the artists that were part of the Cos Cob Colony, the finest gardener was John Peter Twachtman, who bought a domain for his family and created a garden whose bridge between the organised abundance of the upper garden and the naturalistic lower gardens predate Monet's. The chosen centrepiece has to be the poetic, colourful, sensory pleasures of Appledore and its poet-proprietor Celia Thaxter, where the small garden still blooms.

Apart from her training as an artist, author of eleven books, creator of the fifteen acres of gardens at Munstead Wood and crafter of much of its interior, Gertrude Jekyll undertook over 500 design commissions, three of which were for American gardens. The voluptuous perfection of her borders and woods have earned her the moniker of 'England's Impressionist Gardener', although they are now a shadow of their former glory, it is her house and the backbone of her garden that stand as testament to her artistic philosophy.

Although Jekyll was a spinster she loved romance and the joys of a contented marriage. The 'happy beyond measure' love between Frederick and Annie McCubbin would have delighted her, as would their large, happy family and open door to students and the great and the good. They named their property Fontainebleau and offered grand times at the

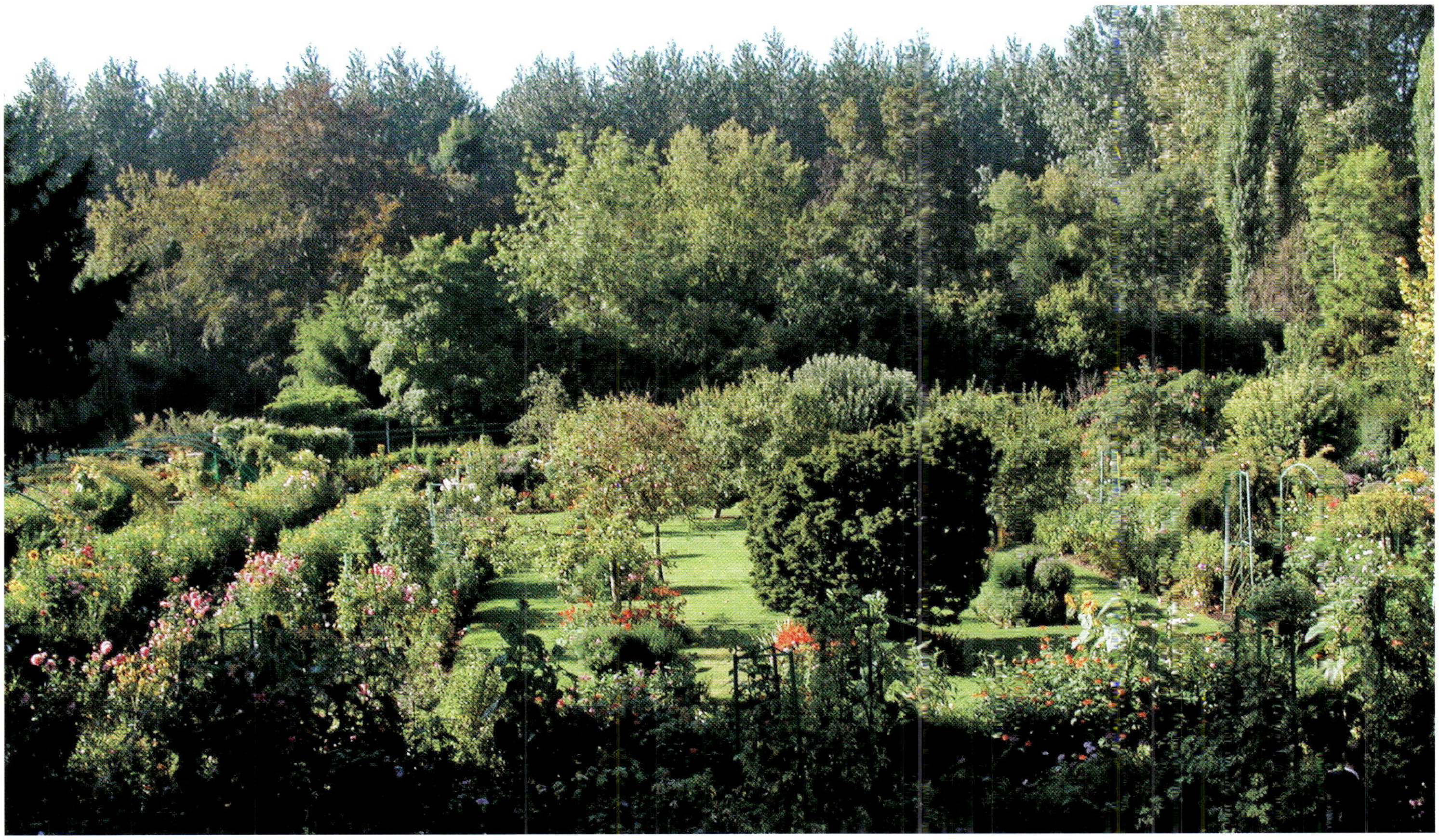

grandest address, its forest source in France the acorn of artistic expression for the Impressionist movement, its Australian namesake the fount around which McCubbin's students camped and drank.

Renoir spent many seasons painting in the Fontainebleau Forest, he rued the way that Paris had spread into Montmartre and the gentrification of towns and villages across France. Poor health encouraged him to spend the winter months in the south of France, as did many of the international *beau monde* whose needs were serviced by the hill settlements nearby. One of these was Cagnes, a village in two parts: one part by the sea where the locals fished, and the other up the mountain where they lived and market gardened. Renoir's arthritis was improved by living in the warm dry climate here, and the family were absorbed into this traditional village whose ways pleased Renoir's philosophy.

The last Impressionist domain is Renoir's final home and garden, Les Collettes, at Cagnes, which he bought to safeguard its ancient olive trees and terraces from being developed into a commercial carnation nursery. The 'lawns' in the gardens the Renoirs created were jewelled with wild flowers and oat grasses, the terraces were nurtured to bring them back into production, the air was filled with the seasonal scent of orange blossom and roses, and there was a fruit for every season. The combination of food for body and soul together with the presence of its artistic master drew visitors from around the world, whilst local girls became accustomed to modelling for him in a setting of Eden-like simplicity.

Above: *Monet's view from his bedroom across the upper garden. The eye is drawn back and forth along the horizontal lines of his allee and down towards the top of the Japanese Bridge and the now mature copper beech. Waving silvery glaucous poplars close the vista, catching the light and adding the sound of the soft swish of their leaves to those of the wild and domestic birds.*

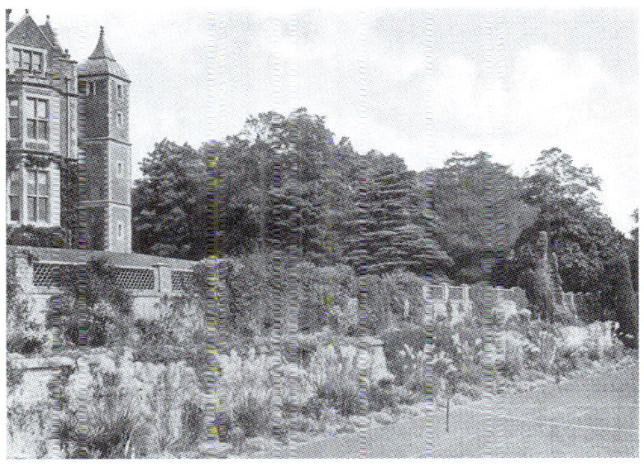

Note the tennis court in the foreground of this anonymous house featured in Jekyll's Wall and Water Gardens. *She admired the background trees that gave texture to the composition, and she praised the salutary effects of rambling growths. But she criticized the monotonous repetition of Uva Grass and Yuccas*

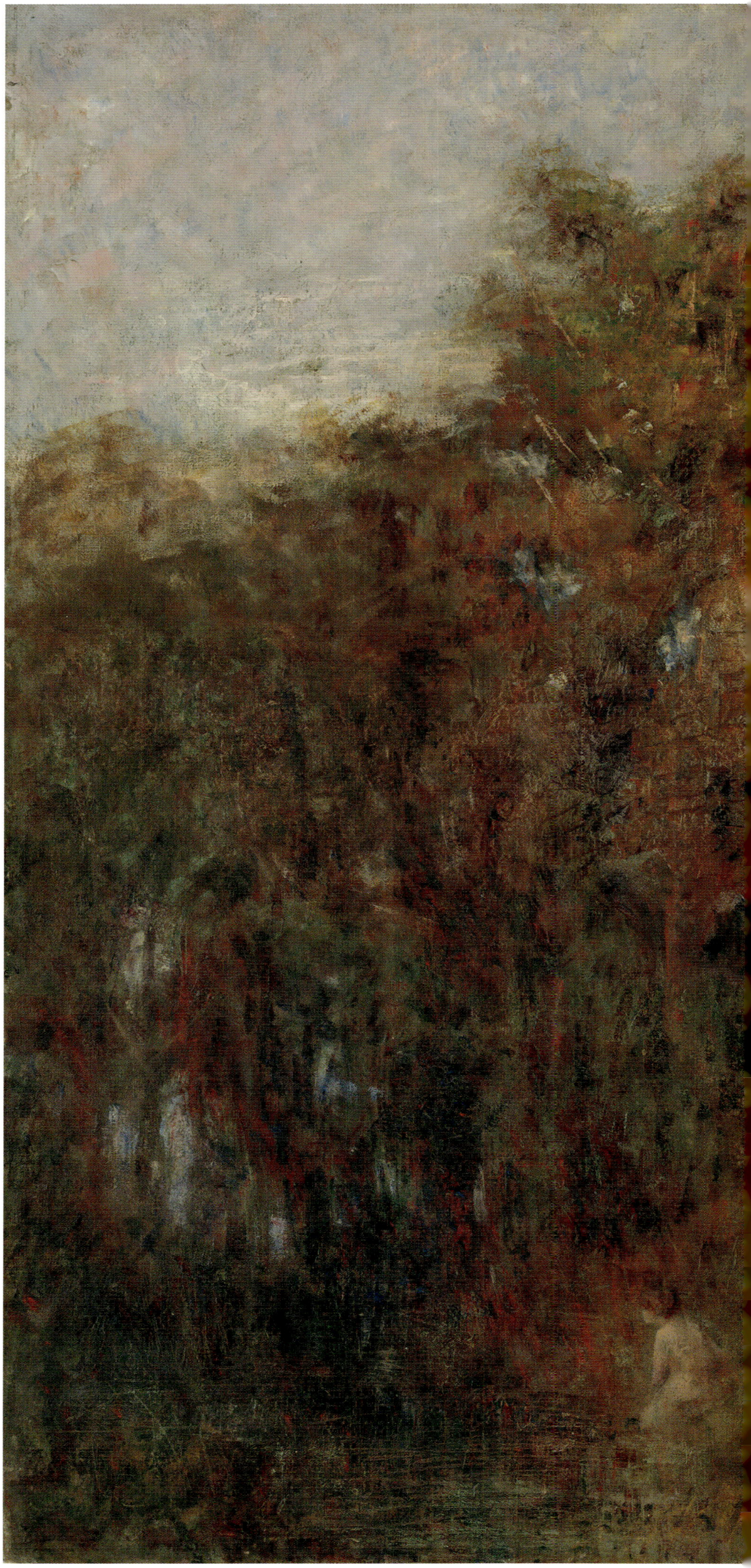

Frederick McCubbin, **Afterglow** *(Summer evening). Oil on canvas, 91.5 x 117cm (36 x 46 in.), 1912*

The remains of the day's shimmering heat is reflected in the skies and tree tops. Many of Frederick McCubbin's fellow artists in the Heidelberg School painted bathing scenes by the sea. His glowing bathers are cooling off at Lake Strathmore on the property of Ard Choille which adjoined his own Fontainebleau on Mount Macedon in Victoria. The estate was based on a Scottish model and included a trout hatchery and a resident piper.

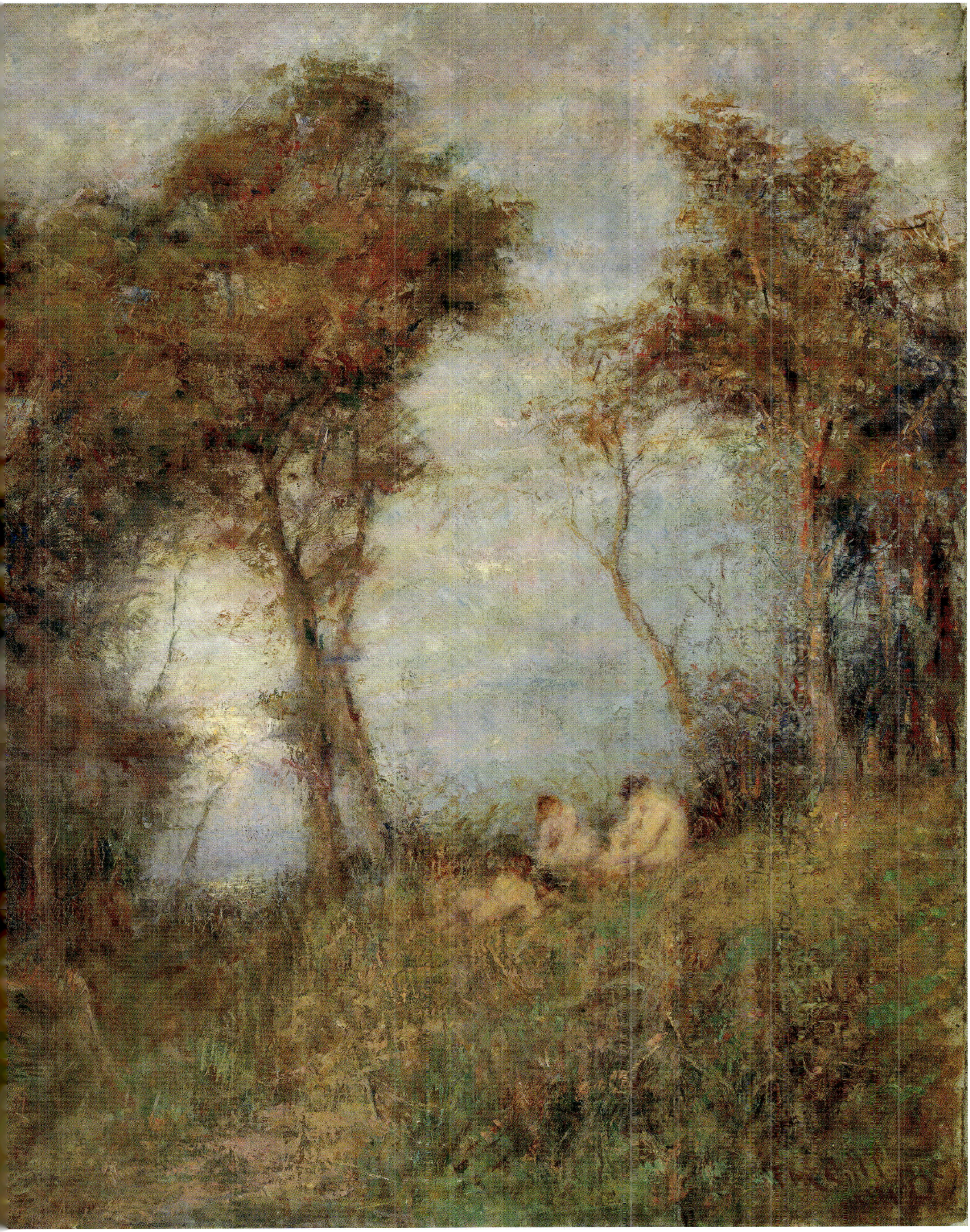

Plants as Paint

I am strongly of opinion that the possession of a quantity of plants, however good the plants may be themselves and however ample their number, does not make a garden; it only makes a collection. ... This does not constitute a picture; and it seems to me that the duty we owe to our gardens and to our own bettering in our gardens is so to use the plants that they shall form beautiful pictures; and that, while delighting our eyes, they should be always training those eyes to a more exalted criticism; ...they may either be fashioned into a dream of beauty, a place of perfect rest and refreshment of mind and body – a series of soul-satisfying pictures – a treasure of well-set jewels; or they may be so misused that everything is jarring and displeasing. In practice it is to place every plant or group of plants with such thoughtful care and definite intention that they shall form a part of a harmonious whole, and that successive portions or in some cases even single details, shall show a series of pictures.

Gertrude Jekyll, Colour Schemes for the Flower Garden, *1914*

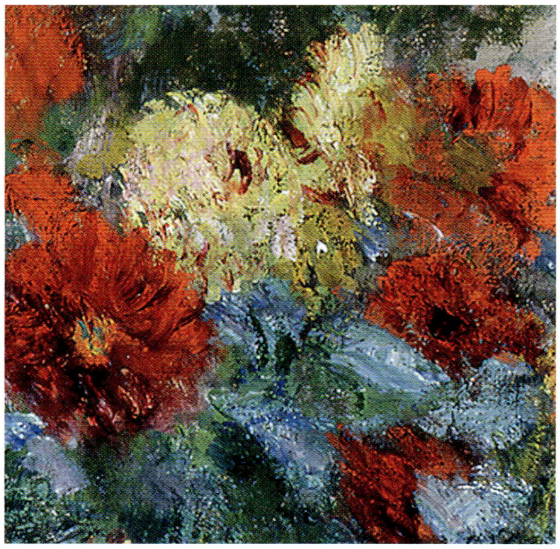

Pierre-Auguste Renoir, **The Garden in the Rue Cortot, Montmartre**. *Oil on canvas, 151.7 x 97.5 cm (59¾ in. x 38⅜ in.), 1876*

Renoir lived in Montmartre where modest apartments were still very cheap. He found a dilapidated house in the Rue Cortot, from which he could also pick up the scent of the dance garden at La Butte. To his delight there was a large garden which he described as 'A mysterious, stately garden, like Zola's paradou – what was once part of a fine residence' with a magnificent view of the countryside right out to St Denis. Amongst numerous paintings, this one depicts the shaggy heads of dahlias amongst the unkempt grass and shrubs. Dahlias – all the rage in France – have a natural proclivity for hybridization leading to flowers of unfeasible proportions. Despite the neglect, these dahlias are thriving, the two men in the background are believed to be Monet and Alfred Sisley.

Historically, gardens were created as places to relax away from the dangers and incursions of wild nature, admitting only its useful and prettier forms to feed and to decorate. As the nineteenth century became increasingly urban, a personal patch of green provided a reminder of the country. Gardening allowed the time to collect personal thoughts whilst giving free rein to the imagination and exercising the senses of touch, sight, scent and sound. Artists (and their agents) paid careful attention to the choice of frames for their paintings and traditionally it was said that just like a painting a garden should have an attractive frame. The framework of Impressionist gardens is subtle allowing the contents to spill out, over and upwards.

When they were students, many of the original French Impressionists had collected Japanese prints, especially those by Utagawa Hiroshige and Katsushika Hokosai, which had arrived as wrappings for imported goods and were then sold very cheaply. Australian artists such as John Russell were geographically better placed to find their own points of reference first-hand. These Japanese landscapes were decorated with wisteria, chrysanthemums, peonies, flowering cherries, water lilies, irises and bamboo. The Buddhist and Shinto philosophy integral to their design was not appreciated in the west but in many respects was imbibed, not least in simple contemplation. Taking time to stare reveals that 'green thoughts in a green shade' actually have many hues. Monet's fame and gardens attracted many international visitors, including General Kuroki Tametomo and his wife, the Princess Matsukata from Japan, who brought with him tree peonies and lilies.

Extremes of weather, pride and joy encouraged the artists to bring the garden into the house. Photographs of Monet show vases of his favourite flowers such as the Etoile de Digoin dahlia in the house and his studio. On the other side of the world in Melbourne, Arthur Streeton, Charles Conder and Frederick McCubbin opened 'The 9 by 5 Impressionist Exhibition' to the public in August 1889 to mixed reviews.

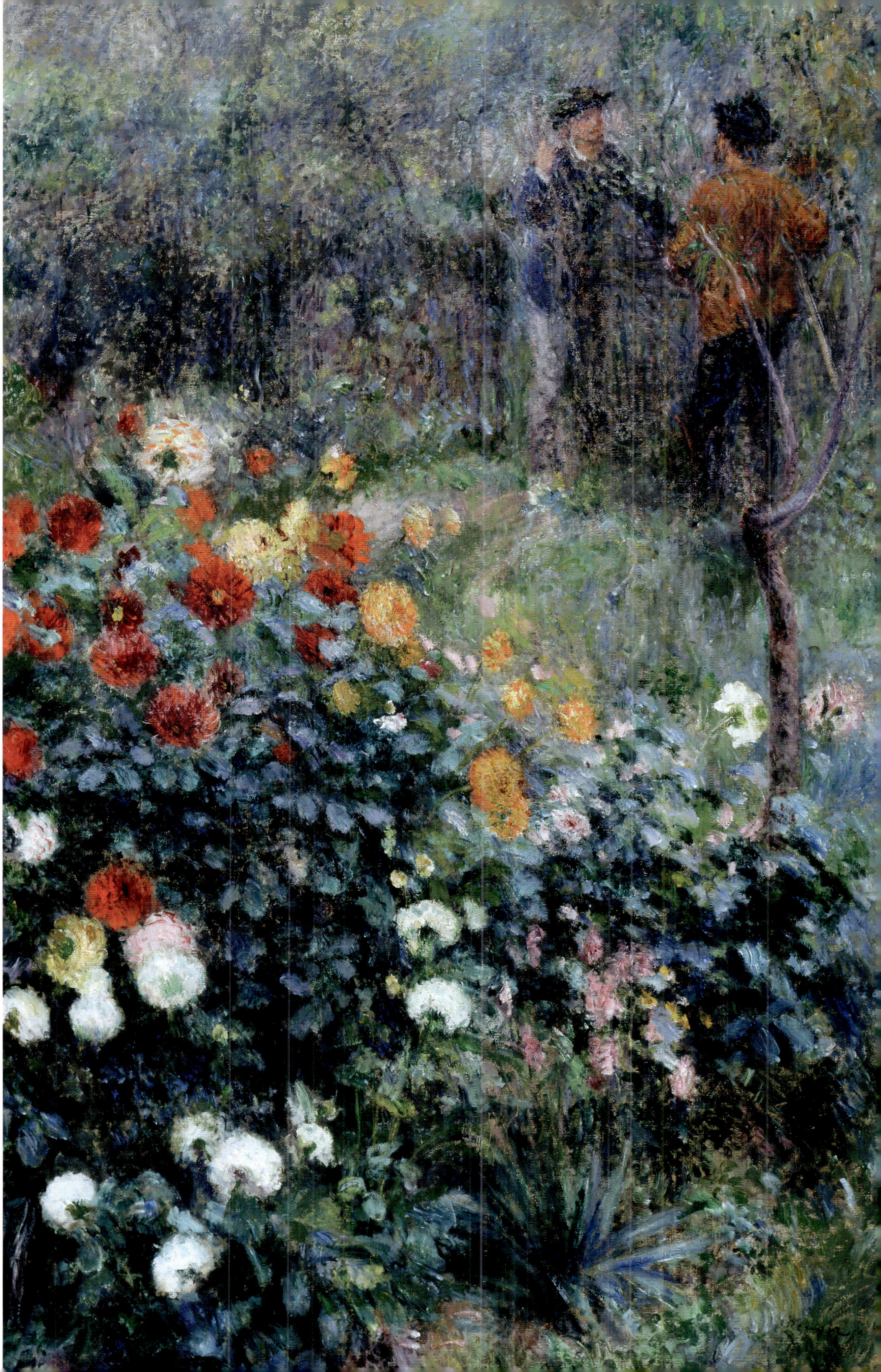

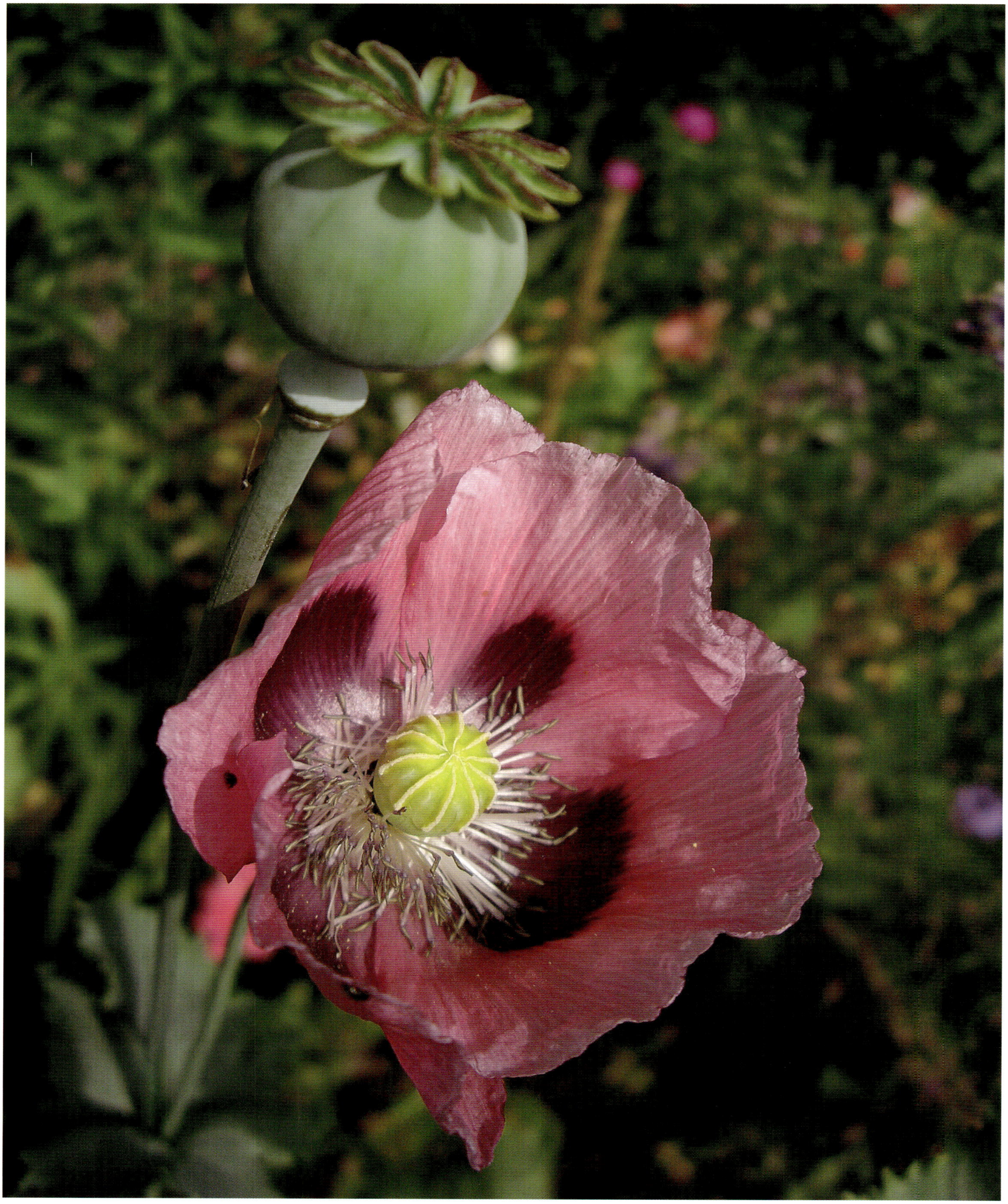

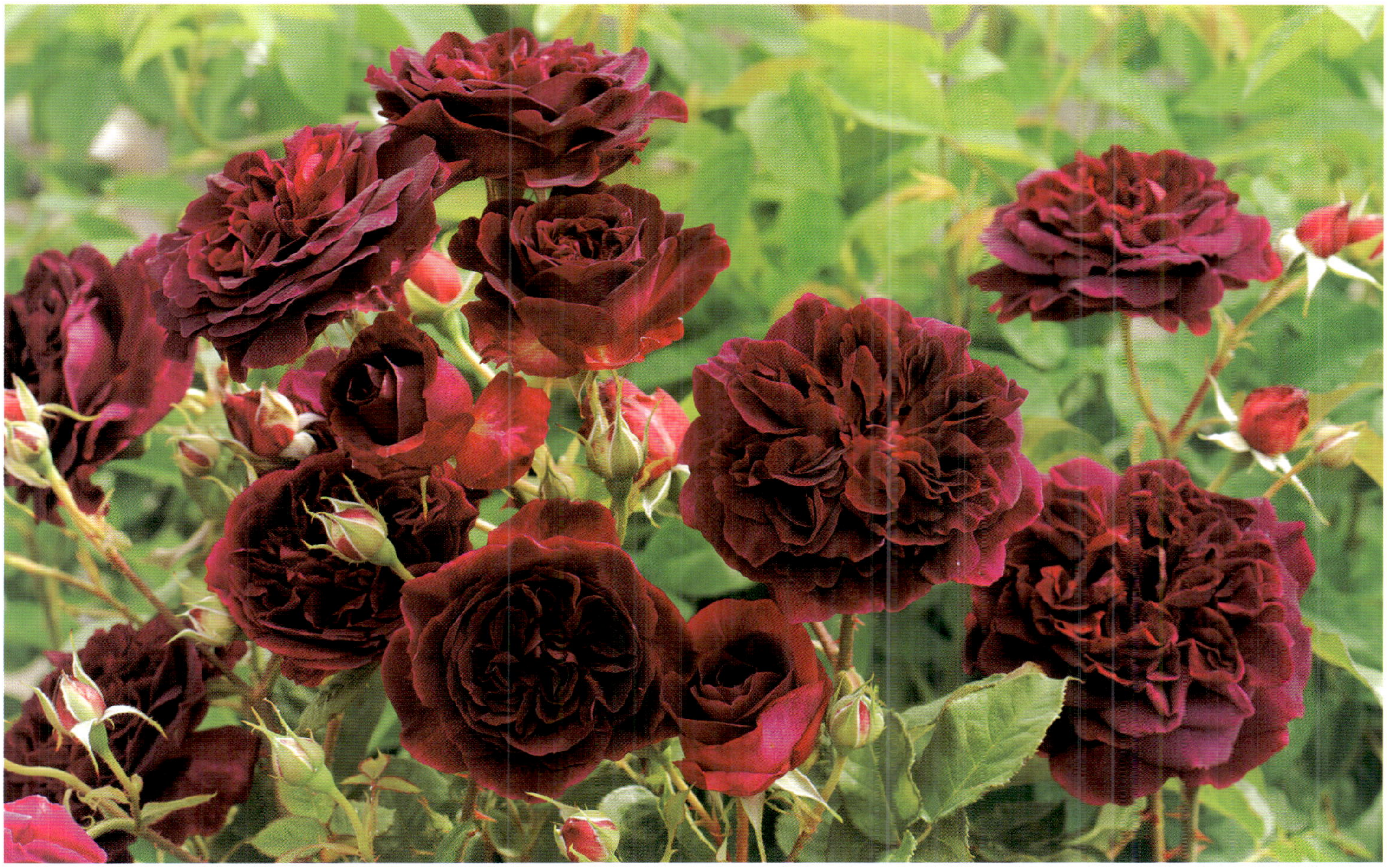

Above: *In* Roses for English Gardens *(published in 1902) Gertrude Jekyll wrote 'No plant is more helpful and accommodating than the Rose in the way of screening ugliness and providing living curtains of flowery drapery.' How she would have rejoiced in the modern rich pink scented Rose 'Gertrude Jekyll' and the 'strong and delicious' fragrance of its climbing form as well as the deep velvety crimson Rose 'Munstead Wood', illustrated above.*

Right: *Forget-me-not flower. "If one but gazes closely into a tiny flower of the pale blue Forget-me-not, what a chapter of loveliness is there!" wrote the poet Celia Thaxter in* Among the Isles. *Forget-me-nots en masse were put to good impressionistic effect to create a blue frothy foam around bulbs such as tulips.*

Opposite page: *"I muse over seed-pods, those supremely graceful urns that are wrought with such matchless elegance of shape, and think what strange power they hold within. Sleep is there, and Death his brother, imprisoned in those mystic sealed cups. There is a hint of their mystery in their shape of sombre beauty, but never a suggestion in the fluttering blossom." The seed-pod Celia Thaxter is musing over is that of any poppy, more specifically it can be seen here emerging from the petals of the Papaver orientale. Sea breezes fluttered the petals of the flowers massed in the island garden of Appledore on the Isles of Shoals, including red, pink, Oriental and Iceland poppies. Poppies come in many forms but have easily identifiable seedlings and seedheads so they can be manipulated to good effect. Famously, they are associated with Monet's red poppies running through the Normandy fields near Giverny and those of Van Gogh scattered across the top of the vineyards at Auvers. Monet used the pink flowering annual Californian or opium poppies to run with lilies in the upper garden, these poppies have a silky sheen to their petals that contrasts with their coal black centres and glaucous leaves.*

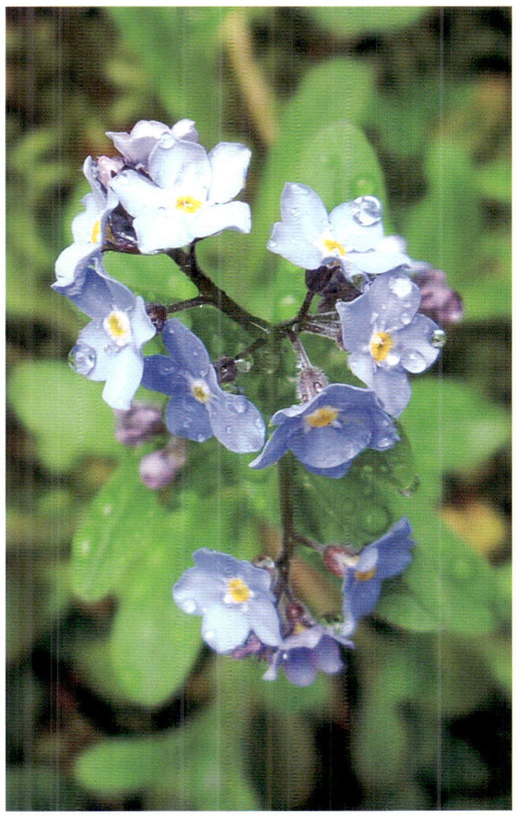

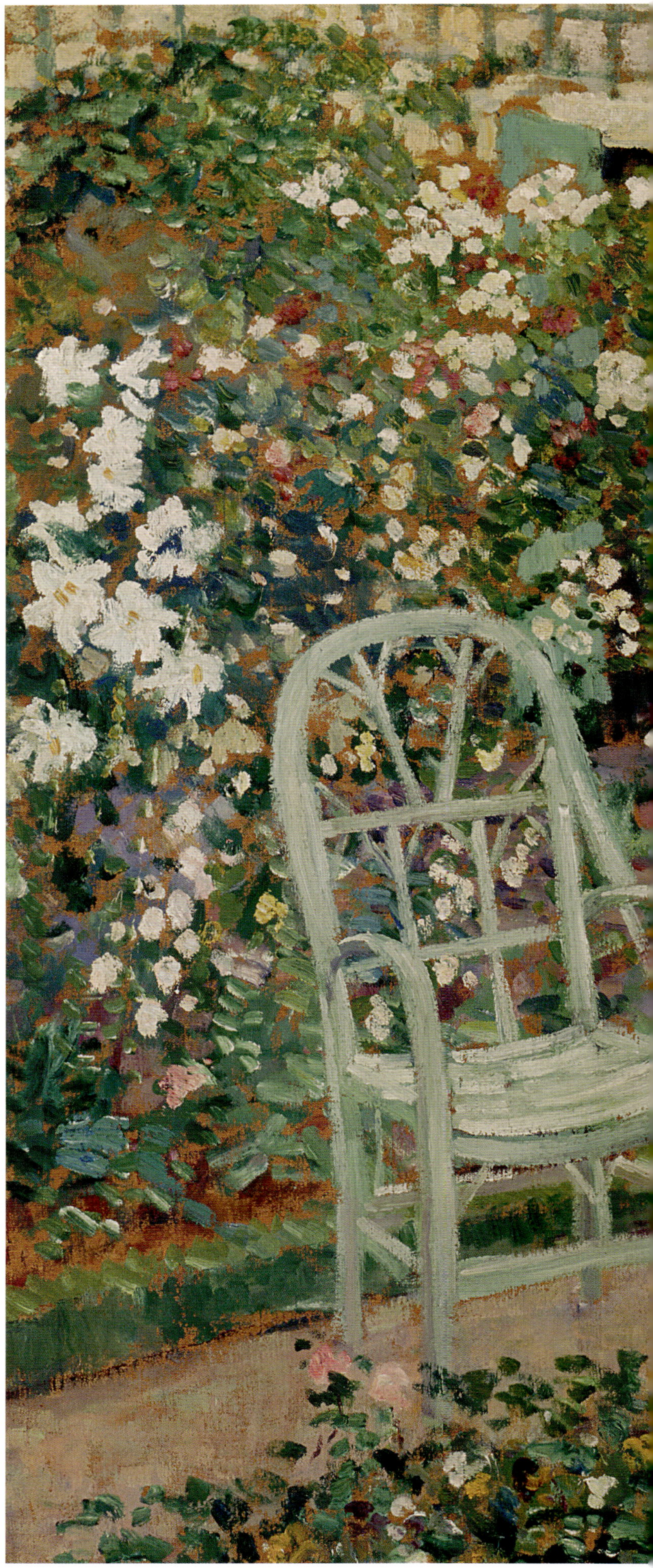

Frederick Frieseke, **Lilies**. *Oil on canvas, 65.4 x 81.6cm (25 ½ x 32 ⅛ in.), by 1911*

Frieseke painted Lilies *in Giverny, featuring his elegant wife Sarah and a friend with a pot of coffee. A jolly planting of pansies forms the narrow border lining the terrace. The woman in white's glance draws the viewer to the tall virginal blooms of the magnificent and newly introduced* Lilium regale *behind her. As well as birdsong, one senses that someone might just be playing the piano inside and its melody is carrying out into the garden. The Friesekes stayed in Giverny throughout World War I and, like Monet, they could hear the sounds of battle from their garden.*

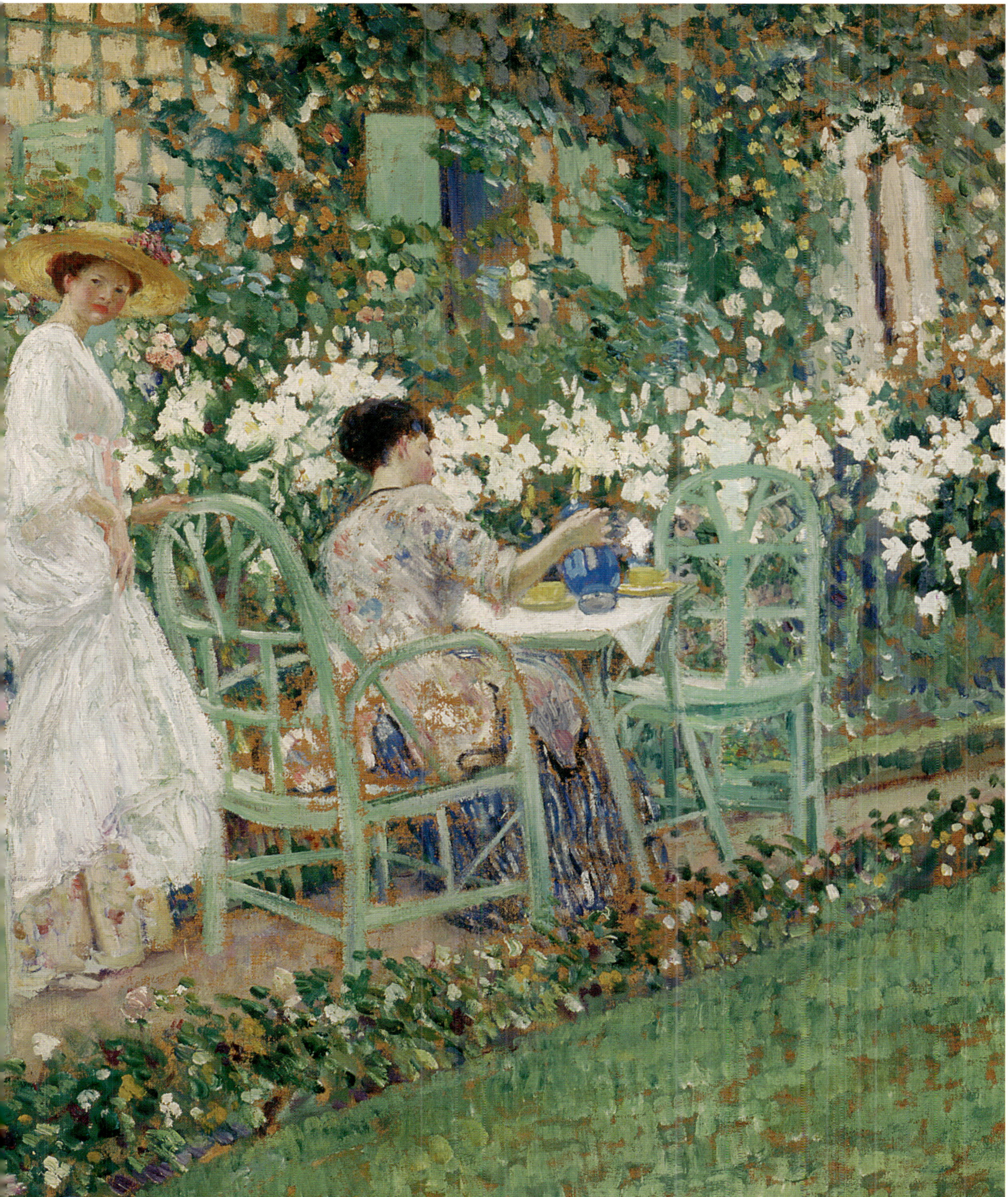

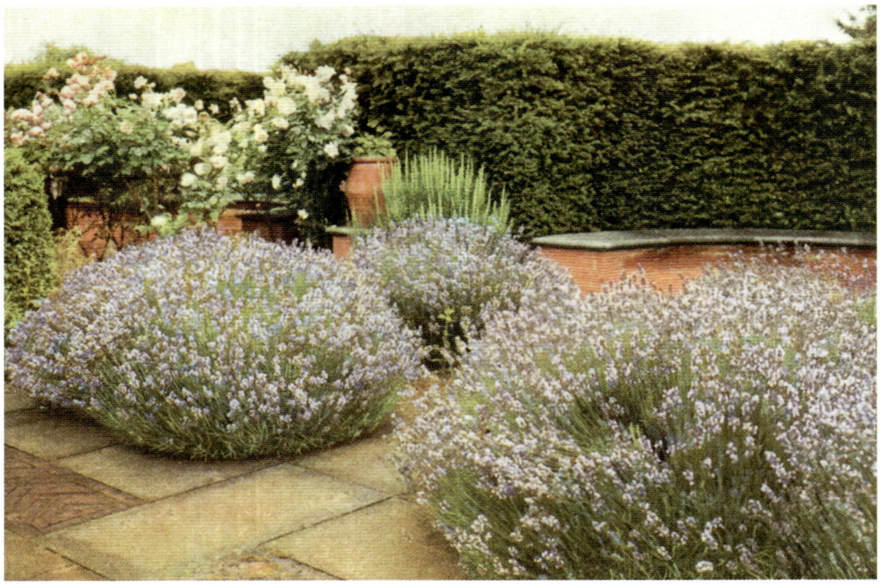

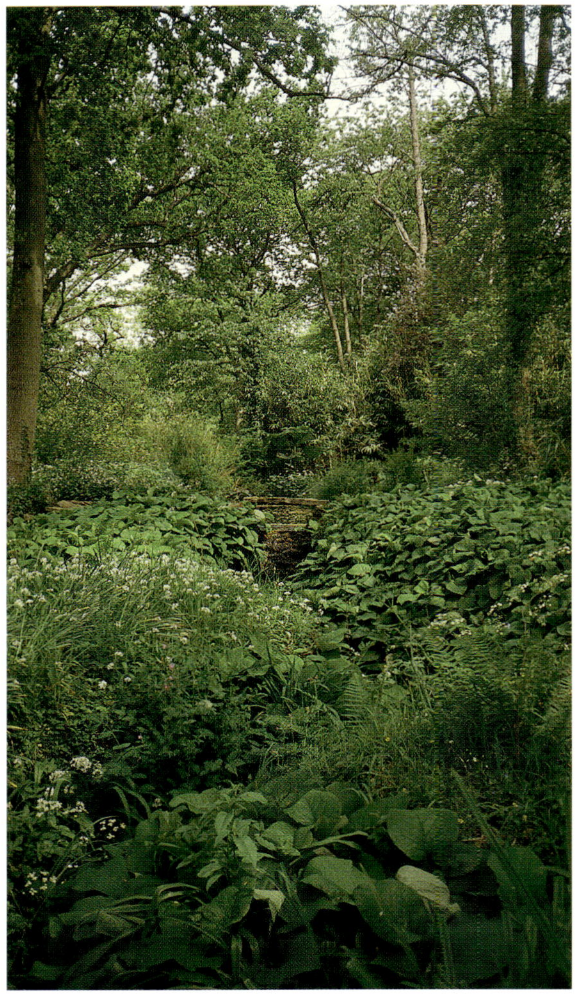

Above: *'White Rose and Lavender' is the frontispiece to* Colour Schemes for Flower Gardens *(1914) by Gertrude Jekyll. There is a delicate pink blush on the white roses that Renoir would have appreciated. The old English white rose shown here is known as Maiden's Blush, the same variety in French is called Cuisse de Nymphe (Nymph's Thigh), both names would suit Renoir who would look at the petals of roses as an aid to capturing the skin tones of children and women (see* Ode to Flowers *page 19). In* Home and Garden *Jekyll writes 'And the Rose, what does it typify? Is not its beauty and sweetness, its bright wholesome gladness, a type of strength, of righteous purpose, and of bountiful beneficence?' Renoir reiterated these virtues in paint to the extent that in 1909 the Rose 'Painter Renoir' was introduced and planted at Les Collettes. Gertrude Jekyll's favourites were the white shades of Climbing Aimée Vibert, Madame Alfred Carrière and the fine crimson Reine Olga de Wurtemburg.*

Top right: *The Arts and Crafts architect William D. Caroe who lived a few miles from Gertrude Jekyll at Vann, Hambledon in Surrey, had designed a pergola extending from his house to a small lake fed by an upper formal rill. In 1911 he approached Jekyll for advice on how to enhance the native trees below the lake, and she introduced her hallmark hosta, Rodgersia, Iris and ferns in drifts that dissolved into naturalistic woodland.*

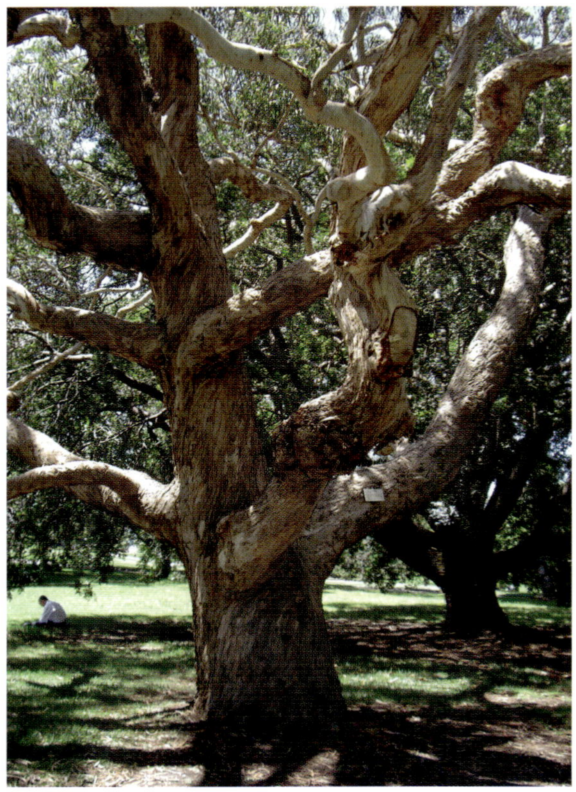

Right: *The bark of trees runs as a visual motif from the Barbizon School based in Fontainebleau Forest south of Paris to transplantion into the garden. The mottled and sometimes peeling bark of the sapling gum tree came to aptly represent The Heidelberg School in Australia. There are over 700 species of Eucalyptus or gum trees and of these only 15 occur outside Australia. The Latin name is derived from the Greek eu kalyptos meaning 'well covered' or in some translations, 'beautiful bark'. Their steel-grey leaves shine metallically against blue skies, and loose beautiful bark can be consumed by bush fires but magically regenerates afterwards. The furrowed bark of the willow trees in Monet's water garden came to symbolize for him the tortured grief of the nation following the First World War.*

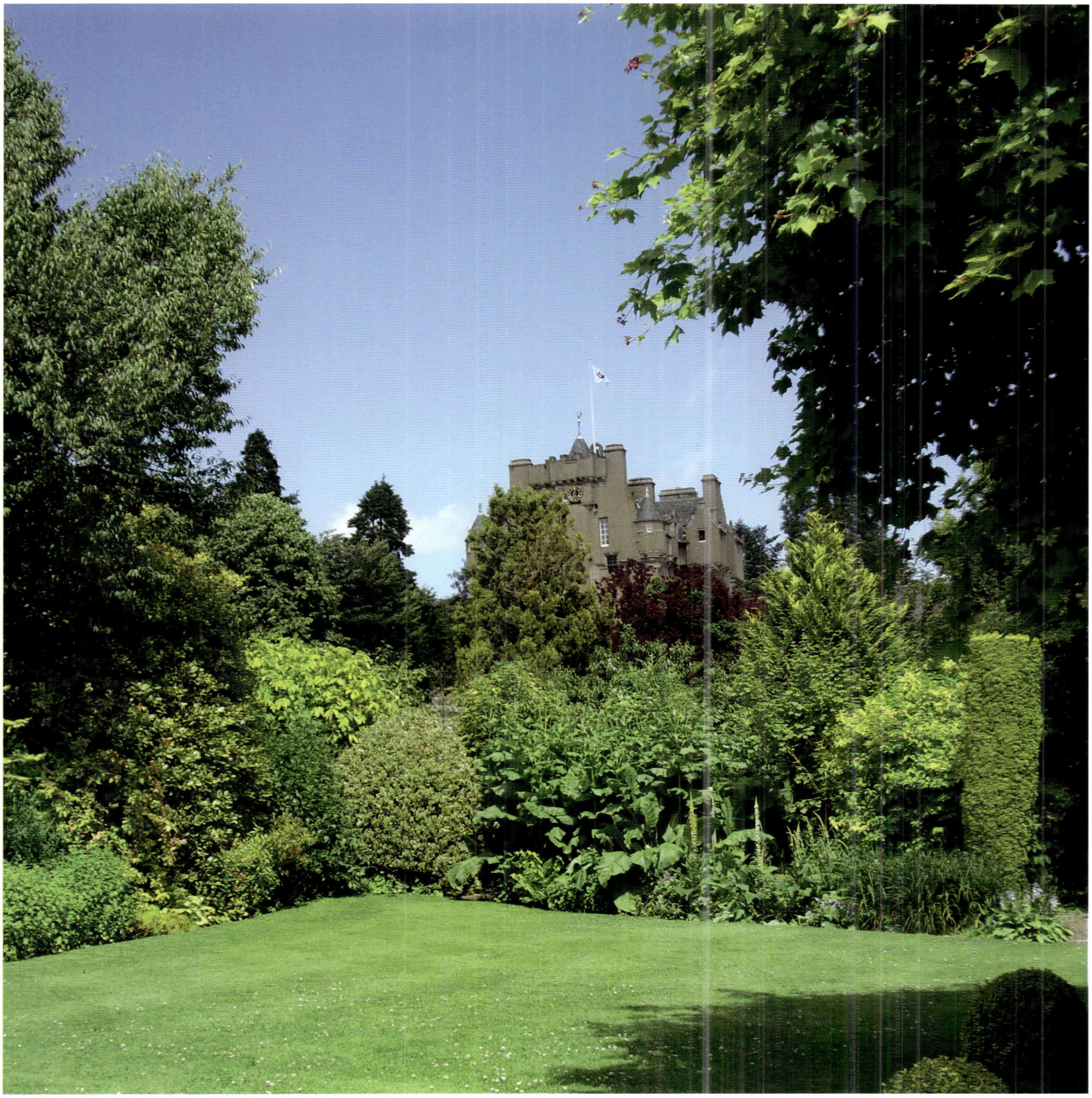

Gertrude Jekyll visited Crathes Castle in north-east Scotland around 1895. The castle can be seen here from the Gold Garden. In 1900 Some English Gardens was published in collaboration with the artist George Samuel Elgood which featured three watercolours he had painted at Crathes. Jekyll worked on around 500 commissions, flowing plant colour into all parts of the garden. The hallmarks of her designs are seasonal borders, deep and drifting – seasonal in the sense of all the plants reaching their apogee together. The crescendos of colour in her long summer borders were inspired by Turner's 1839 The Fighting Temeraire. *The reds and oranges of the dying sun reflected in the sea and clouds in Turner's painting were translated by Jekyll into painterly dashes that run like threads through the beds, shorter plants sometimes running behind taller ones in groups of uneven numbers. The backdrop was either a high wall or clipped yew hedge with the borders placed so that they need only be visited when at their zenith.*

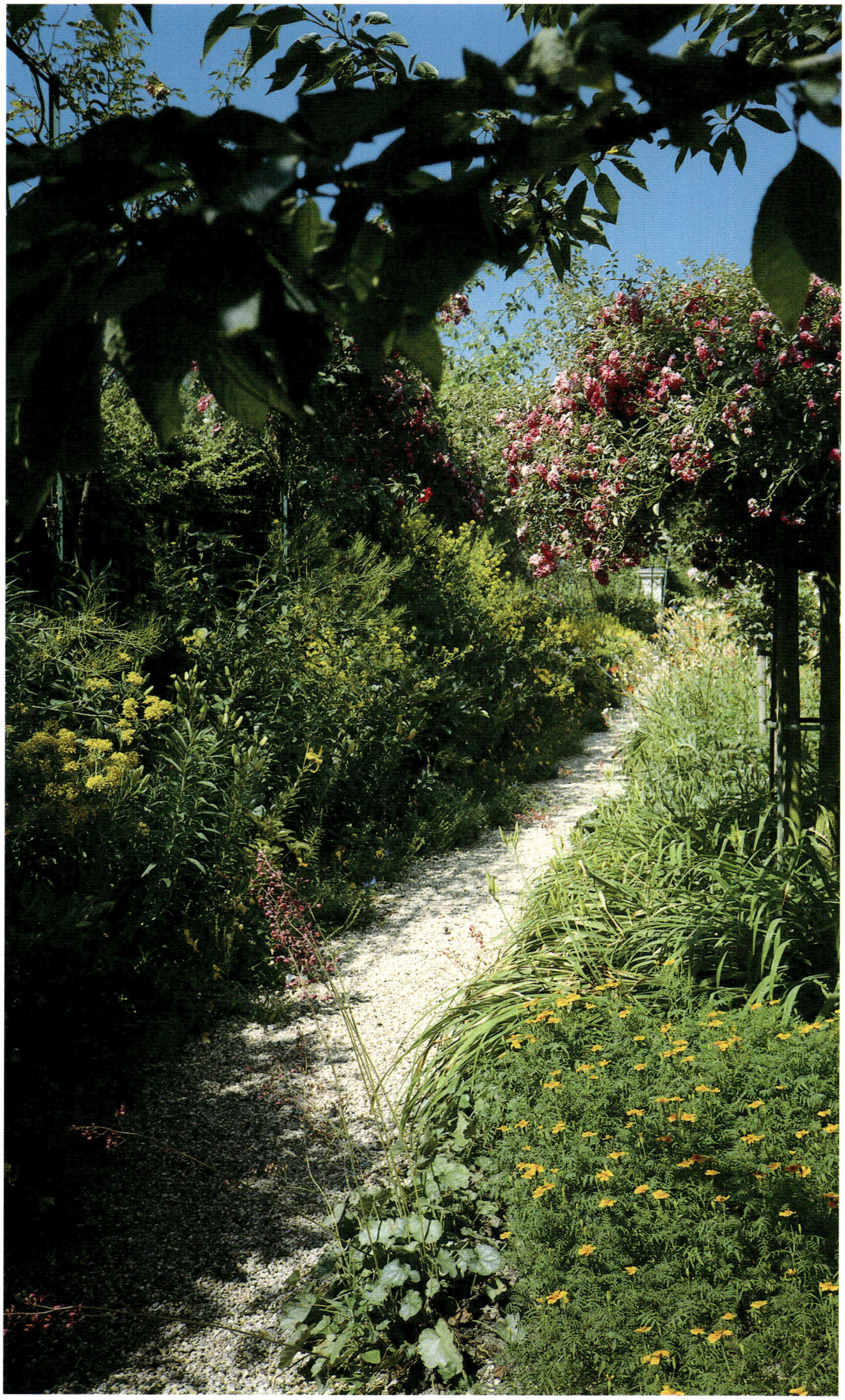

The rose Belle Vichysoisse, underplanted with Escholtzia and Hemerocallis, that are just about to burst into flower, in one of the linear beds in the upper garden at Giverny. The French landscape architect, J.C.N. Forestier praised Monet for popularizing roses which he wrote had been banished to kitchen gardens in France. The only rose to survive at Giverny after Monet's death was Belle Vichysoisse, a weeping standard of pink pompom flowers: the French call them rosier (rose trees). Today most standard roses are budded at little over one metre, in the late nineteenth century it was almost double this, and supported by a good frame the roses gave height and literally cascaded down.

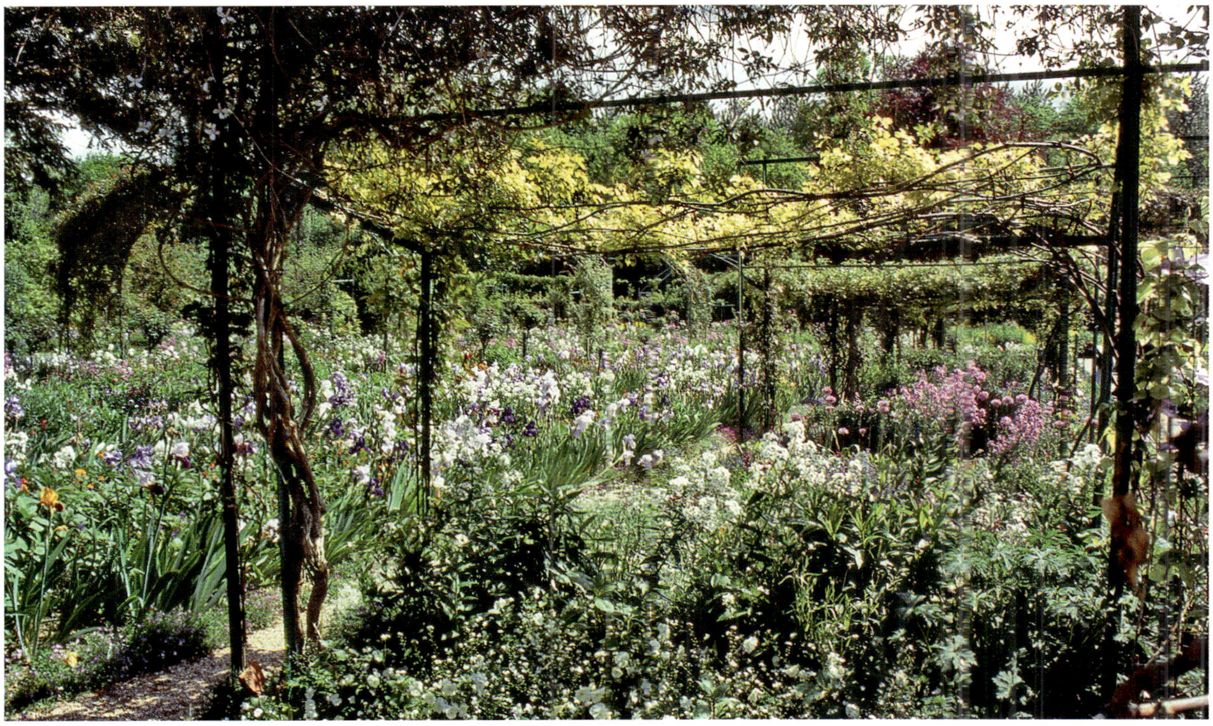

The rectangular beds in the upper garden at Giverny run north to south so that the light plays through their flowers and foliage from dawn to dusk. How appropriate that one of Monet's favourite flowers for these long beds, the iris, derives its name from the nymph who slid down the rainbow bearing messages from the gods. The curved lines of Monet's pond were broken by Flag irises, their bold yellow flowers echoing the sun when mirrored in the water on clear days. Nurserymen were breeding varieties of iris with colours across the spectrum. Textured and often iridescent, the flowers rose elegantly above their architectural sword-like leaves, as evidenced also in the texture and colour that appears carved onto Vincent Van Gogh's eponymous canvas.

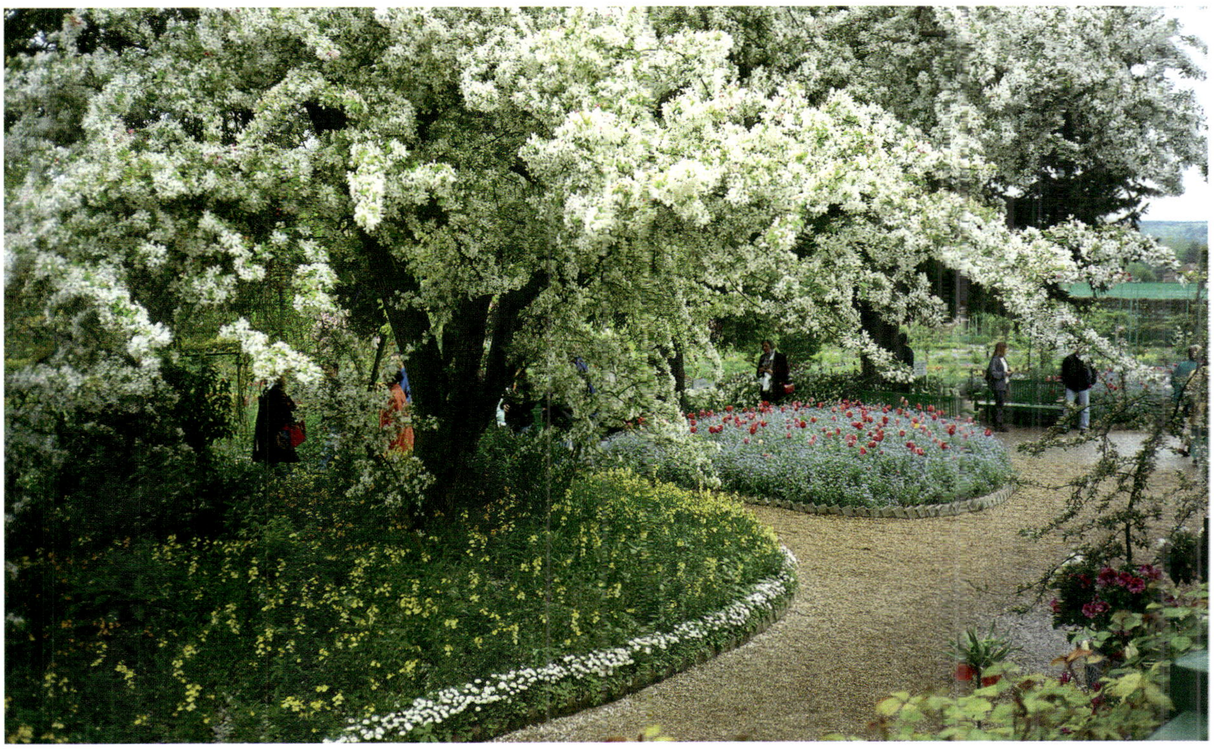

Monet primed his earthly canvas so that it could support massed plants to completely paint the soil. The haze of blossom echoes the waves of forget-me-nots in this image taken in the cool spring of 1996.

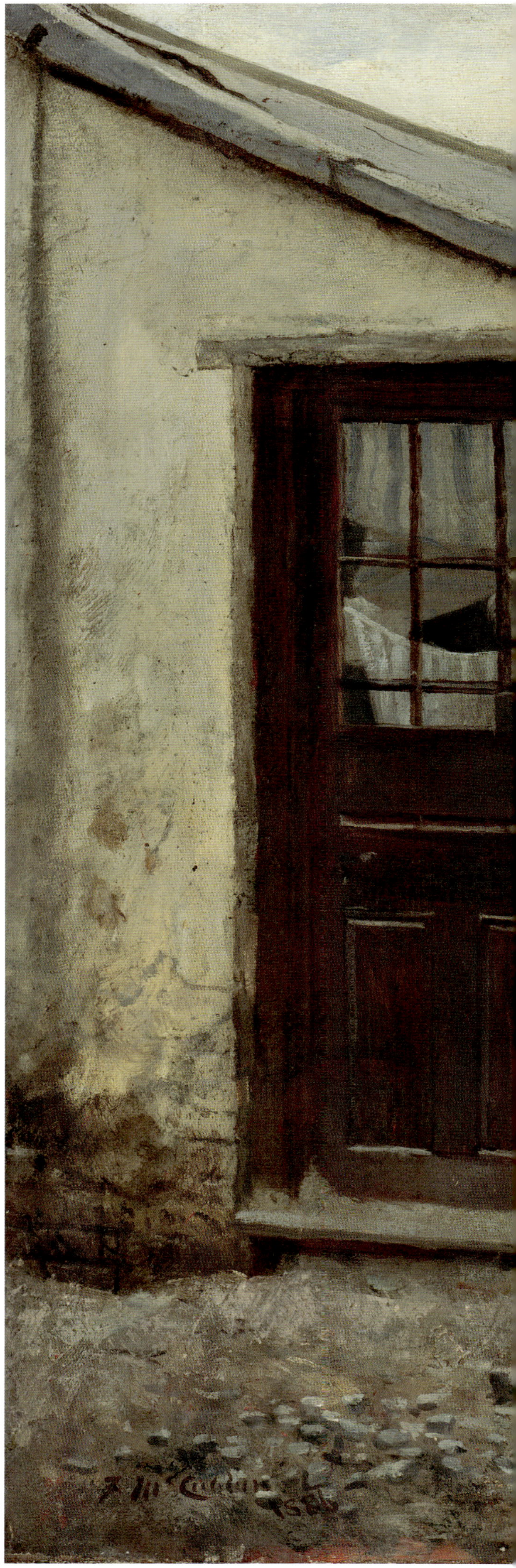

Frederick McCubbin, **Girl with bird at the King Street bakery**. *Oil on canvas, 40.7 x 46cm (16 x 18in.), 1886*

Frederick McCubbin briefly ran the family bakery after his father died, before going on to work at the National Art Gallery School in Melbourne. In the painting a climber provides green and shade, and a bird pecks for insects in the rotting door, while the little girl is absorbed in a book or knitting. Behind her on the wall is a caged bird – is it singing? Despite the dilapidated and drab appearance, there is a sense of oasis.

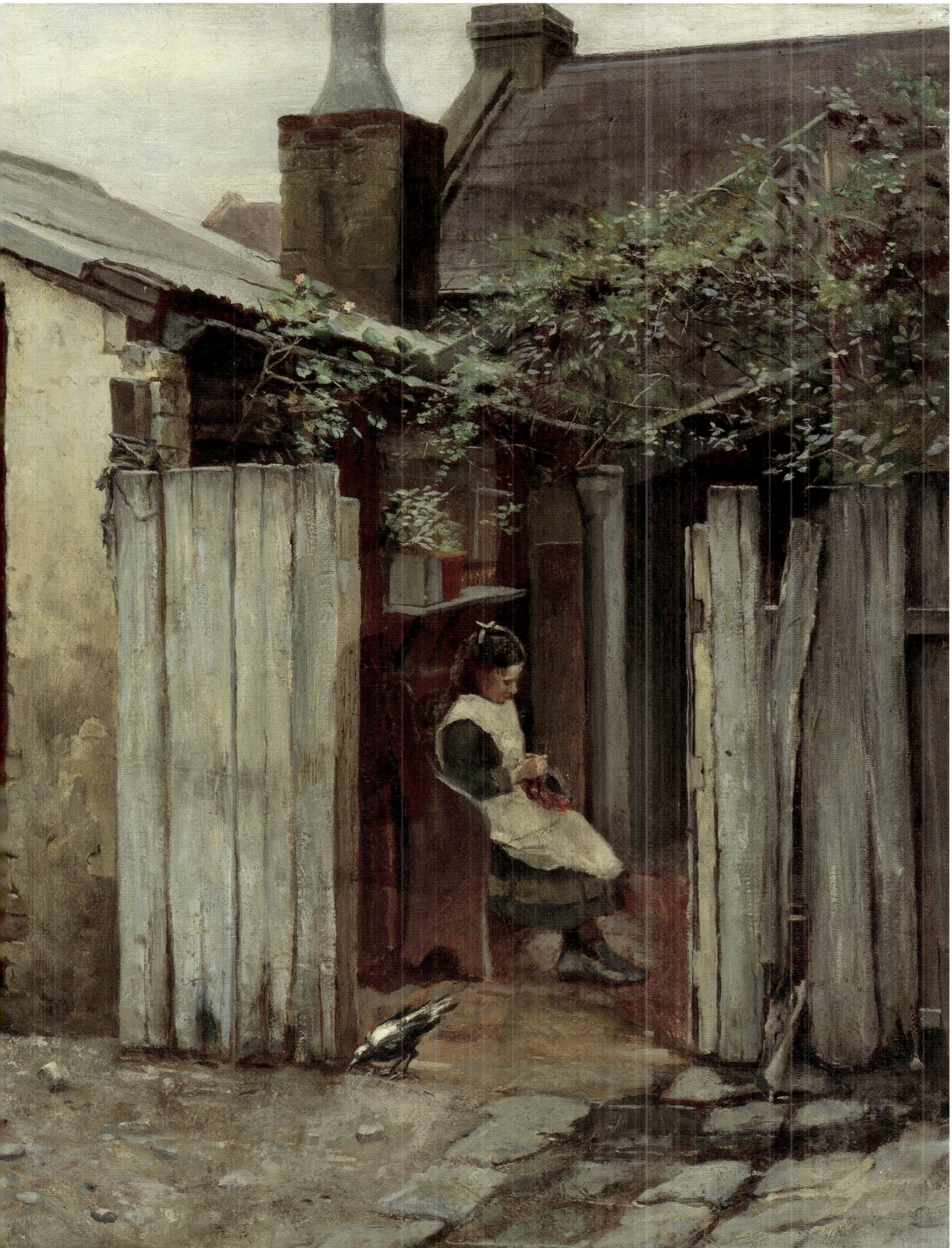

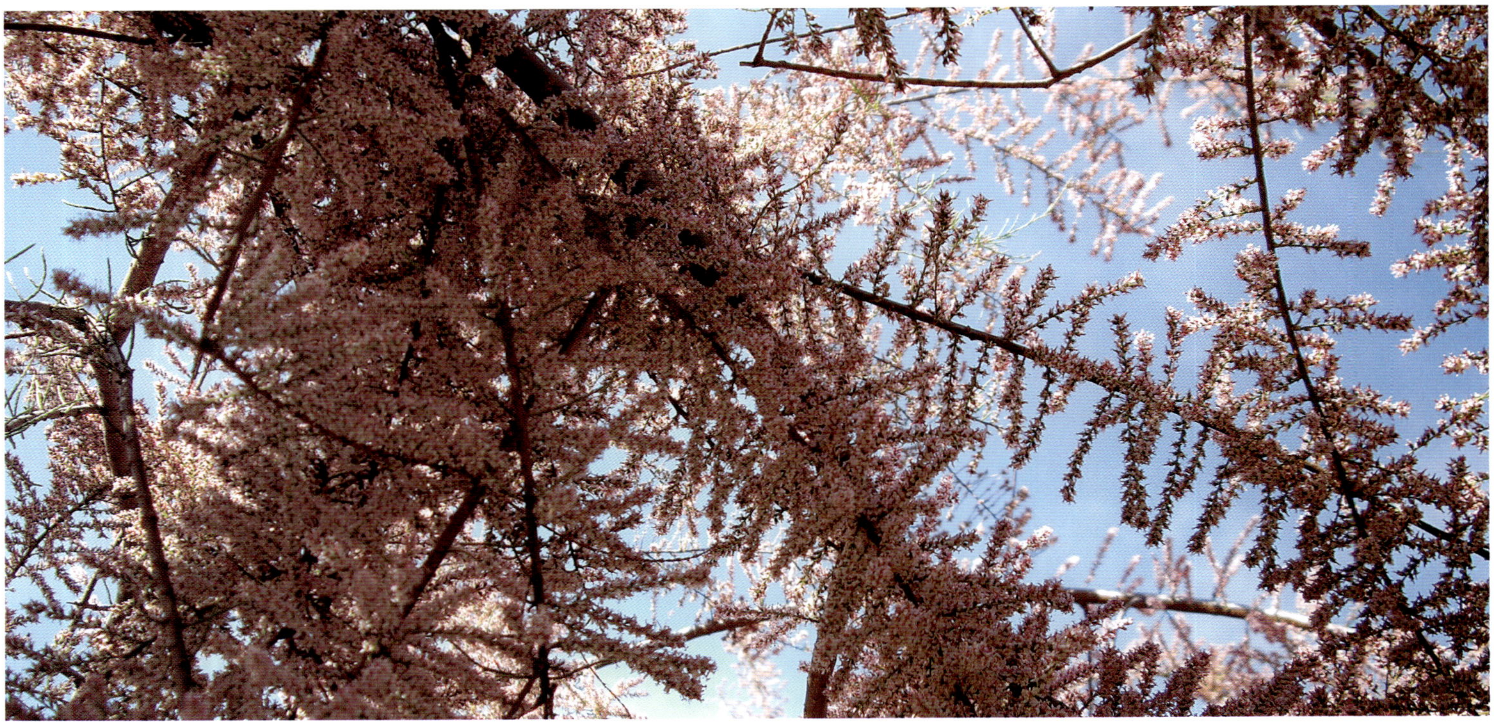

Above: *A Tamarisk flowering in a haze of pink against the blue sky. It thrives in maritime climates such as southern England and eastern Australia. Jekyll's 'grey garden' scheme was so called because most of its plants had grey foliage. To enhance the effect of grey shades, she advised that 'The flowers are white, lilac, purple and pink. … the hedge is of Tamarisk (Tamarix gallica) whose feathery grey-green is in delightful harmony with the other foliage greys.'*

Opposite: *Monet's good friend, the politician Georges Clemenceau, described the view of the pond at Giverny as 'the water lilies, in the mirror of the water garden, were voluptuously lulled to sleep at the breasts of the clouds'. The colour of lily pads changes in different lights from green leaves to a metallic lustre with many shades in between.*

However 'Viva' or Miss Edith Castilla writing for the *Daily Telegraph* enthused: 'The mysterious words "nine by five" … merely refer to the size of the "impressions", which are nearly all 9 inches long and 5 inches broad. To lovers of the beautiful – and beauty is after all, as Browning says "about the best thing God invents" – the arrangements of the exhibition must strongly appeal. Scarves and draperies of soft clinging silk or the reds that Millais has made popular, and the greens, beloved of the aesthetic, hang from picture-frames and overstands and carved cabinets. The great blue and green vases that stand in various parts of the gallery were filled on the opening day with japonica and roses, violets and jonquils, and the air was sweet with the perfume of daphne.'

Of the myriad other plants that could be covered, this chapter cannot close without water lilies, Nymphaea; their name evokes images of water nymphs dancing across still water. Monet created a legacy from his pond, now reproduced onto any product that you can imagine from canvases to consumer ephemera. The source of his lily lies in the hybridising hands of Joseph Bory Latour-Marliac at his nursery in Le Temple-sur-Lot which still thrives. Happily they still possess order books and correspondence in bound editions from 1881-1924, all neatly recorded on 'onion paper'. In 1887 Latour-Marliac wrote to introduce himself to Kew, of whose bedding schemes William Robinson very publicly despaired, enclosing a N.'Marliacea Chromatella foliis hepatic marmoratis' – luckily a name to be simplified later. The Lily House at Kew was originally built to showcase the Victoria amazonica (then known as V. regia) by 1893 it included N. 'Laydekeri'. In the same year Robinson challenged Kew to plant up the lake in front of the Palm House so that it 'might be a garden picture of beautiful water flowers instead of being devoted to the unclean water-fowl that are its only ornament'.

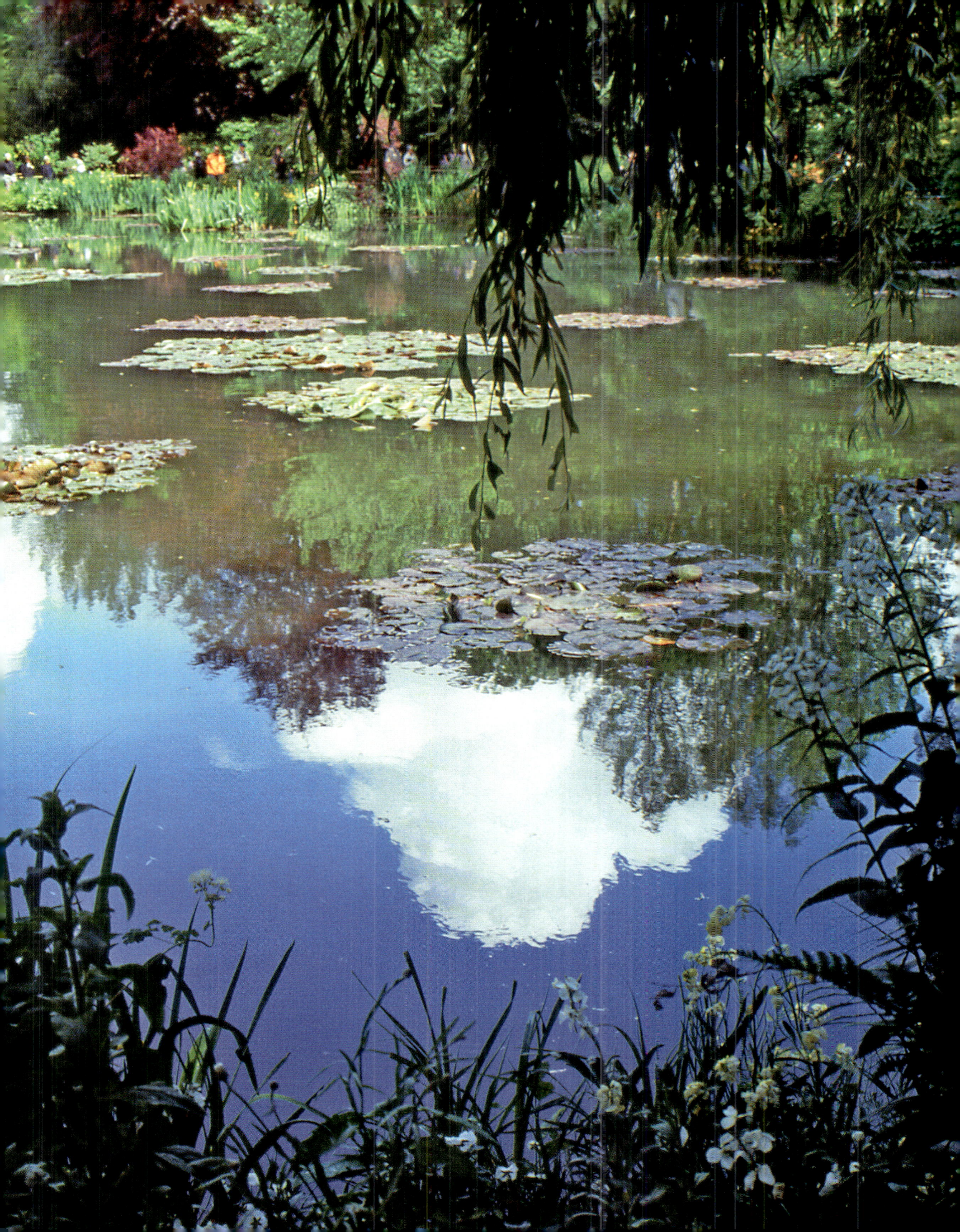

CHAPTER TWO

The Impressionists' Nurseryman

Joseph Bory Latour-Marliac

A field of water, charged with flowers and foliage floating amongst the strokes of the solar blaze, where the effects of a celestial screen are combined with an aquatic mirror, where with the diffusion of sensibilities it seems man can edge ever nearer to objectivity. All the energies of the sky and earth's radiation are called in to appear simultaneously, offering us the stupefaction of a spectacle which words cannot describe where the joys of a dream and a sense of the dawn of mankind merge.

Georges Clemenceau Claude Monet, *1928*

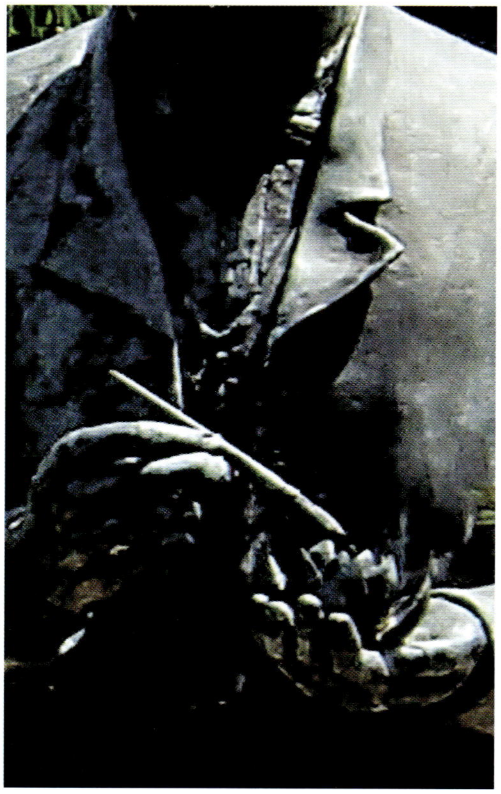

This statue of Latour-Marliac shows him with a fine brush catching the pollen from an open water lily flower. It stands by the large lower lake which has a 'Monet Bridge' at the far end, raised in celebration of the nursery's association with the great painter. Behind are the glasshouses in which the Victoria amazonica is grown.

The world's 'Prune Capital' of Agen lies in the south western French department of Lot et Garonne, where in February white and pink blossoms adorn the glorious patchwork of plum and almond orchards, interspersed with vineyards, and planted along the river basins of the two rivers. About twenty miles north-west of Agen lies Le Temple-sur-Lot, the little-known source of most of the colourful water lilies that adorn the world's ponds. Their progenitor, Joseph Bory Latour-Marliac, was born on 6 March 1830 into a farming family who were keen amateur botanists. He was sent to Paris to study law but returned early in the wake of the 1848 revolution and married in 1852. Although he helped manage the family's properties and the local plum orchards, he exercised his fascination in botany by experimenting with the newly popular Asiatic bamboos, a number of which he introduced from Japan and China. In 1875 he founded his nursery at Le Temple-sur-Lot where there are no fewer than fourteen springs within a circuit of 1000 metres, one of which is thermal. They provided the clean gently-circulating water required by water lilies and the exceptionally good light values that enhance growth and hybridisation – a scientific detail only recently appreciated.

Exotic and tropical aquatic plant displays excited great interest in mid-nineteenth century Europe. Latour-Marliac read about the colourful display of tropical water lilies at the Jardin des Plantes in Paris in an article in *Le Jardin Fleuriste* by Charles Lemaire in 1854. He and other botanists speculated on the seemingly unattainable goal of breeding blue and red varieties that would be as hardy as the white Nymphaea alba and yellow Nuphar lutea. Later Latour-Marliac wrote that hardy water lilies were 'very pretty it is true but too much alike to excite any violent rapture over their cultivation.' The thought of remedying this spurred him into action. He cast his net wide, requesting seeds and rhizomes of water lily species from Sweden, Mexico, America, Egypt, South Africa and India, and got started on experimenting by cross-pollinating them. To his delight he succeeded in producing a hardy red water lily but with the unfortunate drawback that it produced neither seed nor offsets.

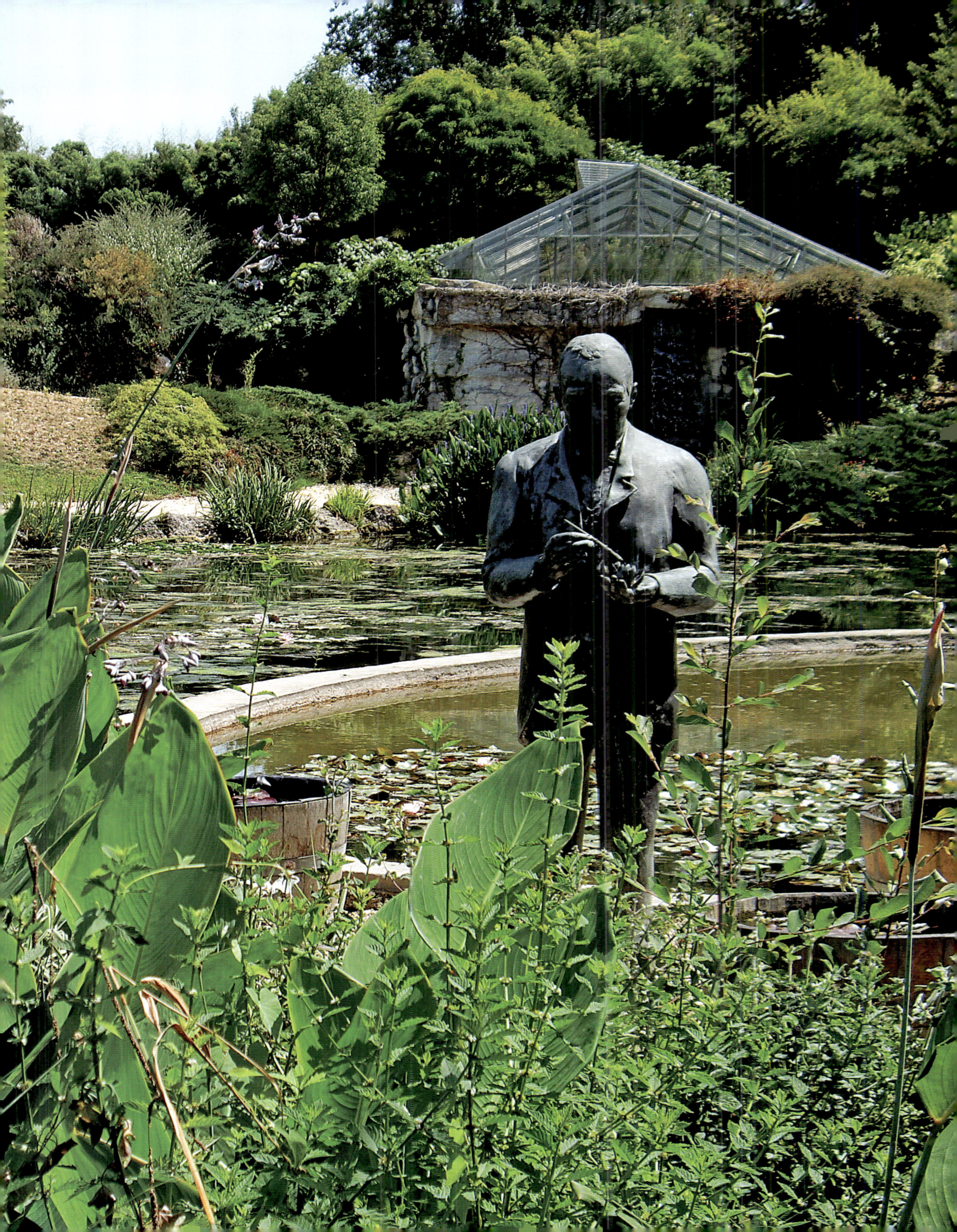

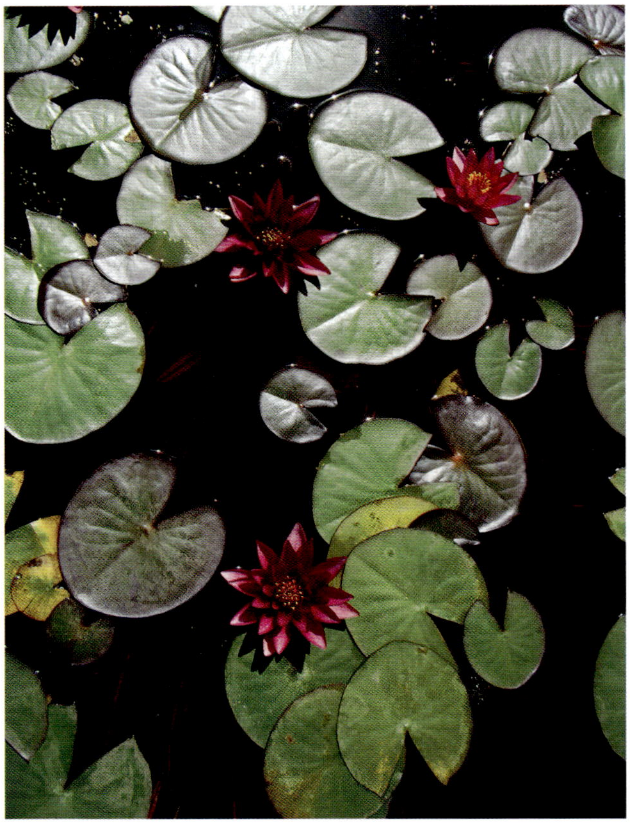

Above: *One of the water lilies bred in 1889, the year of the Exposition Universelle, and still available, is the Nymphaea Marliacea Rubra Punctata. Described as having red-purple flowers mixed with carmine and orange red stamens, its deep colouring was in marked contrast to the customary white water lilies. Latour Marliac died in 1911 and James Hudson, the head gardener to the Rothschilds at Gunnersbury Park, wrote an obituary for him in 'Amateur Gardening': ... his name will live so long as the lovely water lilies that he raised are to be found in cultivation. In 1912 his regular custom was acknowledged with Nymphaea 'James Hudson'.*

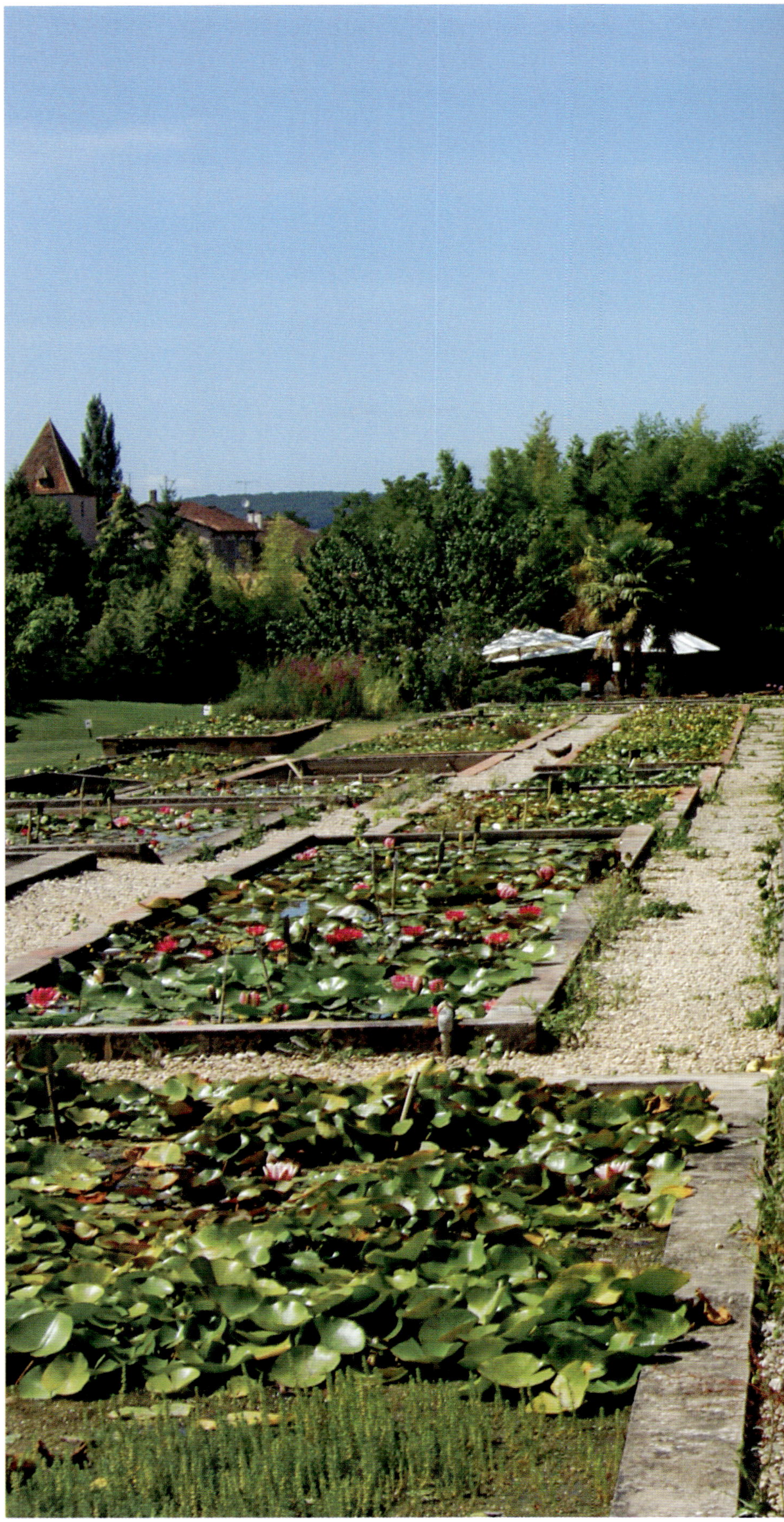

Right: *From the old well head back to Latour-Marliac's house at Le Temple-sur-Lot, the tanks are still filled with water lilies for sale, hybridization and propagation. Nearer the house the tanks are more ornamental. Local legend says that Monet visited the nursery in person, which is possible as he was driven down to Spain in 1905 and it would have been close to his route.*

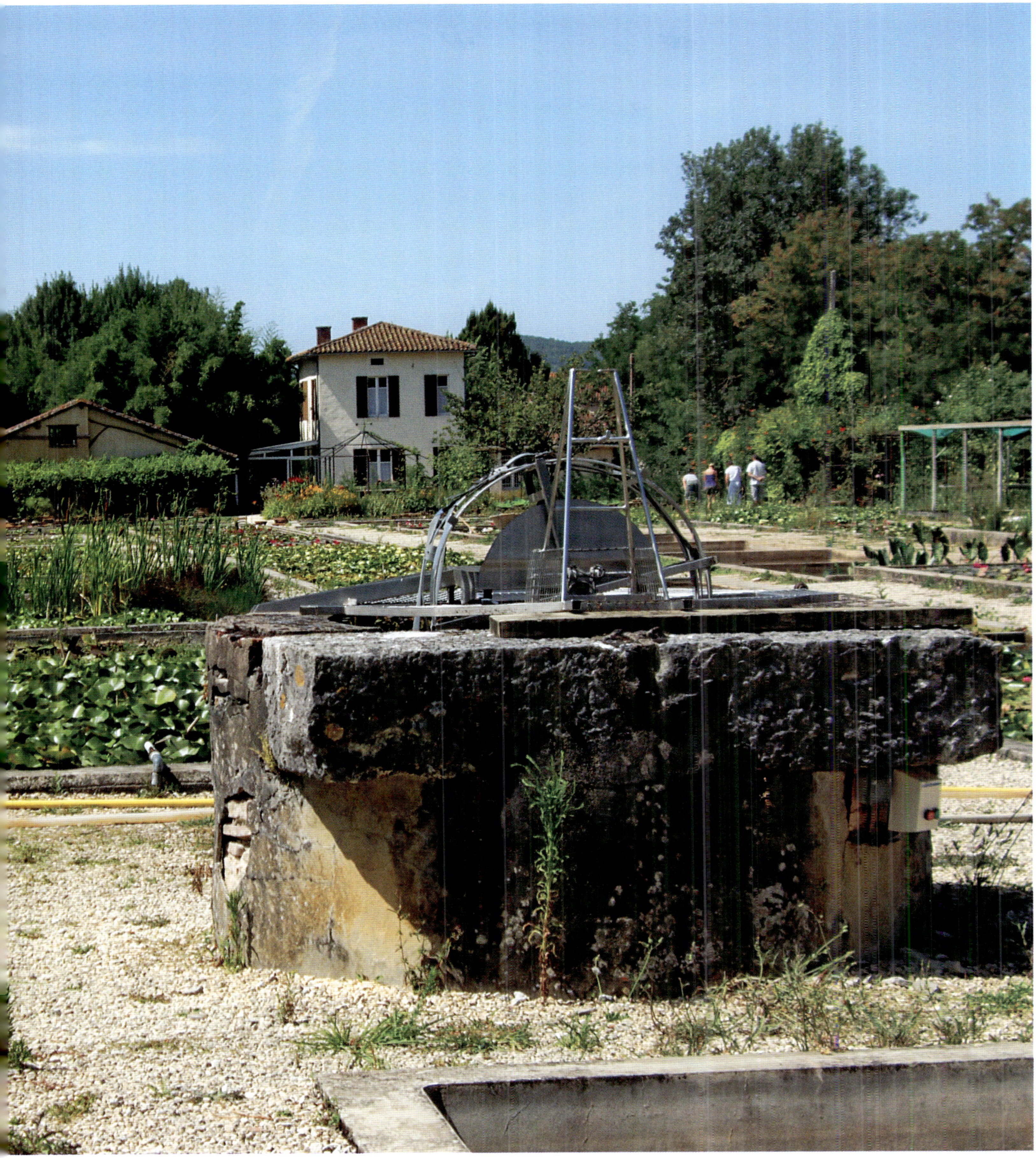

After this he selected only very free-flowering types, observing by means of numerous sowings and strict selections, that the results produced vastly improved varieties. The first yellow (still available) hybrid, from N. alba and the American N. flava, has sulphur yellow stamens set in enormous yellow flowers. It was appropriately named Nymphaea 'Marliacea Chromatella', in addition the leaf surface is marbled with chestnut markings and it has a lengthy flowering period.

In 1882 visitors to Kew Gardens were able to enjoy the premier flowering of Nymphaea marliacea chromatella, which was painted by H.G. Moon for the first coloured plate of water lilies that appeared in *The Garden* on 31st March 1888. Two more varieties were rapidly introduced: the sulphur yellow flowered and stamened N. odorata 'Sulphurea' with brown marbled leaves, and from this the miniature canary yellow N. pygmaea 'Helvola'. Latour-Marliac selected the American species from Cape Cod, N.odorata rubra, as pollen parent and N. alba as seed parent from which gorgeous tints of carmine and red were achieved. In 1887 he offered them as N. 'Marliacea Rosea' and N. 'Marliacea Carnea', as well as launching the now rare carmine pink N. odorata 'Exquisita'. The Rubras were exceedingly rare natural mutations that it took Latour-Marliac many years and much negotiation to procure using his worldwide botanical network.

Precisely when all this work started is unclear. In an 1893 article in *The Garden* he wrote that he commenced work in earnest in 1879 – but current thinking is he had probably started earlier. He was also amongst the first nurserymen to offer bamboo; his records for 1883 show twenty-three varieties, seventeen of which survived, having been introduced from Japan, followed by a further nineteen varieties the next year. The layout

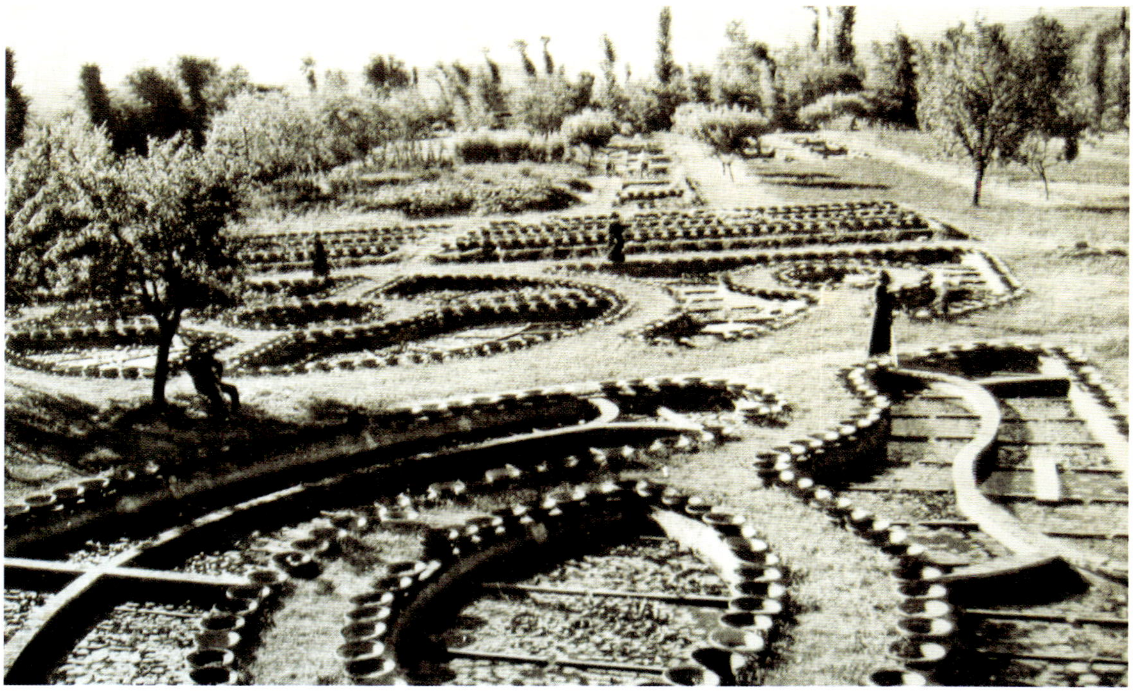

An early photograph of the sinuous Art Nouveau-inspired basins of the Latour-Marliac nurseries, local terracotta cooking pots frame the basins artistically. The site has twenty springs which provide the constant source of fresh water so essential to water lily breeding and hybridization. Lilies were dispatched by train to ports for onward delivery all over Europe as well as to Russia.

of the still-flourishing nursery consists of a series of sinuous and rectangular pools looking like palettes for a water lily colour box. Along the edges are local earthenware cooking pots that are used to hold the plants when they are lifted from the water. Delivery (and receipts) within Europe and beyond were feasible thanks to the railway having reached Villeneuve-sur-Lot, a town about fifteen kilometres down the river.

William Robinson made his first trip to Paris in 1867 as Special Horticultural Correspondent to *The Times* for an exhibition and it is interesting to speculate whether Latour-Marliac also went to the same exhibition as an embryo hybridist. In 1871 Robinson founded *The Garden* magazine and would enjoy a long working relationship with Latour-Marliac, reporting any new varieties. Robinson included the new water lilies in his book *The English Flower Garden* (1883), commissioned an article on them in 1888 for *The Garden* and Latour-Marliac was both featured in and contributed to later articles in 1893, 1894 and 1898.

Latour-Marliac's decision to exhibit at the 1889 Exposition Universelle in Paris was what really brought him to public notice. There he displayed his first collection over a six month period, from which, as he later wrote: 'I came back radiant with the distinction of first prize.' Famously, his display was spotted by Monet, also an exhibitor. Latour-Marliac's 1889 booklet *'Les Aquariums de plein air, de serre et d'appartement'* anticipated Monet's interest when he wrote about growing water lilies, 'so this picture full of seduction has provoked massive enthusiasm amongst the happy owners of lakes, fishponds, streams and pools ....'

In the company archives at Le Temple-sur-Lot are Latour-Marliac's correspondence, articles and the results of his decades-long work hybridising water lilies. These records also show that from 1887 to 1906 Robinson ordered eighteen different varieties; sometimes repeating orders such as for the red N. 'Gloriosa' with very double, perfumed cherry red and palest pink tipped flowers, the now rare pink N. 'Arc-en-Ciel' and the 1904 miniature copper yellow N. 'Graziella'. In January 1894 Robinson dedicated the bound volumes of *The Garden* for 1893 to 'Mons. B. Latour-Marliac who has brought the colours and forms of the water lilies of the east to the waters of the north.'

W. Goldring writing for *The Garden* in February 1894 excitedly reports on more new reds in several shades, the Latour-Marliac catalogue from that year shows N. 'Laydekeri Purpurata' whose flowers range from carmine pink to crimson centres; the brilliant vermilion hues darkening towards the centre of N. 'Lucida'; and the blousy purple-red flowers tipped with white of N. 'Marliacea Flammea' along with the now rare copper coloured N. 'Fulva'. The planting of water lilies in readers' gardens invoked strong opinions on both sides of the Atlantic: in 1894 Robinson reported in *The Garden* that Mr. L.W. Goodell of the Massachusetts Horticultural Society had advised: 'In planting large, artificial or natural ponds, do not, above all things, set the Nymphaea in regular rows at equal distances apart, as though it were an agricultural crop needing cultivation with a horse hoe'. Today it seems unimaginable

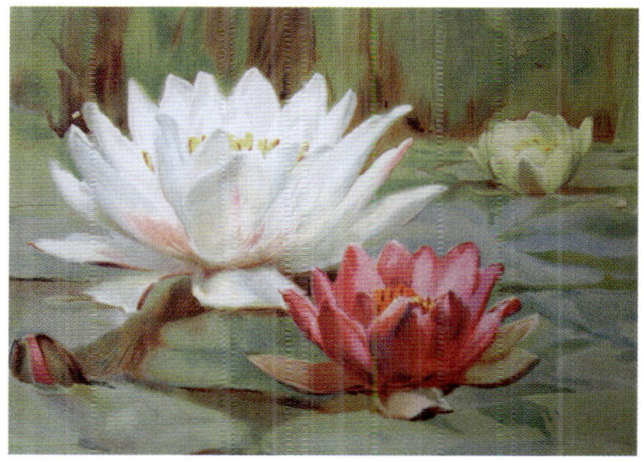

Colour plates appeared in magazines and books from the early 1880's. This is a typical example illustrating the new Nymphaea chromatella (yellow), N. carnea (pale pink) and N. ignea (red). Latour-Marliac was awarded first prize and a gold medal respectively for his displays at the 1889 and 1900 Expositions Universelles. In 1898 the Royal Horticultural Society awarded him the Veitch memorial medal.

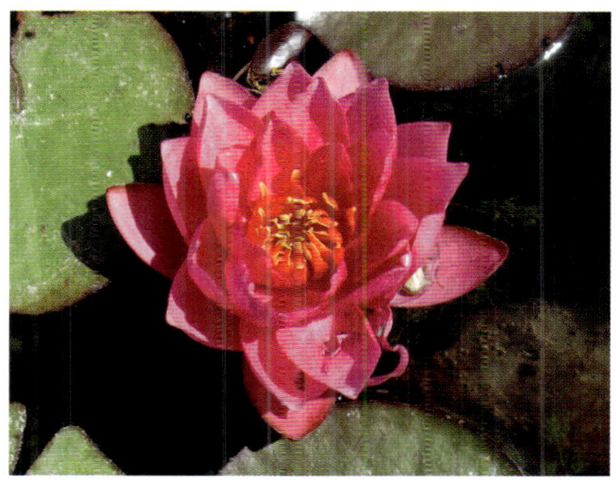

Nymphaea James Brydon was one of the water lilies Monet ordered from the Latour-Marliac nurseries in 1904. Latour-Marliac swapped water lilies with the American breeder Henry Dreer who had bred and introduced N. James Brydon in 1899.

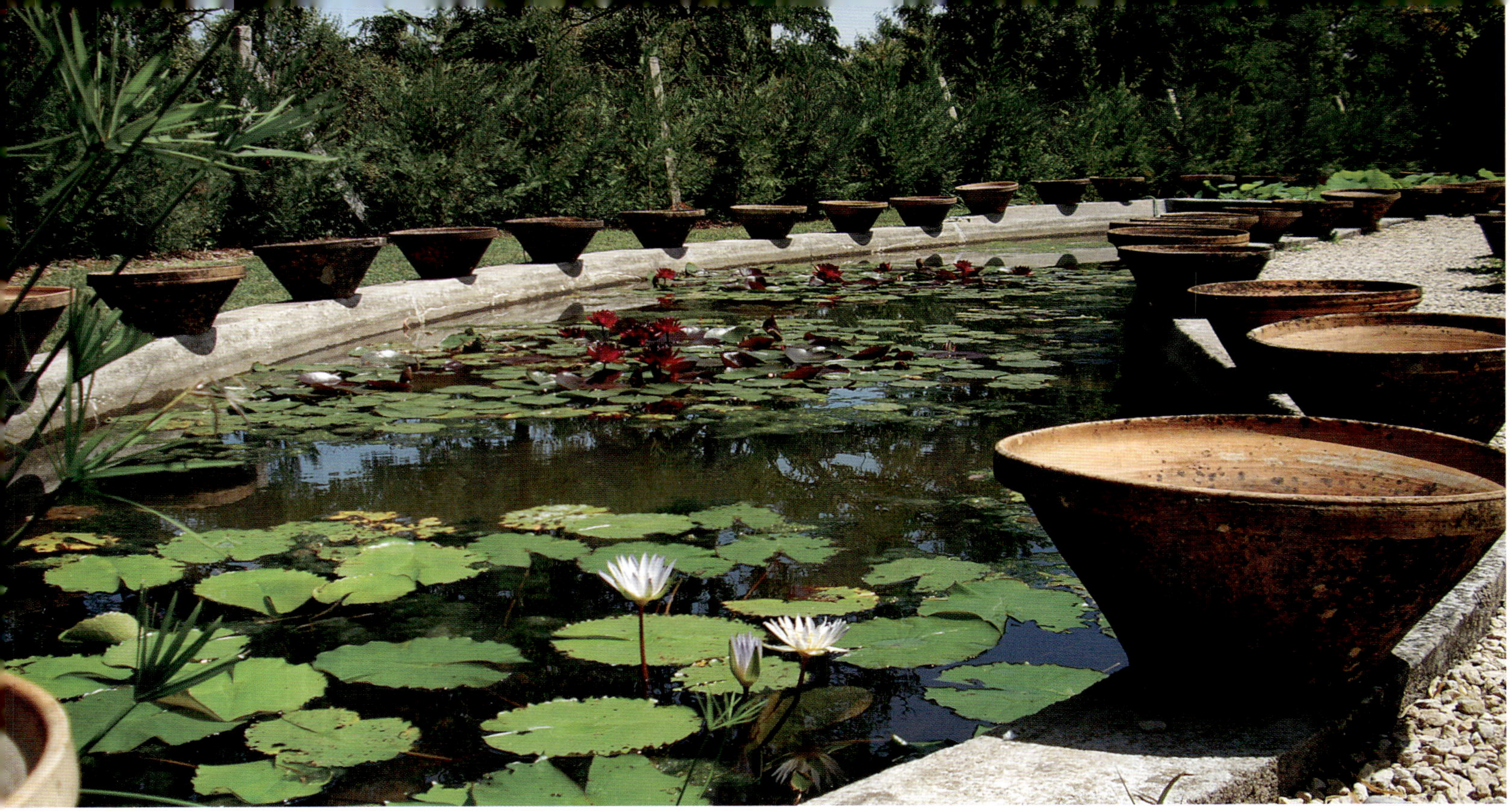

Latour-Marliac's tanks are still used today, as are the local terracotta cooking pots. The ogival tanks have a decidedly tadpole shape and appropriately are home to large colonies of toads.

to grow water lilies in anything other than sinuous asymmetry but evidently this was not the case for Victorian gardeners raised on the neat row mentality. Robinson firmly adds: 'In such ways we shall get gardens of lovely colour and form, free from the pastry cook gardener.'

The new century was marked in Paris by the 1900 Exposition Universelle, where, despite its cold aspect, Latour-Marliac's tanked display by the newly built rococo Petit Palais was considered successful. He showed forty-one varieties of hardy water lilies and six blue exotic Nymphaea.

Latour-Marliac cleverly named many of his new hybrids after his most enthusiastic customers: Robinson's support was recognised in the introduction of N. 'Robinsoniana', about which Latour-Marliac wrote in *The Garden* (1893): 'The acquisition of a red-flowered hybrid Nymphaea which yields seed has opened up a new prospect by affording the means of effecting crossings with the yellow-flowered kinds, the result being the production of quite a legion of Nymphaeas bearing flowers which exhibit singular shades of colouring, such as orange, vermilion, gold colour, etc. Some of these splendid kinds have been already introduced to the public, the first of them which flowered being named after the editor of *The Garden*, a compliment due to him in return for the great interest which he has taken in the advancement of the culture of hardy Nymphaeas.' Indeed, Latour-Marliac's customer list reads like a Who's Who of the late nineteenth and early twentieth century gardening world.

Year after year orders were despatched to English nurserymen such as James Backhouse of York, Veitch and Sons in both Chelsea and Exeter, James Cocker & Son in Aberdeenshire, William Cutbush and Son Ltd., Barnet and Amos Perry at Enfield. Many of them went on to sell Latour-Marliac varieties, sometimes under different names, which created some sharp exchanges. In 1900 E.T. Cook who was newly editing *The Garden* with Gertrude Jekyll, was sent an order with which Latour-Marliac enclosed a flower of N. 'Atropurpurea' which was to be introduced the following year. Other regular English customers were A. Paul and Sons, Cheshunt,

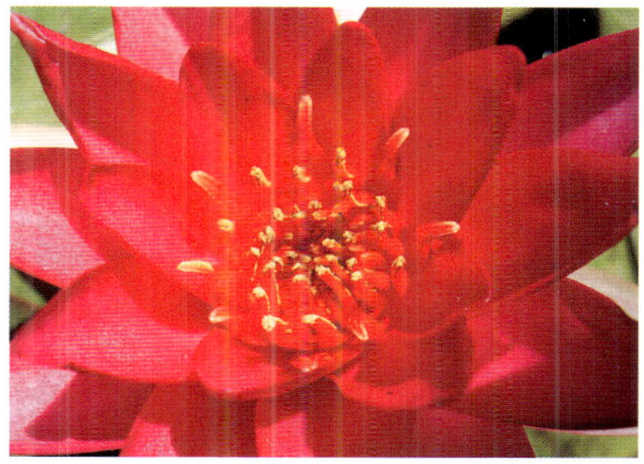

Nymphaea marliacea Ignea. The glorious new shades of pink and yellow that Joseph Bory Latour-Marliac had managed to hybridise were marketed from the 1880s onwards. He exported water lilies throughout Europe, into Russia, the United States and even back to Japan. His surviving records show orders from both Monet and Jekyll.

Hertfordshire and Kelways of Langport, Somerset, the latter also supplied Monet with herbaceous plants. Although today's most celebrated customers Monet and Jekyll ordered small amounts, Monet chose more expensive varieties whilst Latour-Marliac wrote to Jekyll regarding cultivation of tender and hardy varieties. The origins and dispatch of coloured hardy water lilies lie with Latour-Marliac but the international legacy and association of water lilies rests with Monet.

The secret of Latour-Marliac's successful hybridisation has yet to be discovered, however, crosses raised by him were still being introduced as late as 1937, a legacy of over seventy varieties. After his death in 1911 the nursery with its specialist pools and nursery pans was run initially by his son Édgard. Beset by poor health, Édgard died in 1924, and the business continued under his sister Angèle, brother-in-law Maurice Laydeker and their descendents until the 1990s. Ray and Barbara Davies then bought and renovated the site which they sold to Robert Sheldon under whom it continues to flourish as SARL Latour-Marliac.

Where would a Jekyll-Lutyens design be without a lily tank or pool around which the models for Frederick Frieseke and Rupert Bunny could elegantly drape themselves? The austere stone-edged pools provide the perfect frame for a colourful display, a design idea that from the outset could be decanted down to very modest proportions. The greatest proponent of the water garden in art is, unquestionably, Monet, through his water garden and his canvases, whether first hand or in the manifold commercial replications.

In conclusion, the white-fading-to-pink water lily, N. 'James Hudson', was named for the head gardener at Gunnersbury Park, London. One of Hudson's watchwords was 'Variety is infinitely better than repetition', and he worked firstly with Leopold Rothschild, then his son Lionel, beautifying their gardens with nature and colour. Leopold had fifty different varieties of prize-winning water lilies, as well as tender blue ones in specially heated tanks, notably the Australian water lily, N. gigantea 'Hudsoni'. On 20 May 1911 Hudson wrote the obituary in *Amateur Gardening* to Latour-Marliac: 'his name will live so long as the lovely water lilies that he raised are to be found in cultivation.'

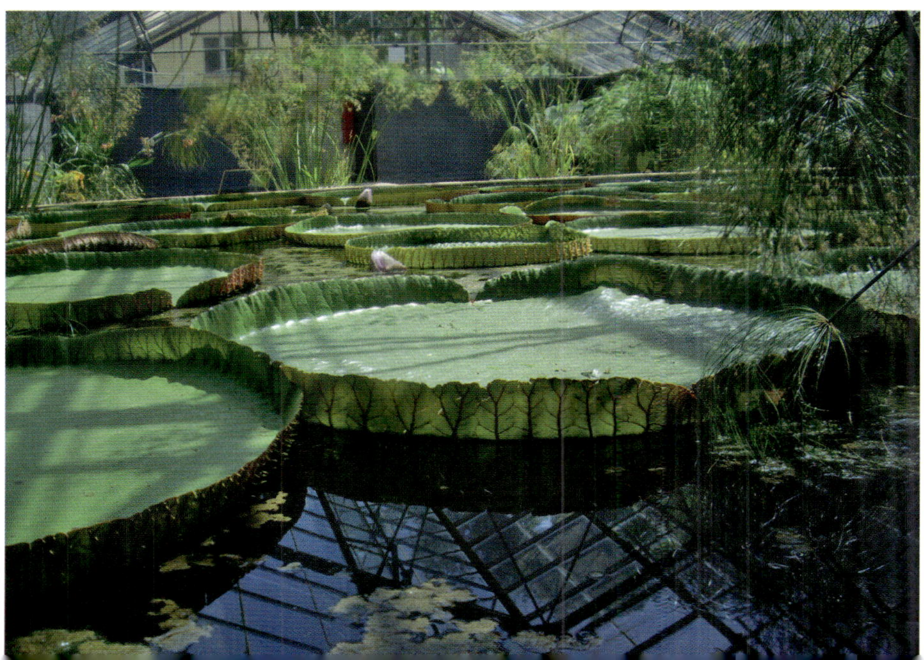

The Victoria amazonica under glass at SARL Latour-Marliac today. Its vast leaves and substantial ribbed understructure inspired Joseph Paxton's design for the Crystal Palace in London. Seeing exotic water lilies in conservatories at botanic gardens was the genesis of Latour-Marliac's quest to breed their colours and variety into hardy forms.

Food for Love

They painted, discussed art matters, criticized each other in a healthy manner and, imbued with Roberts' enthusiasm, all worked tirelessly and joyously throughout the long summer day. Late in the afternoon in the shade of the pine trees, the long trestle tables which always stood there for such occasions were set out by the ladies with a feast 'fit for the gods' awaiting the return of their men folk. Then there would be exclamations of admiration at the work achieved during the day and all would settle down to a merry feast accompanied by laughter and badinage while a marvellously-happy spirit of camaraderie prevailed among the members of the big family. Many a quick sketch was made on the spot with brilliant colour and rich contrasts of light and shade.

Anna Fraser, c.1889

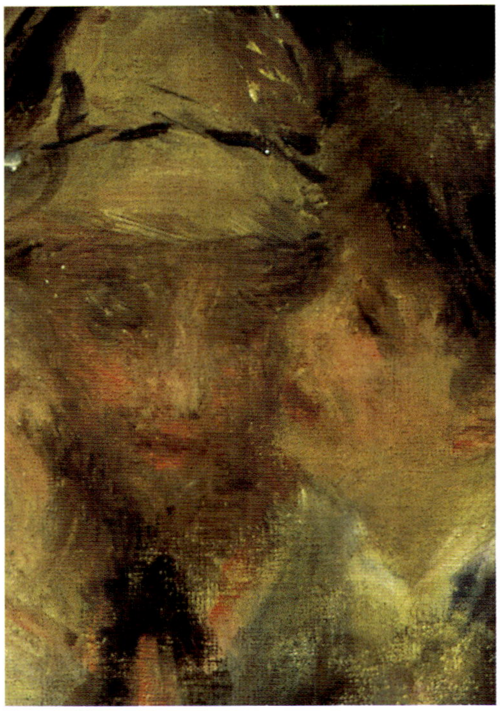

Pierre-Auguste Renoir, **In the Garden**, *or* **Under the Trees of the Moulin de la Galette** *(Sous la Tonnelle, au Moulin de la Galette). Oil on canvas, 81 x 65cm (32 x 25 ½in.), 1875*

The enclosure of entwining arms and branches creates a delicious sense of intimacy. Art critic and good friend to Monet and Renoir, Geffroy captures this perfectly in his description of this as 'meals in the open air set in the brilliant atmosphere of fine weather where the colour of their eyes and traces of their smiles were lost in a haze of smoke, with the light inebriation of conversation.' The formal garden cannot be seen but the light plays brightly on the blue and white dress of the girl in the foreground, and catches the upturned faces of the couple at the table.

Anna Fraser's description encapsulates the joys of Bohemian life in Australia. Love, divine or profane, inspirational or not, is a part of life, and for European culture it started in the Garden of Eden with God, lust and food or was it food before lust? Religious faith amongst the Impressionists ranged from devoutly spiritual to simply divining the genius of the place. According to the mores of the time, many of the artists were profane in the sensuality of romance that infiltrates their paintings. Food amongst family, friends and strangers is a form of loving which was enjoyed with relish by Impressionists around the globe.

As a teenager Monet had been introduced to the freedom of painting *en plein air* by the landscape artist Eugène Boudin, who also initiated and nutured Monet's tastes for eating good food, toasting friends and enjoying robust conversations at La Ferme Saint Simeon in Honfleur. In painting terms Monet developed this simple pleasure into an act of rivalry with his friend Edouard Manet by elegantly clothing his picnickers. In his 1865 *Dejeuner sur l'herbe* he even includes a well-behaved dog, quietly looking at the spread of raised pies, crockery and bottles. The weight of the picnic hamper, the delicacy of the ladies' dresses and the fact that this was Monet's first complete canvas *en plein air* suggest the party had only taken a very short walk. Manet's original raises lasciviousness to an art form where painted luscious fruits and freshly baked breads pour carelessly out of the basket, drawing the eye in turn to the naked delights of pale womanly flesh, in contrast with the rather overdressed young men engaged in conversation.

Monet's lover, and later wife, Alice Hoschedé, was an excellent cook and hostess who widened Monet's circle of friends. A meal at Giverny was always preceded by a tour of their gardens. Whether lunching, wining or dining, Monet shared his passion, exchanging plants and nursery catalogues, with his two dearest friends the politician Georges Clemenceau and the art critic Gustave Geoffroy as well as journalist and author Octave Mirbeau. Much to the amusement of his friends, Mirbeau became fanatical about gardening.

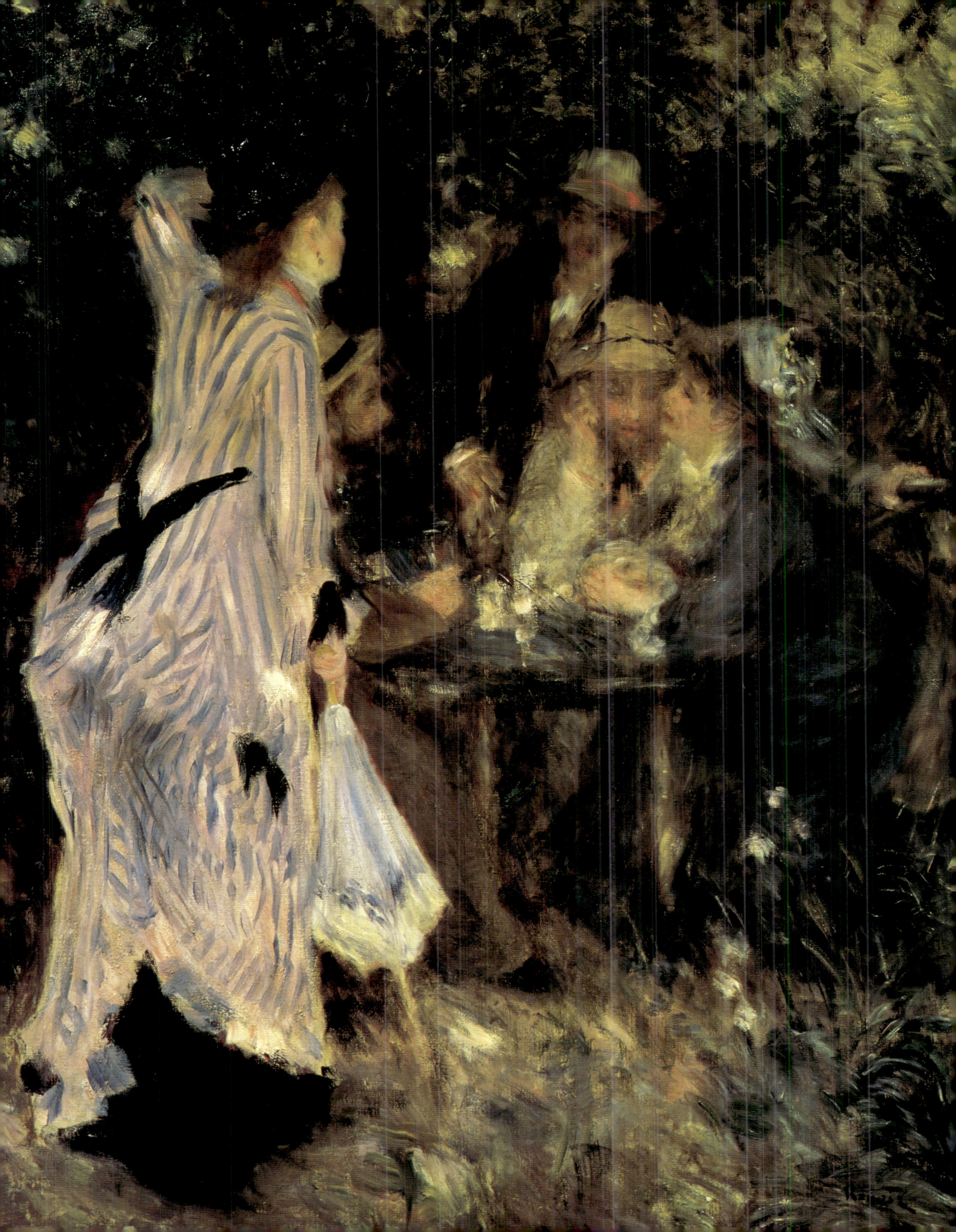

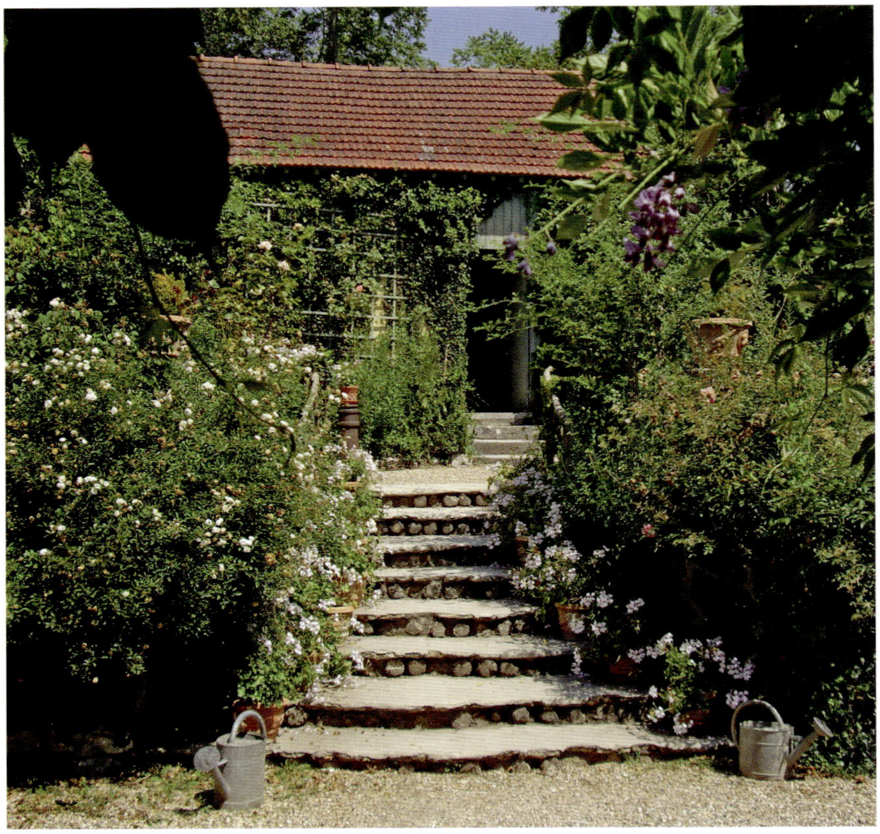

Left: M. and Mme Baudy ran the local village bar and grocery in Giverny. As their business increased with the visiting artists they decided to invest in building rooms which opened in 1887, followed by a studio in the gardens which can be seen in this image. Later two tennis courts were built and maintained by American Impressionist Stanton Young, and despite Monet's disapproval his stepdaughters would come to play tennis with the artists. John Leslie Breck painted a wonderful picture of M. Baudy sitting at the café cash desk-cum-bar at the Hotel Baudy in 1888. It is a table covered in bottles and decanters with a large mirror on the wall behind so that he could keep an eye on what was going on when his back was turned. The scene is completed by a cat snoozing on the floor.

Below: The garden appears to be growing within the Hotel Baudy studio. It provided the Givernyists with room to finish their canvases after a day in the Normandy countryside. The Hotel Baudy and its studio still exist, today excellent coffee and a slice of lemon tart can be taken in front of the hotel. There are no longer tennis courts, just a pleasant circuitous walk around the gardens up the flowerpot-lined path into the original studio. The Musée des Impressionismes dedicated to the American Impressionists in Giverny is just up the road.

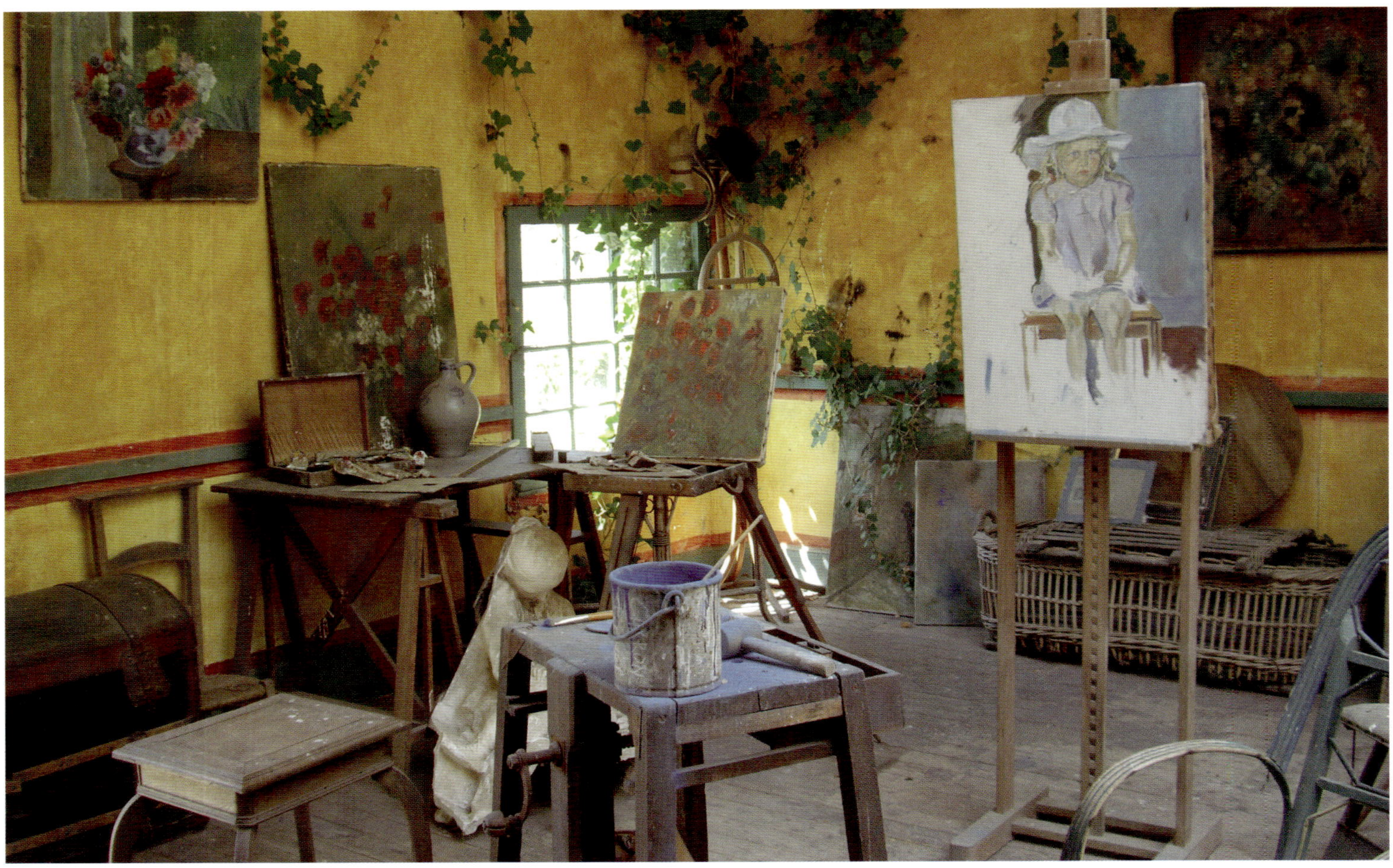

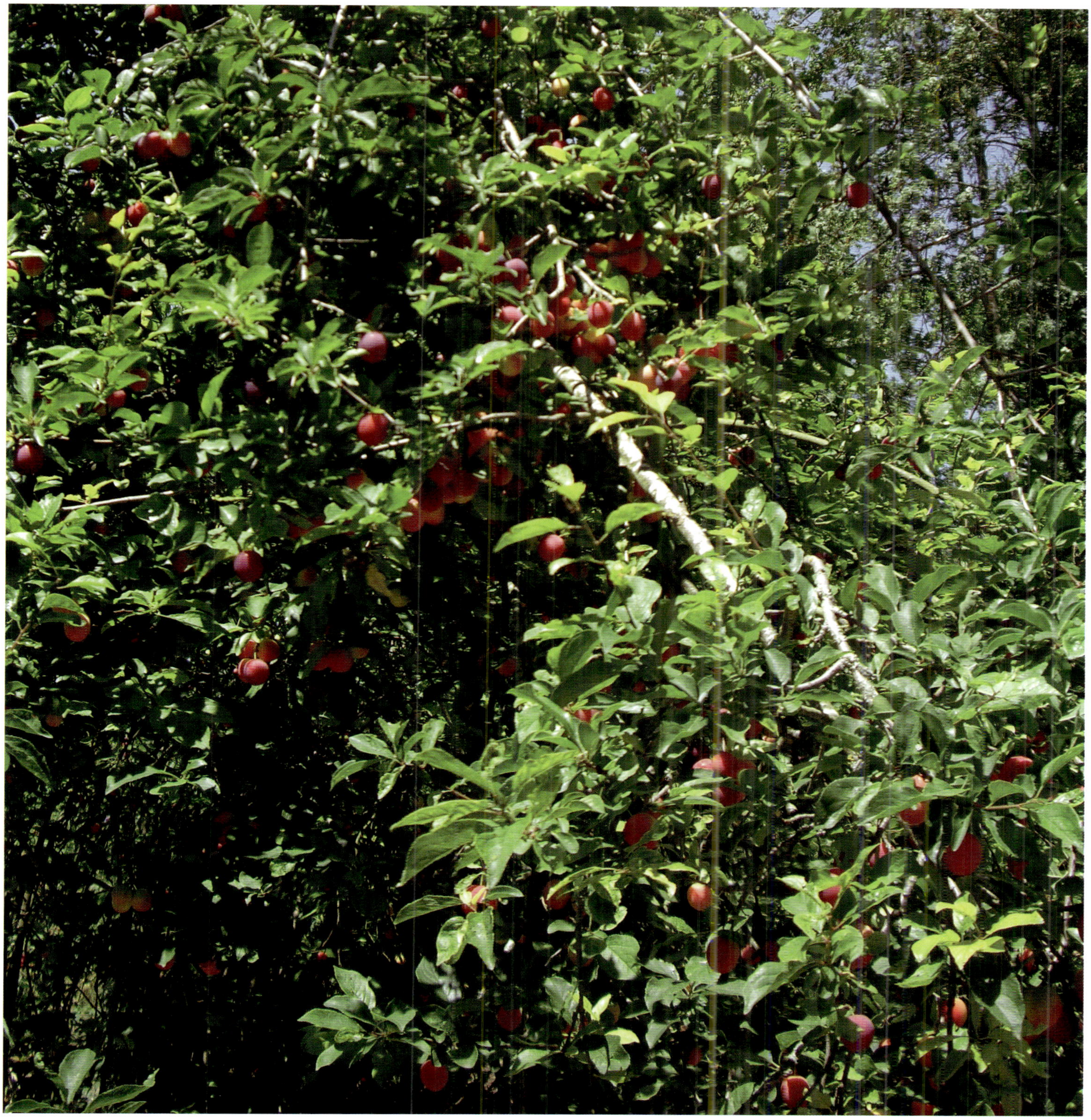

Ripe cherry plums against a sunny blue sky. On Saturdays there might be masked balls and dancing to the piano and banjo, and tennis matches were followed by suppers eaten under Chinese lanterns in the bower with copious amounts of wine, and cherries off the Baudys' trees. Mme Baudy even learnt how to cook a Thanksgiving Dinner, though presumably not to be served in the garden. Seven hundred names were recorded between 1887 and 1899, other notable guests included Paul Cézanne, Bernard Berenson and Alexander Calder. As Giverny became a pilgrimage centre for Impressionism, the hotel and the village both thrived on its new tourist industry. Not everyone benefited, however; indeed the neighbouring Frieseke's grew their own fruit and vegetables because they had become more expensive in Giverny than in Paris.

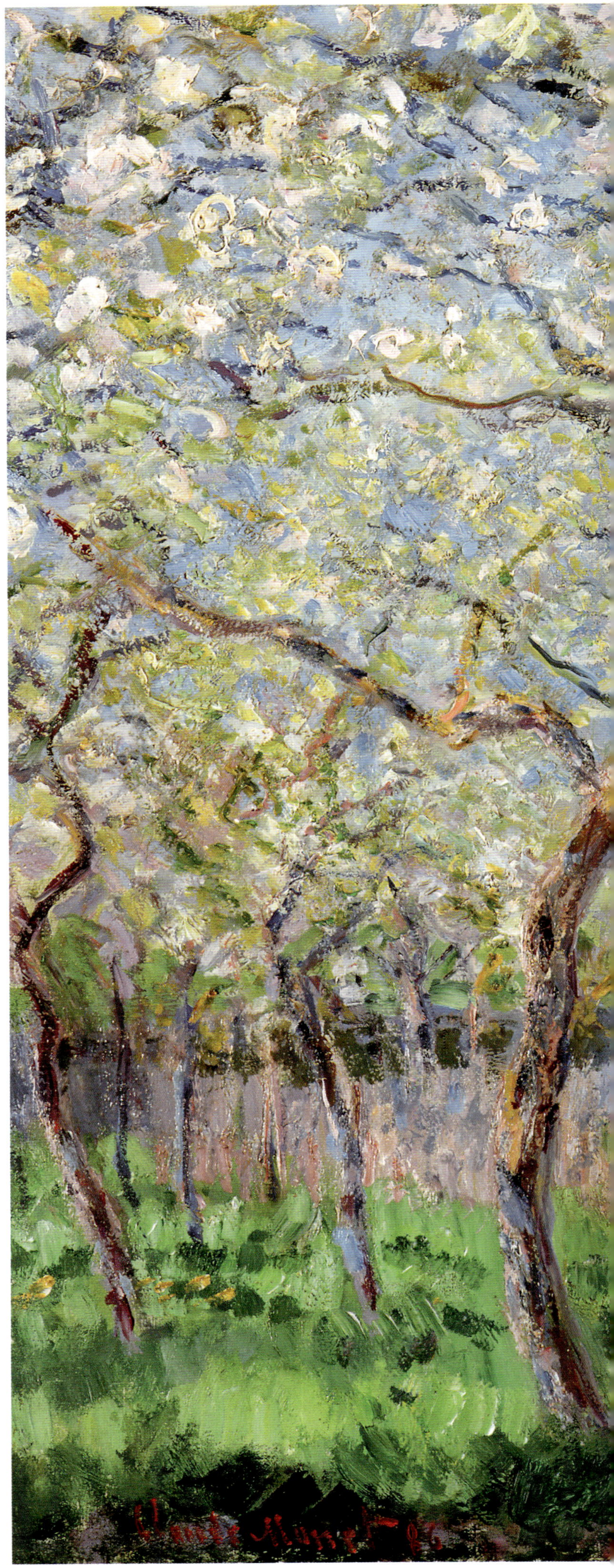

Claude Monet, **Le Printemps** (Springtime). *Oil on canvas, 64.8 x 80.6cm (25½ x 31¾ in.), 1886*

When ordering food 'à la Normande' it is almost certain to include apples; Monet found his house at Giverny in late April 1883 just as its apple orchards were bursting into blossom. The Garden of Eden where 'out of the ground made the Lord God to grow every tree that is pleasant to the sight, and good for food'; and the tree of life in the midst of the garden remained an aspirational setting. One senses the hope of an earthly Eden when Monet painted his elder son Jean with his favourite stepdaughter (to be) and model Suzanne under the canopy of apple blossoms, embraced by the outer wall of the garden at Giverny. Some years later Jean Monet married Blanche Hoschedé, Suzanne's elder sister who nursed first Jean and then Monet in their final years. Over the following decades these gardens were the setting for many happy family meals al fresco under the shade of the lime trees close to the house.

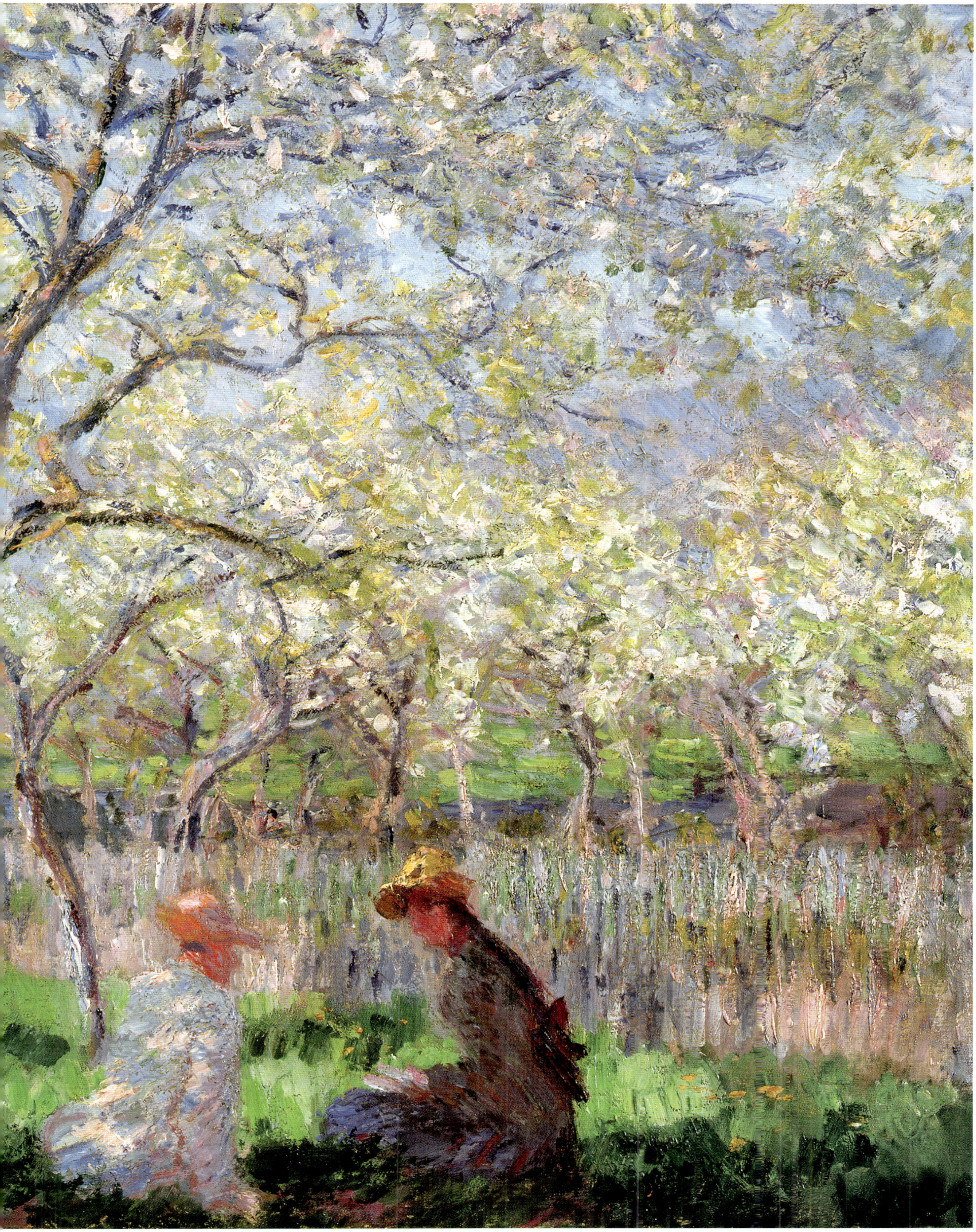

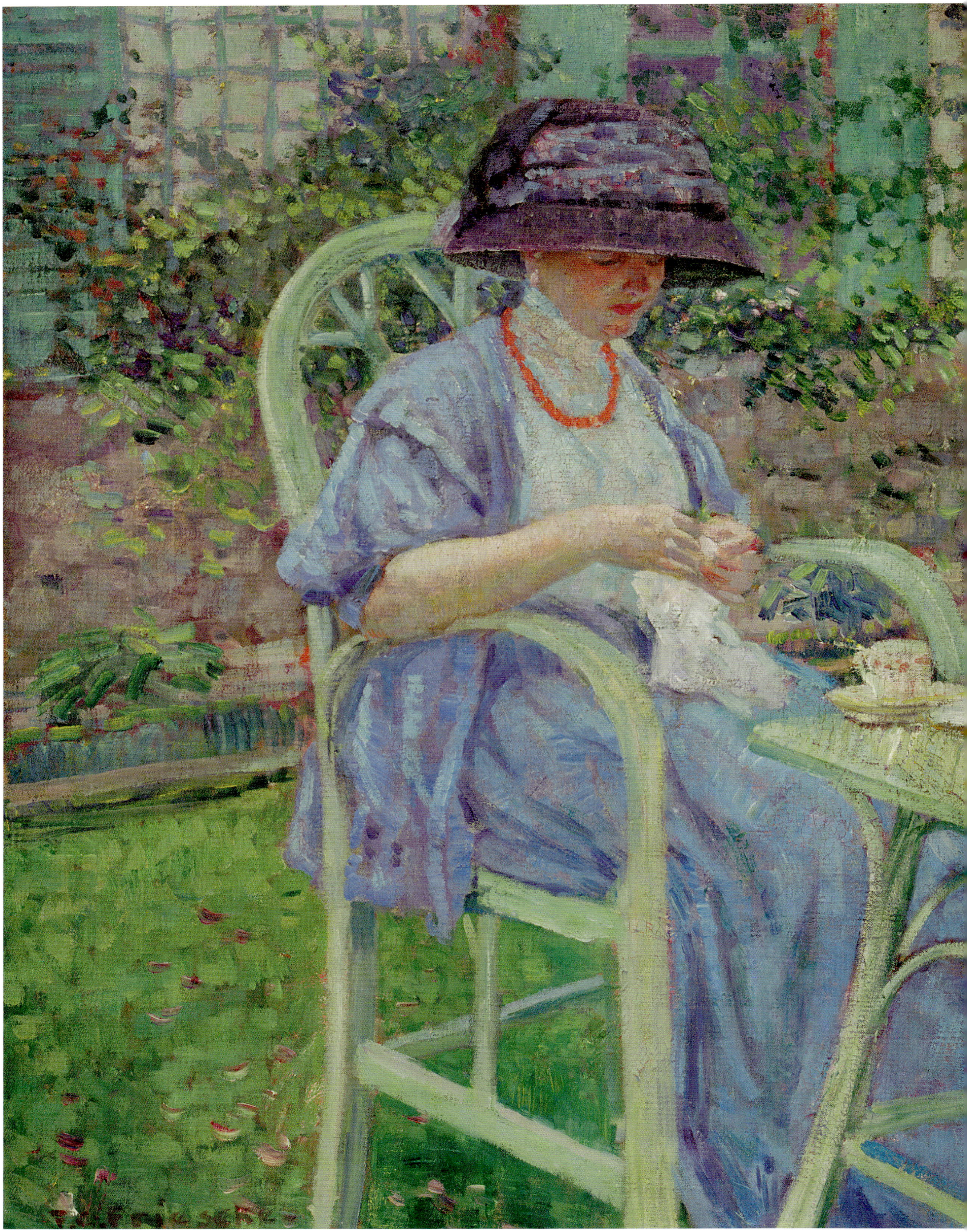

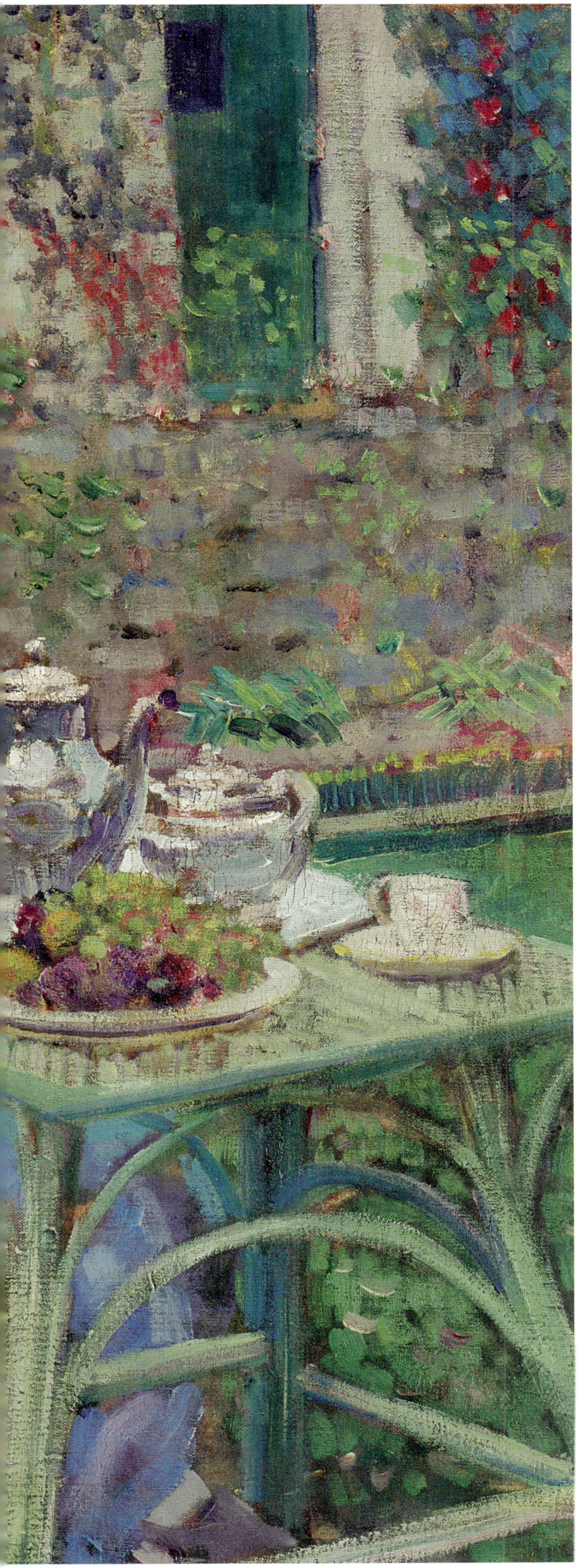

Frederick Frieseke, **Breakfast in the Garden**. *Oil on canvas, 66 x 82.1cm (26 x 32 5/16 in.), c.1910*

Finding the right spot is essential for enjoyable meals al fresco – in spring one needs a sun trap; in summer the shade of trees and climbing plants; whilst in simmering heat, a breeze is like heaven. Breakfast in the Garden is a harmony of blue and green, it captures the warmth of the day and the thoroughly pleasant scene. The earlier flamboyant dresses of Camille Monet and other Impressionist women evolved into the serenely simple style, seen here on Mrs. Frederick Frieseke at the breakfast table, exuding a calm air of glorious elegance. She is probably sitting in the decorative garden of Le Hameau, a house in Giverny that was leased to the artist and educator Mary C. Wheeler from Rhode Island. In 1906 Wheeler began bringing her students to Giverny, where they were tutored by Frieseke and Richard E. Miller. The wall behind is a perfect example of Edwardian wall gardening as described by Gertrude Jekyll. Did the Friesekes have copies of Jekyll's books? Both her books and those of William Robinson sold well in the United States. Sarah Frieseke was a keen gardener and the Friesekes lived in Giverny until 1920 where they were part of the second generation of 'Givernyites'.

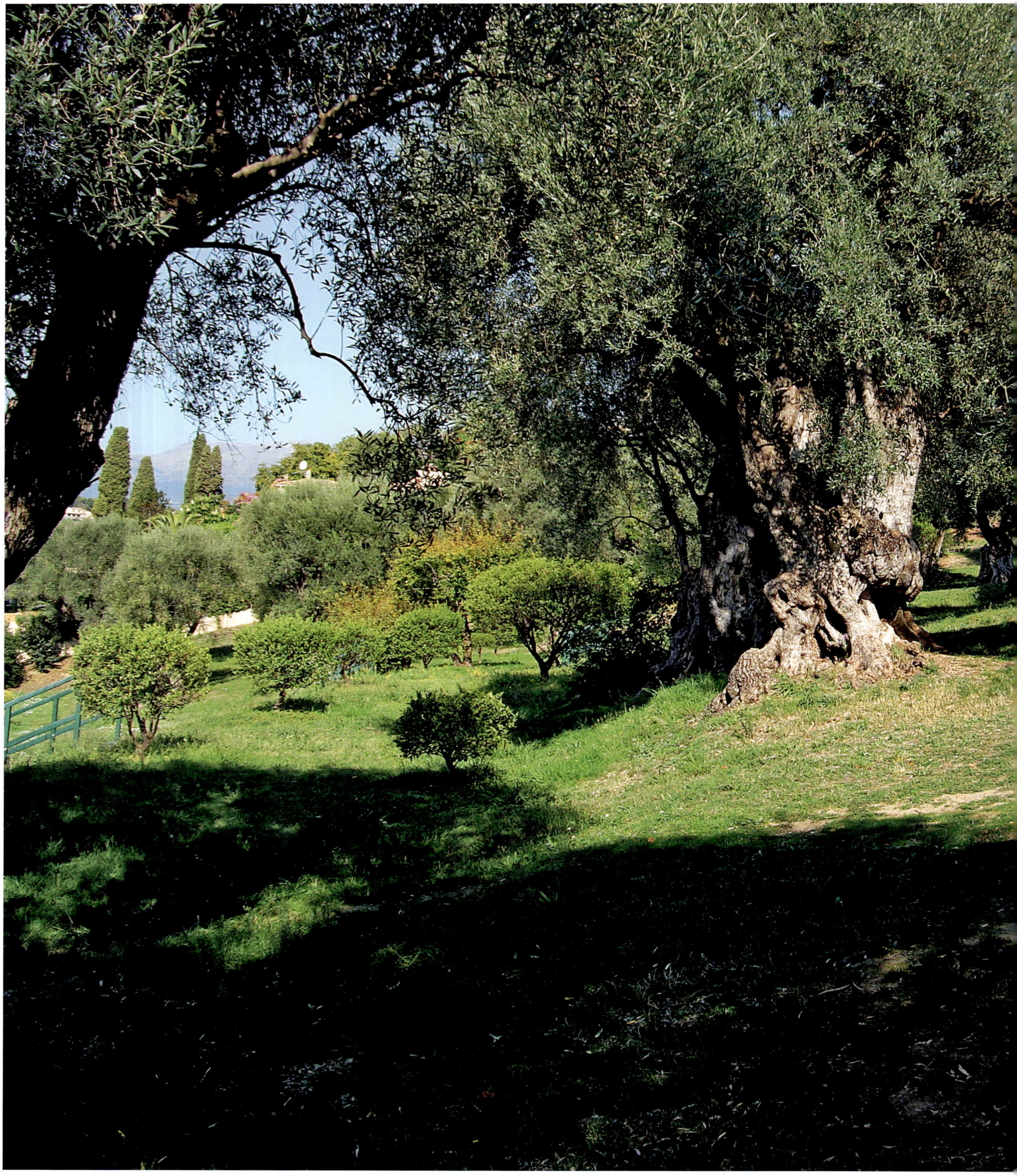

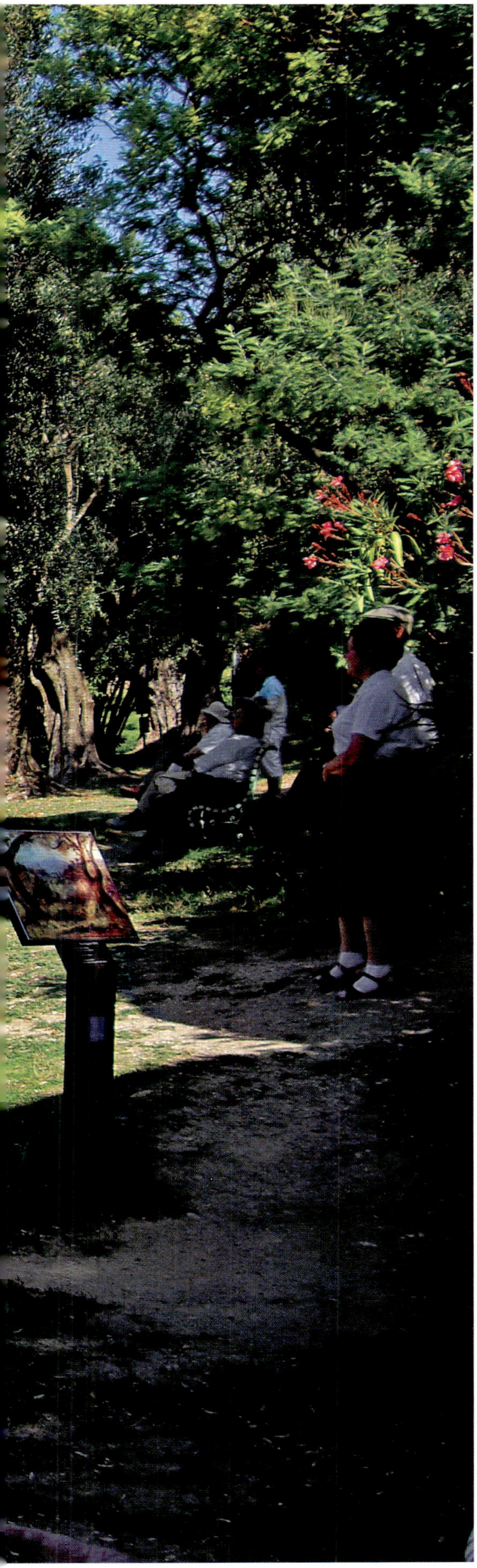

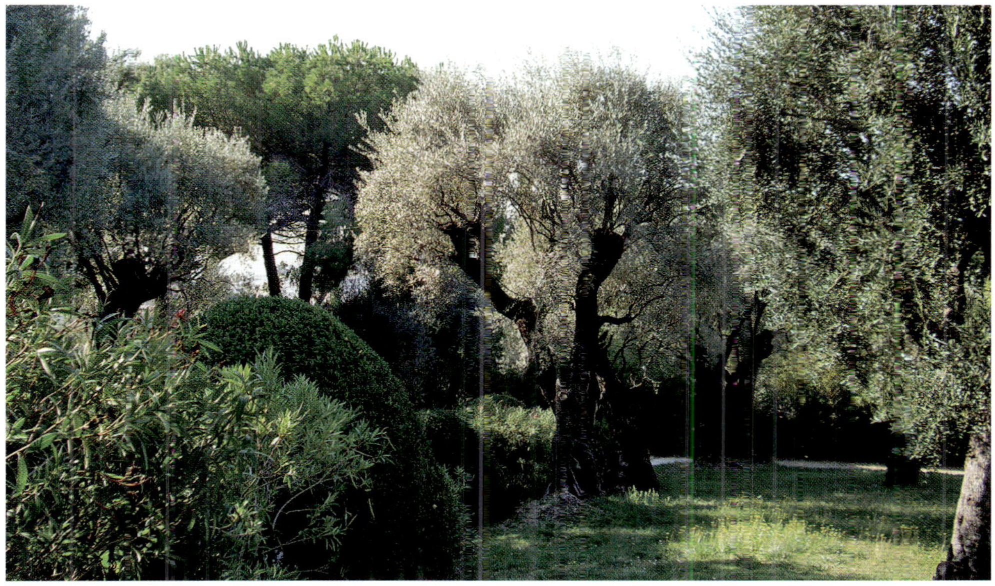

Above: *Beauty and utility unite in the silver heads of the venerable olive trees under the Mediterranean sun. Renoir's wife Aline was a robust cook of local produce and made an annual pilgrimage for the vendange to her family's vineyards near Essoyes in Burgundy, and Renoir painted many canvases of communal eating, both indoors and outside. The Renoir family and their friends would eat under the shade of the lime (or linden) trees to the west of the house at Les Collettes. The mature, fruiting olive trees, which were harvested in November, provided the Renoirs with their own olive oil. The green and gold of the pure oil and the black and green of the olives created their own impressionistic colours through Aline's cuisine.*

Left: *During Renoir's lifetime, visitors and admirers came from all over the world to watch the master at work. The legacy of Aline Renoir's generous hospitality continued after her death in 1915. Today, Les Collettes is open to the public where the olive trees provide shade from the September heat for modern visitors experiencing a Renoir moment.*

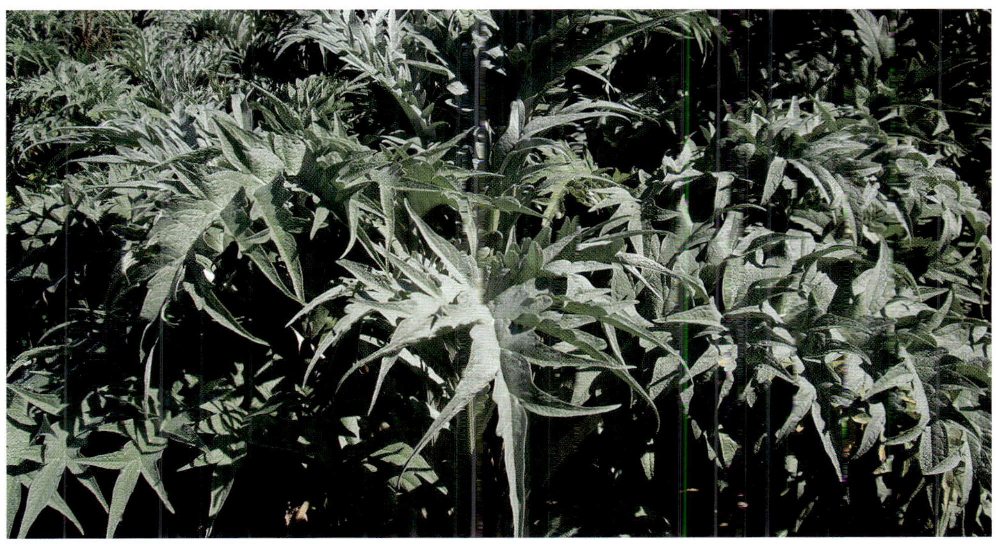

Not only are artichokes delicious to eat but they are gorgeous to look at, each stage offering new colours and shapes. The Renoirs spent time in Brittany, famed for its artichokes, where this photograph was taken. At Les Collettes Aline created a sizeable globular and glaucous artichoke patch. On a less poetic but equally sustaining note, the Australian artist, John Langstoff visited John Russell in Brittany and painted Cabbage Plot, Belle Ile in 1889. The blue-green healthy globes are ample proof of the maritime origins of cabbages, known in France as the poor man's medicine chest.

At the end of the nineteenth century Mirbeau published *Le Jardin des Supplices*, a gothic horror novel where the setting of the garden took on a macabre tone as the trees are used to hold dead bodies, and the water lilies are actually decapitated heads. On a happier note, the group wedding photo of the marriage of Theodore Butler and Marthe Hoschedé on 31 October 1900 was taken on the steps of the house canopied by the climbers over the verandah.

During the nineteenth century, the sight of picnicking day trippers escaping the urban smoke became increasingly common, not just in Europe but the United States and Australia. In 1882 the railway line from Melbourne had reached the fourteen kilometres to Box Hill, thus accelerating the rapid disappearance of virgin bush. Local artists Tom Roberts, Frederick McCubbin and Louis Abrahams managed to pitch a tent a mere kilometre from the station in a setting that was still evocatively naturalistic. Large canvases were propped up against trees so that the artists were on terms of the greatest intimacy with nature, this and working up an appetite for chops cooked over a fire of gum twigs was painted by Tom Roberts in *The Artists' Camp* around 1886. Out in the bush, the trees – especially the blue gum (boxwood or red gum) sapling in the foreground – provide a sense of garden enclosure, and the more shrubby seedling looks like a local gum known as mallee, the Eucalyptus cretata.

Productive gardens and the ability to create food from the fruits of the land are a common theme amongst many of the Impressionists, and such images of plenty are at discord with the well-worn vision of the artist starving in his garret. At the fore were the regional specialities of Aline Renoir, finer French cuisine was the preserve of Alice Monet and cuisine with an American seasoning came from Celia Thaxter. Whether the barbie was born in Australia or not, the McCubbins used their own gardens to cater on a large scale for their extensive family, his students from the National Gallery of Art School in Melbourne, and the great and the good who beat a path to their door at Fontainebleau.

Mary Cassatt, **Young Women Picking Fruit**. *Oil on canvas, 130.8 x 90.2cm (51 x 35in.), 1891*

Cassatt's women exude a warm independent air, as the older woman sits engaged in leisurely conversation with the younger as they harvest pears. This was part of the series of painted murals Cassatt produced for the Columbian Exposition in Chicago with symbolic imagery such as Young Woman Plucking the Fruits of Knowledge *and* Young Woman Pursuing Fame. *The pears being picked are barely visible but their shape is symbolically more female than that of apples. The body language of the women imbues them with a gentle innocence, almost like New World 'Eves' in a latter-day Garden of Eden. The women seem to be chatting, the older woman turns a loving face to the younger one, as she lifts up her immaculate white apron to hold the pears she has picked. The older one looks as if she is turning hers over in her hand before eating it – hopefully they are Jekyll's favourite variety, the Jargonelle, which ripens on the tree. The perfect pear to eat whilst walking amongst the fruit trees.*

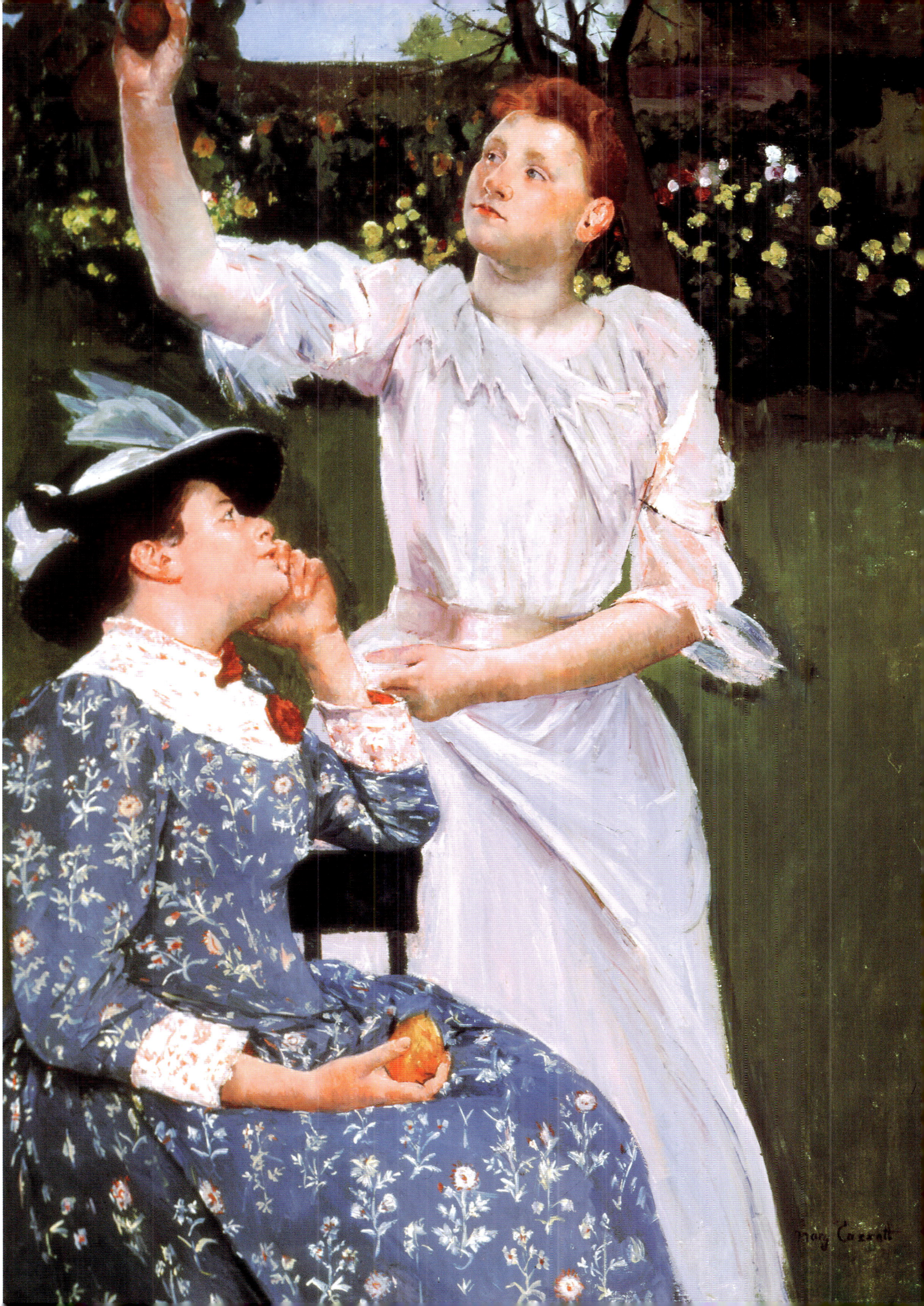
Mary Cassatt

Rest and Relaxation

There is sweet music here that softer falls
Than petals from blown roses on the grass,
Or night-dews on still waters between walls
Of shadowy granite, in a gleaming pass;
Music that gentler on the spirit lies,
Than tir'd eyelids upon tir'd eyes;
Music that brings sweet sleep down from the blissful skies

Alfred, Lord Tennyson, The Lotos Eaters

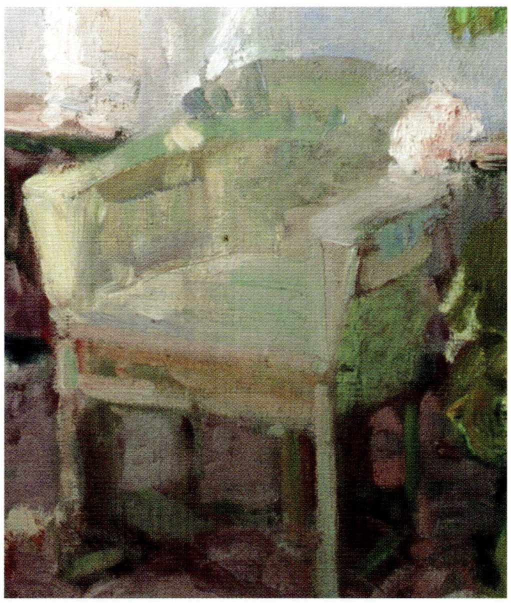

Joaquin Sorolla y Bastida, **The Gardens at the Sorolla Family House** (Jardin de la Casa Sorolla). *Oil on canvas, 105 x 81.5cm (42 x 32½in.), 1920*

The Spanish Impressionist Joaquin Sorolla y Bastida and his family bought a property in Madrid in 1911, and spent the next seven years creating gardens inspired by Spain's Moorish past that were a cool haven from the madrileño heat. The Gardens at the Sorolla Family House *was painted in 1920. Shades of pink reflect from the terrace, the columns and the house. The blue and white tilework cools the effect, the light silver of possibly a mimosa catches the sun, whilst the sombre greens of a cupressus provide shade. At the centre lies La Fuente de las Confidencias, a stone and tile fountain that still exists today. The colours used act like a balm that encourage the viewer to sit down and relax in the empty chair next to a large flowering geranium.*

Most of us have lost the art of the siesta – the delights of a good lunch followed by a snooze to then awaken renewed and revitalised. The bright dashes of light in Cézanne's portrait of *The Gardener* dozing in his chair exudes the sensation of someone who has been active, has had a bite to eat and is now ready just to relax and digest. Monet, a very early riser, always took an afternoon nap after lunch and when the weather was warm the Monet-Hoschedé family would spread out for a rest under the canopy of the flowering Prunus and Malus in the upper garden at Giverny.

In all three continents the Impressionists were daring, thinking groups of people in touch with new ideas, mixing with writers, musicians and philosophers. The houses and gardens of Monet, Renoir, Thaxter and McCubbin and, to a lesser extent, Jekyll were regularly used for entertaining. All were well stocked with books, papers, magazines and even plant catalogues for reading and referral, and at Giverny the Monet family built up a considerable library of literature as well as an essential selection of gardening tomes and art books. Host or guest could take themselves off to a quiet corner of the garden to read. Monet's early canvases of Camille, his first wife, portray an elegant woman at leisure or gentle occupation in the garden; her outfits extravagant and gorgeous, like overblown flowers.

The Australian Impressionist John Russell was both talented and wealthy, and his financial security enabled him to make constructive relaxation and sociable pleasure an art form. He was born at Darlinghurst, Sydney, in 1858: at the time of the first Impressionist Exhibition in Paris he was travelling around Fiji, Tahiti, China and Japan, from whence he returned with several Japanese woodblock prints. His father, the owner of a successful engineering company, sent Russell to Robey and Co., Lincoln in England for three years as a gentleman apprentice; he qualified as an engineer in 1879, also the date of his first known painting. Russell returned to Australia in 1880; his father died later

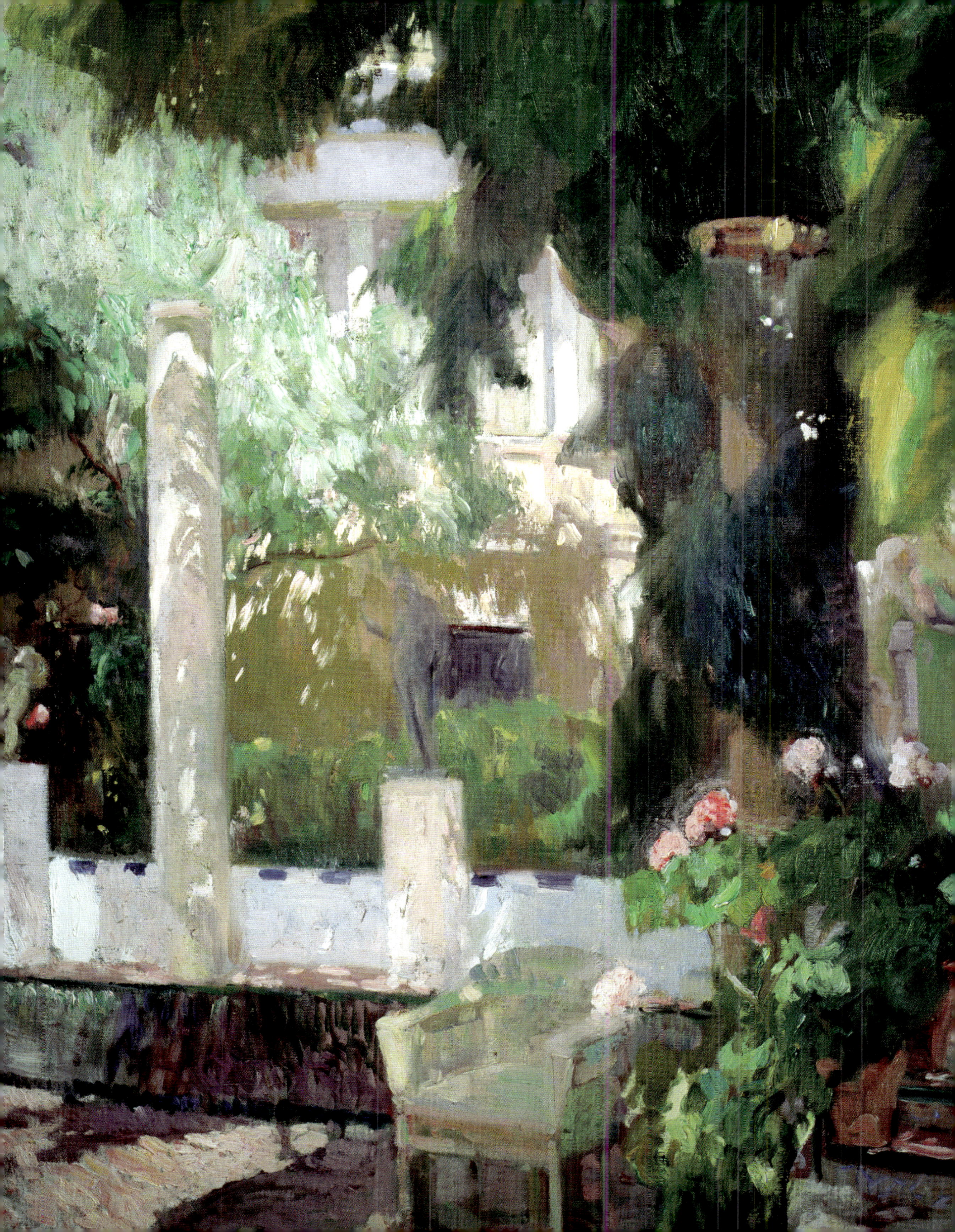

that year, making him financially independent. His inheritance enabled him to return to London to enrol at The Slade in January 1881 where he continued off and on until 1884.

His financial security meant he was able to travel extensively. During the winter and spring of 1882-3 Russell undertook a walking tour of Spain with Tom Roberts, Will Maloney and his architect brother, Peter Russell. In 1885 he visited the *plein air* sites of the Newlyn School in Cornwall whose brushwork evoked a lifestyle closer to nature and was to become an inspiration for Australia's Heidelberg School. After this he entered the Paris atelier of Fernand-Anne Piestre for three years. In Paris he mixed with many progressive artists but in the context of the Impressionists, Russell's interactions with Vincent Van Gogh and Auguste Rodin are of the greater interest. It is fair to say that if an Impressionist catches the sensations in nature then a portrait should be a flash card to the sitter's character. In Russell's 1886 portrait of Van Gogh there is a storm warning in the eyes and a sense of alienation in his body language that presages Van Gogh's own self portrait.

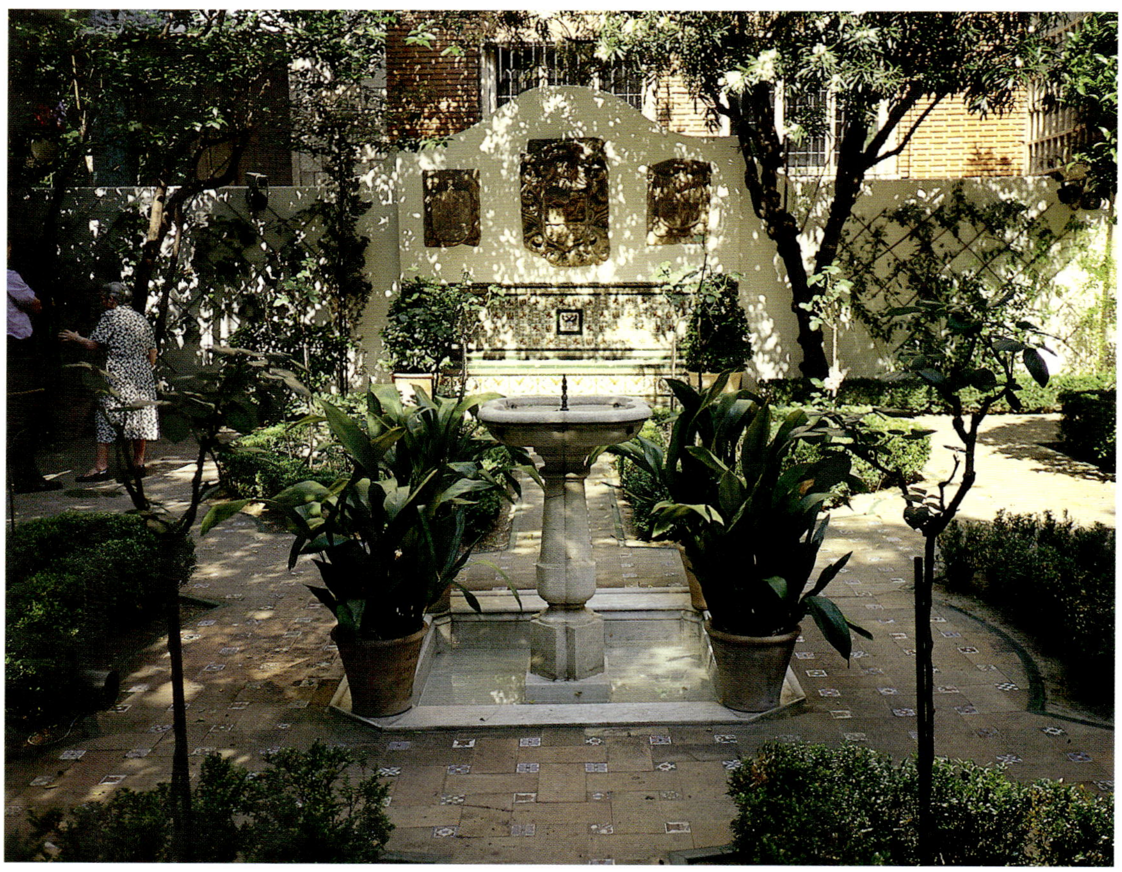

Left and opposite
The Sorolla family house and gardens now form the Museo Sorolla, where their setting still provides a haven from the summer heat of Madrid and shelter from the winter cold. The geometric Moorish design is softened by trees, shrubs and pots around the ornamental rills and pools. The rills that Jekyll designed into the Grand Plat at Hestercombe, Somerset were inspired by Moorish water features and traditional strapwork embroidery.

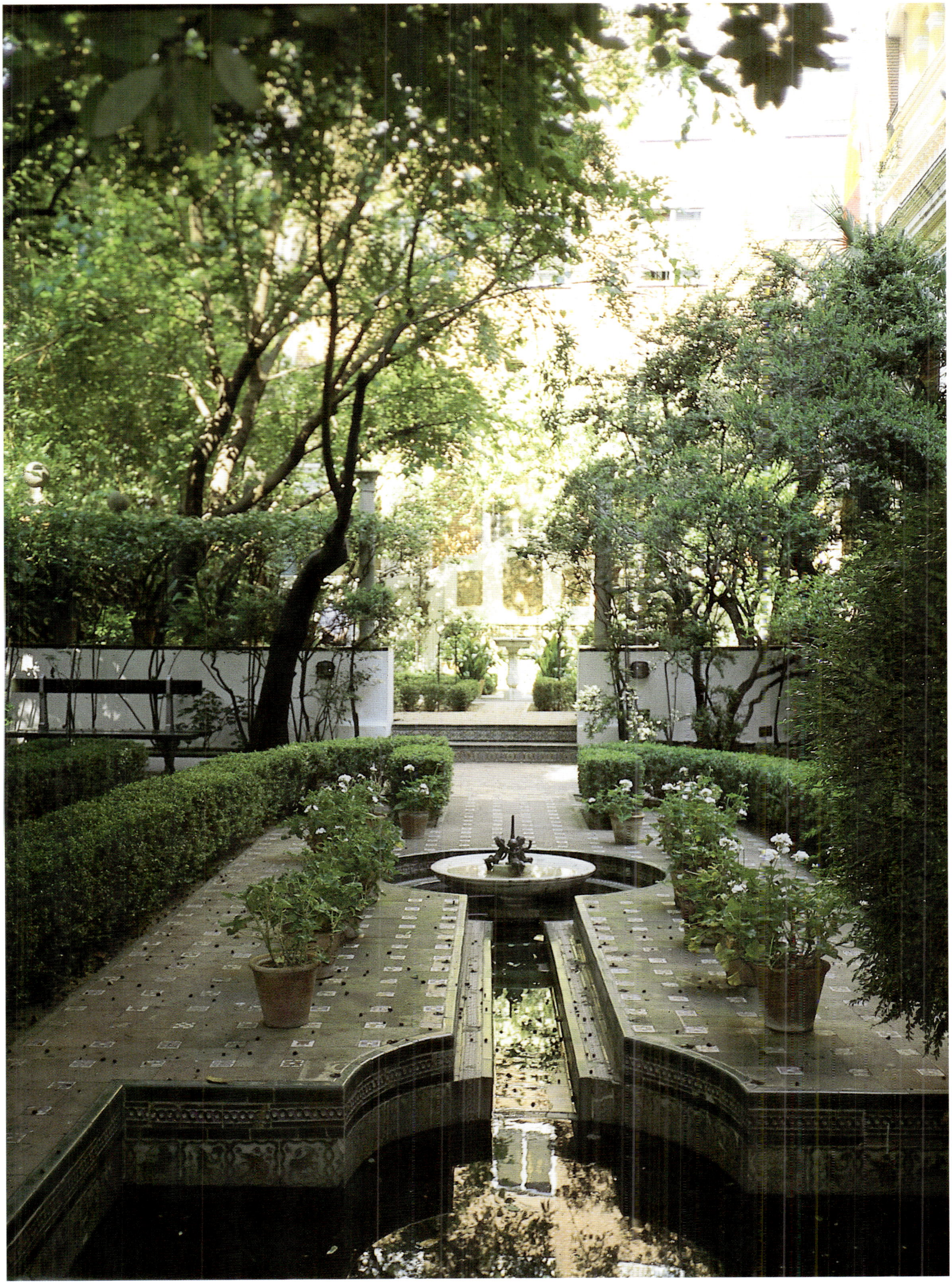

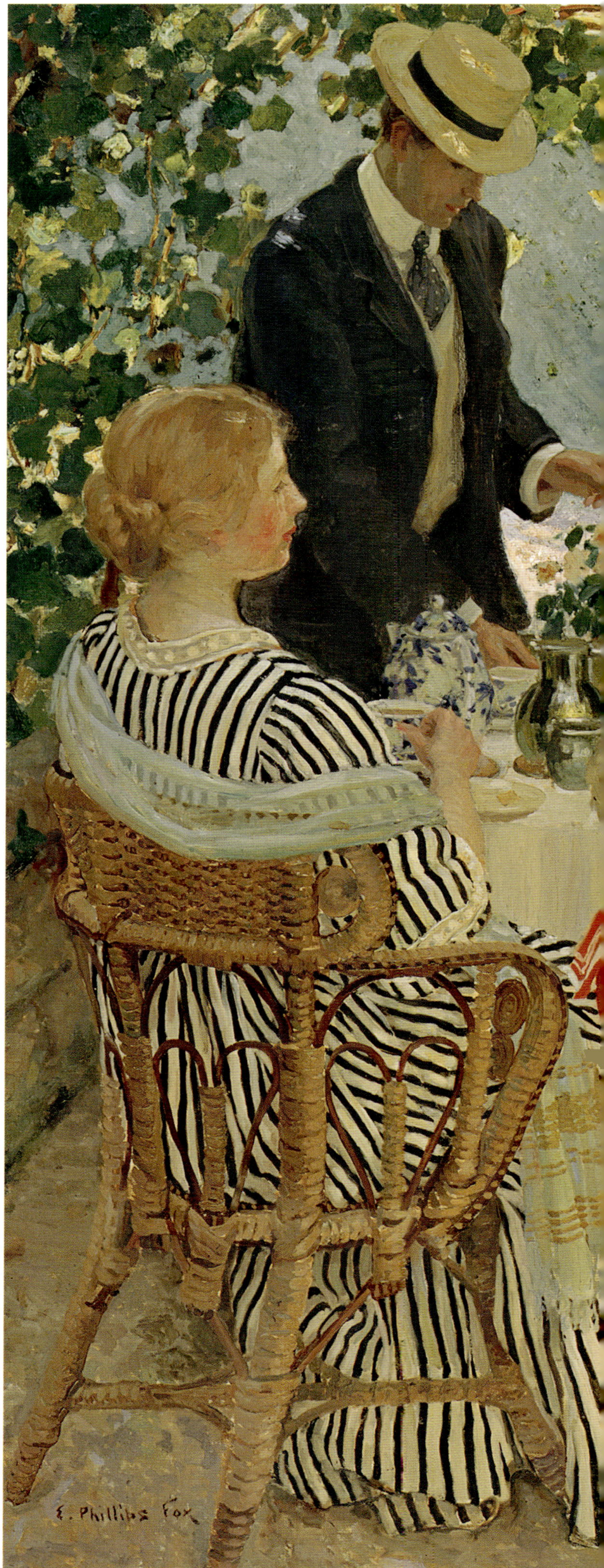

E. Phillips Fox, **The Arbour**. *Oil on canvas, 190.5 x 230.7cm (76 x 92in.), 1910*

Solitude could be hard to attain in large households, so the garden arbour was a place where a little privacy might be ensured for a tryst, reading or quiet contemplation. E. Phillips Fox portrays the Edwardian garden arbour at its elegant apogee of dappled shade, furnishings and conversation. The children are so perfect that it could almost be a Pears soap advert. There is an air of repose, however, the little boy looks like he has had enough inactivity and is ready to run with his hoop (but will he be allowed to dirty his white socks?) E. Phillips Fox was born in Melbourne in 1865, and spent many years in France. In 1910, the year The Arbour *was painted, he became the first Australian to be elected a full sociétaire of the Société Nationale des Beaux-Arts.*

E. Phillips Fox's garden arbour is rivalled by the leisure and elegance of Rupert Bunny's The Garden Bench *five years later. Two ladies are relishing the shade, one is florally dressed sitting and sewing whilst the other, in blue and white stripes, stands gently fanning herself. The balm of the shade is in sharp contrast with the fate of soldiers dying on the other side of the world in 1915. Bunny had lived many years in France, a year later he painted* The Letter *for which his French wife Jeanne modelled, in which two women are reading a letter from the front. Knowing as we do of the contrasts between the comforts of the safe enclosure of the garden and the battleground of the trenches, the painting is charged with poignant emotion.*

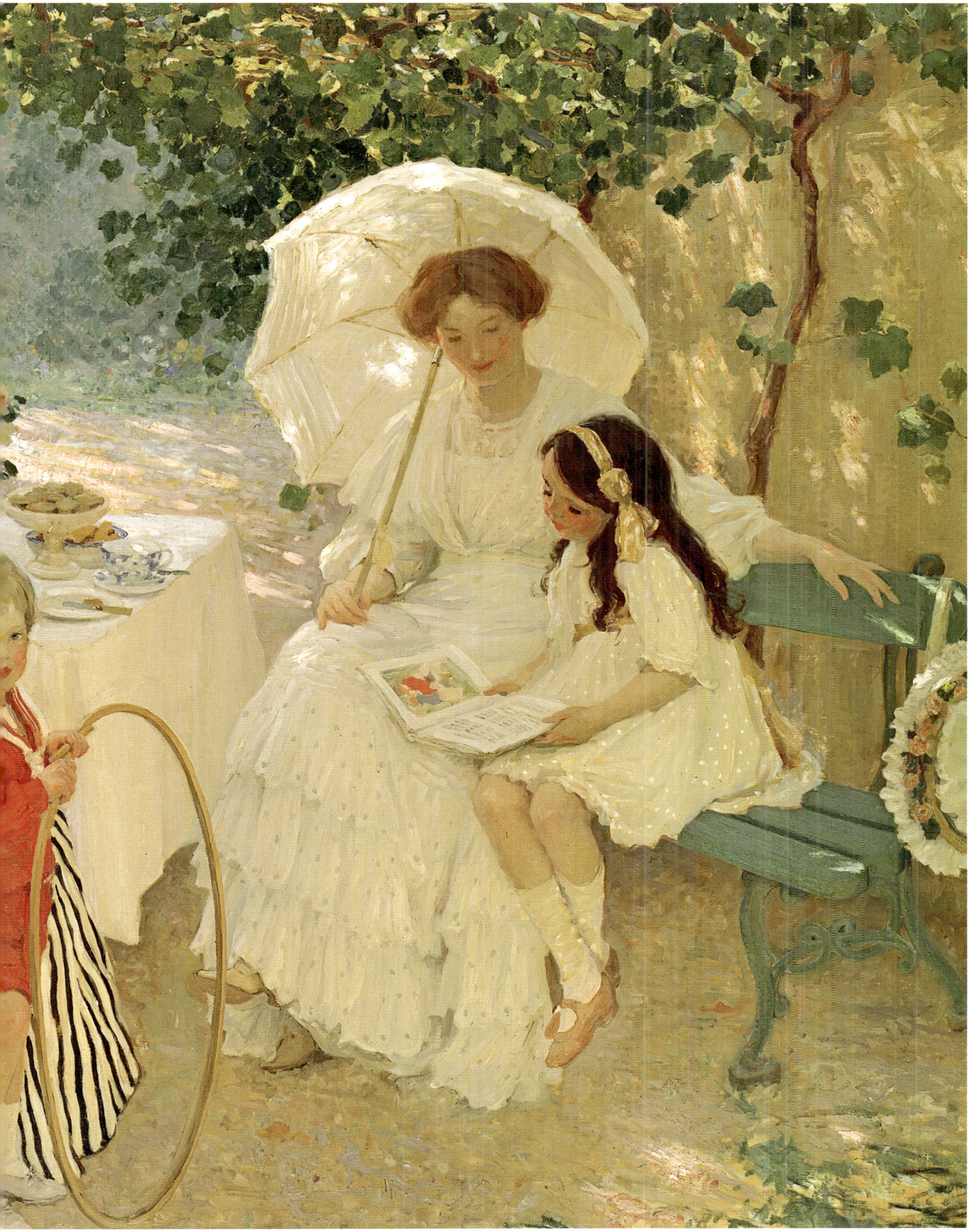

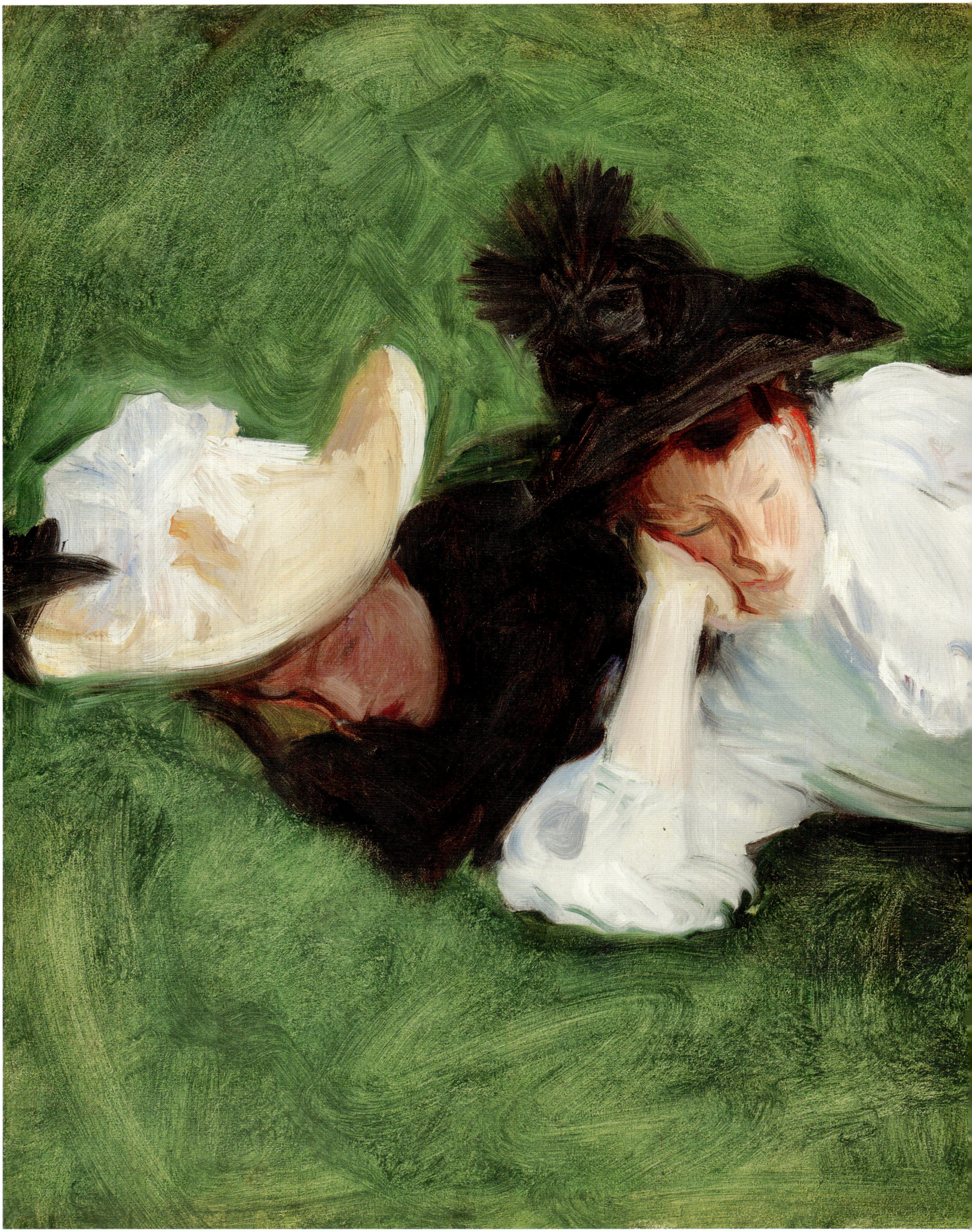

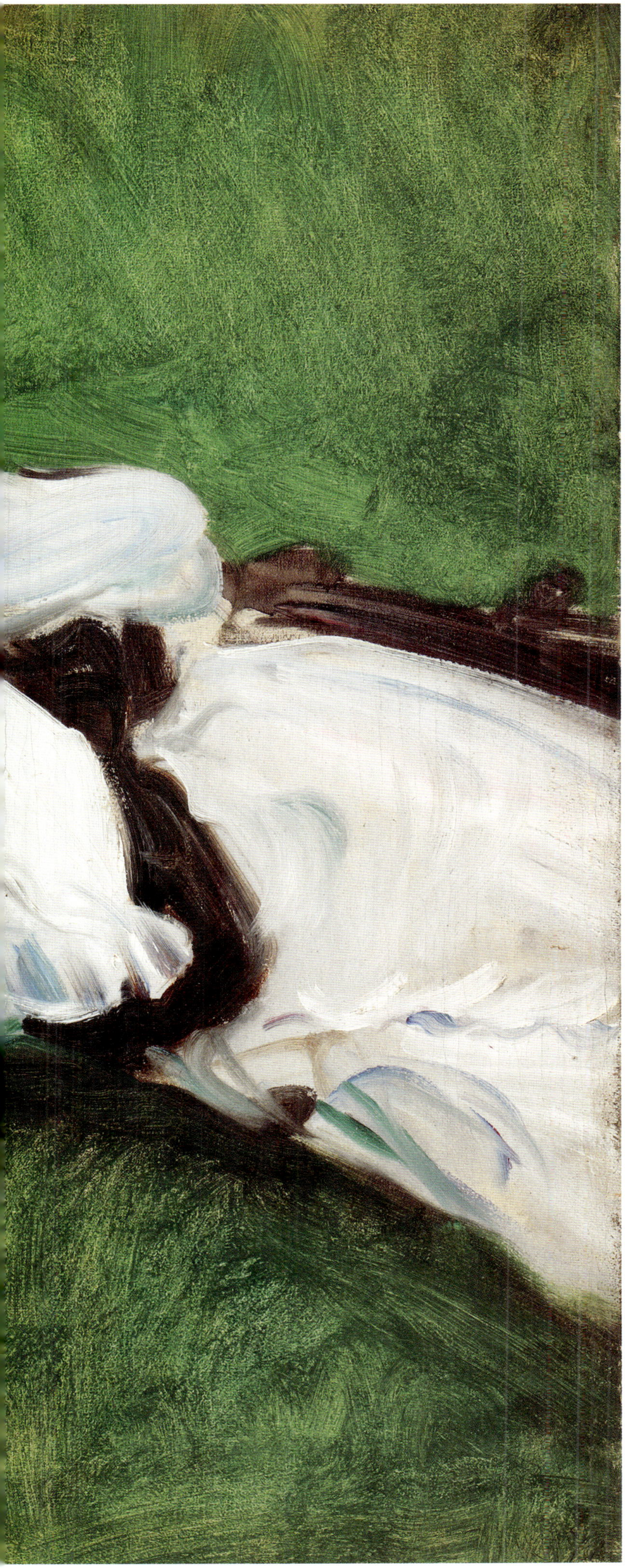

John Singer Sargent, **Two Girls on a Lawn**. *Oil on canvas. 53.7 x 64.1cm (21⅛ x 25½ in.), c.1889*

'Languid' is the adjective that comes to mind when looking at so many of John Singer Sargent's elegant portraits and vignettes. After 1885 he settled in the Cotswold village of Broadway, noted for its 'Henry James' Americans, and in 1889 he rented Fladbury Rectory, an old house about ten miles from Broadway with his recently widowed mother and two sisters, Emily and Violet, and it is Violet who is portrayed here in black. It is thought that he probably got the two girls to swop their bonnets to make a better composition. The girls' sinuous bodies in black and white dresses rest against the soft green of the lawn, almost carving an S horizontally across the canvas.

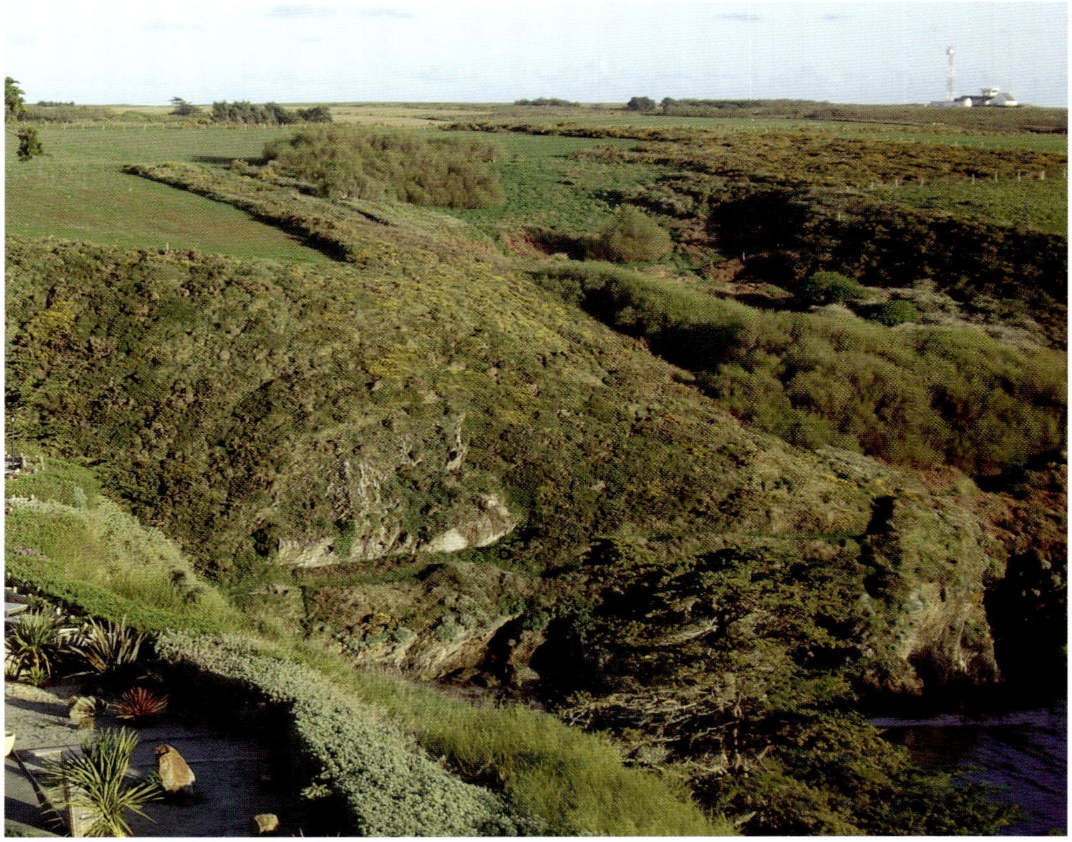

The hotel Castel Clara now occupies the footprint of the Chateau Anglais *at Port Goulphar on the south Côte Sauvage of Belle Ile. The terraces today are in much the same place overlooking the sheltered inlet. The original battered pine trees (below) stand as testament to the relentless winds of the Bay of Biscay. The jagged rocks painted by Monet, the Aiguilles de Port Coton, are a ten minute walk along the coast.*

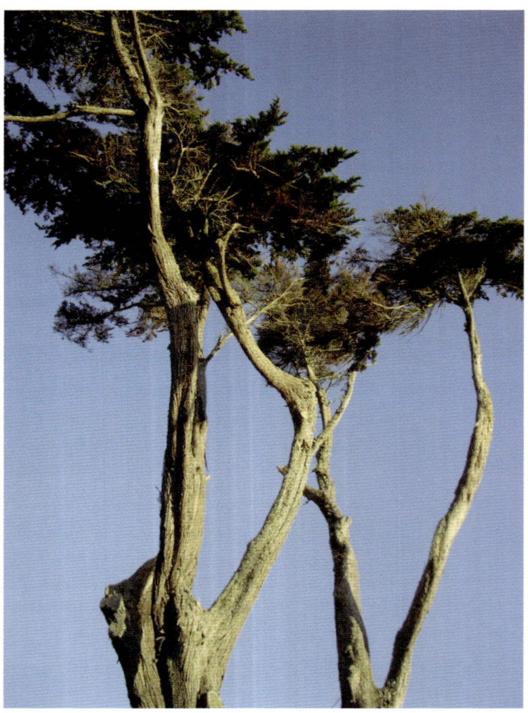

The rugged coasts, rural landscapes and cottage gardens drew many, many Impressionists to Brittany and after John Russell's marriage to Marianna Antoinetta Mattiocco they summered there, wintering either in Paris or the South of France. Their house at Port Goulphar on Belle Ile became known as *Le Chateau Anglais* was also a sojourn for Monet, Sisley, Matisse and fellow Australian Impressionists such as John Longstaff and Bertram MacKennal (both later knighted). In many respects Russell is more important for his artistic connections and hosting a guest list that reads like a 'Who's Who', than for his own creative output. Russell's fellow Australian Impressionist Tudor St George Tucker painted *Springtime*, at Etaples in Brittany during 1887-1892. This sensual siesta exudes a delicious sense of gay abandon in the way the arms are flung out and the legs tucked up. He transported the canvas back to Melbourne where it was exhibited in the Victorian Artists' Society exhibition of 1893. Health reasons had brought Tucker to Australia as a very young man from England, at the height of the aesthetic craze he would saunter down 'The Block' in Melbourne with a lily or sunflower in his hand. Not content with this he combed his golden locks into beautiful curls and would sport a great flopping sunhat with a huge sunflower embroidered across it when playing tennis.

Frederick Frieseke had started his studies at The Art Institute of Chicago in 1893, before heading east to the Art Students League, New York City in 1897. At that time the painting of nude models was

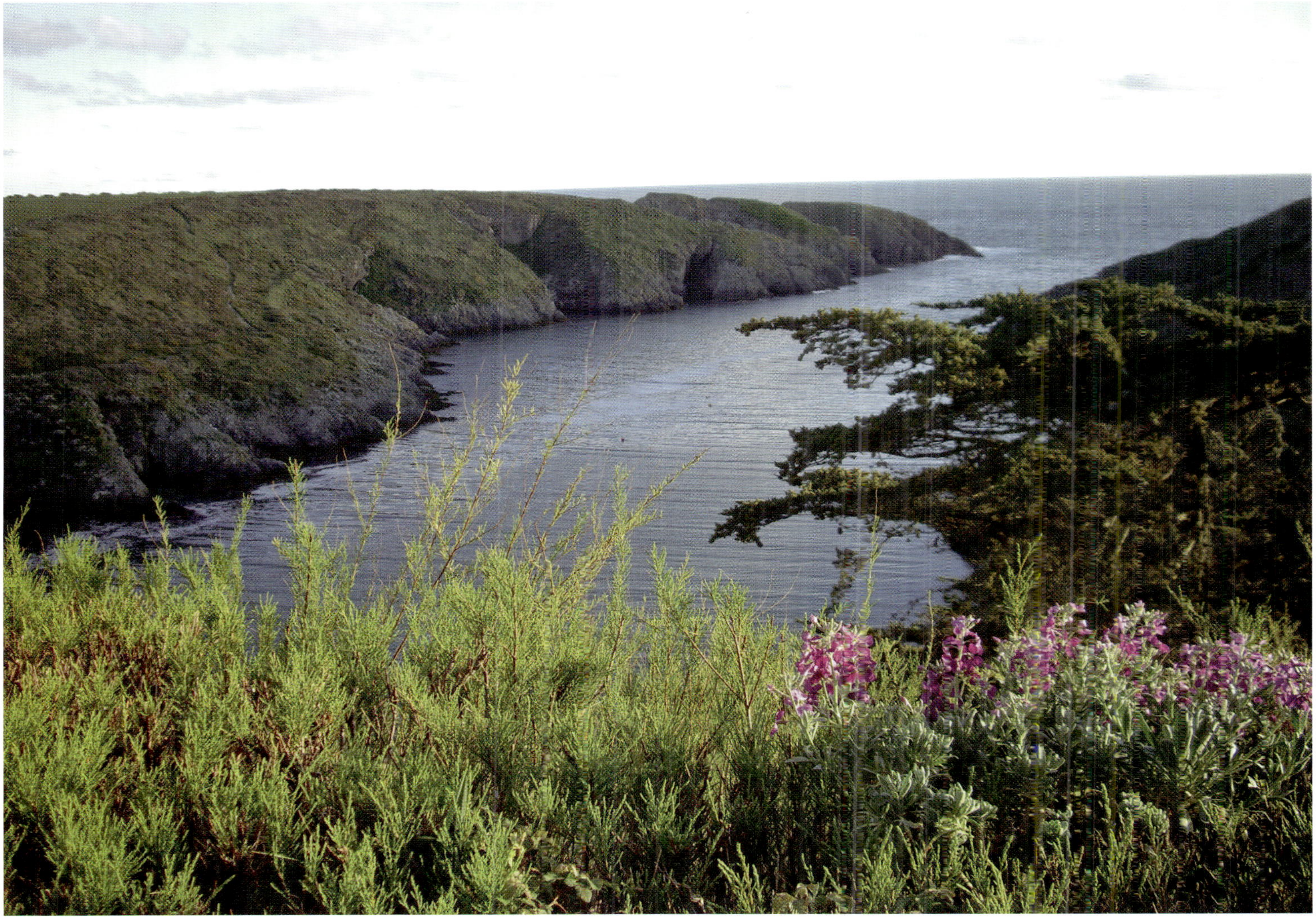

Port Goulphar, Belle Ile in late afternoon. John Russell frequently painted this view from his house. The shape curiously echoes that of the garden in the Place Lamartine sketched by Van Gogh. Russell's engineering training enabled him to cast his own keel for the yacht he moored here.

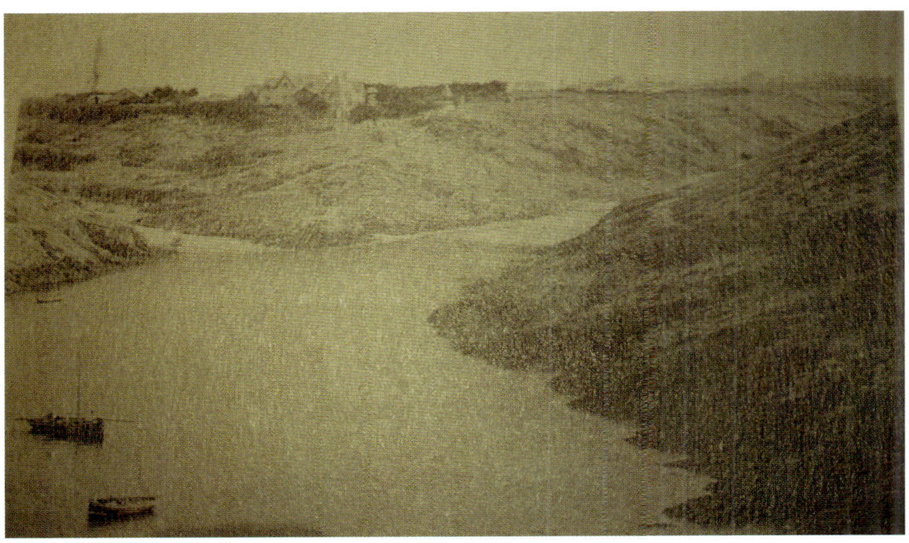

A faded postcard of Le Chateau Anglais. In 1888 John Russell had married Marianna Antoinetta Mattiocco, Rodin's favourite model, and the next year they built a house at Port Goulphar on Belle Ile, off the south coast of Brittany, which was known as Le Chateau Anglais. The Russells spent their summers here, entertaining friends and artists until Marianna's death in 1908 on Belle Ile where she is buried. This artistic hospitality was revived with his second wife, Caroline de Witt Merrill after their marriage in 1912. The hotel Castel Clara now occupies the same footprint with much the same terraces and original gnarled pine trees.

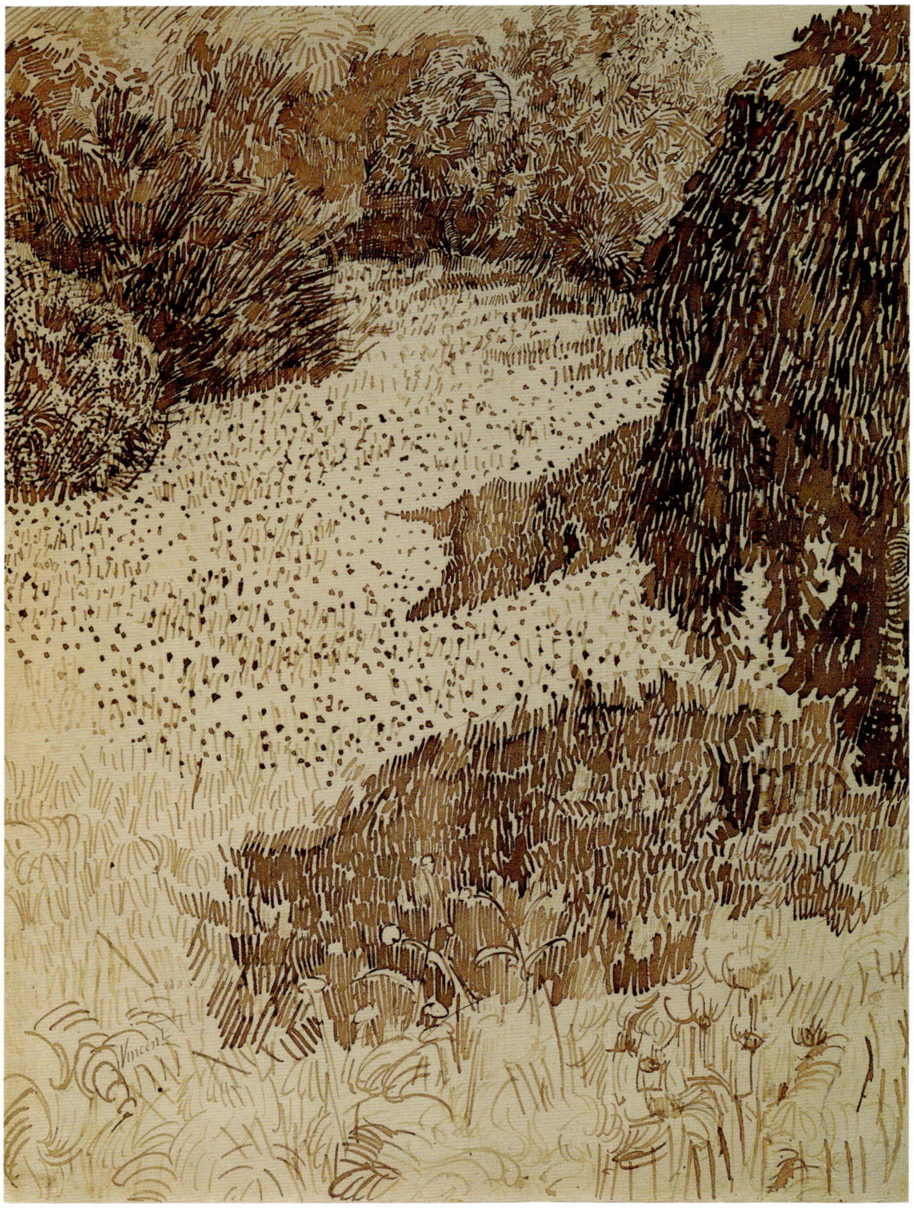

Vincent Van Gogh, **A Corner of a Garden in the Place Lamartine**. *Reed pen and ink over graphite on wove paper, 31.5 x 24.5cm (12½ x 9¾in.), 31 July–3 August 1888*

The ever congenial Russell corresponded with Vincent Van Gogh, and their letters reveal a good friendship. In one of his letters Van Gogh enclosed this sketch of his painting of A Corner of a Garden in the Place Lamartine. *As was typical of Van Gogh he added the colour in words: 'Here's a new motif. A corner of a garden with shrubs clipped in balls and a weeping tree and at the base coiffed oleanders. And the grass awaiting mowing after which the long blades will be left to dry in the sun. Above a little corner of blue sky …' Russell had several of Van Gogh's paintings, and they were in touch in the months leading up to Van Gogh's suicide. Many of the letters survive in the Van Gogh archive.*

Private Collection, courtesy Thomas Gibson Fine Art.

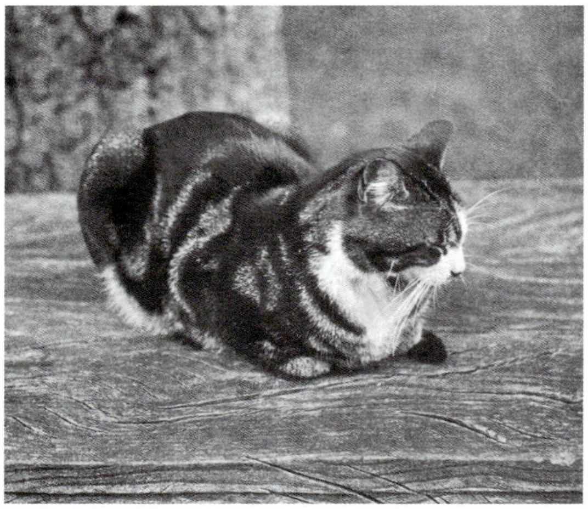

Cats have never lost the art of the siesta. Pinkieboy, one of Gertrude Jekyll's cats, was photographed for Home and Garden *on the Cenotaph of Sigismunda (see page 188). She writes: 'It is a favourite resort of the pussies, sheltered, and receiving the alternate benefits of full afternoon sun and its milder filtration through the still taller Birches opposite. Pinkieboy's portrait was done there while he was enjoying his after-dinner siesta.' Jekyll also clipped a large topiary cat that could be admired from the drawing room window.*

forbidden in the States, this and the irresistible draw of the world's art capital drew him to Paris a year later. Here he studied at both the Académie Julian and briefly with James Abbott McNeill Whistler at the Académie Carmen. Later he wrote: 'As there are so few conventionalities in France, an artist can paint what he wishes, I can paint a nude in my garden … and not be run out of town.'

His time in Giverny coincided with that of fellow resident and performing artist, Isadora Duncan, who danced naked on her lawns in the morning, surely a bonus. That said, Frieseke's depictions of the fully-clothed woman such as his elegant wife Sarah who appears in various garden scenes are elegantly relaxed. In contrast, the body language of his nude in *Summer* seems awkward, restive and ready for lovemaking rather than a siesta. By comparison the Junoesque qualities of Renoir's nudes in and around the garden are portrayed with both a classical and naturally earthy repose.

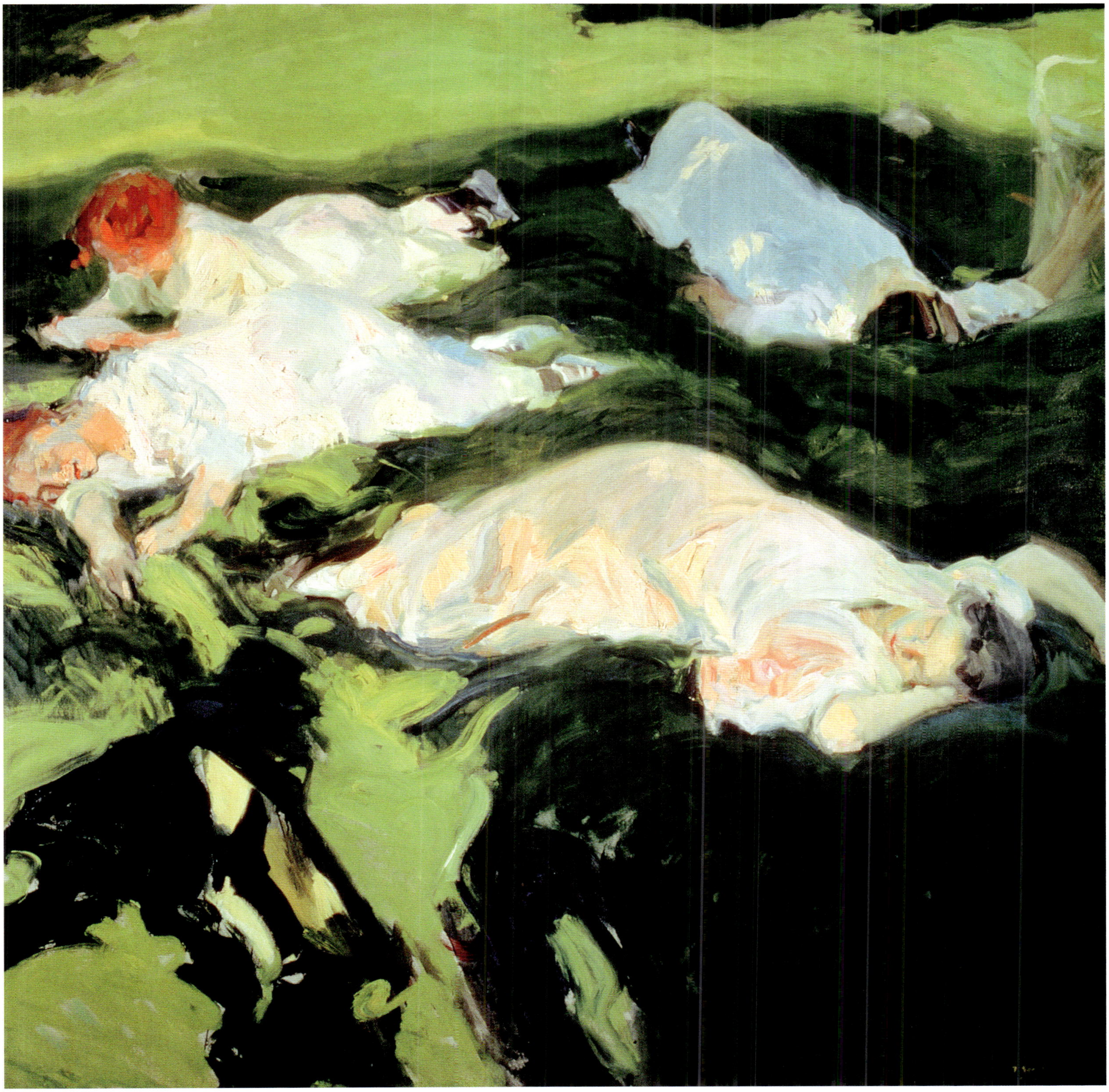

Joaquin Sorolla y Bastida, **La Siesta**. *Oil on canvas, 300 x 300cm (118 x 118 in.), 1911*

Here are the languid recumbent bodies of Sorolla's wife Clotilde, who lies with her two sisters and cousin on flower-spangled meadow grass in the gardens of Dr. Madinaveitia's farm in San Sebastian in northern Spain. One reads, whilst the rest look gloriously relaxed on the soft, spongy grass. Although it was painted in the spring they still seek the cooling shade of the trees. Sorolla admired John Singer Sargent and presented him with one of his paintings.

CHAPTER THREE

Impressions under Norman Skies

Monet at Giverny

You must go to Giverny to see Monet so that you can know him, understand his character, his lifestyle, his inner self. He is a man who has lived, known deep affections, family responsibilities, paternal anxieties, the loss of his friends Caillebotte, Sisley, de Bellio, Pissarro, Renoir, Mirbeau, Degas, the terrible bereavement of his nearest and dearest which broke his heart and ravaged his spirit: he has survived because of an inner strength, an invincible force that was not just physical but animated by the burning desire of art. … This house and garden is also a work of art, and Monet has put all his life into creating and perfecting it.

Gustave Geffroy, Memories of Monet (Monet, Sa Vie, Son Oeuvre), *1924*

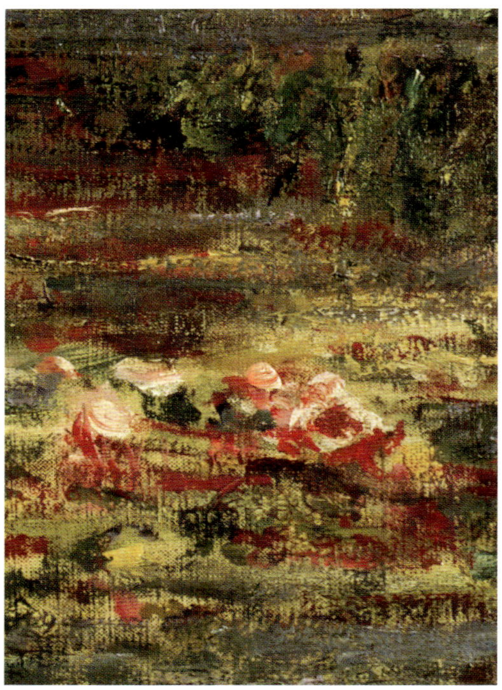

Claude Monet, **The Waterlily Pond (Symphony in Rose)**. *Oil on canvas, 90 x 100cm (36 x 40in.), 1900*

Initially the bridge over Monet's modest first pond in 1893 had no canopy. He waited until 1899 before painting the pond and water lilies when he felt the scene was sufficiently mature. The surface of the water and the smooth green banks are invisible as the bridge spans the gap. The eye is deceived by shades of yellow and carmine water lilies nestling against their green leaves; rushes and irises masking the foreground and the willow curtains closing the picture.

So to the most famous of the Impressionist's gardens: that of Monet at Giverny. Here the skills of the great artist and gardener fused together, as Monet's glorious planting schemes were captured on canvas in a kaleidoscope of living colour and light. His good friend Octave Mirbeau reported that Monet had told a budding artist seeking his advice that he didn't teach painting, he just did it. Pointing to the sky he said that it was the only teacher and if the novice failed to hear and understand its message, he would be better employed in a notary's office copying out registers. Monet could have given exactly the same advice to a budding gardener.

One April day in 1883, oppressed by family and financial worries, Monet was walking from the small town of Vernon along the Epte valley. En route his heart was lifted by the massed fruit blossoms and wild flowers in the small Normandy village of Giverny. His eye was further drawn by the unusual sight of a gloriously pink house with blue green shutters, in stark contrast to the usual Norman taste, owned by Louis Singeot who had spent many years in Guadeloupe. The village nestled under hills to the north, sheltering this house, Maison du Pressoir, and its gardens which faced south. Despite no visible means, Monet immediately agreed to rent it, and then begged and borrowed funds so that his family was installed by May. Imagine the shock to the Givernois; a widowed artist with his two children living with a still-married woman (Alice Hoschedé) and her six children. Daubing was hardly a proper occupation, their lifestyle was beyond the pale and as for their Parisian clothes – it was if aliens had arrived from another planet. Initially the Monet household were outcasts, the walls of the garden literally shielding them from the harsh outer world, as well as providing sustenance – vegetables were sown immediately followed by flowers in early June. Ultimately Monet's presence would change Giverny but not directly; his

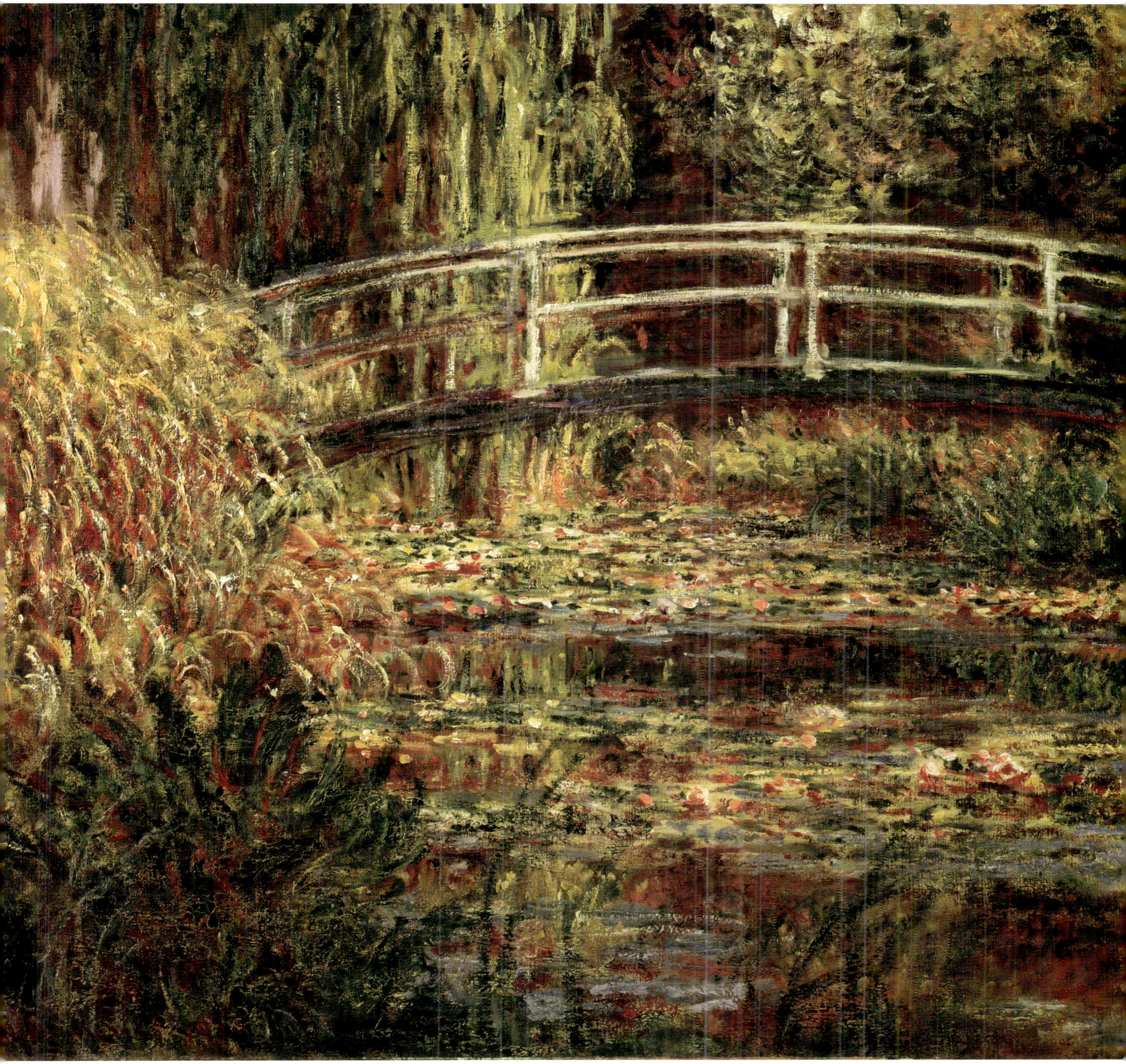

Claude Monet, **Chrysanthemums**. *Oil on canvas, 80.3 x 120cm (32 x 48in.), 1897*

No soil, no sky just a picture full of colour that anticipates the onset of autumn. Gertrude Jekyll recommended chrysanthemums for gold gardens. Pierre Loti's book Madame Chrysanthème *was read avidly by Van Gogh in 1888 with its insight into Japanese customs (from a very European perspective). In China they are one of the 'Four Gentlemen', the others being favourites of Monet's, namely orchid, plum blossom and bamboo.*

presence and its setting drew an influx of artists. It was the Givernistes, the artistic community, that would have a radical effect on the village, its economy and the Givernois.

The Maison du Pressoir gardens had been laid out as a formal potager with clipped dwarf boxwood hedging and a central allée of cypress and spruce trees, that led from the central garden door to the Chemin du Roi. Monet immediately removed the hedging, however, after much argument Alice won the right to retain at least the spruce trees, whose trunks Monet trimmed into poles for roses. The apple trees were gradually replaced with ornamental blossoming crab apples and Japanese cherry trees, and the grass softened with wild plants and spring bulbs. This little orchard along with the Lime Allée between the house and second atelier provided places for the family to eat and take a siesta. Monet finally bought the property in 1890 for 22,000 francs, and the ground for the water gardens was bought in two stages in 1893 and 1901. Along its boundary he planted poplars that swayed like a glaucous sea, terminating his view of the garden from his bedroom window.

In my previous book, *Monet at Giverny*, I suggested that despite Monet's loathing for French formal gardening of the heroic period, he and France's most celebrated gardener, Andre Le Notre, shared a sense of landscape known by the Baroque term *pourtraiture*. It stems from *'pour'*– to or in order to and *'traire'* – to milk or draw out, a revealing: altogether meaning a bringing forth by removing accidents of nature to reveal the essential nature underlying all things. The earth was the primed canvas. Le Notre's consummate skill was his mastery of perspective, manipulating it by varying the distance between the cross axes, using the chemistry of light filtered or reflected by trees, hedges, pools and fountains to create powerful landscapes. The garden became a geometric extension of the house, whose embroidered parterres were designed to give a visual release. Monet too was quick to remove irregularities from his garden, whether natural or manmade, coaxing his plants into an eye-catching masterpiece of design, indeed Giverny became a portrait of the man. Inspired by Japanese prints, Monet manipulated perspective to such an extent that he excluded it altogether in the water garden, and revealed the nature underlying his garden by his painterly plantsmanship.

In the upper garden Monet prepared his earthly canvas and created a 'grille' of rectangular beds that blazed a vertical and horizontal visual release of light and colour in faint parallel lines, running across from the existing central axis. Just as Monet avoided a dark primed canvas, so the rich soil that supported these plants did not show. The horticultural priming took the form of low cushioning plants, elaborated by the rich weave of hooks and dashes of floral colour that clambered for the light. From dawn to dusk the flowers and leaves reflected and caught the light in myriad ways. The west facing beds were planted in yellow, orange and red flowers that would glow in the setting sun. Under the shrubs and trees Monet planted blue flowers in circles – shades of his earliest

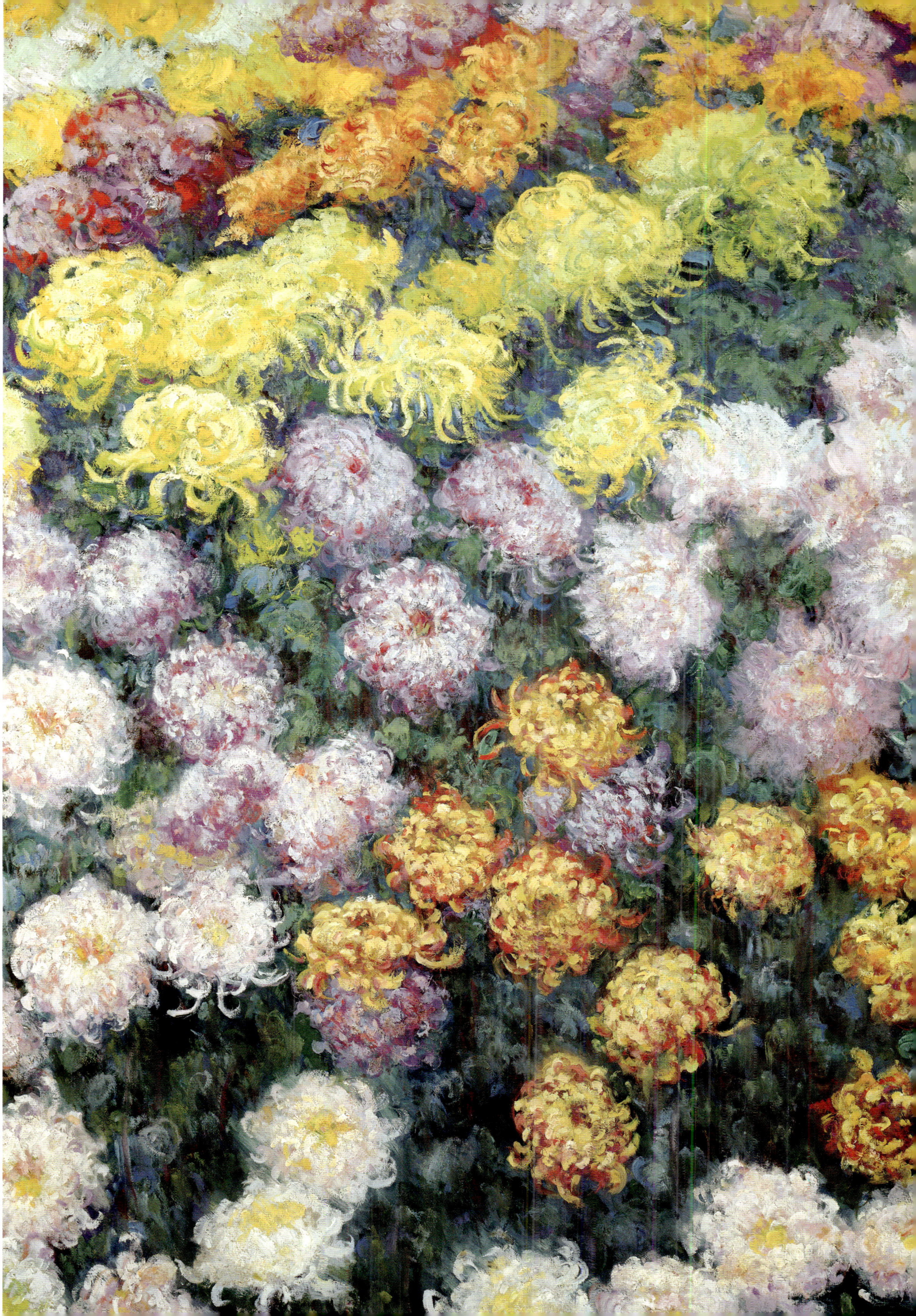

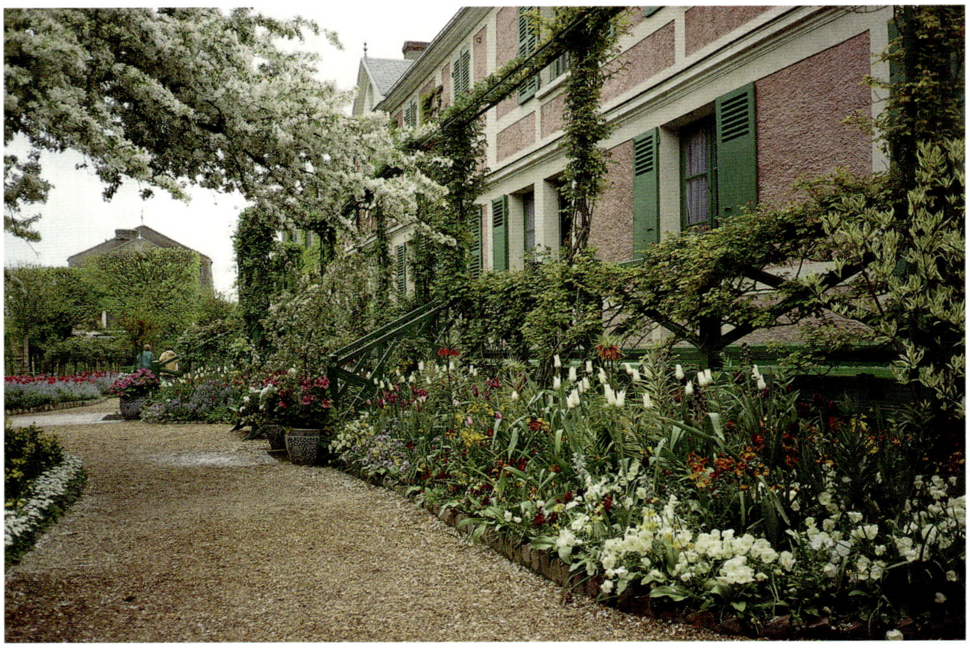

The house at Giverny seemingly afloat in an ocean of flowers and bulbs in early May. In the foreground expensive rare tulips are mixed with pansies, whilst taller Crown Imperials stand in majestic orange and red above the other flowers. Note Monet's blue and white ceramic pots and beyond the pink tulips in a haze of forget-me-nots.

paintings. The fulsome planting around the house and verandah ensured that the effect was like a ship on a tide of flowers, no statuary but an array of cleverly devised iron, green painted supports that took the pictorial composition into the sky.

The trunks of the spruce remained the support for the roses along the Grand Allée until they were replaced by the now famous iron arches in the 1920s. The earth at the base of the allée was built up to create what are known as 'carp's back' beds. This maximises the soil available for massing plants, the flowers climb up to seek the light, spread and cascade down, and the floral effect was completed by nasturtiums at the base which then scrambled across the central path. The iron arches form the backbone of the upper garden but deceive the eye away from its symmetry and perspective. By the end of summer the interior has become a green tunnel – no earth and no sky. When viewed from the bedrooms the eye darts back and forth across its arches before being taken on to the roof of the Japanese Bridge and the copper beech in the lower water garden.

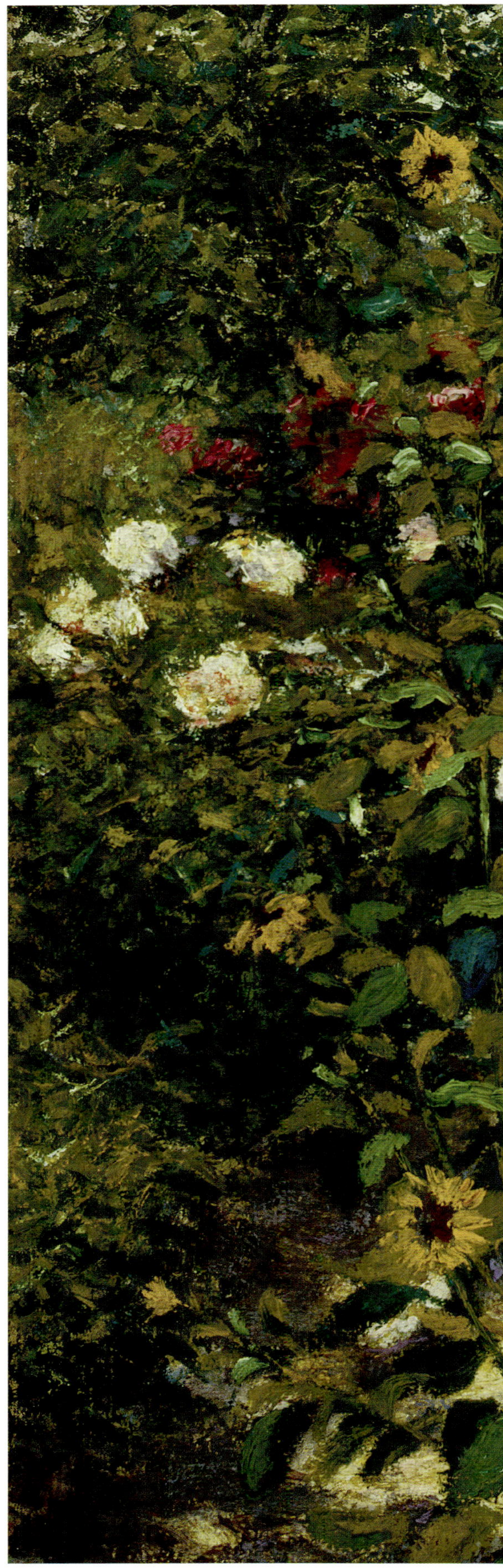

John Leslie Breck, **Garden at Giverny (In Monet's Garden)**. *Oil on canvas, 46 x 55.6cm (18 x 22in.) Frame 64.5 x 74cm (25 x 29in.), between 1887 and 1891*

In 1887 Breck settled in Giverny, where he was invited by Monet to paint the garden, a rare incident and a great privilege. His small brushstrokes plump up the flowers and enhance their light sensations. The sunlight running along the path also reflects up into the flowers, showing how the flower gardens had developed in the first five years. The effect is less linear than can be seen today.

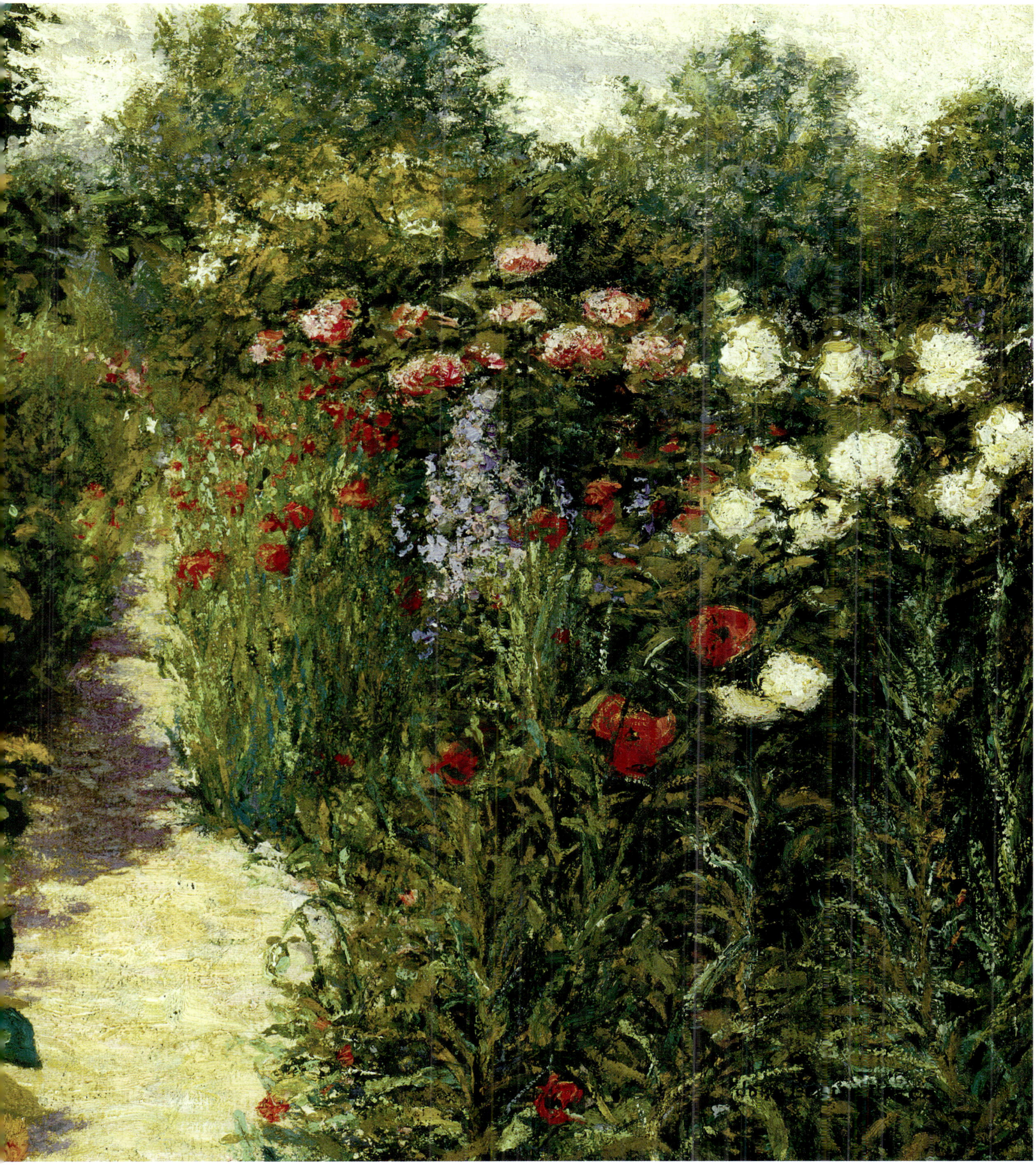

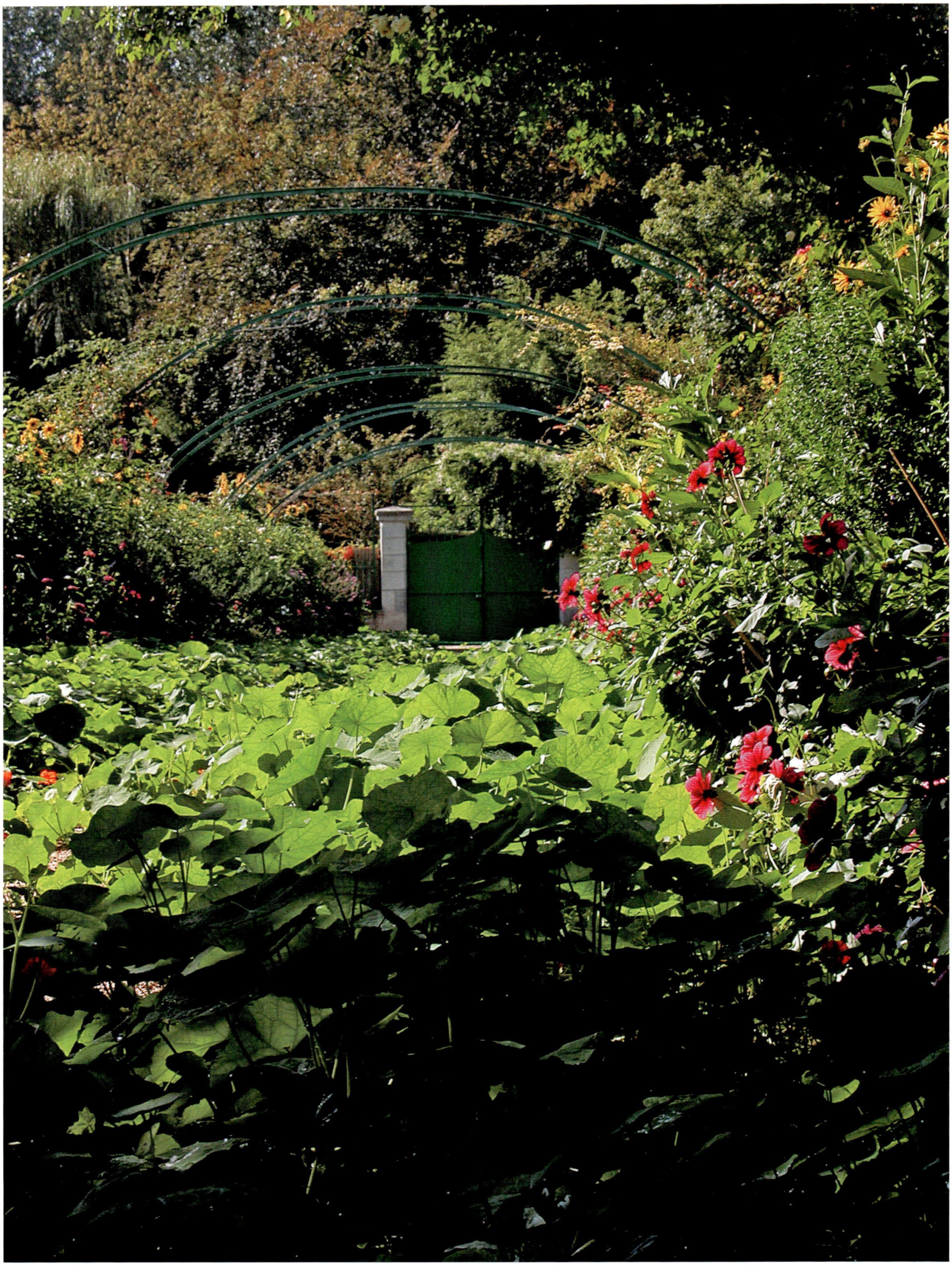

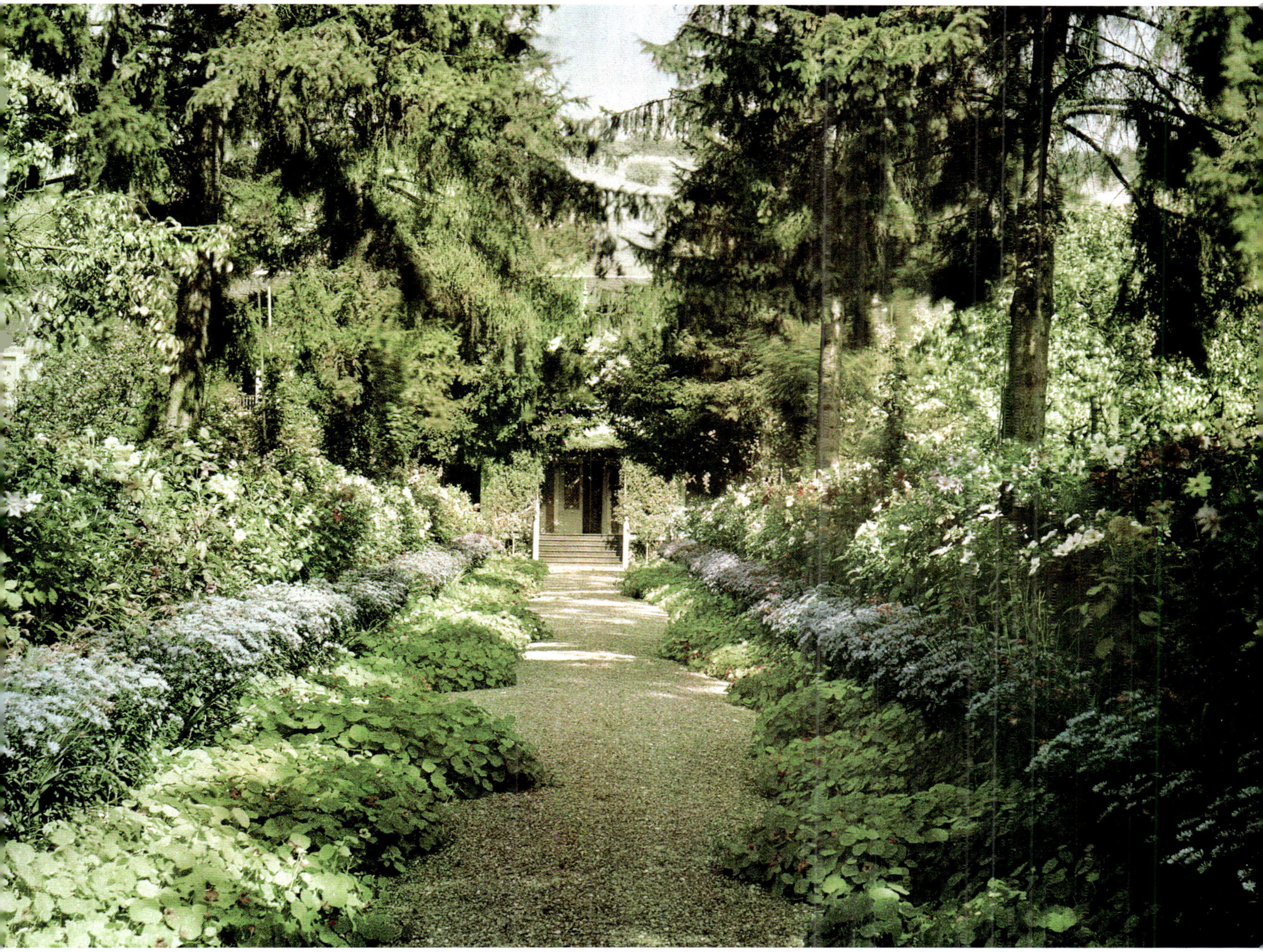

The roses grown by Monet to scramble over his Grand Allée included the climbers Paul's Scarlet Climber, Dorothy Perkins, New Dawn, Albertine, Sympathie and Maréchal Niel. Although Monet travelled, his roots and heart were in France. Little did he know that in America Childe Hassam's painting *The Maréchal Niel Rose* features a vase of them blooming on a highly polished surface, whilst a blond girl gazes at them and a brunette appears in the mirror behind. The large yellow rose was named for Napoleon III's secretary of war and Hassam wished to express its hybrid beauty as a symbol for American culture which had absorbed the best of European and Asian history. Monet actively tried to protect, and indeed stopped, his step-daughters from forming new hybrids with visiting American Impressionists, the exception being Theodore Butler.

Above: *This tinted photograph was taken in the early 1920s. You can see that the iron hoops so famously associated with the Grand Allée have yet to be installed. The plants across the path and over the tree stumps have practically met to form a green tunnel. The upper branches of the spruce give additional texture and practically hide the house.*

Opposite: *The Grande Allée in late summer. The nasturtiums have covered the path creating a tide of green, the edging borders are raised into a carp's back so that the marginal flowers both cascade down and grow up towards the light. The iron frames support several different colour climbing roses – the allée becomes a green tunnel.*

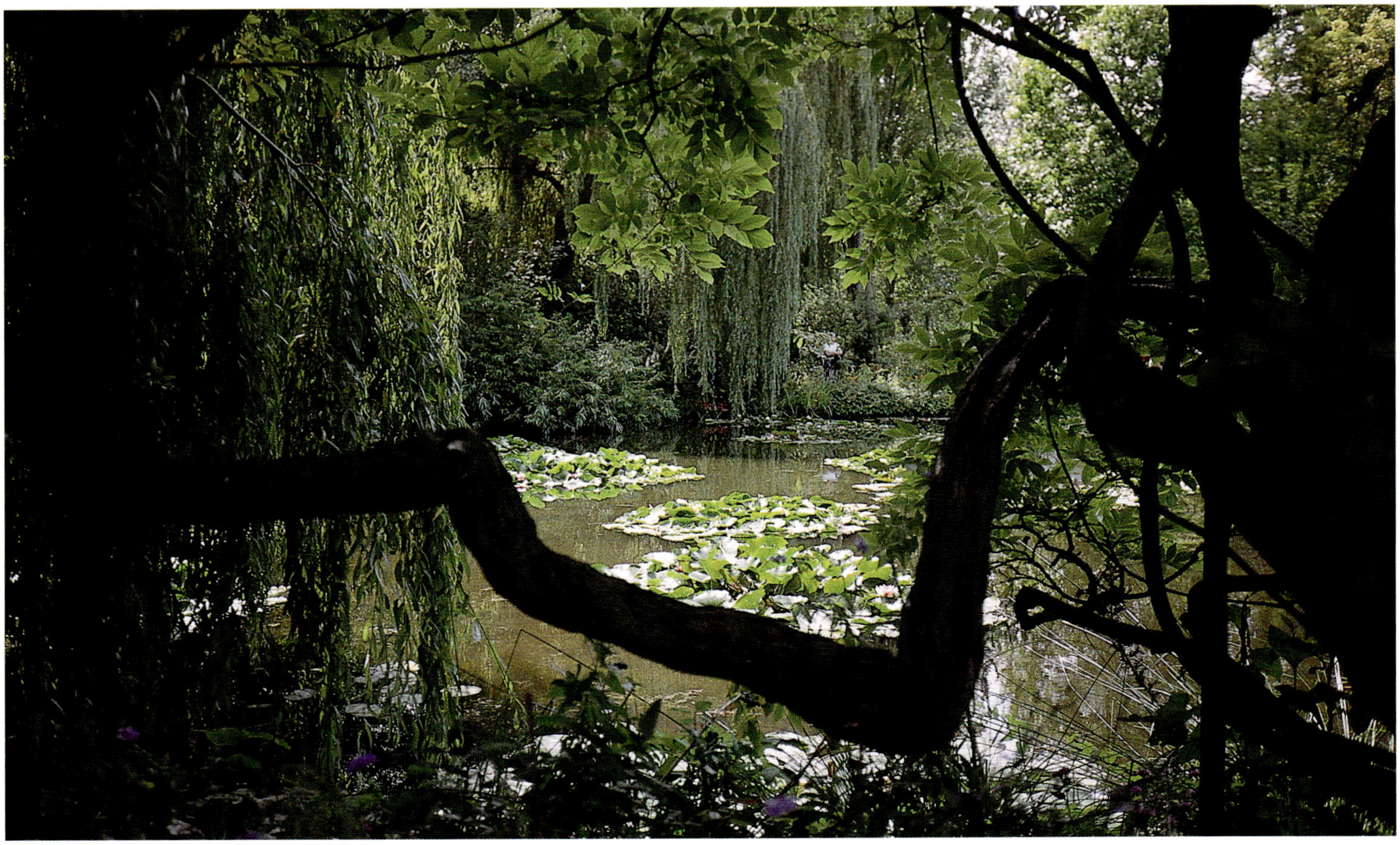

Above: *A glimpse across the etang through one of the original wisterias. It was trained along the furthest bank from the Japanese Bridge. Very few plants survived the decades of neglect after Monet's death and the etang was particularly badly damaged by gnawing rats.*

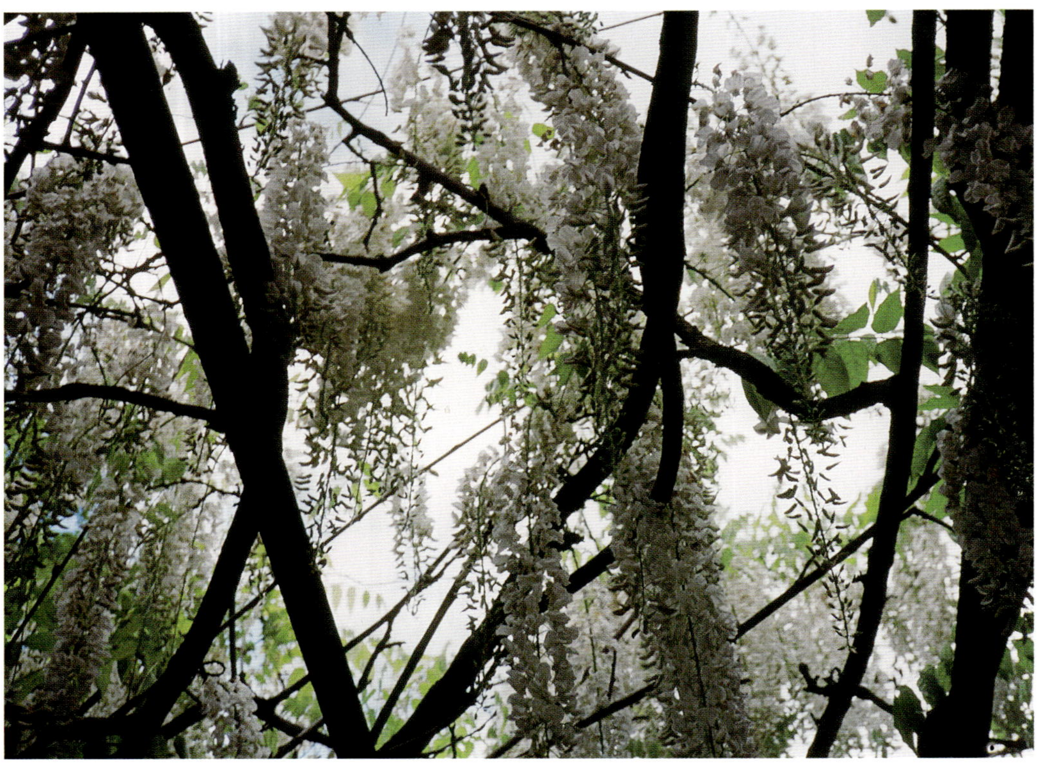

Opposite: *As his wealth grew, Monet expanded his gardens, including a second one, Maison Bleue, also in Giverny. He employed eight gardeners, and amongst their tasks was the compositional arrangement of the water lilies. The view here is from the Japanese Bridge through a curtain of wisteria, to a weeping willow.*

Left: *Taking the pictorial composition into the sky. A view through the white wisteria that is trained over the upper canopy of the Japanese Bridge. The flowers are at their best in late April/May, when the flowering panicles hang down in profusion.*

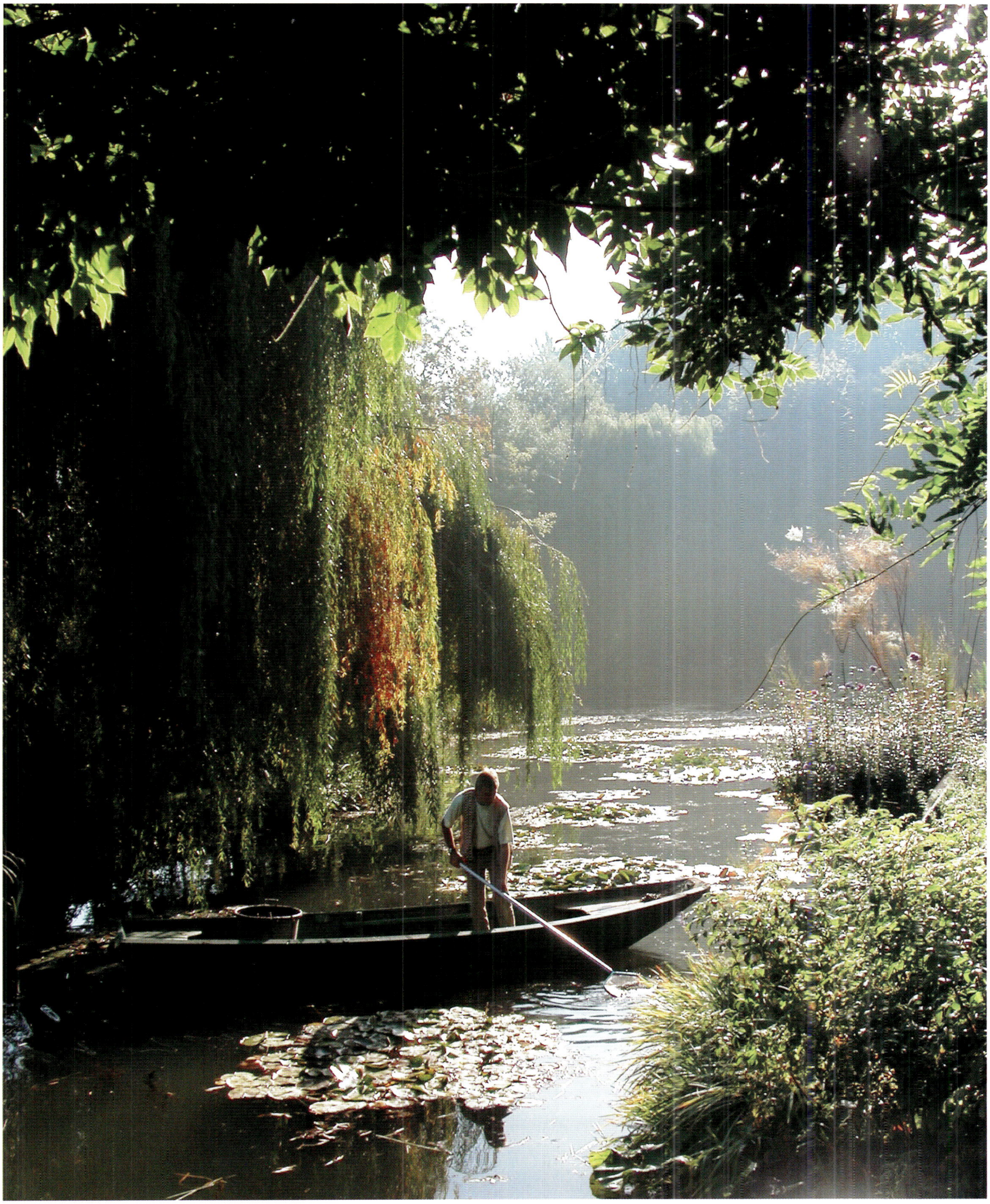

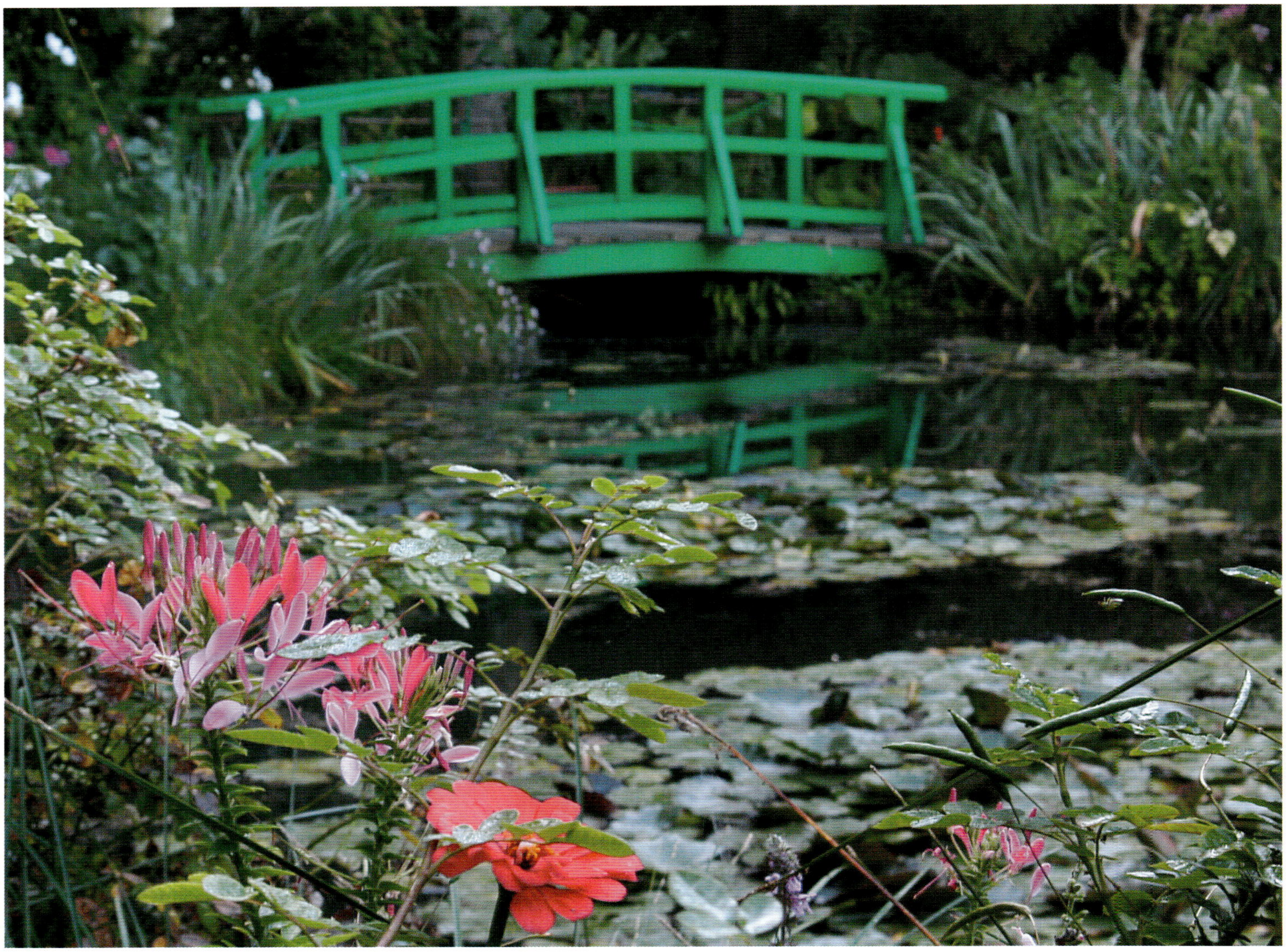

Apart from the Japanese Bridge there are small bridges over the diverted streams from the River Ru which can be lifted for maintenance. Visitors were taken on a tour of the gardens and a circuit of the pond before lunch or dinner. Today all the banks are planted up, however in Monet's time he planted clumps to alternate with the grass melting into the water. The bright pink cleomes light up the corner.

The long rectangular beds at Giverny were spectacularly filled with irises, followed by helianthemums, dahlias, rudbeckias, and cleomes whose shaggy flowers seem to reach for the sky, making it almost impossible to walk up the narrow beds that divide them. Actually today you are no longer allowed to even try. To the east of the Grande Allée a series of ironwork 'pavilions' provide small rooms over which primarily varieties of Clematis montana are trained. One variety that Monet painted can be identified as Clematis 'Marie Boisselot' which is also sold as C. 'Mme le Coultre'. This hybrid was created around 1900 and remains to this day one of the best white-flowered forms (for its size).

Monet enjoyed a successful exhibition at the 1889 Exposition Universelle in Paris and, of course, was inspired by Joseph Bory Latour-Marliac's six-month display of the colourful new varieties of hardy water lilies. These and his long standing admiration of Japanese prints fed his desire to create a sinuous water garden, so in 1893, after a little local resistance, Monet bought the meadowland below the Chemin du Roi to divert the tiny River Ru into a pond for the pleasure of the eye and also for motifs to paint. He ordered water lilies and other aquatic plants from the Latour-Marliac nurseries in 1894 and spanned the small pond with a Japanese bridge. Nursery records of 1898, 1904 and 1907 show that he ordered more plants but was a slow payer and gossip says he propagated Latour-Marliac's stock and then sold it. The pond was extended in 1901 from twenty to sixty metres in length and the bridge gained its upper canopy a year later, whilst the lily pads rapidly materialised the immaterial water surface. The horizon was deftly manipulated, through the vertical accents of the weeping willows which drew the eye up from the margins of the pool, whilst their leaves and branches took the eye inexorably back into the limpid water.

The winter of 1909/10 witnessed severe winter flooding. On 10th February Monet wrote to Paul Durand Ruel 'I thought for a while that my entire garden would be destroyed … although I've lost a lot of plants, it will probably be less calamitous than I feared.' In fact it was a dark year. Not only was Alice's health very fragile, but in a letter dated 5th August to Gaston Bernheim-Jeune he wrote 'to add to my miseries an appalling storm has created havoc in my garden. The weeping willows I was so proud of have been torn apart and stripped; the finest entirely broken up.' The following year he rationalised the damage by further extending the pond.

Over the years Monet hosted a select few American Impressionists at Giverny, and took on Lilla Cabot Perry and Theodore Butler as students. In 1885 Theodore Robinson was introduced to Monet and established himself in the village two years later. J.Carroll Beckwith, friend and fellow student of John Singer Sargent, and who had exhibited at the 1889 Exposition Universelle, spent the summer of 1891 in France staying with John Leslie Breck who tried to woo Blanche Hoschedé. Monet put a stop to the relationship as he considered Breck penniless and without prospects. Robinson took Beckwith to meet Monet and see the Poplar series which he found remarkable and profoundly interesting. The Impressionist effect of Beckwith's time amongst the Giverny colony can be seen in the brushwork, use of colour and composition for his portrait of John Leslie Breck.

Another regular visitor was Mary Cassatt, who in November 1894 brought Paul Cézanne to meet Monet as well as his good friends Georges Clemenceau and Gustave Geffroy, and to Cézanne's amazement was introduced to Auguste Rodin.

Theodore Butler had arrived in 1888, and after some protest from Monet he married Suzanne Hoschedé on 20 July 1892. Butler's paintings received high accolades and his home in Giverny became a great social centre.

Red and yellow helenium and rudbeckia. On the left hand side the flat pink flowerheads of hydrangeas have died back. The light plays all round the petals, the conical centres of the flowers and the leaves. The effect is boisterous and bright.

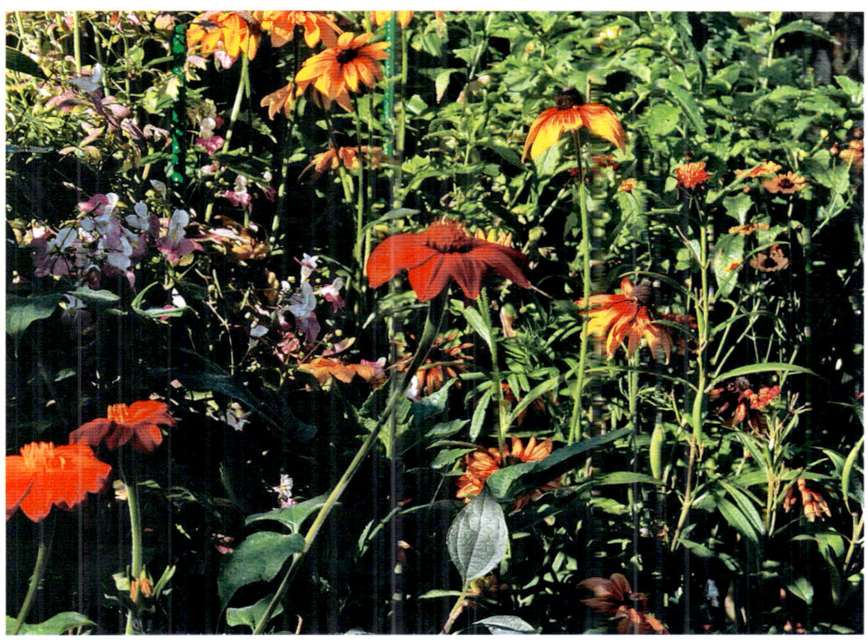

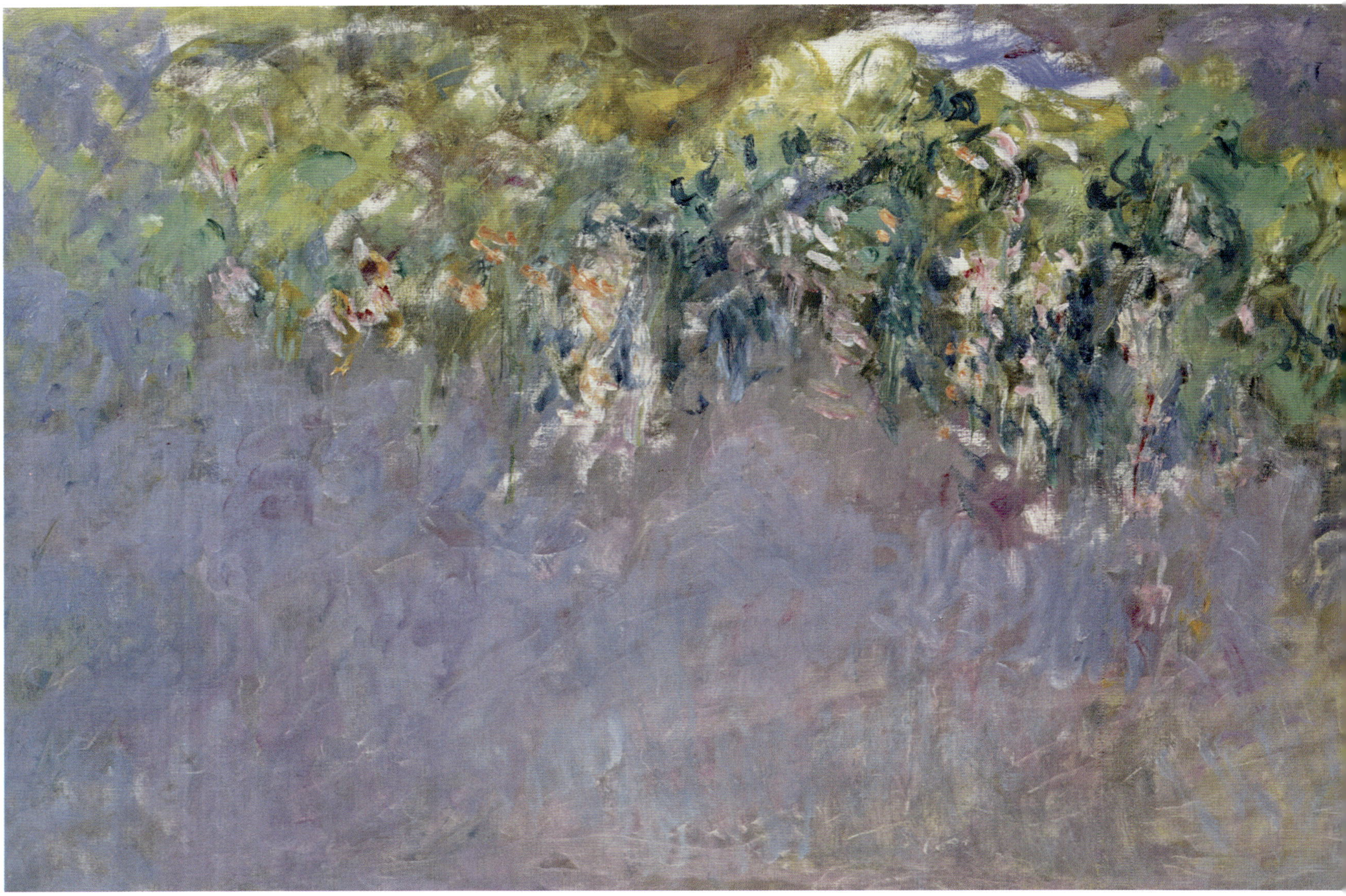

Claude Monet, **Wisteria**. *Oil on canvas, 100 x 300cm (39 x 118in.), 1919-20*

The original name for Wisteria was the same as the French – Glycine – which sounds so appropriate. Monet trained them over the Japanese Bridge, with purple flowering varieties swathed along the lower section and white varieties over the canopy. He also trained wisteria over a framework around the north-east end of his pond. Renoir had planned to clothe the stone walls of Les Collettes with wisteria. For English Edwardian designers it was the hallmark plant for festooning over walls, pergolas and loggias. At the time there was an alternative spelling of 'wistaria', as used, for example, by Celia Thaxter.

John Singer Sargent and Monet had first met back in 1876, and renewed their friendship when he visited Giverny in 1885, 1887 and possibly also in 1888. In addition Lilla Cabot Perry and her family rented a property next door for ten summers and her accounts of her friendship with the Monet household are invaluable.

Although often called his 'Japanese Garden' Monet did not follow the Japanese custom of shaping pools into animal or bird shapes, however, the perimeter willows he planted echoed the backdrop of gnarled trees favoured in Japan. Monet carved a semi-circle within the bamboo thicket that provided a sheltered view point across the water. Although resolutely without a Christian faith and (unlike John Twachtman), he did not study Zen philosophy nor seek the dematerialisation of reality, his hours of contemplation and obsession with light do equate with deep meditation. One might ask whether staring at water lilies drove Monet to Abstraction? The very late angry abstract paintings of the bridge and the house are revolutionary in the way they challenge the viewer, and in the twentieth century, Jackson Pollock, Mark Rothko and Gerhard Richter

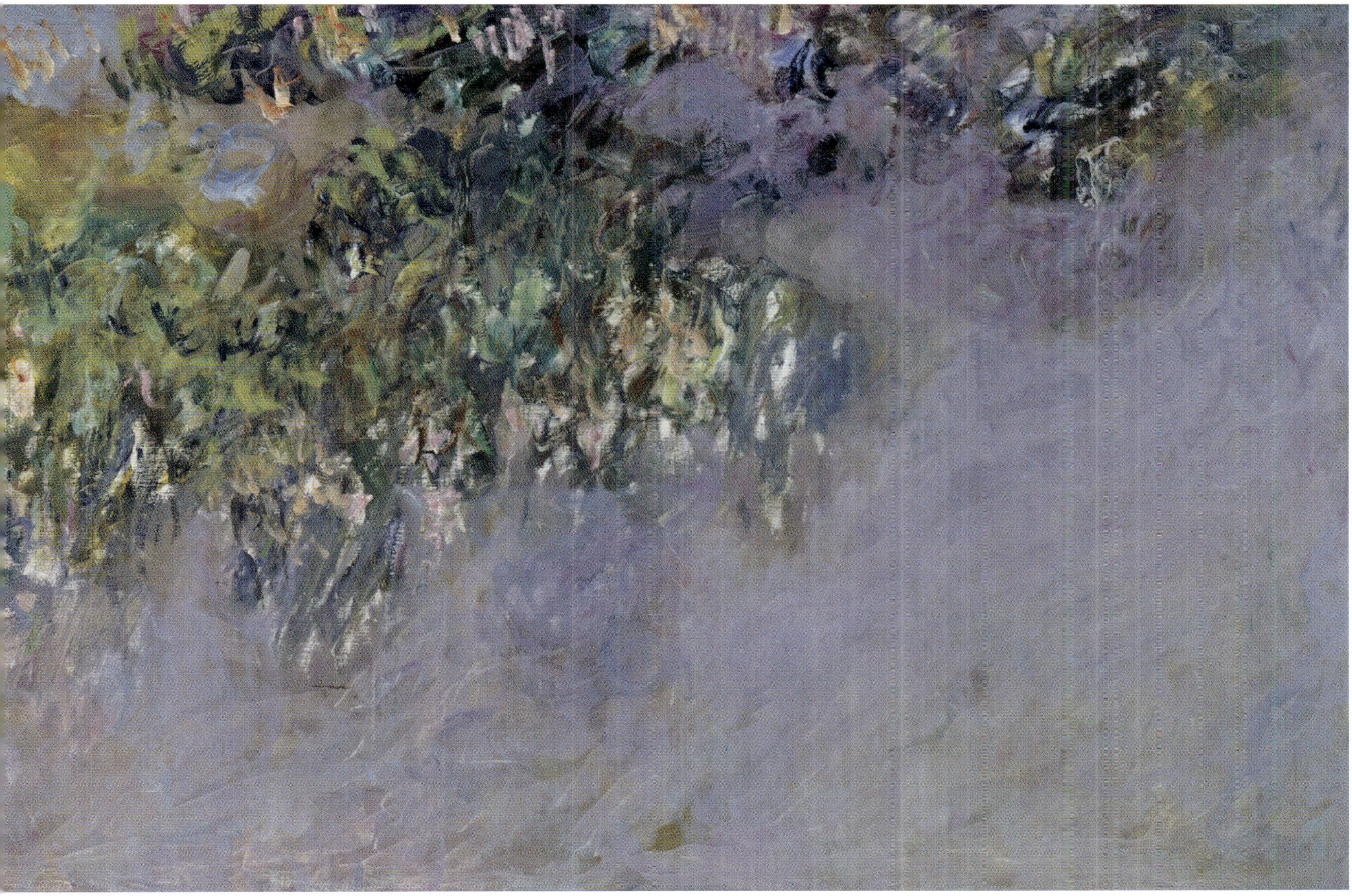

picked up the baton and ran.

Apart from walking through the gardens at Giverny, a visit to the oval basements of the Musée de l'Orangerie, on whose long walls hang Monet's water lily series, totally immerses you in the sensation of his pond and, as Geffroy wrote, his terrible bereavements. The gardens were maintained by his devoted step-daughter Blanche until her death in 1947. She painted many images of the garden including a border with those fashionable female shrubs, hydrangeas. Blanche's 1942 painting, *Hydrangées, le jardin de Monet à Giverny* provides testament to the survival of the garden nearly twenty years after Monet's death and includes one of his favourite flowers, a bright clump of yellow dahlias.

Nearly seven years after Monet's death, Stephen Gwynn visited and wrote an article for *Country Life*. It was published on 7th October 1933, entitled 'Claude Monet's Lily Garden'. Gwynn's photographs and words capture Giverny's serenity and beauty: 'Lilies floating among the reflection of clouds, the reflection of trees: that is the theme; and it is created even more by the grouping of trees than of flowers.'

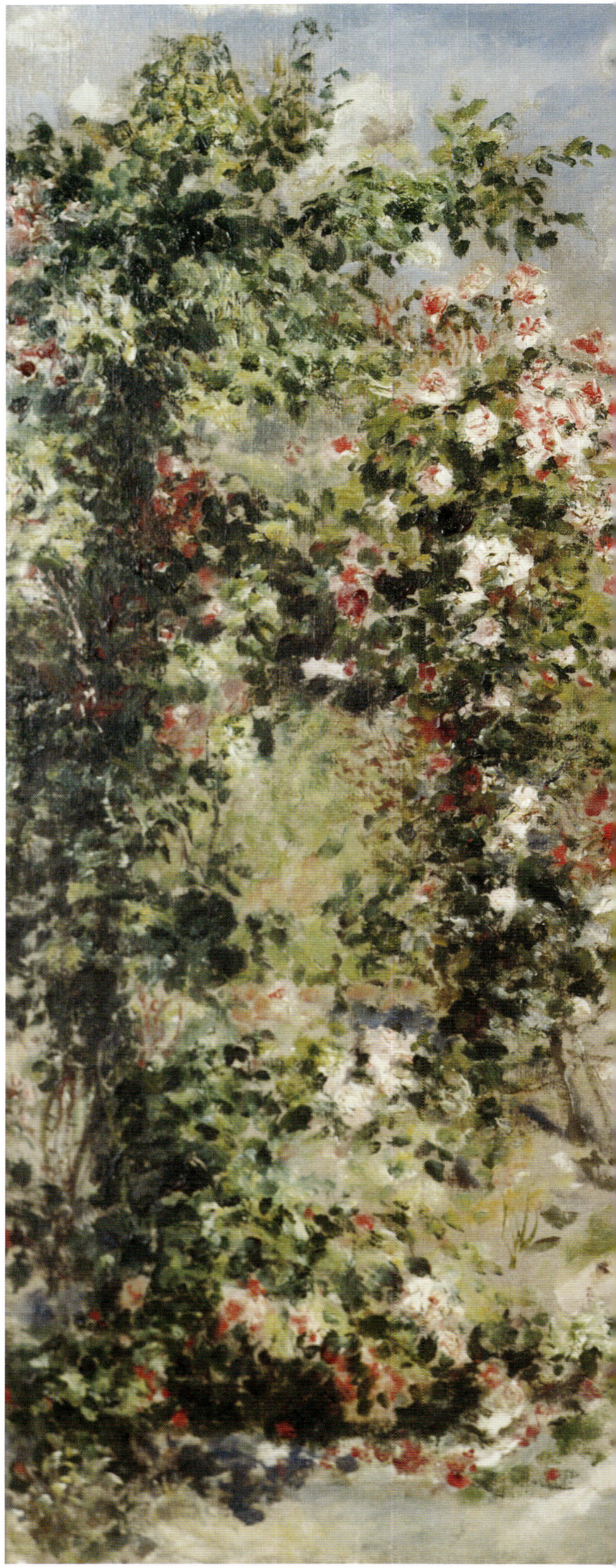

Pierre-Auguste Renoir, **The Greenhouse** (or The Conservatory). *Oil on canvas, 1880s*

Embowered by flower beds, The Greenhouse *by Renoir is very much as the view of the gardens at Giverny towards the Second Atelier would have been. Monet had extensive glass in the form of greenhouses and cold frames, and was a keen collector of orchids and other exotic plants through regular exchanges with the Jardin des Plantes in Paris. His American neighbour Lilla Cabot Perry wrote that on the arrival of new heating Monet insisted on sleeping in the greenhouse in case it broke down. Alice and his step-daughters were concerned that he should not be alone (and his step-daughters were as concerned for their mother), so in the end they all spent the night keeping watch over the plants. The heating did not fail!*

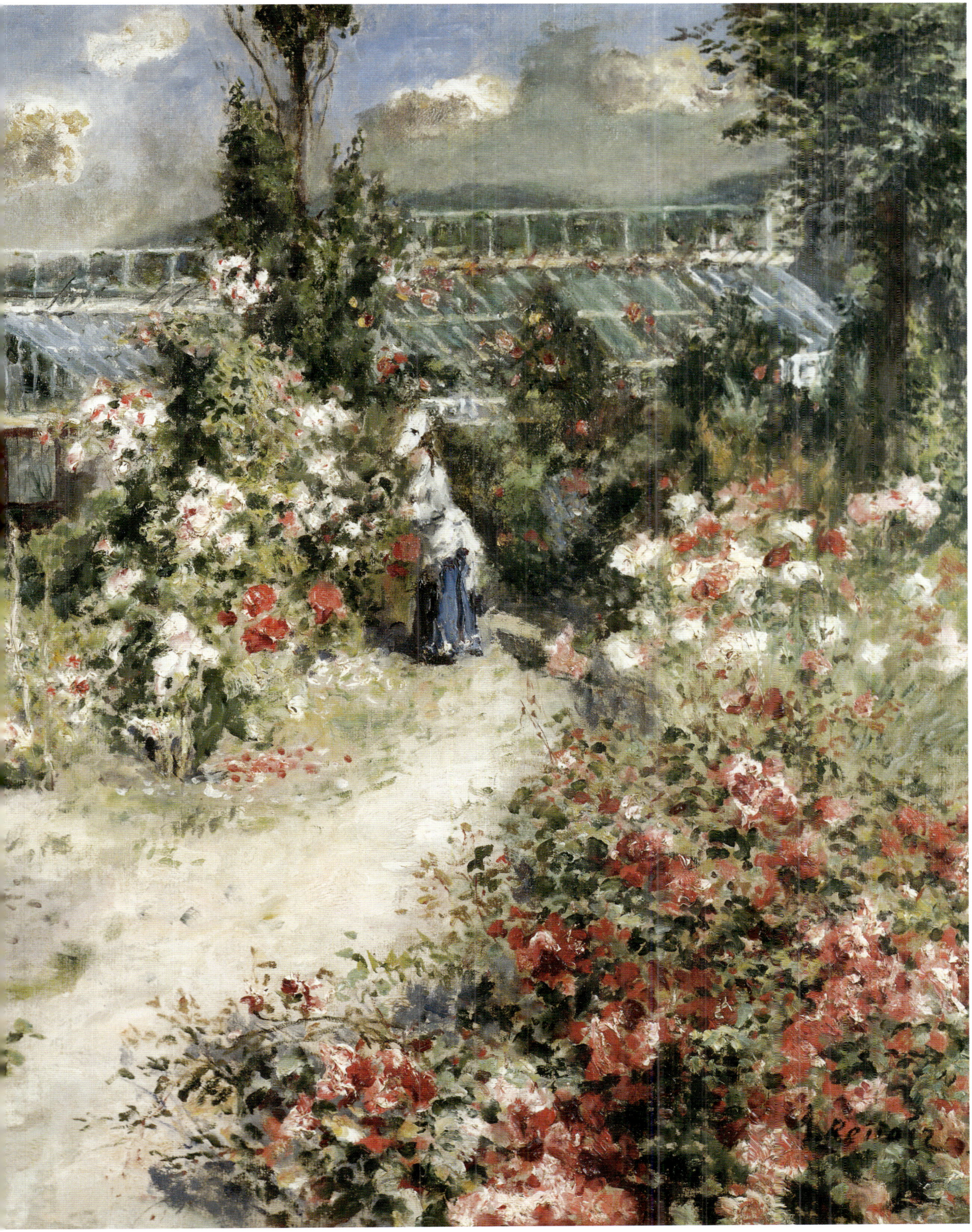

Harnessing the Light

An effect is only momentary; so an impressionist tries to find his place. Two half hours are never alike, and he who paints a sunset on two successive evenings must be more or less painting from memory. So, in these works, it has been the object of the artist to render faithfully, and thus obtain first records of effect, widely differing and often of very fleeting character.

Arthur Streeton

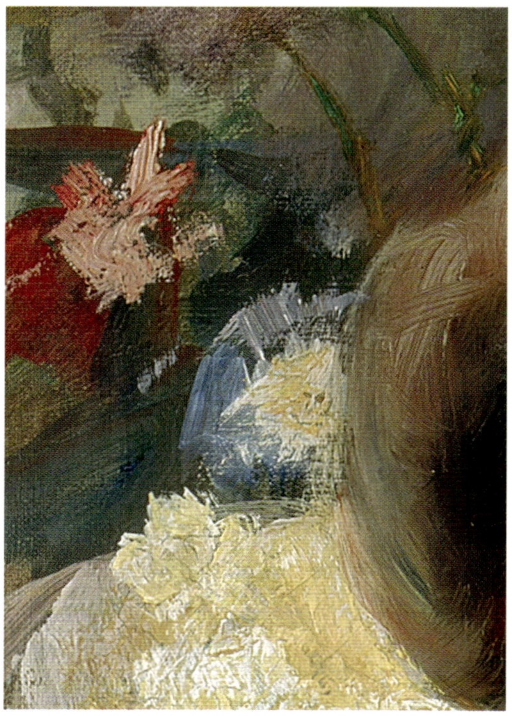

Mary Cassatt, **On a Balcony**. *Oil on canvas, 89.9 x 65.2cm (35 ½ x 25 ⅝ in.), 1878/79*

So often Cassatt leaves the viewer wanting to question the bigger picture: where are they? What are they talking or thinking about? There is no sign of any structure in On the Balcony, the young woman reading the newspaper is surrounded by roses with a pink rose on her bosom. In the centre of the rose blooms behind her head there appears to be one blue and white Morning Glory, which beautifully encapsulates the sitter and her setting. Cassatt achieves this enigma again in the face of Young Woman in the Garden, as she concentrates on some fine stitchery leaving one to wonder what is running through her mind?

One of the hallmarks of the Impressionists is their finely-tuned awareness of capturing the nuances of day or moonlight in their paintings. The miracles of gas and then electric light were transforming the urban scene but were far slower to illuminate more rural districts. This was equally highlighted in work of the Australian Impressionists, typically depicting a rural scene in the foreground with the bright lights of Melbourne, a distant dream, on the horizon.

Away from the convenience of urban technology, daylight was harnessed whenever possible to lighten (in every sense) daily chores, as well as the relaxations of reading, writing and a smoke – Monet is rarely photographed without a cigarette in his hand.

Aline Renoir personified the traditional country wife skilled in mothering, cooking, gardening and domestic crafts, celebrated by Renoir not least in his paintings of Aline breastfeeding their babies. The Renoirs could afford a wet-nurse – which was customary practice for the middle classes upwards at that time – but unusually Aline choose to nurture her children herself. Almost every year the family would summer in her home town of Essoyes and in early autumn she would take the children to help with the vendange of the family's vineyards.

Chopping the wood to keep the home fires burning was considered man's work. Splitting the logs and piling them neatly was a source of pride for the householder, and for the artist it became an art form. Childe Hassam liked subjects that endorsed his Yankee roots and sense of tradition, which is perfectly portrayed in *Woodchopper* (1902) in which a man carefully piles his split logs to bring warmth to hearth and home. In Australia, the bush on and around Mount Macedon provided all the wood that the McCubbin family needed for fires, building and fencing for their Fontainebleau property, as well as the backdrop for many of his paintings.

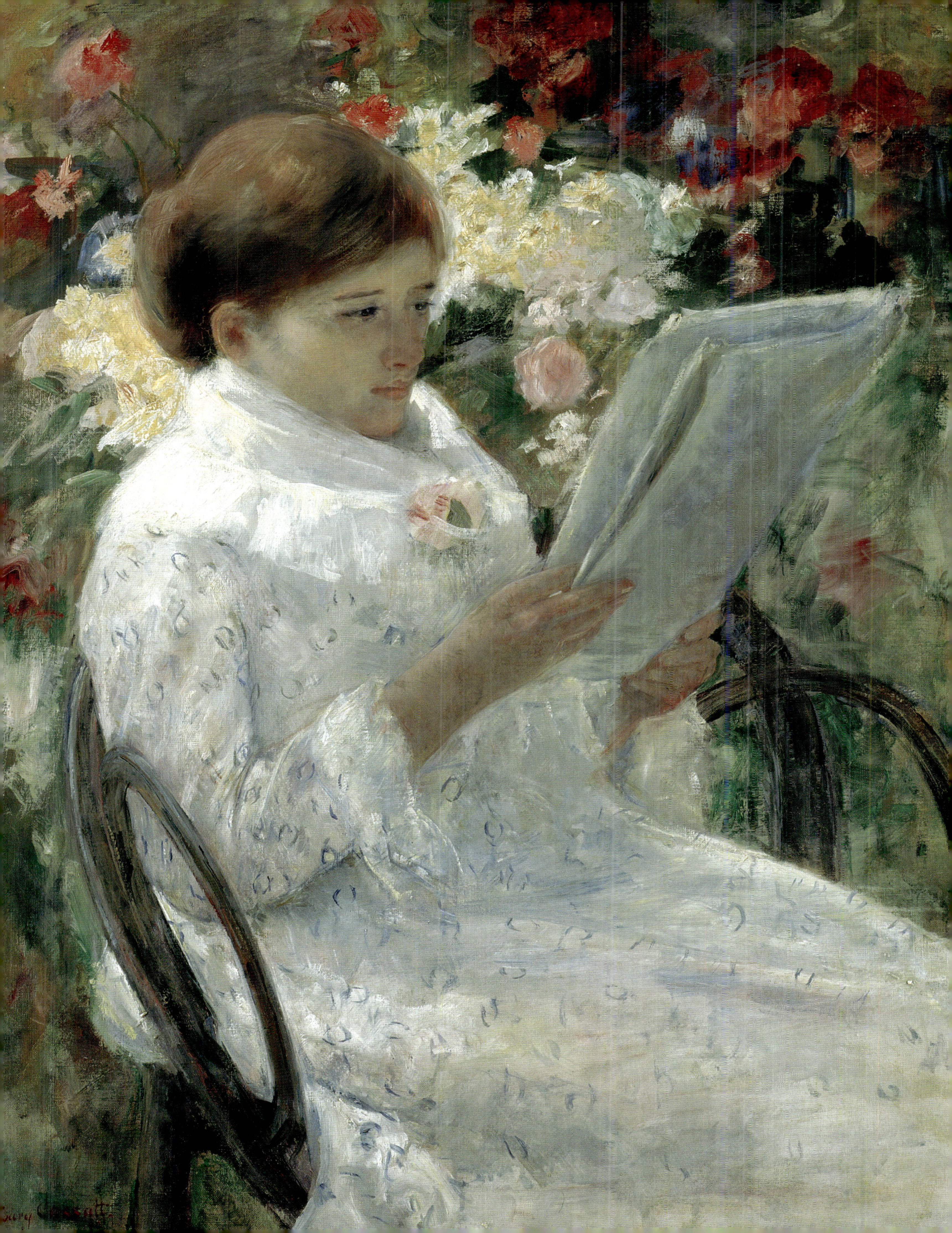

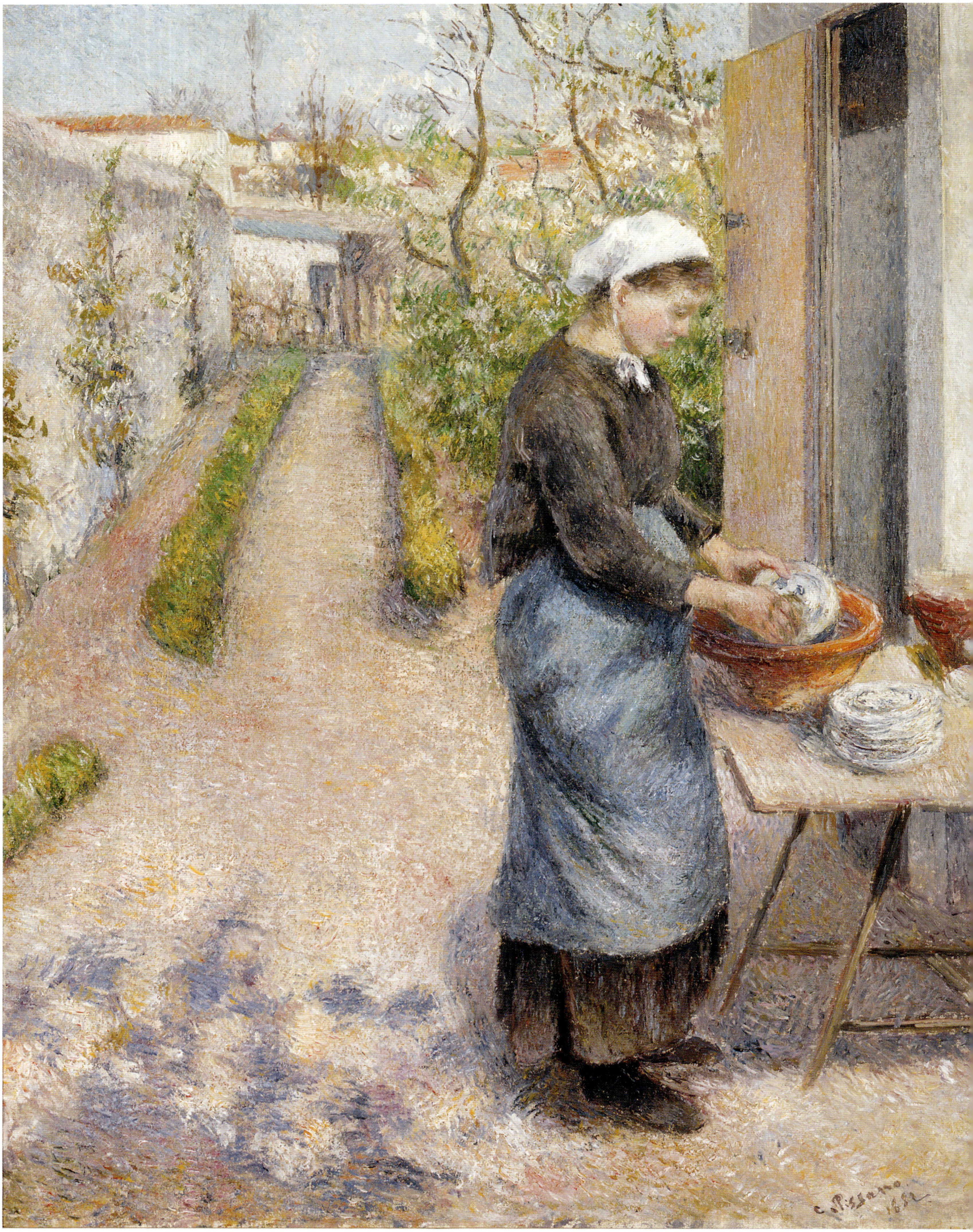
C. Pissarro
1882

Opposite: *Camille Pissarro,* **In the Garden at Pontoise: A Young Woman Washing Dishes.**
Oil on canvas, 81.9 x 65.3cm (32 x 25in.), 1882

In 1882 Van Gogh and Camille Pissarro both captured the drudgery of domestic chores: Van Gogh's self absorbed (probably interior) Woman Peeling Potatoes *seems to relish sitting with her feet on a stool absorbed in her task; whereas Pissarro's* In the Garden at Pontoise: A Young Woman Washing Dishes *shows a solemn maid washing up standing by a doorway, the spring blossom just touching the trees with white over her shoulder. If the water had to be drawn from the pump it may have been easier and pleasanter to wash up outside, especially in a little spring sunshine. The box-hedged path leads one's eye into the garden with its promise of fruit in the white blossoms of the pear trees. Can she see the blossom or appreciate the fan-trained pear trees? Is she lost in thought or just vacantly carrying out the task? The combination of a large family and Pissarro's strict adherence to his Impressionist principles meant that they lived much of their lives in penury. Mme. Pissarro was a keen gardener, mostly of essential vegetables; on a visit to Giverny she admired Monet's irises, and later when he was lifting them he despatched a generous collection to her.*

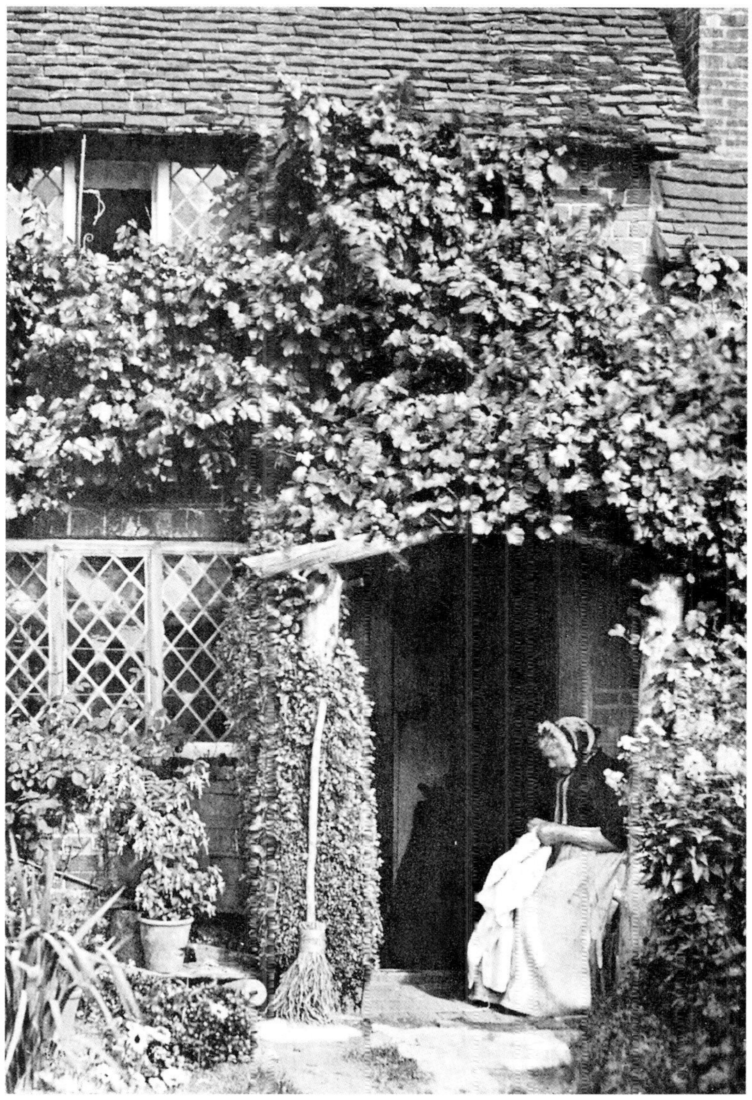

Right: *Cottage housewives would carry out many domestic tasks sitting in the doorway where the light was better, whilst ladies of leisure would sew on a terrace or in an arbour. For many women, working outside was often a communal task with a chance for chat and gossip whilst supervising small children at play. This black and white photograph 'The Cottage Porch' was taken by Gertrude Jekyll for an illustration in* Old West Surrey *(1904). In the text she describes that the daily routine was almost identical for all cottagers, but occasionally 'it was a pleasure to find some cottage housewife with a distinct taste for some occupation or general aptitude for wider interest. … beautiful plain needlework; a thing that by long practice became almost an extra sense'. She added that she knew an old lady who could still stitch shirt-fronts, though now totally blind.*

Claude Monet, **Madame Monet and a Child in the Artist's Garden in Argenteuil**. *Oil on canvas, 55.3 x 64.7cm (21 x 25in.), 1875*

There is a world of difference between darning and embroidering. The first is domestic in the extreme, but both are enhanced by sitting under the dappled shade of a tree on a warm day. The great bank of flowers behind Camille Monet and the unknown child looks remarkably like the dahlias that her husband had painted in their gardens at Argenteuil two years earlier. The boisterous flower bed was filled with roses followed by dahlias, a scheme that was popular with English garden writers such as William Robinson and Gertrude Jekyll. The light is brightest on the white linen in her lap, the blues of her dress and that of the child frame the centrepiece. The two figures are together and yet separated by their absorption in their tasks.

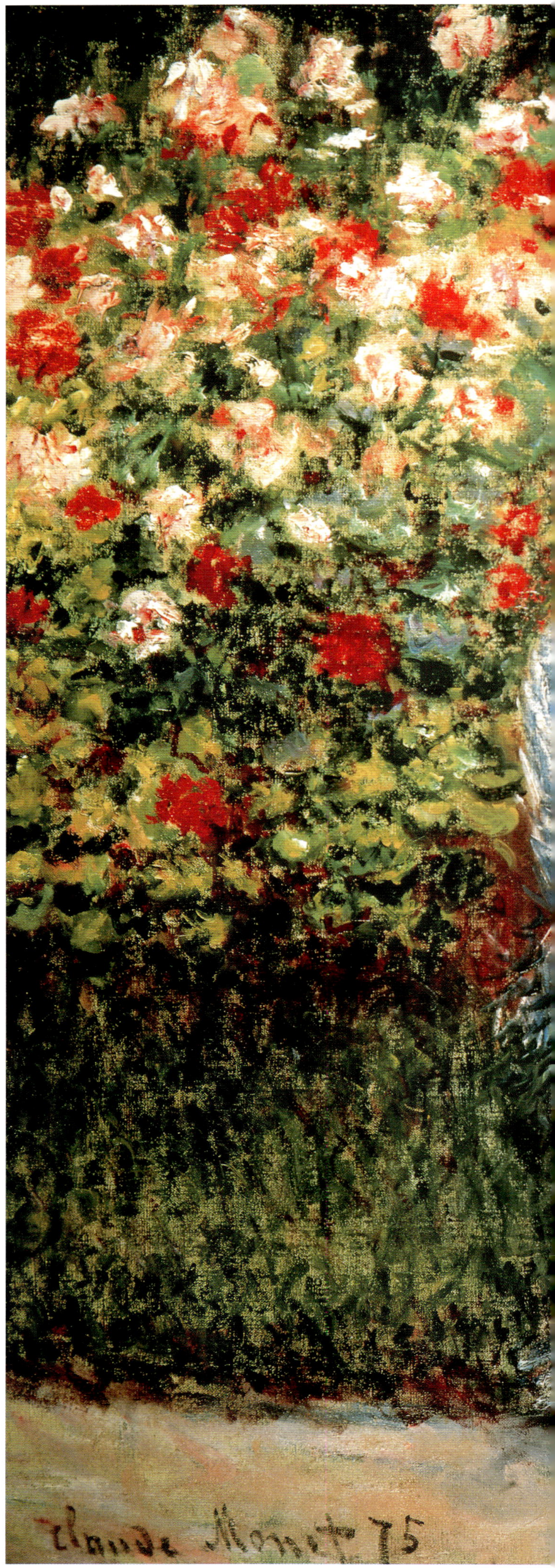

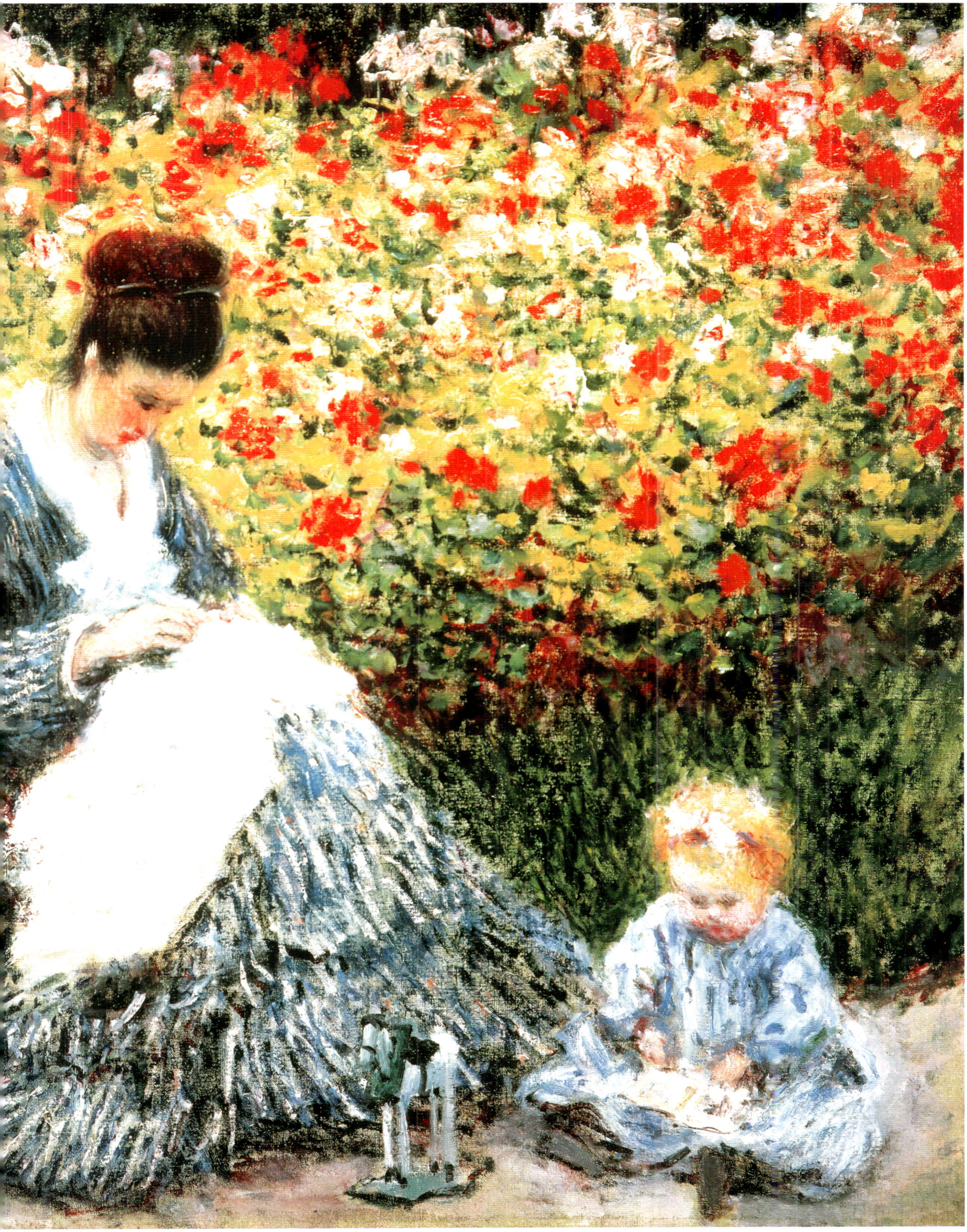

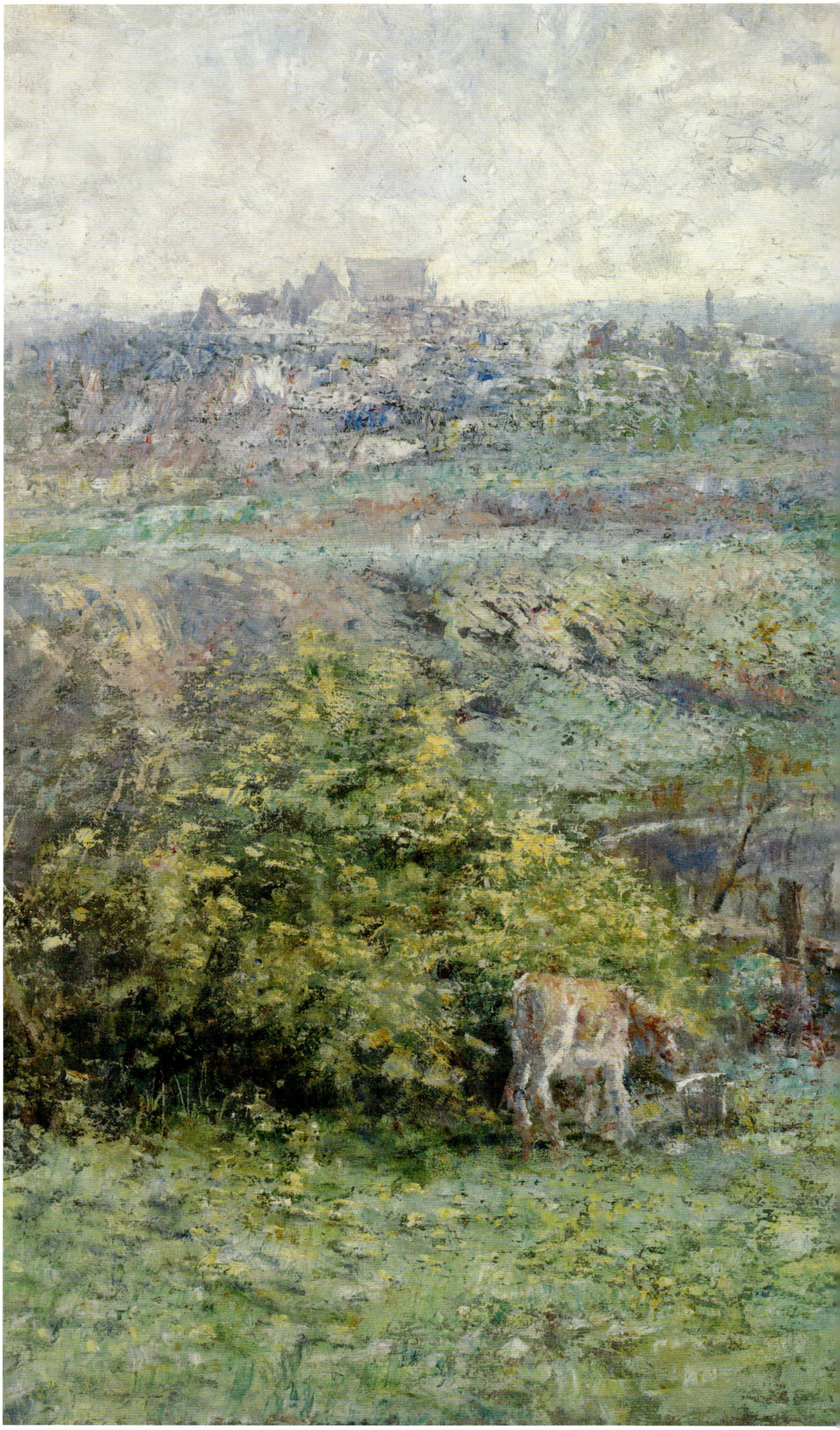

Frederick McCubbin, **The Coming of Spring**. *Oil on canvas, 68.8 x 102cm (27½ x 41in.), 1912*

The clear bright light of spring illuminates McCubbin's garden on Kensington Road in Melbourne's South Yarra, from the green fresh blades across the fields to the suburbs of Richmond. The Coming of Spring *with its luminescent colours and rich, textured finish expresses his words: 'It is precisely the pictures of things familiar to us of homely subjects... which most appeal to us and more often therefore rise to true greatness ... the farm with its neighbouring clump of gum trees, the fields that merge into wayward forests, the winding road ... and all things that savour of man.'*

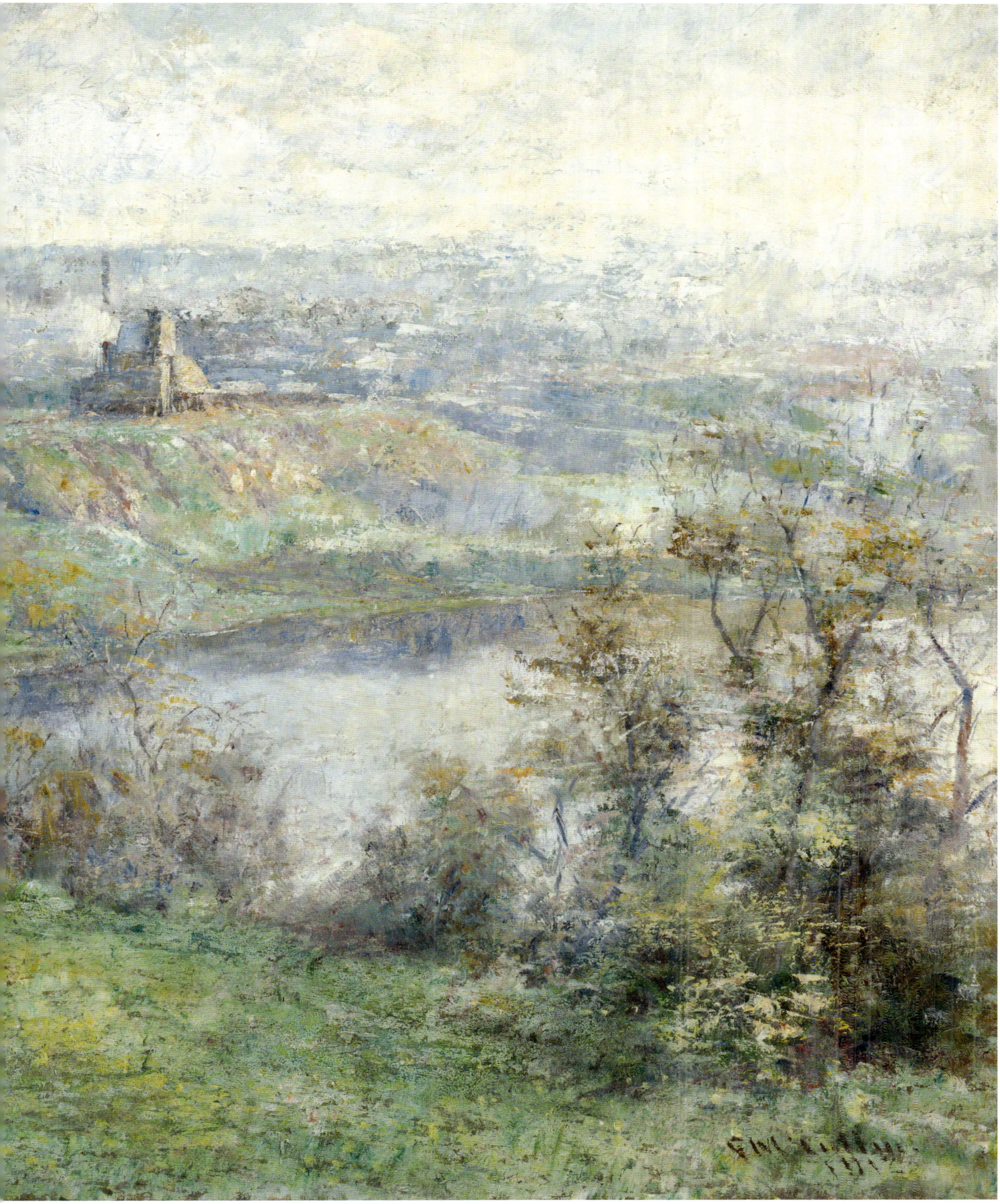

The house and gardens of Joaquin Sorolla y Bastida in Madrid, so enjoyed by his wife and daughters (see pages 62-63) are now a museum. The Islamic courtyards crossed by rills, with small fountains and bounteous shade still make it a pleasure to visit. Sorolla shared with many Australian Impressionists an admiration for the work of the French Realist Jules Bastien-Lepage, who at the end of his career returned to his rural roots to paint the fruits and vines growing in his grandfather's garden.

Sorolla was born in Valencia where he began to study painting, then went to Madrid and Rome where he spent four years. He also spent several months in Paris in 1885. His paintings were exhibited at the Columbian Exposition in Chicago in 1892 and the Exposition Universelle in Paris in 1900, and the Hispanic Society of America commissioned him to paint decorative scenes for its New York City Library. The harsh unrelenting sun captured in so many of the Australian paintings of the period match many of Sorolla's Spanish works, and like so many Impressionists, he also frequently painted beach scenes. His sun-filled work has an elegiac quality that is joyous whether harnessing the light at work, rest or play.

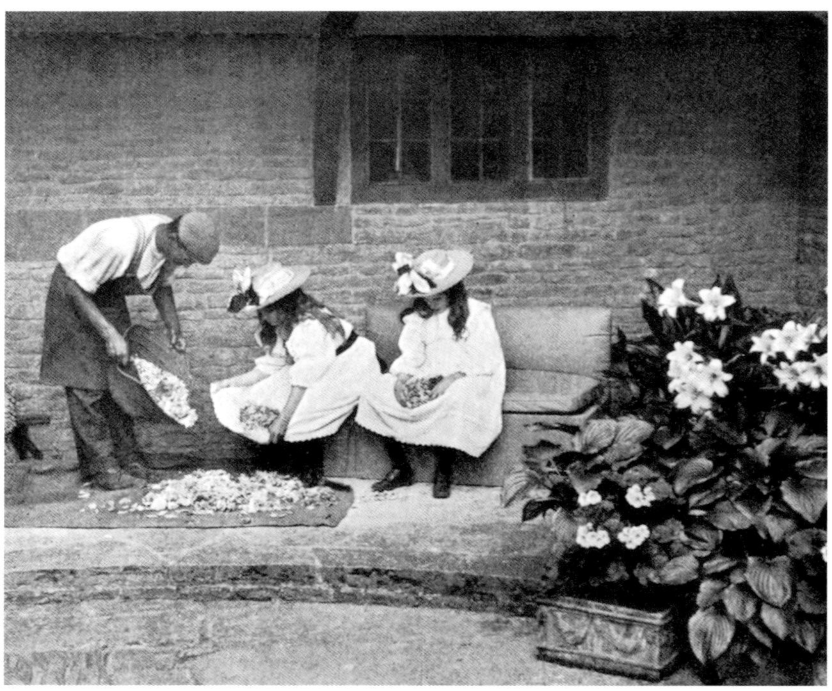

Home and Garden, *1900. Gertrude Jekyll devoted one chapter of her book* Home and Garden *to Pot-Pourri in which she writes: 'Sometimes visitors are pressed into the service, sometimes the little nieces come down from their home … plunging hands or face into the mass, delicious alike to scent and touch, one calls to mind how such generous measures of plucked Roses played their part in the feasts of Ancient Rome.' Jekyll used the courtyard below her north-facing jetty at Munstead Wood in Surrey for mixing pot pourri, gathering a bushel-basket (8 gallons or 35 litres) of roses from her garden every two to three days. Then the petals would be separated from their base and spread out on a cloth to partially dry, a job that Jekyll advised could be done with or without daylight. They were then gently crammed into 'various odds and ends of jars' at the rate of two handfuls of petals to a good sprinkling of salt. The garden also provided sweet geraniums, sweet verbena, bay leaves, rosemary and lavender, to which she added spices, sweet gums and orris root powder as well as shavings of sandalwood or sweet cedar. The enclosure of the courtyard must have channelled the scents up into the windows above and through the house.*

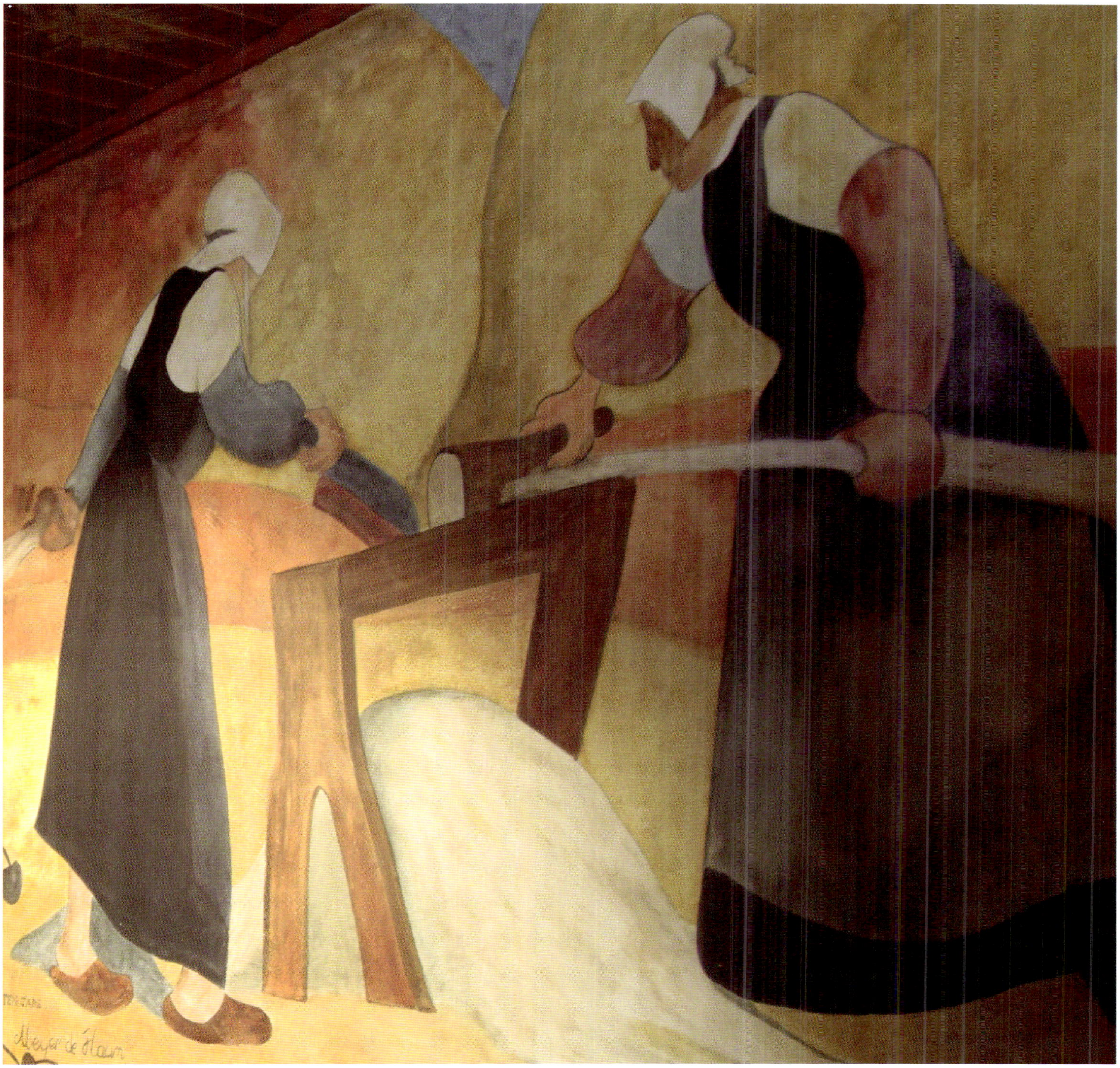

After Paul Gauguin and Meijer de Haan, **Breton women processing hemp**. *Mural*

Paul Gauguin and the Dutch artist Meijer de Haan lodged with Marie Henry, the owner of the Buvette du Plage in Le Pouldu, Brittany. Gauguin wrote to Vincent Van Gogh around 13th December 1889: 'My dear Vincent, I know how isolated you are in Provence and that you like to receive news from the friends who interest you, and yet many circumstances have prevented me from doing so. Among others, a rather large job which De Haan and I have undertaken together: a decoration for the inn where we eat. You begin with one wall, then you end up doing all four … De Haan has done a large panel on the actual plaster … Peasant women from around here working with hemp against a background of ricks of straw. … Here in Brittany the peasants have a medieval look about them and don't appear to think for a moment that Paris exists and that we're in the year 1889 – quite the opposite of the south.' The impressionist-style murals were papered over in the 1920's, rediscovered, then sold. Today, as can be seen in this image, Marie Henry's mural has been meticulously recreated in another traditional Breton cottage in Le Pouldu.

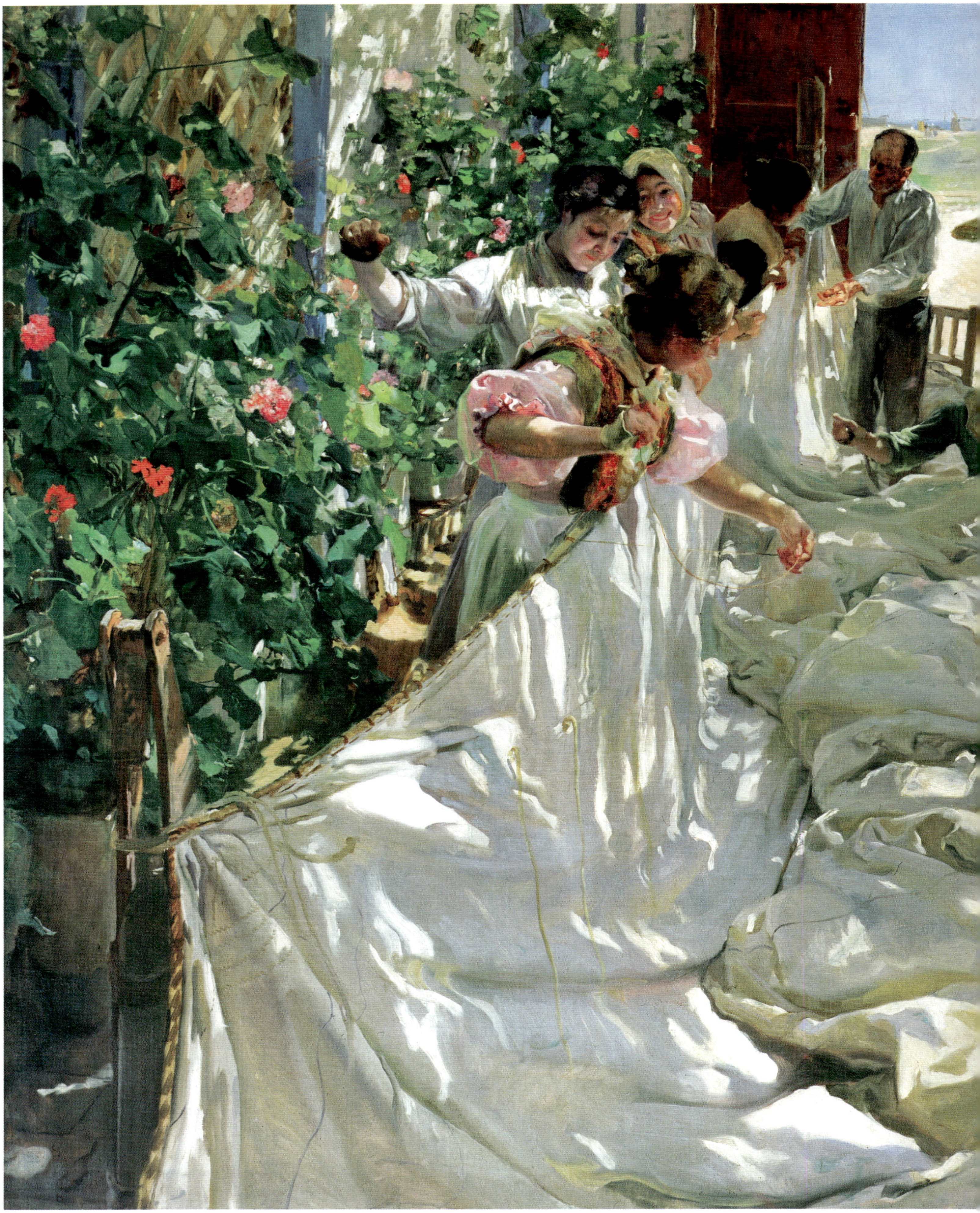

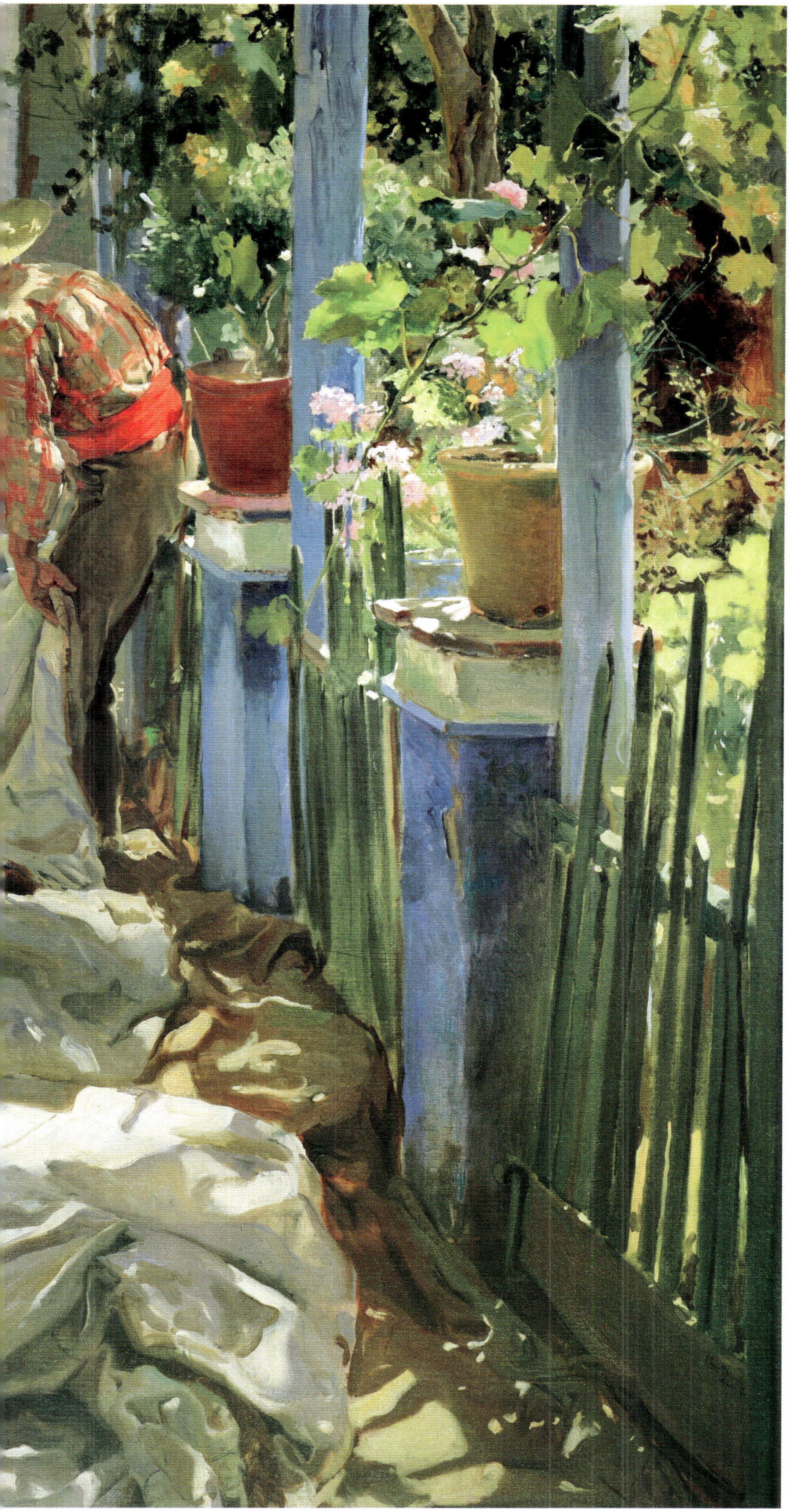

Joaquin Sorolla y Bastida, **Cosiendo la vela** *(Sewing the Sail). Oil on canvas, 302 x 220cm (118¾ x 86½ in.), 1896*

Sewing the sail on the terrace is clearly a project for a team and makes a great link to the sea. This space between the house and garden looks as if it has been designed for the purpose, as the white sail billows along the ground, its whiteness catching the light as if it is already heading for the sea. The path is covered by a pergola over which a vine is growing, offering dappled shade, the deep pink of the climbing rose echoed in the seamstress's sleeve. The busy composition evokes the sounds of industrious chatter and the sea beyond. The garden door looks out onto the sea whose proximity probably accounts for the poor sandy soil and the fact that all the showy flowers are in pots. Many of the Impressionists were keen sailors or observers of sailing, indeed Gustave Caillebotte owned fourteen yachts, of which eight were designed by him. He chose his house at Petit Gennevilliers for its double assets of the garden and the mooring.

CHAPTER FOUR

American Impressions

Childe Hassam and Celia Thaxter at Appledore

Often I hear people say, "How do you make your plants flourish like this?" as they admire the little flower patch I cultivate in summer, or the window gardens that bloom for me in the winter; "I can never make my plants blossom like this! What is your secret?" And I answer with one word, "Love". ... For though I cannot go so far as a witty friend of mine, who says that when he goes out to sit in the shade on his piazza, his Wistaria vine leans toward him and lays her head on his shoulder, I am fully and intensely aware that plants are conscious of love and respond to it as they do to nothing else. ... Like the musician, the painter, the poet, and the rest, the true lover of flowers is born, not made. ...Given a little patch of ground, with time to take care of it, with tools to work it and seeds to plant in it, he has all he needs, and Nature with her dews and suns and showers and sweet airs gives him her aid. But he soon learns that it is not only liberty of which eternal vigilance is the price; the saying applies quite as truly to the culture of flowers, for the name of their enemies is legion, and they must be fought early and late, day and night without cessation ... the flower lover must seek all these with unflagging energy; and if possible exterminate the whole. So only may he and his precious flowers purchase peace.

Celia Thaxter, An Island Garden, *1894*

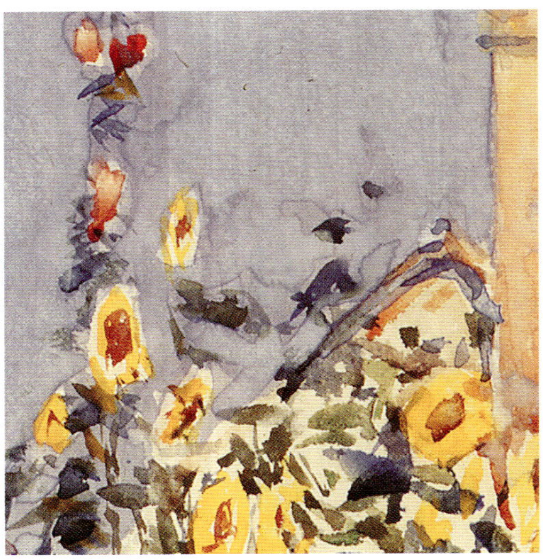

Childe Hassam, **Thaxter's Garden**. *Watercolour on paper sheet: 50.2 x 35.8cm (19 x 14in.), 1892*

Hassam is looking up from the north east of Thaxter's garden, towards the corner of the white clapboard cottage. Beyond the fence and gate the eye is drawn to the arched trellis. Celia Thaxter's garden at Appledore is like a smaller version of the upper garden at Giverny. Ripened seedheads from the island garden are volunteered all over the surrounding rocky hillsides and cliffs, carpeting them in flowers.

Childe Hassam is often cited as 'America's foremost Impressionist', however, he vehemently rejected any suggestion that he was inspired by Monet. Despite his protestations he may well have been informed by the publicity and articles generated by Durand Ruel's first American Impressionist Exhibition in New York in 1886, after which Ruel opened a gallery. In 1883 Hassam had visited Europe, travelling around England, Scotland, Holland, France, Switzerland, Spain and Italy – the very year Monet acquired Giverny, and Jekyll Munstead Wood. Hassam's shift to Impressionism appears to have been consolidated in *Peach Blossoms* painted between 1887 and 1889. This peach tree was growing on the Villers-le-Bel estate, owned by the Blumenthal's; Madame Blumenthal was the daughter of Thomas Couture who coincidentally had taught Monet and Mary Cassatt. Hassam's picture shows a peach tree in need of a good prune but its gnarled bark and new blossoms echo Japanese prints as well as symbolising the passage of time. This shift towards Impressionism can be contrasted in two of his paintings at Villers-le-Bel: the figures of a woman with a large bunch of roses and a man reading are decidedly wooden in the first painting: *Gathering Flowers in a French Garden* (1888). The scene is certainly floriferous – baskets and bushes of roses viewed through a canopy of white horse-chestnut candles but it fails to draw you in. The second, *Geraniums* (1888/9) captures his wife Maude engrossed in sewing under bright sunlight in the top left hand

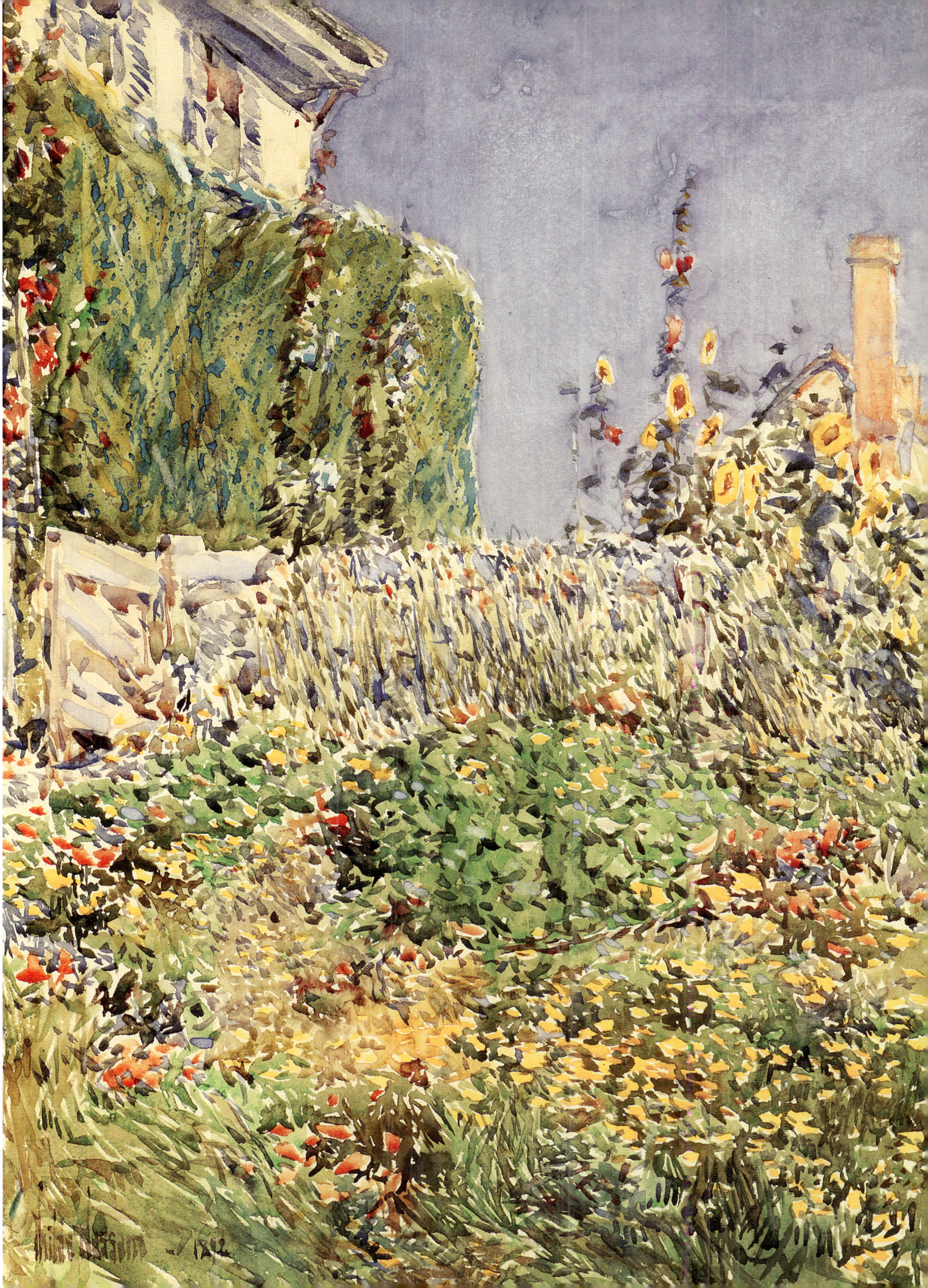

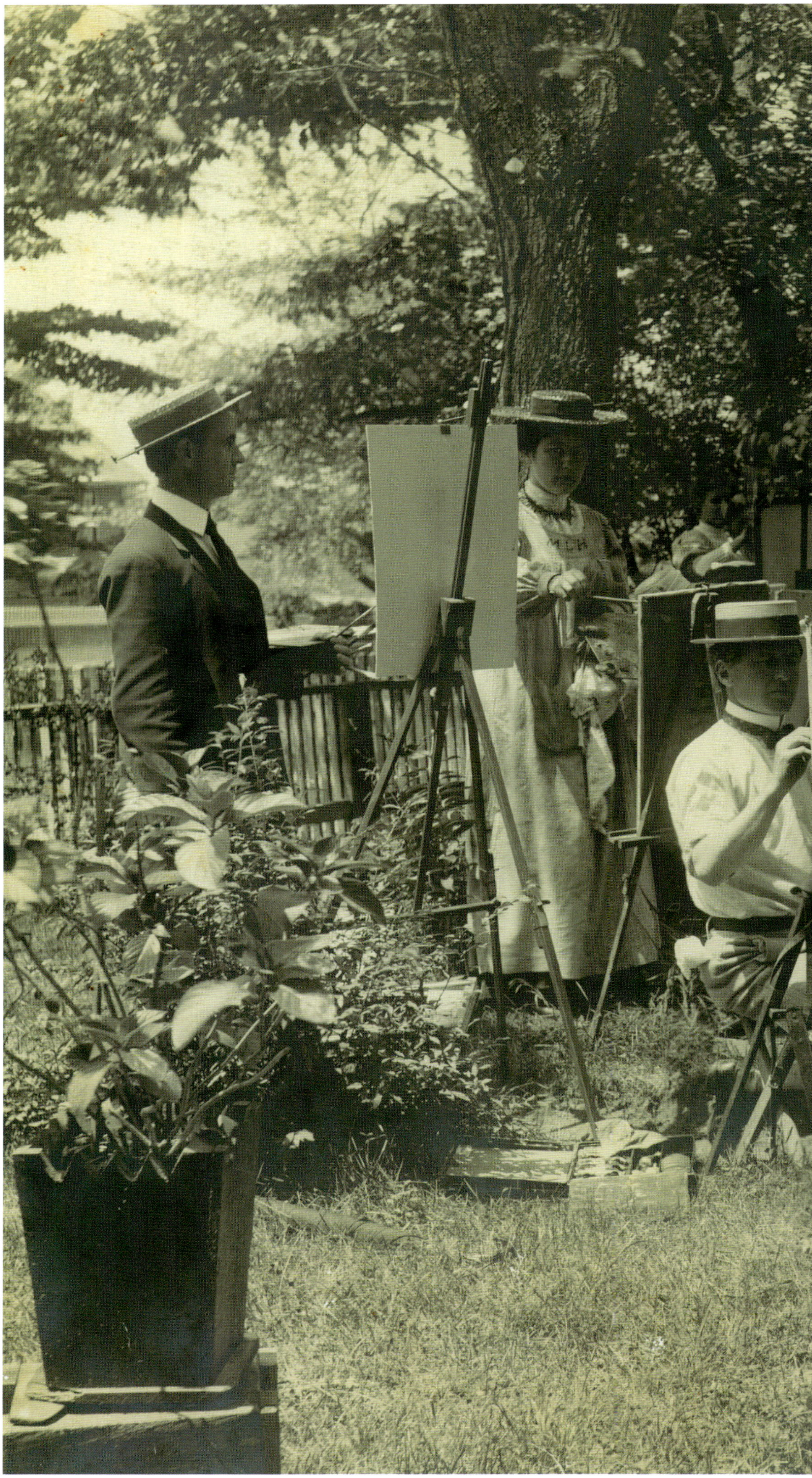

A summer painting class circa 1904. A positive battery of artists and easels recapturing their earlier plein air *experiences in France, often at the Hotel Baudy in Giverny. The class are painting in the gardens of Florence Griswold's boarding house, at Old Lyme in Connecticut, where the paintings created by the visiting artists on the doors and walls still survive. The site was known as 'America's Giverny', and Childe Hassam painted here from 1903.*

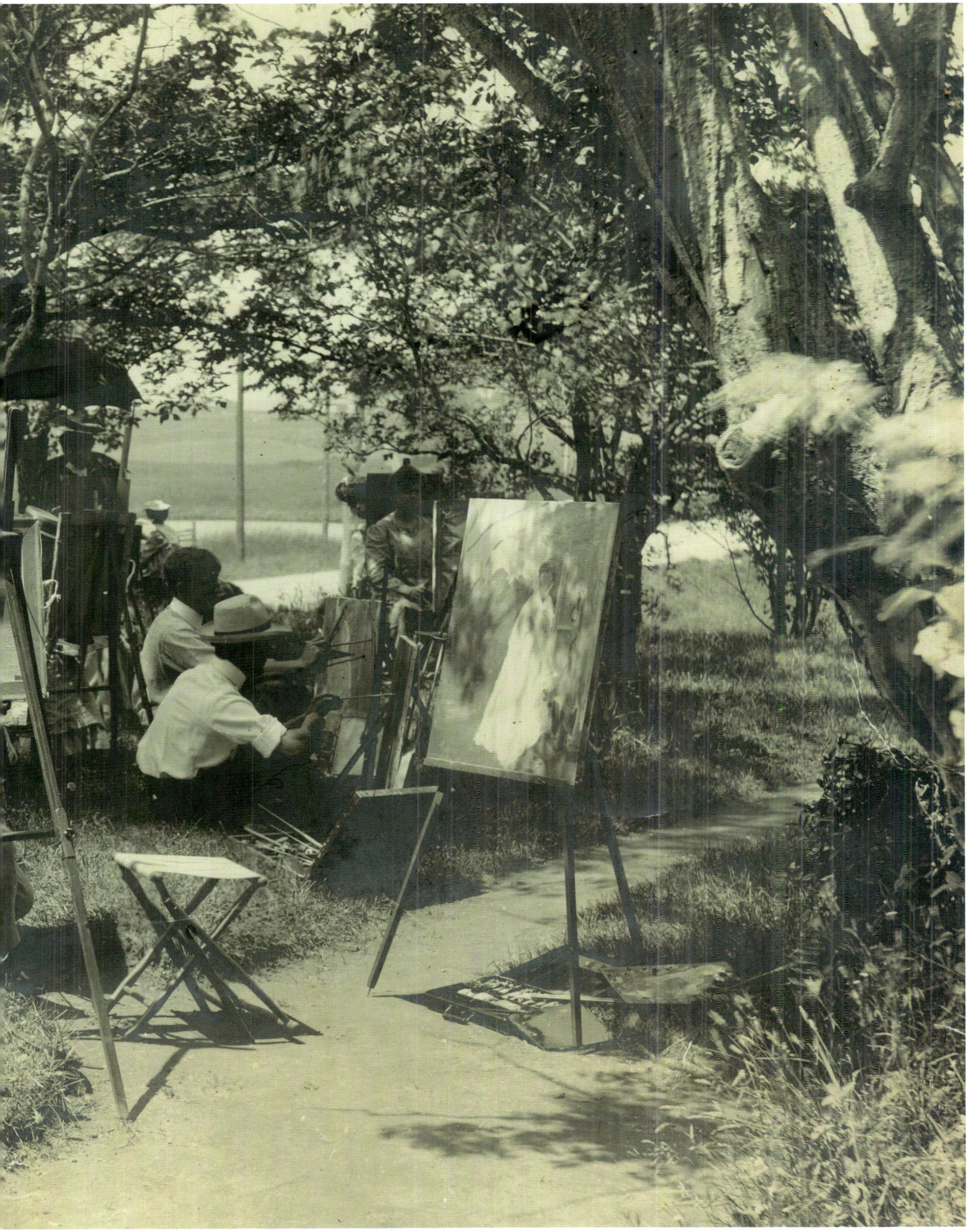

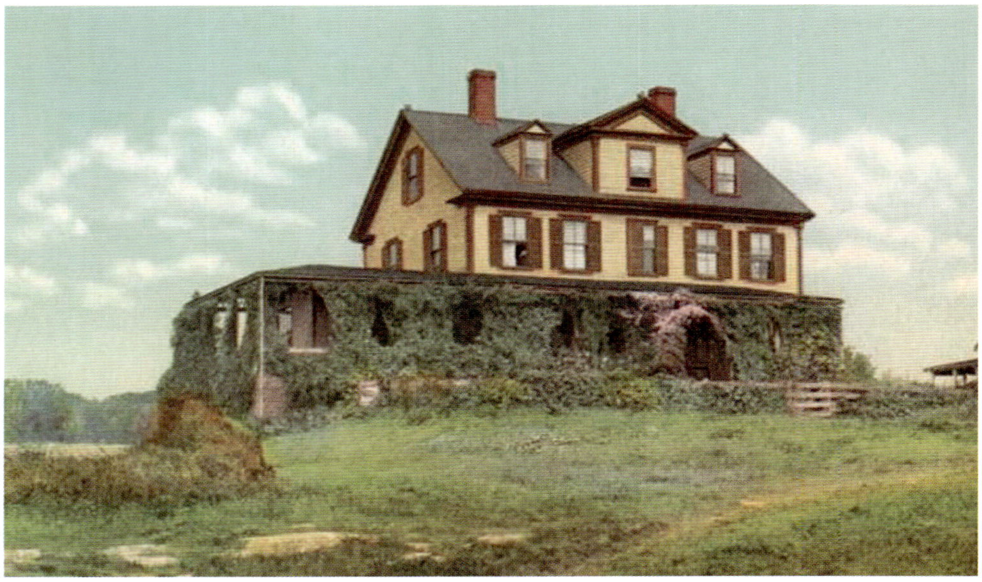

This picture was taken seven years after Thaxter's death in 1894, but the vine-wreathed verandah still flourishes, as does the flower-canopied doorway where Hassam painted her holding the hand of her grandchild Elliott (see page 139). Both flowers and vines acted as a filter for the sea winds and allowed a warm perfume to infuse the interior. You also appreciate just how exposed and rocky the terrain was that surrounded Appledore Cottage.

corner of the canvas, she is framed by pots of red geraniums on shelves which lead the eye down (or is it the other way?) to two stout watering cans. A vivid sensual balance of beauty and utility.

Hassam painted in three art colony gardens closely associated with American impressionism, Old Lyme and Cos Cob (Cos pronounced Cahs) in Connecticut, but he found his greatest inspiration at Appledore where the poet Celia Thaxter lived from spring to autumn. The setting of Appledore is one of wild beauty on the Isles of Shoals, a granite outcrop off the coast of New England. Thaxter's house was framed in a colourful sea of flowers which were transported into her sunny house where the sounds of garden birds were accompanied by music and readings by her eclectic guests including artists, writers and musicians. The floral compositions of Thaxter's plantings were arranged in harmony with the vases that were placed on every surface. In David Park Curry's 1990 *An Island Garden Revisited* he wrote: 'Appledore was a place where the imagination could flourish. Inspired by Impressions of the parlor's cultured atmosphere, the garden's brilliant color, and the landscape's wild beauty. Conversation and discussion were key threads in the colourful weave of stimuli circulating in Celia Thaxter's domain.'

The childhoods of both Celia Thaxter and Gertrude Jekyll had been spent observing nature, especially plants, which they both write about in touching detail. Thaxter's father, Thomas Laighton, had bought four of the islands in 1839, including Hog Island which he renamed Appledore, and he also acted as keeper of the White Island Light. As a child Thaxter studied Shoals' seaweeds which she later used to decorate porcelain.

Laighton and Levi Thaxter, an ornithologist and Robert Browning scholar set up Appledore House as an off-shore hotel. Thaxter acted as tutor to the young and beautiful Celia, wooed and married her; they built Appledore Cottage and had three children. Her cottage parlour was extended in 1887, the porch and verandah were swathed in climbing plants such as wisteria, hops, blue and white clematis, Cinnamon Vine, nasturtiums, and the beautiful and picturesque Wild Cucumber which wafted its scent on the warm summer breeze. Van Wyck Brooks wrote that amongst other poets at Appledore John Greenleaf Whittier read his poems aloud and she read hers. '… Celia Thaxter's poems were literary water-colours … graceful, touching, fragile, evanascent.

Celia wrote that 'a special invitation was issued In the name of the Prophet, Toads: … a force of only too willing boys was set about the work of catching every toad within reach, … three dry and dusty toads, wearily gazing at nothing. …I took up the hose and turned upon them a gentle shower of fresh cool water, flooding the box. … The dry, baked earth heaved tumultuously; up came dusky heads and shoulders and bright eyes by the dozen. A sudden concert of liquid sweet notes was poured out on the air from the whole rejoicing company. It was really beautiful to hear that musical ripple of delight. I surveyed them with eager interest as they sat singing and blinking together.' She carefully lifted them out into her garden for a fine feast of slugs.

The simplicity of the garden's layout belies its gentle manipulation of views in and out of the garden, and the sun's effects as it runs its course over petals, leaves and stems. Hassam captures this with his painting *In the Garden* (see page 106). Thaxter stands at the West Gate, framed by tall hollyhocks whose reds and pinks are echoed in the petals of full-blown poppies that are beginning to scatter, whilst the asters offer pinks with tinges of red. The yellow of the Coreopsis draws your eye across this multi-coloured spume of informality, out into the blue of the ocean beyond the pale blue fence. Colours captured by Hassam, in what Park Curry describes as 'painterly accumulation of pigments dragged over and through one another to create a sense of luxuriant bloom'. In many paintings Hassam took the theme of a grid of verticals and horizontals but

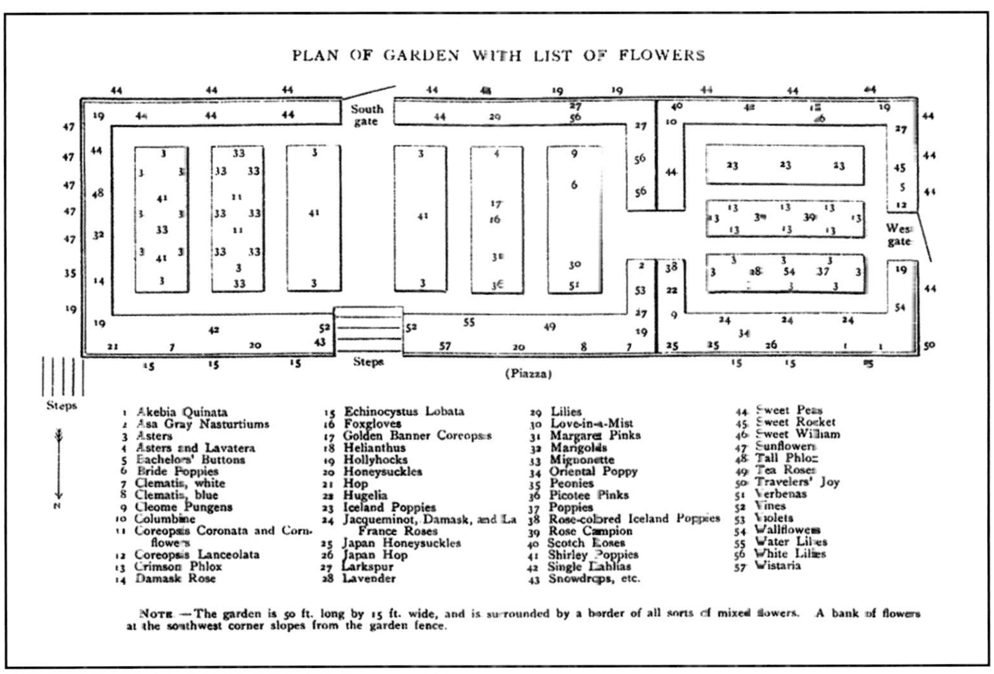

The plan of the flower garden at Appledore Cottage from An Island Garden (1894). The dimensions are 4.5m (15 feet) x 15m (50 feet). The first impression is of a rigid almost monastic formality, until you fill the board-edged rectangular frames with flowers. Note the centrepiece beds fitted with an ocean of Iceland Poppies, with asters taking the drifting colours into late summer. Height came from the climbing akebia, clematis, honeysuckle and wistaria with scent wafting from roses, sweet peas and sweet rocket in the evening. Stark primary colours adrift in pastel pinks, creams and mauves, or is it the other way round? Over 100 bouquets were picked from the garden each week for the house.

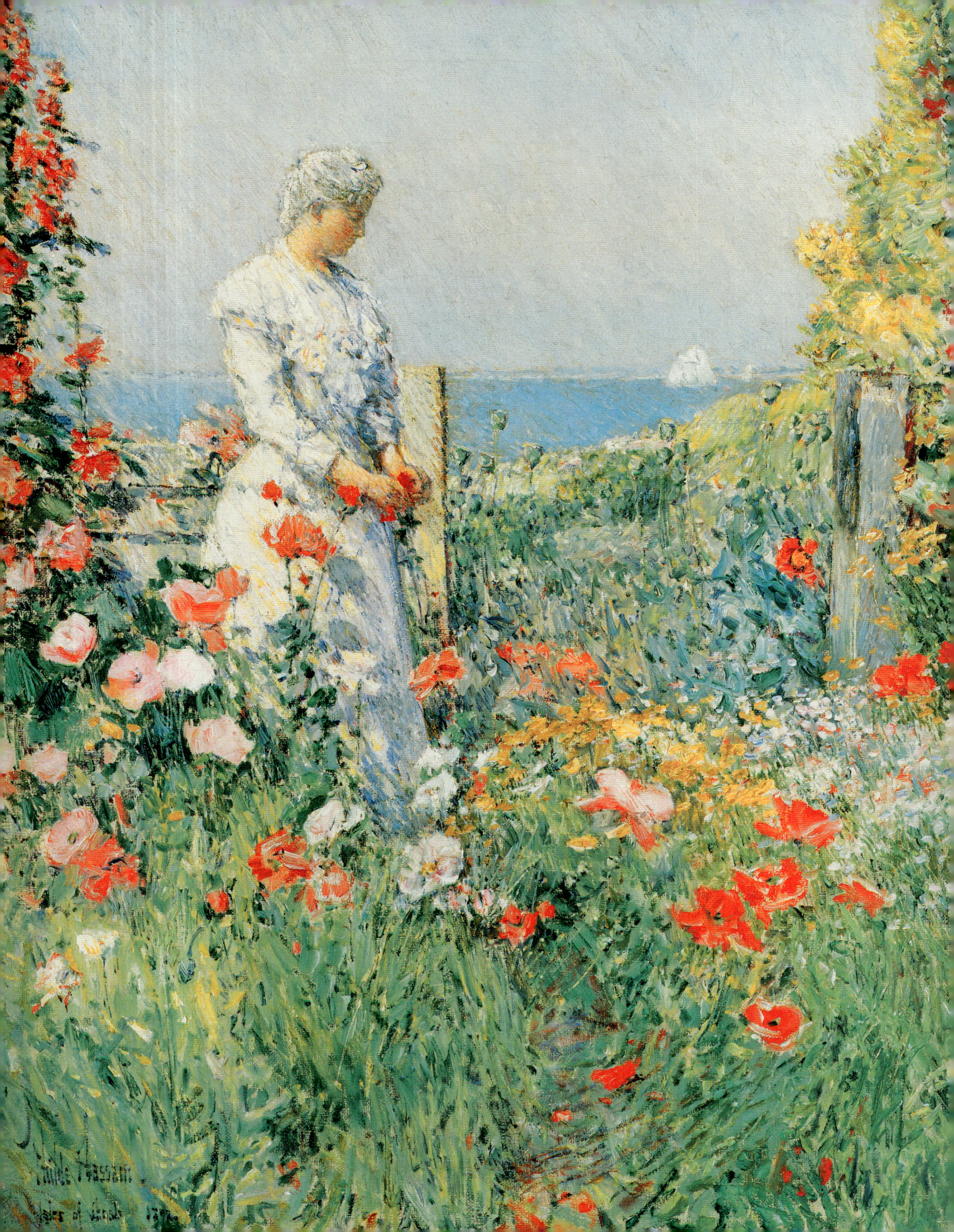

reinterpreted them for artistic effect, the spires of hollyhocks being an especial favourite but not necessarily in the beds to which they were assigned. One of Thaxter's favourite flowers was the Iceland Poppy, whose mix of yellow, orange and pink flowers filled two central beds where '… the ardent light has wooed a graceful company of drooping buds to blow, and their cups of delicate fire … sway lightly on stems as slender as grass.' She also planted these hardy and promiscuous plants without the garden fence, creating a kaleidoscopic torrent down to the sea, that Hassam painted again and again.

This summer colony of artists was hosted by Thaxter and frequented by Hassam from 1889. The Appledore gardens and flowers inspired his paintings in the years 1889-94, not least as illustrations for *An Island Garden* published in 1894. The full wording of the title page is *An Island Garden by Celia Thaxter with Pictures and Illuminations by Childe Hassam*, which perfectly encapsulates Hassam's work. There is a magical chemistry between his paintings and Thaxter's poetry – he perfectly synthesises the sensations of her words – as do the flowers on a bright, sunny day.

Think of the glory of color! The red of the rose,
Green of the myriad leaves and the fields of grass.
Yellow as bright as the sun where the daffodil blows,
Purple where violets nod as the breezes pass.

Think of the manifold form, of the oak and the vine,
Nut, fruit, and cluster, and ears of corn;
Of the anchored water-lily, a thing divine,
Unfolding its dazzling snow to the kiss of morn.

Thaxter died in 1894, but Hassam continued visiting Appledore after her death for another two decades, increasingly drawn to painting the waters that surrounded this sea-walled kingdom.

In the years 1896-1918 he also spent summers in Newport Rhode Island, Provincetown and Gloucester Massachusetts, Old Lyme and Cos Cob Connecticut. Hassam's family roots went back to the seventeenth century, and his landscapes often included churches serving as icons for American religious freedom and the deep-rooted traditions of his Yankee forefathers.

Old Lyme was christened 'America's Giverny' because so many of the artists such as Theodore Robinson and Willard Metcalf had also stayed at the Hotel Baudy in Giverny. Like Giverny, it was still rural and also became a mecca for New York artists searching for *plein air* opportunities. The heart of the colony was Florence Griswold's boarding house, now the Florence Griswold Museum.

John H. Twachtman, Theodore Robinson (who had been a student of Monet at Giverny) and J. Alden Weir all joined Hassam to paint at the Cos Cob Colony, Greenwich, which flourished between 1890

Childe Hassam, **In the Garden (Celia Thaxter in her Garden)**. *Oil on canvas, 56.5 x 45.7cm (22 x 18in.), 1892*

In her youth Thaxter was a noted beauty, looks which matured into an attractive serenity as can be seen in this painting. She is framed by hollyhocks in an earthly sea of poppies with the ocean beyond. Hassam illuminates her words:

Think of the delicate perfumes borne on the gale,
Of the golden willow catkins's odor of spring,
Of the breath of the rich narcissus waxen-pale,
Of the sweet pea's flight of flowers, of the nettle's sting.

Strange that this lifeless thing gives vine, flower, tree,
Color and shape and character, fragrance too;
That the timber that builds the house, the ship for the sea,
Out of this powder its strength and its toughness drew!

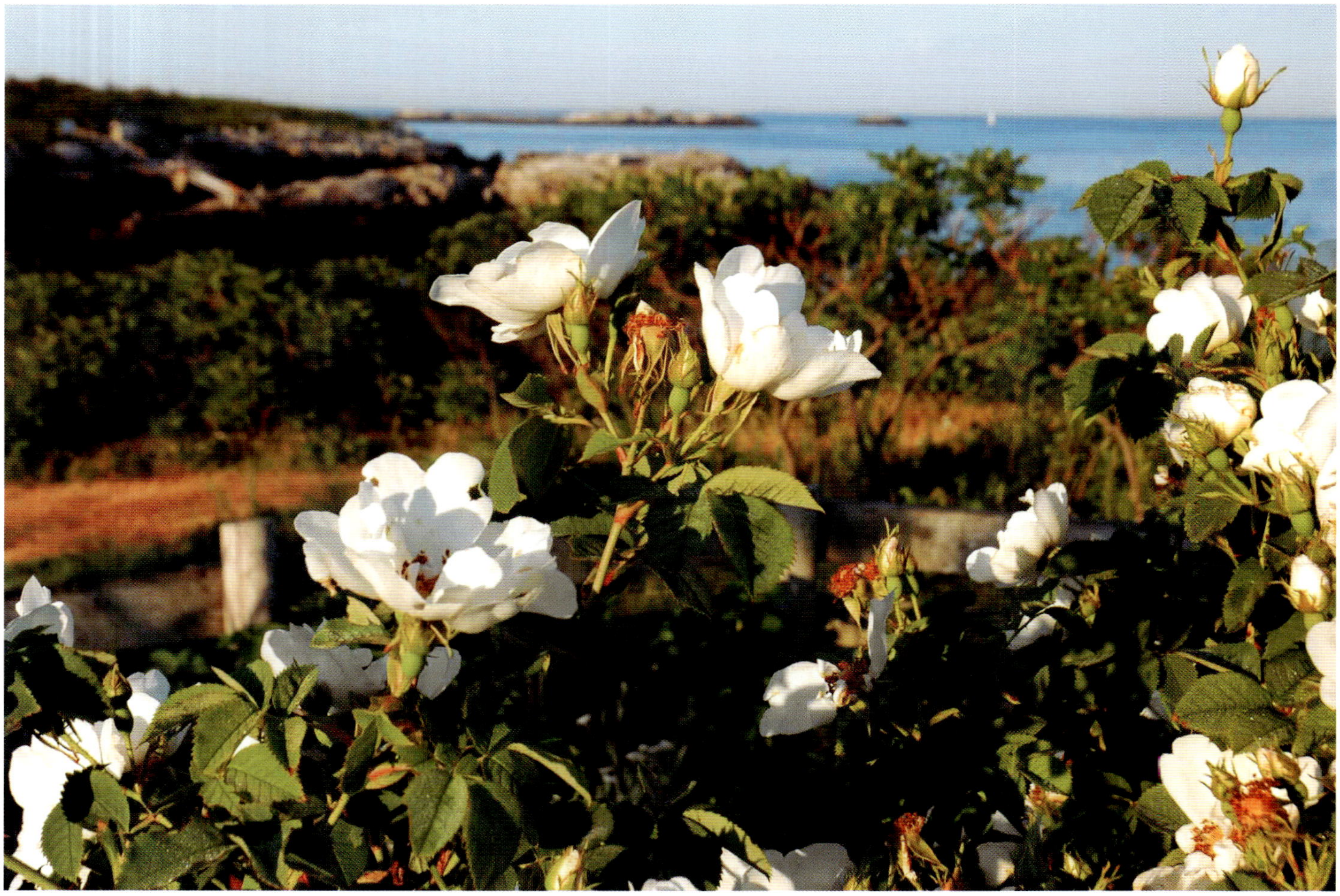

White Rosa Rugosa on Appledore today '... and the strong white Rosa Rugosa, a Japanese variety which bears very large single flowers in the greatest profusion. This Rose is extremely valuable, easily obtained, so hardy as to be almost indestructible, and absolutely untroubled by any disease or insect plague whatever. Its foliage is always fresh and handsome, and its seed vessels are huge scarlet balls as large as an average Crab-Apple, most ornamental after the flowers are gone.' An Island Garden, *Celia Thaxter.*

and 1920. Holley House, situated on the waterfront, followed in the mould of the Hotel Baudy and Florence Griswold's boarding house – comfortable, well placed and reasonably priced.

Gregarious and introspective, restless and serene, Twachtman was both artist and gardener. Like Renoir he was concerned about modernisation, as he saw the original Greenwich farms were being divided up for new development, and the old dry stone walls that had been the principal form of farm fencing were simply torn down or left to fall into ruin. Twachtman bought a house and seventeen acres on Round Hill Road, and he enclosed the property in traditional style, three acres of which were gardens as can be seen in his late 1890's painting *Summer*. This shows the house with stone walls that were laid so that they looked like natural outcrops. The formal area near the house can be seen in *On the Terrace* (see page 134) in which his wife cradles their new-born son whilst their two daughters hover in close attendance. The shelter of this area has allowed a magnificent bed of lilies to flourish, which appear to become pinker nearer the house, drawing your eye through the arch and out into the rest of the gardens.

Twachtman gardened naturalistically, encouraging large trees to shade the front and back of the house, whilst smaller trees offered privacy and he devised 'mysteries and quaint nooks' along the brook. He put up a white footbridge over Horseneck Brook along which he planted willows and sowed wild flowers in the banks, to mark the transition between the domestic and natural parts of his garden. Monet's bridge at Giverny was surely unknown to him, as *The White Bridge* is post 1895 and *The Little Bridge* is c1896, predating any exhibition of Monet's Japanese Bridge in France or America by several years. His gardens were featured in *Country Life* in America on 8 October 1905 under the title of 'An Artist's Unspoiled Country Home'. The white he loved best was snow, he wrote to J. Alden Weir: 'We must have snow and lots of it. Never is nature more lovely than when it is snowing. Everything is so quiet and …all nature is hushed to silence.'

Mention should be made of another great American Impressionist, William Merritt Chase, who led his own (very much one man) art colony at Shinnecock, New York. Like Twachtman he studied at the Royal Academy of Fine Arts, Munich and later they travelled to Venice together.

Thaxter's cottage burned down with Appledore House Hotel in 1914, however, her naturalised plantings survived over the rocks whilst within the garden the season still opens with her snowdrops, followed by Coreopsis, Centaurea and day lilies. In 1977, using her plan, the garden was reconstructed by Dr. John M. Kingsbury, the founder of the Shoals Marine Laboratory. It is now a summer garden, open from the end of June through August tended by a devoted group of volunteers. You can no longer experience the music or the readings, but as the colourful flowers blow in the ocean breezes, Celia Thaxter's words bring music to your ears:

'This island garden of mine is so small that the amount of pure delight it gives in the course of a summer is something hardly to be credited. It lies along the edge of a piazza, forty or fifty feet long, sloping to the south, not more than fifteen feet wide, sheltered from the north winds and open to sun.'

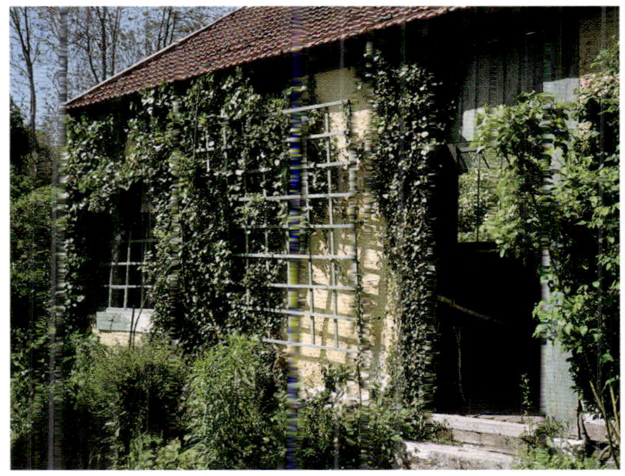

An atelier was built in the gardens of the Hotel Baudy in Giverny as one of the studios for visiting artists. Inside today there is a signed photograph of American artist Henry Fitch Taylor who also painted with the Cos Cob Colony in Connecticut.

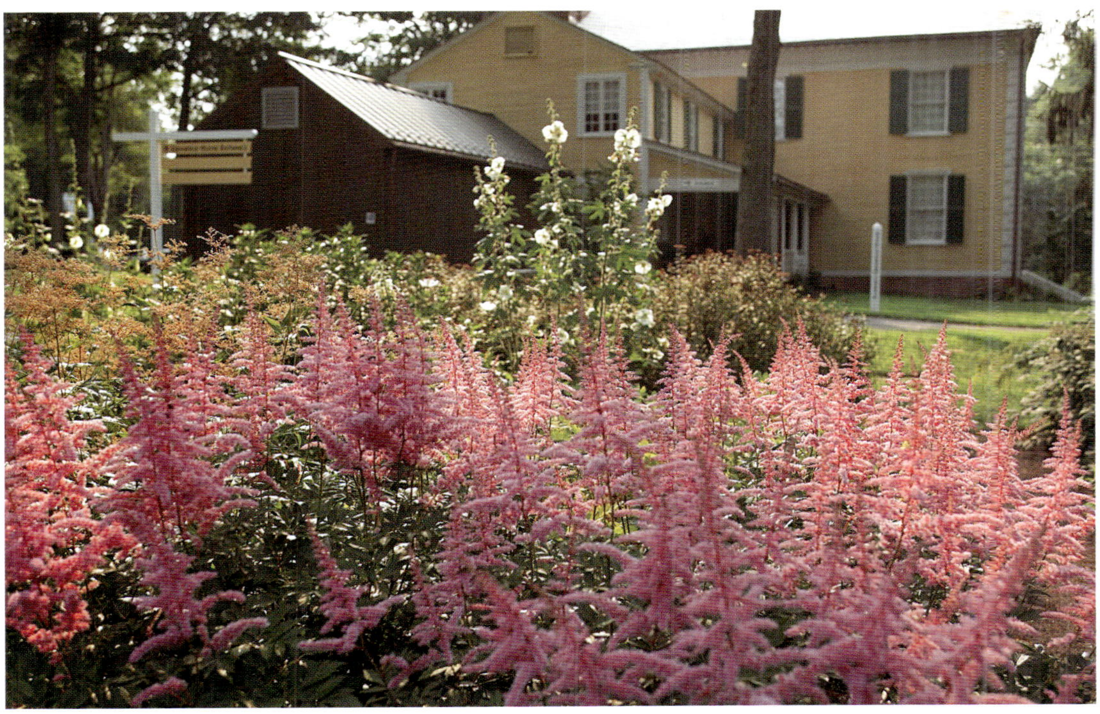

A haze of pink filipendula in the gardens today at Florence Griswold Museum in Old Lyme, Connecticut. The artists that formed the Old Lyme Art Colony found the New England countryside inspiring and organized 'summer annuals' to exhibit and sell their work, a tradition which effectively continues through the Museum.

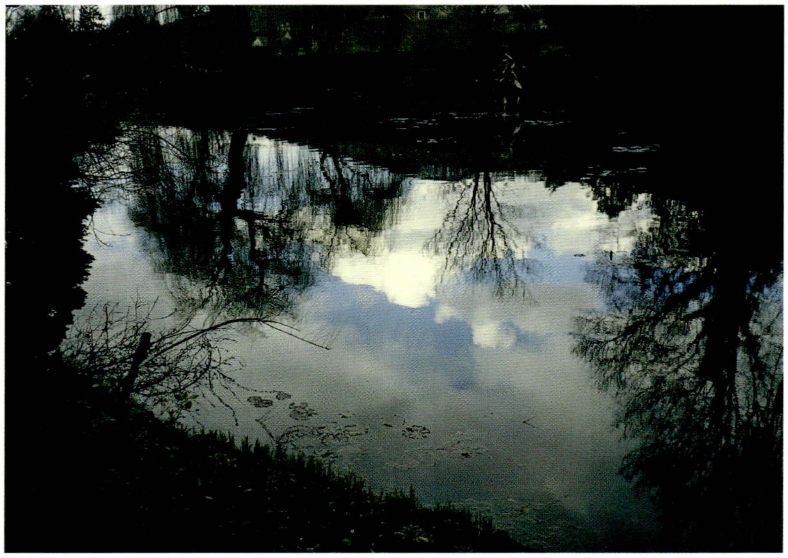

Monet shared Twachtman's fascination with the effects of winter, initially in the landscape and then his garden. The pond at Giverny truly becomes a mirror for the sky and leafless trees in February. The water has the same icy navy blue that Twachtman painted.

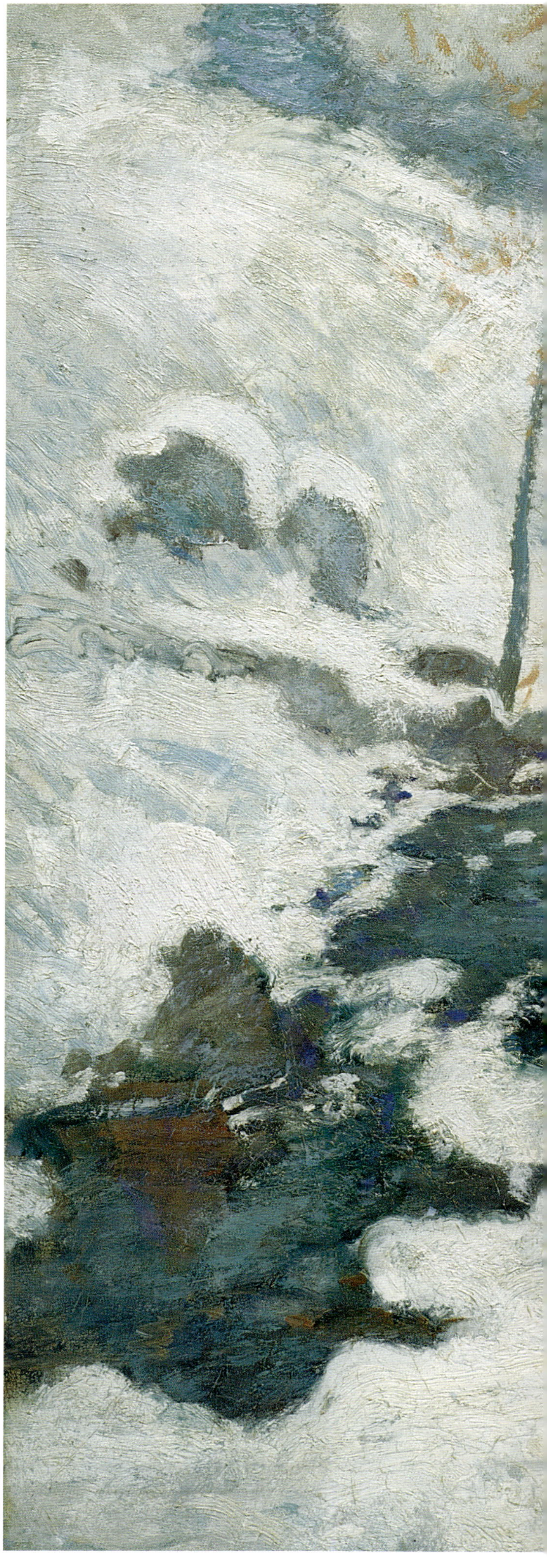

John Henry Twachtman, **Icebound**. *Oil on canvas, 64.2 x 76.6cm (25 x 30in.), c.1889*

Twachtman would meditate on the patterns and flow of the brooks that flowed through his garden in Connecticut. Icebound shows how the freezing weather has sculpted Horseneck Brook, as the flow of the water swirls under the constrictions. The brook divided his upper and lower gardens, and you can see the last tenacious vestiges of autumn in the orange brown leaves. The icy whites and blues contrast with the radiant colours of Celia Thaxter's summer garden at Appledore.

In 1894 the following report appeared in the Greenwich Graphic: 'On we go through Hayroot ... a locality filled with rocks and trees and Horse Neck Brook making its way between, to the delight of that famous artist, J.H. Twachtman, who some years ago became so enamored of the spot that he settled there in a house that you will recognise immediately as the home of an artist. And it has been said that his pictures of these artistic nooks and rugged rocks have brought him, in hard cash, much more than all the land about them is worth.'

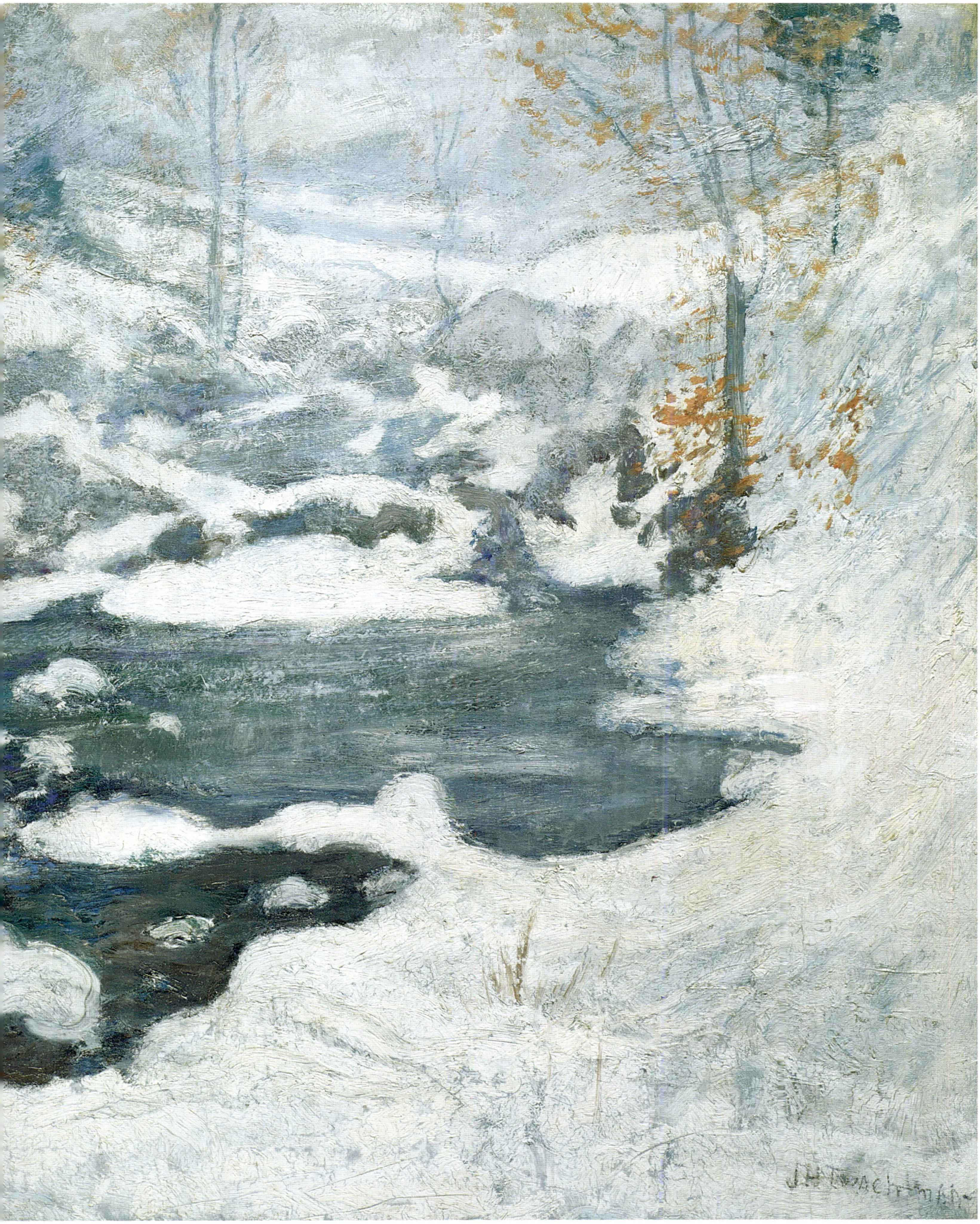
J.H.Twachtman

Sound Sensations

The wild bird's song that breaks from without into the sonata makes no discord. Open doors and windows lead out on the vine-wreathed veranda, with the garden beyond steeped in sunshine, a sea of exquisite color swaying in the light.

Celia Thaxter, An Island Garden

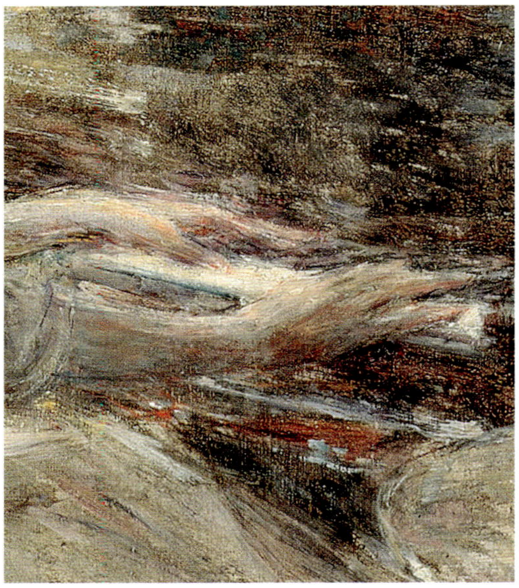

Childe Hassam (1859-1935): **Improvisation**. *Oil on canvas, 76.3 x 86.2cm (30 x 34in.), 1899*

Childe Hassam painted Celia Thaxter's neice, Margaret Laighton, at the piano in her parlour, for Improvisation. *All guests were welcome to play what they enjoyed; with the windows thrown open, the scent of the honeysuckle would waft through the windows, allowing the garden to pour into the room. The portrait shows Thaxter's genius for filling the house with cut flowers which were chosen to match vases and offered their own arrangement. James MacNeill Whistler advocated coordinating vases with their flowers and then laying the vases out in linear arrangements, Thaxter followed these principles. She evokes Debussy in her harmonic description of the Princess Beatrice sweet pea: 'a divine pale pink, a shade of rose refined and exquisite, there are glasses of clear pink that repeat the hues of the flowers with magical gradations and reflections'. A year later Hassam painted* The Sonata at Appledore *inspired by Beethoven's Apassionata that evokes the seas crashing on the Isles of Shoals. At Appledore, the man-made music was often accompanied by the trills, chords and carolling of the summer visiting and resident birds.*

The fine singing of the choir of the church of Saint Eustache in Paris was celebrated during the late 1840s, strands of music woven under the direction of the then unknown Charles Gounod. He took an especial interest in a talented young chorister to whom he offered private lessons, a grounding in musical composition and the opportunity to sing solos, as well as tickets to the opera for all the family. Gounod proposed to the parents that their son should have a full musical education whilst earning his living singing in the chorus of the opera. Unfortunately for Gounod, at the same time a M. Lévy, the owner of the porcelain works in Rue Vielle du Temple, offered the thirteen-year-old Pierre Auguste Renoir an apprenticeship which he accepted. Renoir may have recalled his earlier training when almost forty years later on 15 January 1882 he took a mere thirty-five minutes to paint a portrait of Richard Wagner with a disquietingly prominent chin, averted eyes and overstuffed cravat, not in a garden but with an angry blue backdrop that seems in tune with the thunderous ride of the Valkyries. It becomes apparent which subject he prefers when you compare it with the sparkling light and colour of his vignettes of real life dancing, chatting and flirting, such as the 1876 *Dance at the Moulin de la Galette* in the popular dance garden on La Butte, Montmartre, or equally in 1892, the radiantly gentle domestic scene of *Girls at the Piano*.

Amongst many radical innovations, the rhythm of nineteenth-century life had been revolutionised by rail travel and the advent of photography; evocatively the latter seems to record the notations in groups of garden plants. Gertrude Jekyll in England and Tom Roberts in Australia were both gifted photographers, Roberts as a professional. Evidence suggests that Roberts was influenced by James McNeill Whistler's penchant for giving paintings musical names such as Allegro con brio – not just a great painting that is 'quick and lively with spirit', but also possibly referring to the four dramatic strokes that open the First Movement of Beethoven's Fifth Symphony. In 1884 whilst in London, Roberts had seen Whistler's 'Notes

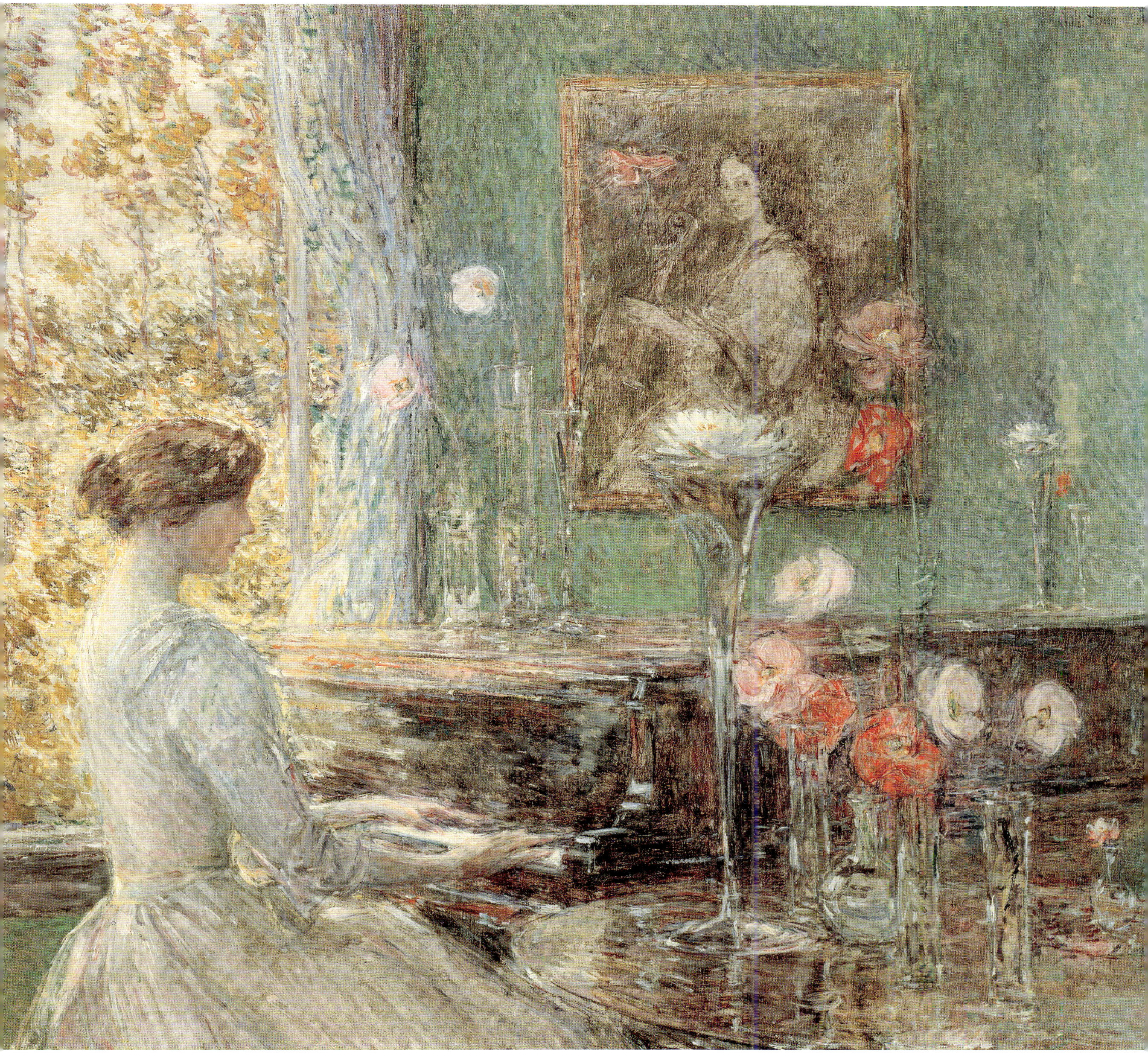

– Harmonies – Nocturnes' exhibition which may also have inspired his 1889 '9 by 5 Impression Exhibition' in Melbourne. Whistler's *A Note in Blue and Green* was exhibited by the Anglo Australian Society in 1885, but despite being an invaluable visual experience for local artists (which it is not known if Roberts saw), the critics were not tuned into it.

The expert advice of Roberts was called on for the design of purpose-built artists' studios called The Grosvenor Chambers at the smart end of Collins Street in Melbourne. Although they were without gardens as such, the studios were filled with cut flowers and pot plants and extended back to a lane from Little Flinders Street. Each studio had large windows, as far as possible facing south (for European readers this is the equivalent to a northern light), commanding views over Hobson's Bay and the City. They were rapidly taken up by artists and sculptors, and Roberts instigated a series of *conversaziones* at which 'the latest French and other art journals were inspected, singing and artistic conversation indulged in'. Roberts own *Allegro con Brio, Bourke St. W.* was painted around 1886. It is a bustling urban scene whose title evokes the musical properties of its colours. The three small figures stepping lightly from the left-hand corner were modelled by Anna and Lottie Fraser on the verandah of their house at Heidelberg. As it was unsold at the time Roberts gave it to the McCubbins. In 1920, hearing of his financial difficulties in England, Annie McCubbin sold it and sent him the proceeds.

The newspaper *Table Talk* and surviving correspondence from Anna Fraser have left boisterous descriptions of musical exploits amongst numerous students, wives and girlfriends over the weekends at Eaglemont. *Table Talk* reported that the visiting members of the Victorian Artists' Society in December 1889 enjoyed a picnic lunch and afternoon

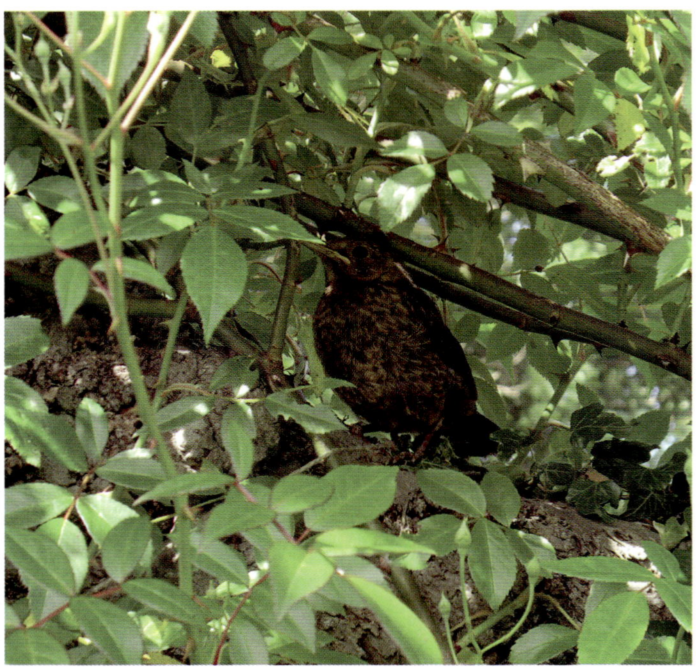

Blackbirds were not her favourite bird but Celia Thaxter rejoiced in the soundscape of her island garden. Here a fledgling blackbird awaits further instruction from its parent. You can hear the birdsong described by Thaxter in An Island Garden*: 'Then out of the high heaven above, at once one hears the happy chorus of the barn swallows; they come rejoicing, their swift wings cleave the blue, they fill the air with woven melody of grace and music. Till late August they remain. Like the martins', their note is pure joy; there is no coloring of sadness in any sound they make. The sandpiper's note is pensive with all its sweetness; there is a quality of thoughtfulness, as it were, in the voice of the song-sparrow; the robin has many sad cadences; in the fairy bugling of the oriole there is a triumphant richness, but not such pure delight; the blackbird's call is keen and sweet, but not so glad; and the bobolink, when he shakes those brilliant jewels of sound from his bright throat, is always the prince of jokers, full of fun, but not so happy as comical. The swallows' twittering seems an expression of unalloyed rapture,—I should select it from the songs of all the birds I know as the voice of unshadowed gladness.'*

On Thaxter's plan (see page 105) they are marked as violettas, today they are known as pansies. Their name is a corruption of 'pensée' so they symbolise thoughts. Every part of the Appledore experience was thought provoking. In An Island Garden she wrote: 'Some morning in the first of May I sit in the sunshine and soft air, transplanting my young Pansies and Gillyflowers into the garden beds, – father and mother martin on the fence watching me and talking to each other in a charming language, the import of which is clear enough, though my senses are not sufficiently delicate to comprehend the words. The song-sparrows pour their simple, friendly lays from bush and wall and fence and gable peak all about me. Down in a hollow I hear the brimming note of the white-throated sparrow, – brimming is the only word that expresses it.'

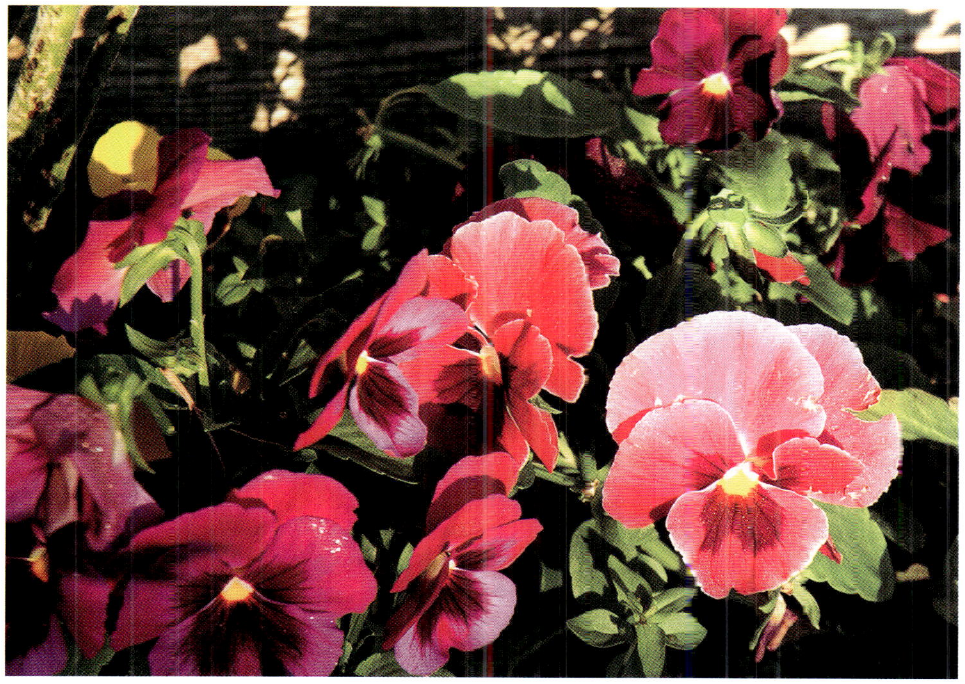

tea to the accompaniment of an orchestra of silver whistles, after which they lit their way back to station with dozens of coloured Chinese paper lanterns. Fraser wrote: 'Dancing was accompanied by the music of fiddles, mouth organs, jews harps and any other instrument which could be persuaded to play dance music. Couples wandered off into the garden to 'cool off' while admiring the effect of the moonlight on the old fountain or sampling the filberts on the old nut tree. Finally, a rush was made for the last train leaving Heidelberg by those obliged to return to the City, and arrangements were made for another "picnic dance" in the near future.' One musician, Louis Lavater, who stayed over on one occasion reported finding a tiger snake in his bed which he dispatched with his walking stick. In 1890 fellow Australian artist Charles Conder wrote to Roberts from Montmartre: 'I feel more than sorry that [those] days are over, because nothing can exceed the pleasures of that last summer, when I fancy all of us lost the 'Ego' somewhat of our natures in looking at what was Nature's best art and ideality. Give me one summer again with yourself and Streeton – the same long evenings, songs, dirty plates, and the last pink skies. But these things don't happen, do they? And what's gone is over.'

When painting at Cos Cob, Greenwich in Connecticut, Childe Hassam visited Holley House where he painted twenty-three images of women. One of the most evocative, painted in 1902, is *Listening to the Orchard Oriole*. A woman, dressed in a kimono that seems both as traditionally Japanese as it is thoroughly twentieth century, stands on the upper porch of Holley House, gazing over a mill pond towards the tree-shaded village, her body straining to the song of the unseen bird. The idyll is perfected by the exclusion of any modern intrusions.

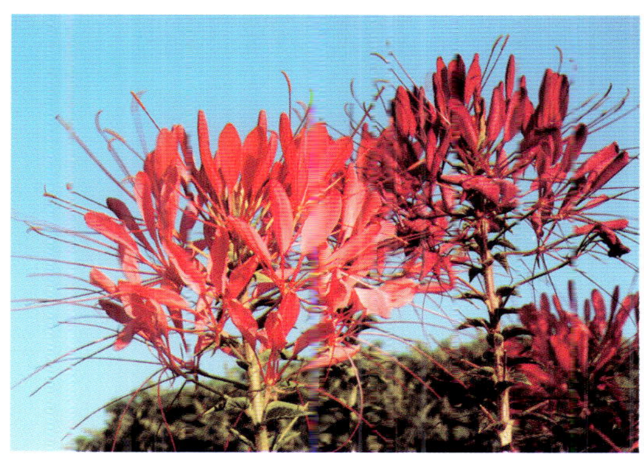

A close up of the flower heads of Cleome pugens as they shine out against the blue sky of Appledore. Thaxter included them in the flower garden plan in An Island Garden and would have selected one of their crimson hues to be matched to her flower vases indoors. The buzz of bees, curlew calls and the lapping of the waves would have provided additional music.

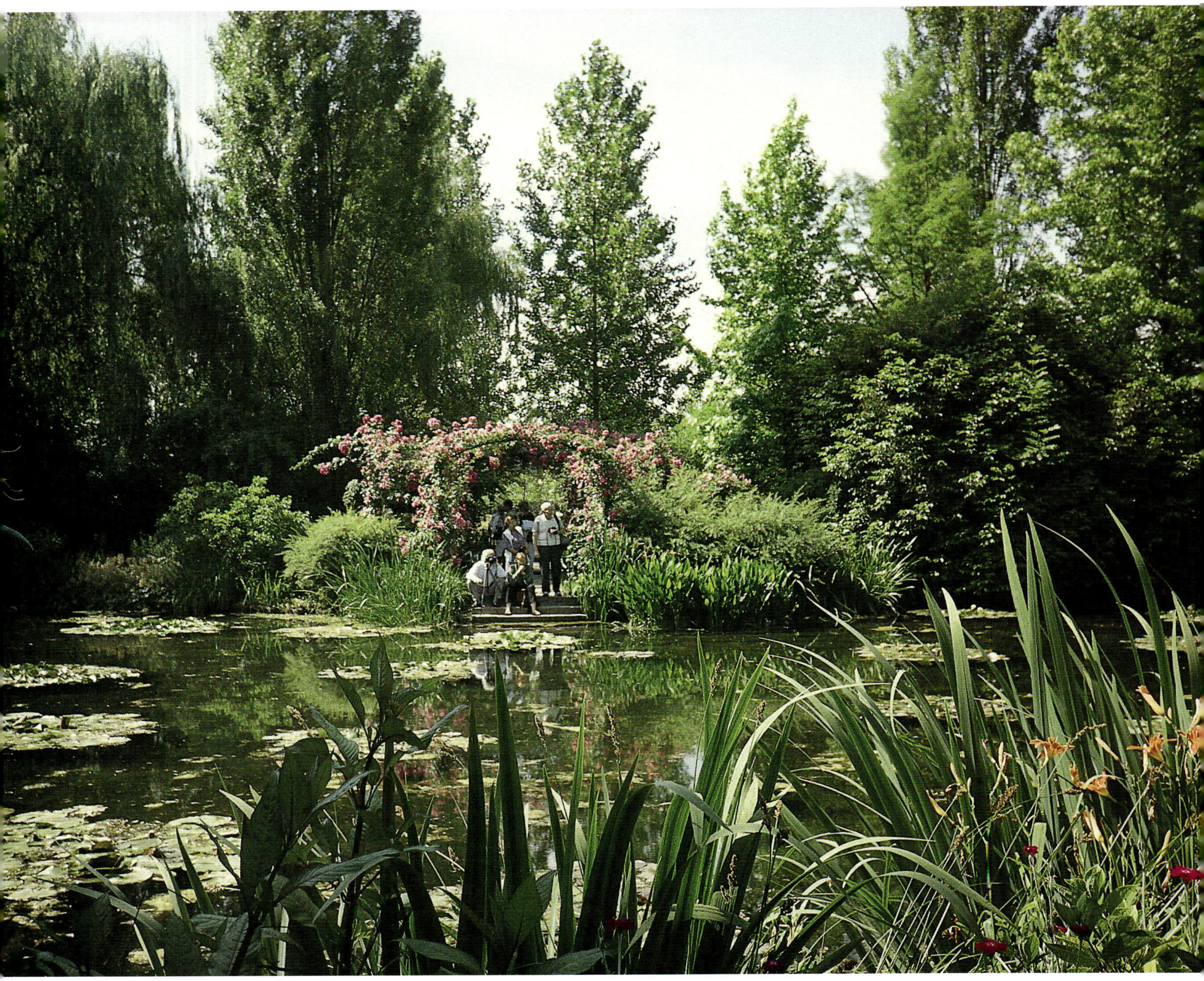

Listening to the natural sounds of the gardens at Giverny can be a challenge with the constant touristic background banter, however, the swish of the poplars still contrasts with the peace of the pool. Although strictly beyond the realms of the garden, at the heart of Monet's series of poplar paintings was the trees' potent symbol of France's grace, spirit and youth. He planted them at the base of his water garden where their canopy moved like an ocean swell in the breeze and imitated the sound of waves breaking on the shore. Novelist and good friend Octave Mirbeau was unstinting in his admiration for Monet, he was so enraptured by the poplar series exhibited in March 1892 that he said he wanted to hug him in thanks for such profound joy. Less joyous was an evening with the melancholic poet Maurice Rollinat that closed with a song about poplars, Mirbeau wrote to Monet: 'We had anticipated music that would sound like the rustling of leaves, svelte and light to express the yearning, the grace, the delicious, airy melody that is the poplar. And what did we get, my dear Monet, but verses that had a terrifying and absurd roar. It was as if the Himalayas were crumbling or trains crashing ... I was thrown into a daze and didn't know where I was ... The truth is that M. Rollinat has no feeling for nature.'

The flowers of the iris harness the light in such a way that they have become one of the key plants associated with the Impressionists. They also attract bees whose gentle buzzing evokes associations of hazy, warm days

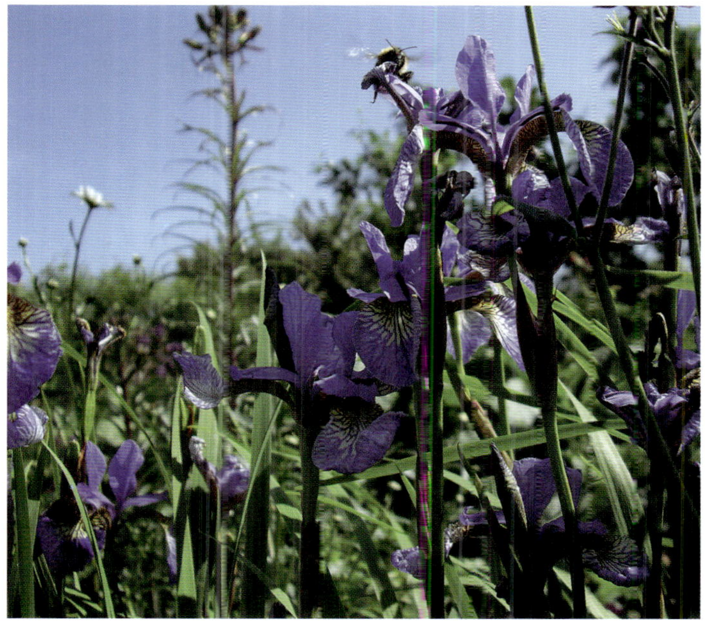

Below right: *The White Lily in a cottage garden. In Gertrude Jekyll's* Flower Decoration for the House *(1907) she criticised 'the lack of available 'flower-glasses of simple shape that would hold plenty of water and ... be moderate in price'. The London firm of James Green & Nephew responded by introducing a new range of 'Munstead' vases. Jekyll kept a separate cutting garden at Munstead Wood for flowers for the house, not that she had any success with the White or Madonna Lily, Lilium candidum. This illustration entitled 'The White Lily in a Cottage Garden' appears in 'Lilies for English Gardens' 1901. A year earlier she had published* Home and Garden *in which she wrote 'Ever first and best comes the White Lily, emblem of spotless purity, and noblest and loveliest of garden flowers. To my great regret this grand Lily is almost impossible to grow in my poor, hot soil, even in well-prepared beds. It thrives in chalk and nearly all rich loams, and I am full of a pardonable gardener's envy when I drive down into the clay lands of the neighbouring weald and see how it thrives in every cottage garden.'*

The earliest recording of the American lyric soprano Marguerite Namara was when as a teenager she sang the 'Flower Duet' from Delibes' opera *Lakmé*. Later she appeared at the Opéra-Comique in Paris and numbered Auguste Rodin, Debussy, Picasso and Isadora Duncan amongst her friends. She insisted on singing beside Monet's water lilies and there are photographs to prove it, however, myths and legends of operatic proportions have grown up around her visit. One is that Theodore Robinson organised for the piano to be carried down to the water's edge so that she could sing *en plein air*, however, surviving photographs only show the piano by the canvases in the Third Atelier. The other is that she sang in exchange for painting lessons. She signed a photograph in 1922 dedicated 'A vous tres grand et cher Maitre in the happiest recollection of my life ... to have met you and to have chantait pour vous' – obviously the lessons did not include French.

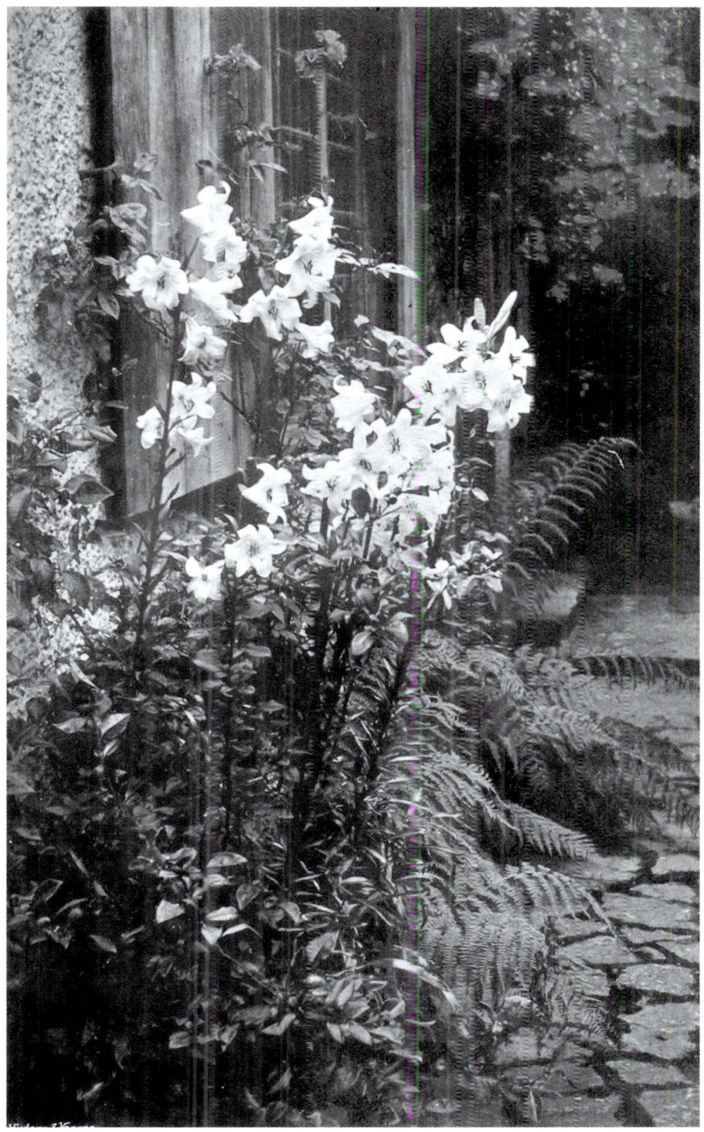

Decades before when the Monet family were all still at home, the artist and Alice would listen to the phonograph or to Marthe playing the piano and, when in the mood, Monet would sing with an apparently excellent voice. He introduced the symbolist writer and poet Stephan Mallarmé to Whistler who wrote 'As music is the poetry of sound, so is painting the poetry of sight, and the subject-matter has nothing to do with harmony of sound or of colour.'

CHAPTER FIVE

English Impressions

Home and Garden with Gertrude Jekyll

Miss Jekyll is a lady of such regular and remarkable accomplishments ... clever and witty in conversation, active and energetic in mind and body, and possessed of artistic talents of no common order, she would have at all times shone conspicuously bright amongst other ladies. The variety of her accomplishments, however is far more extensive ... – carving, modelling, house painting, carpentry, smith's work, repousse work, gilding, wood inlaying, embroidery, gardening, and all manner of herb and flower knowledge and culture; everything being carried on with perfect method and completeness. Her artistic taste is very great, and if it had not been for the extreme near-sightedness of her vision, I have little doubt that painting would have predominated over all her other talents.

George Leslie, RA Our River, *1881*

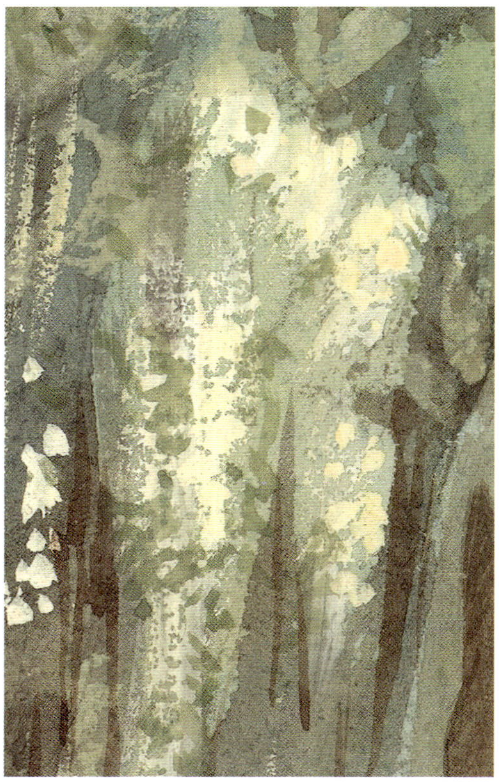

Gertrude Jekyll, **Clematis cirrhosa, Texheraim**. *Watercolour, c.1873/4*

This scented winter flowering clematis can be grown on sheltered walls in southern England but originates from North Africa where Jekyll travelled during the winter of 1873/4 and where she painted this watercolour. The billowing white Arab dress of the central figure emphasizes the sense of movement as he passes along a track lined with tall plants.

In 1874, at the time that the Impressionists held their first exhibition, the sandy land of Munstead Heath in Surrey was a wild place frequented by gypsies and a hideout for footpads and smugglers. That a widowed lady and her daughter should contemplate buying eighteen acres of bracken there seemed close to lunacy. Nonetheless Mrs. Julia Jekyll bought the land in 1876 and commissioned the architect J.J. Stevenson to design a house. In keeping with its setting on open heath, Munstead House has a faintly Scottish baronial style around which the usual Victorian flower and kitchen gardens were created to provide flowers, fruit and vegetables. Inspired by William Robinson's *The Wild Garden*, her daughter Gertrude worked with the heathland introducing azaleas, alpine areas filled with gentians, saxifrages, campanulas and thymes. The formal lawns faded into the wild heath, where stands of foxgloves and mulleins were encouraged to naturalise amongst the bracken at the edge of the pine wood. In 1883 Gertrude Jekyll bought a fifteen acre plot of her own, over the road, which she called Munstead Wood. It was the same year that Monet found Maison du Pressoir in Giverny, The Foreign Exhibition Association brought Durand-Ruel's canvases of Monet, Renoir, Camille Pissarro, Alfred Sisley et al to Boston, Childe Hassam first visited Europe and William Robinson published *The English Flower Garden*.

Although Jekyll was born in London her family soon moved to Bramley in Surrey. Its cottages and cottagers coloured her childhood memories and informed her sympathetic approach to houses and gardens. In 1861 she was enrolled at the Kensington School of Art, and she exhibited at the Royal Academy in 1865. During the 1860s and early 1870s she travelled around the Near East, North Africa, France and Italy. Her circle of friends and acquaintances included John Ruskin, Edward Burne-Jones and Frederick Lord Leighton. An artist and consummate craftswoman, her increasingly poor eyesight meant she had to stop all arts and crafts except gardening, which became the focus of her creative talents.

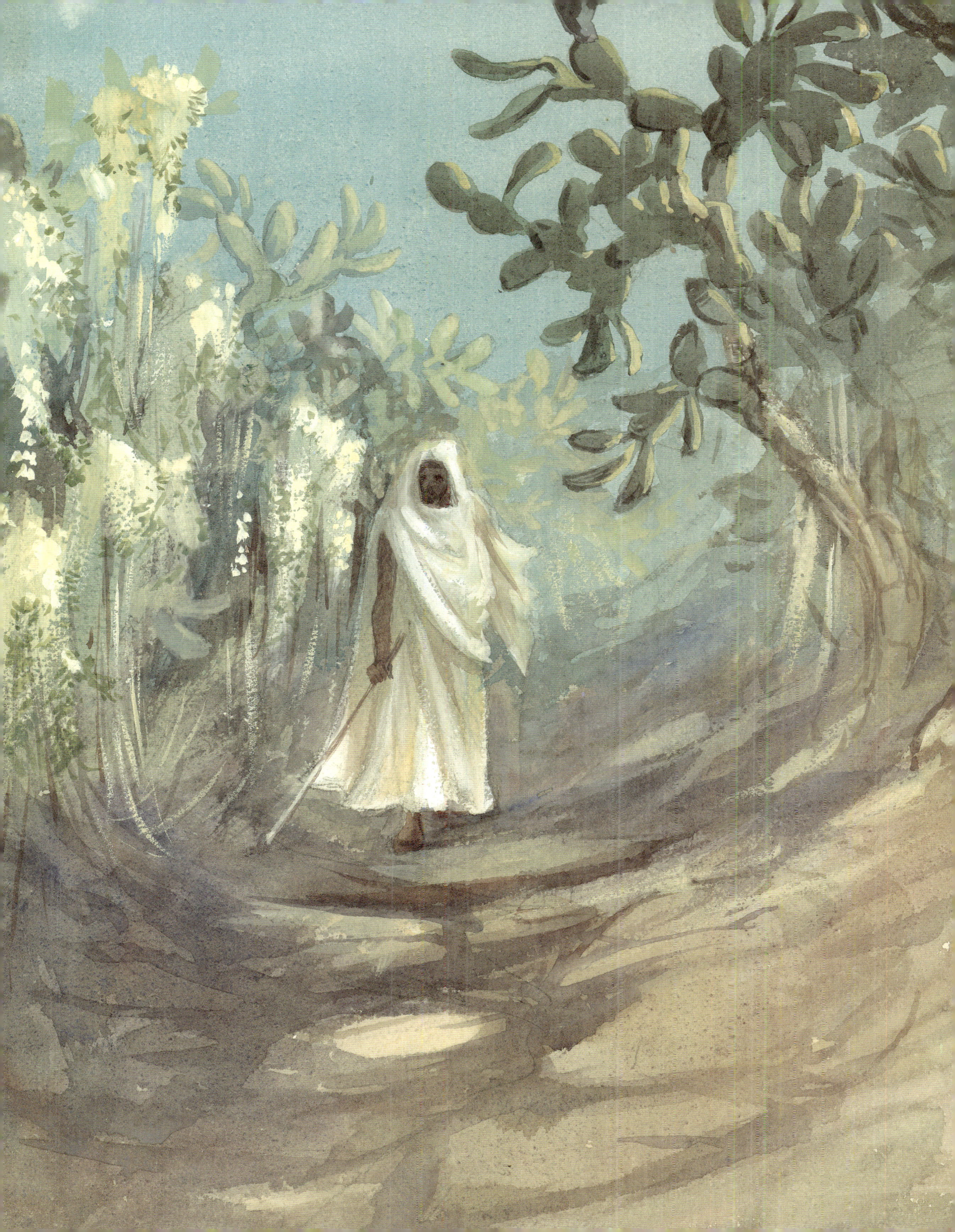

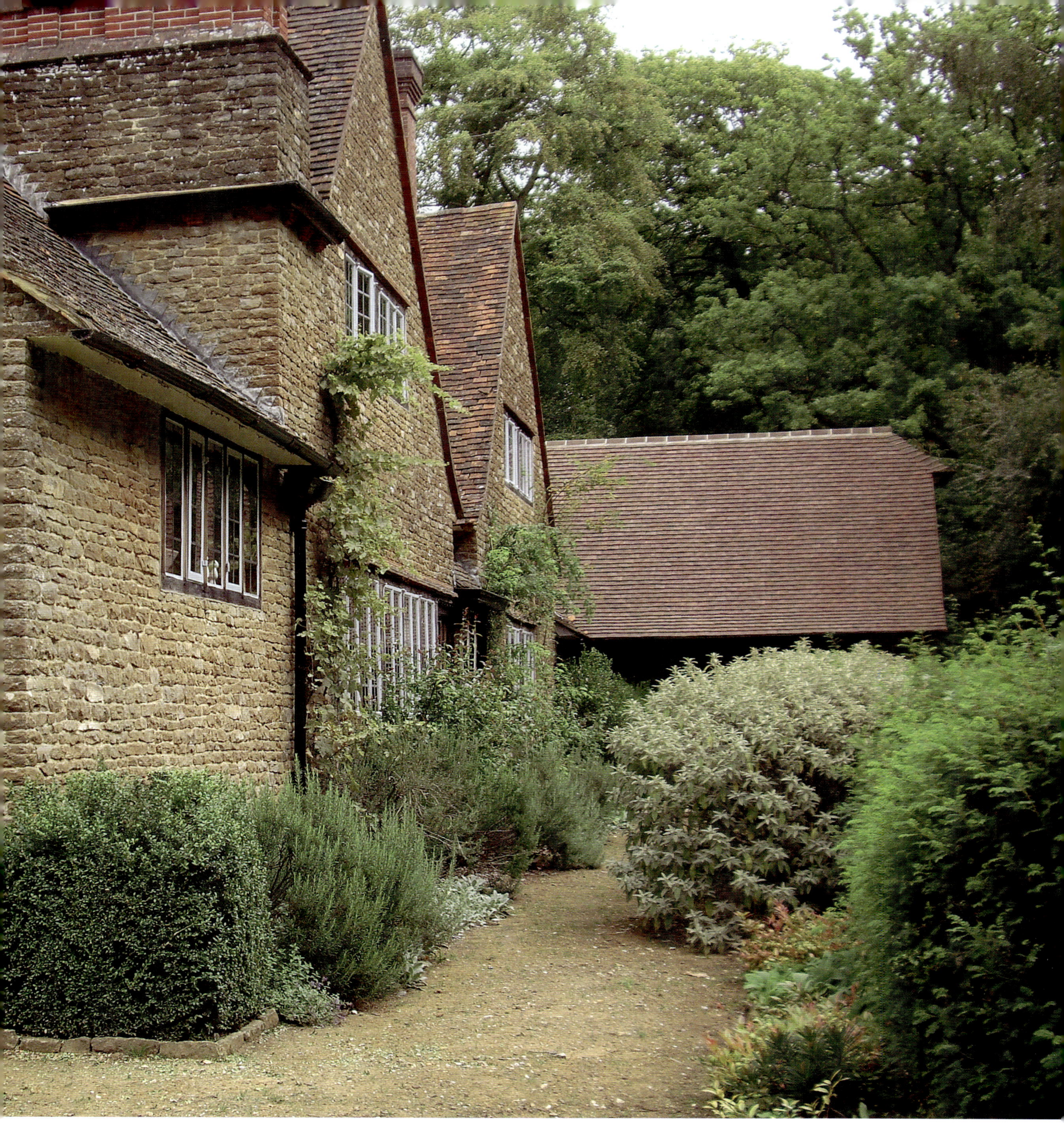

Munstead Wood – a house growing from its own site, the south-facing footings engulfed in rosemary and the walls softened with climbers. In Home and Garden *Jekyll wrote of its creation with Edwin Lutyens 'The architect has a thorough knowledge of the local ways of using the sandstone that grows in our hills, and that for many centuries has been the building material of the district, and of all the lesser incidental methods of adapting means to ends that mark the well-defined way of building of the country, so that what he builds seems to grow naturally out of the ground.'*

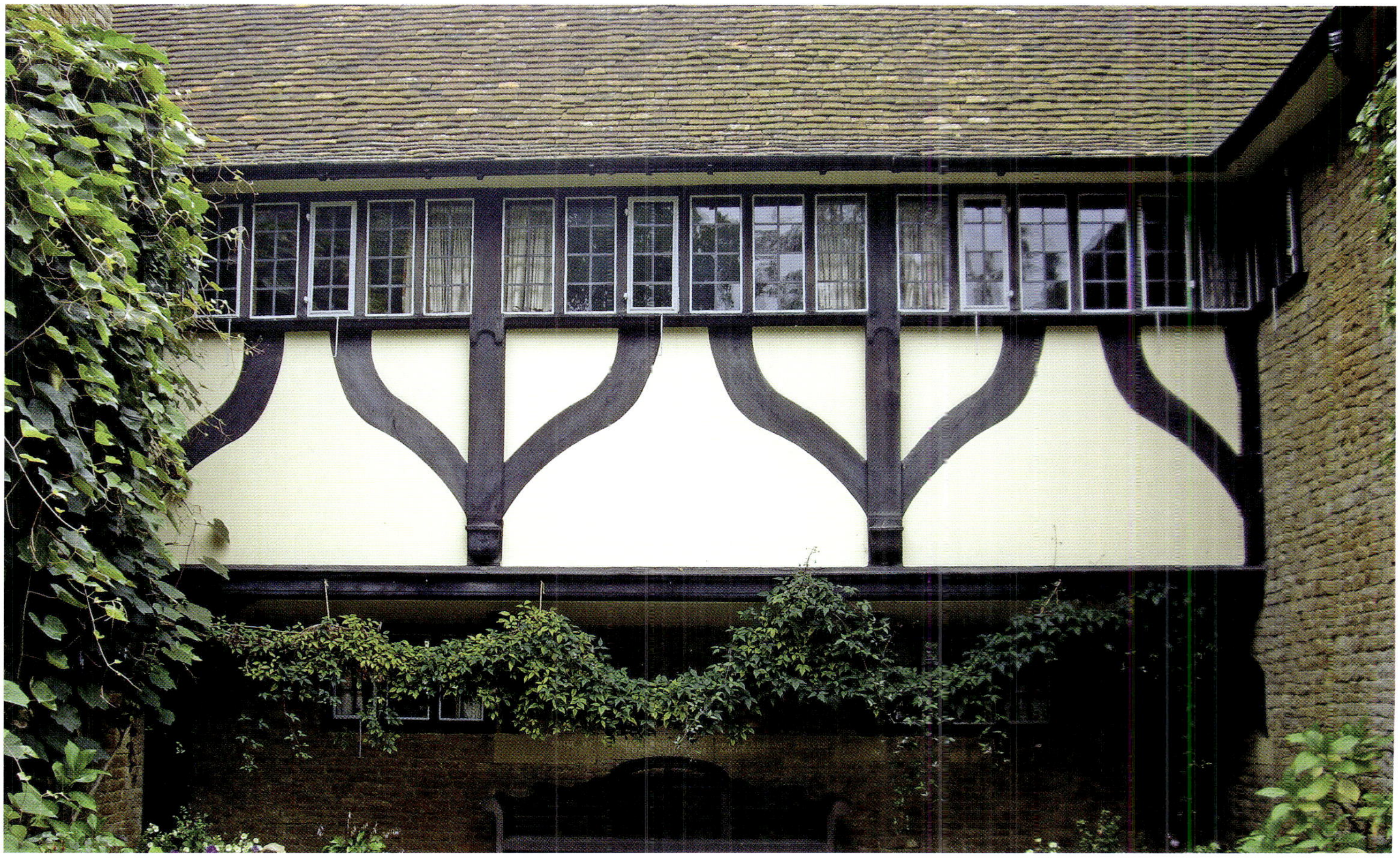

The jetty and paved court at Munstead Wood today, still with a swag of Clematis montana – north facing it provides light for the artist inside and a cool outdoor enclosure for the summer. Jekyll made prodigious amounts of pot-pourri and the ingredients would be heaped here for drying and mixing (See page 96). This style of garden bench is now known as a Lutyens Seat, the inscription above it reads:

BUILT BY THOMAS UNDERWOOD FOR GERTRUDE JEKYLL
EDWIN L. LUTYENS ARCHITECT 1897

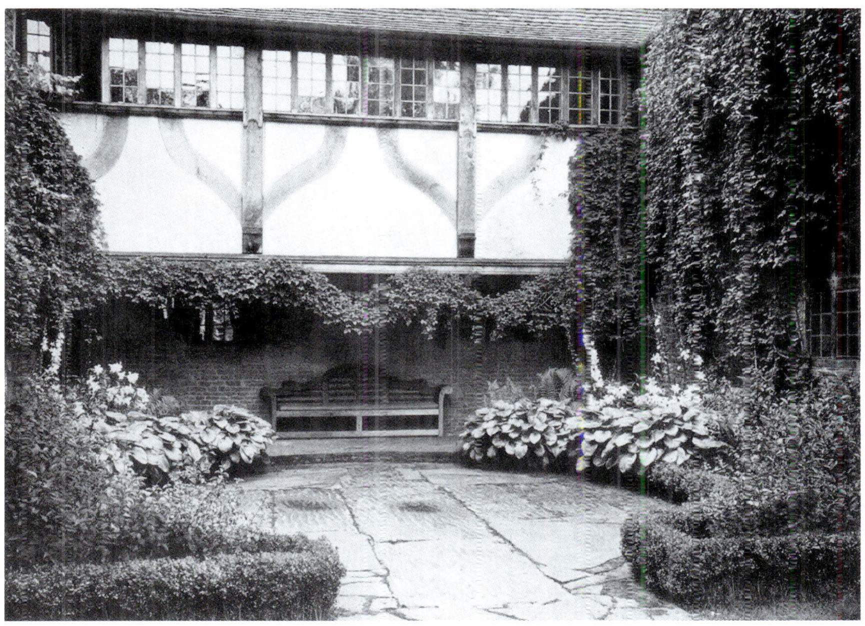

Described as 'a house in West Surrey' in Gardens for Small Country Houses *(1912), Jekyll wrote The court has a circular pavement, partly between two box-edged beds and partly bounded by a raised step next the house. On the sides of the raised pavement stand pots of fern and funkia, forming a good green setting for potted plants in flower – lilies, bellflowers, hydrangeas, etc. …Clematis Montana drapes one side wall and hangs as a garland from the lower moulded beam of the timber-framed overhang. She included an earlier photograph dated 1908 to show how the planting had matured by 1912. The building and creation of Munstead Wood inspired one of her earliest books* Home and Garden *(1900), American John Twachtman would have thoroughly endorsed her plea: 'O! for a little simple truth and honesty in building, as in all else that is present to the eye and touches daily life!'*

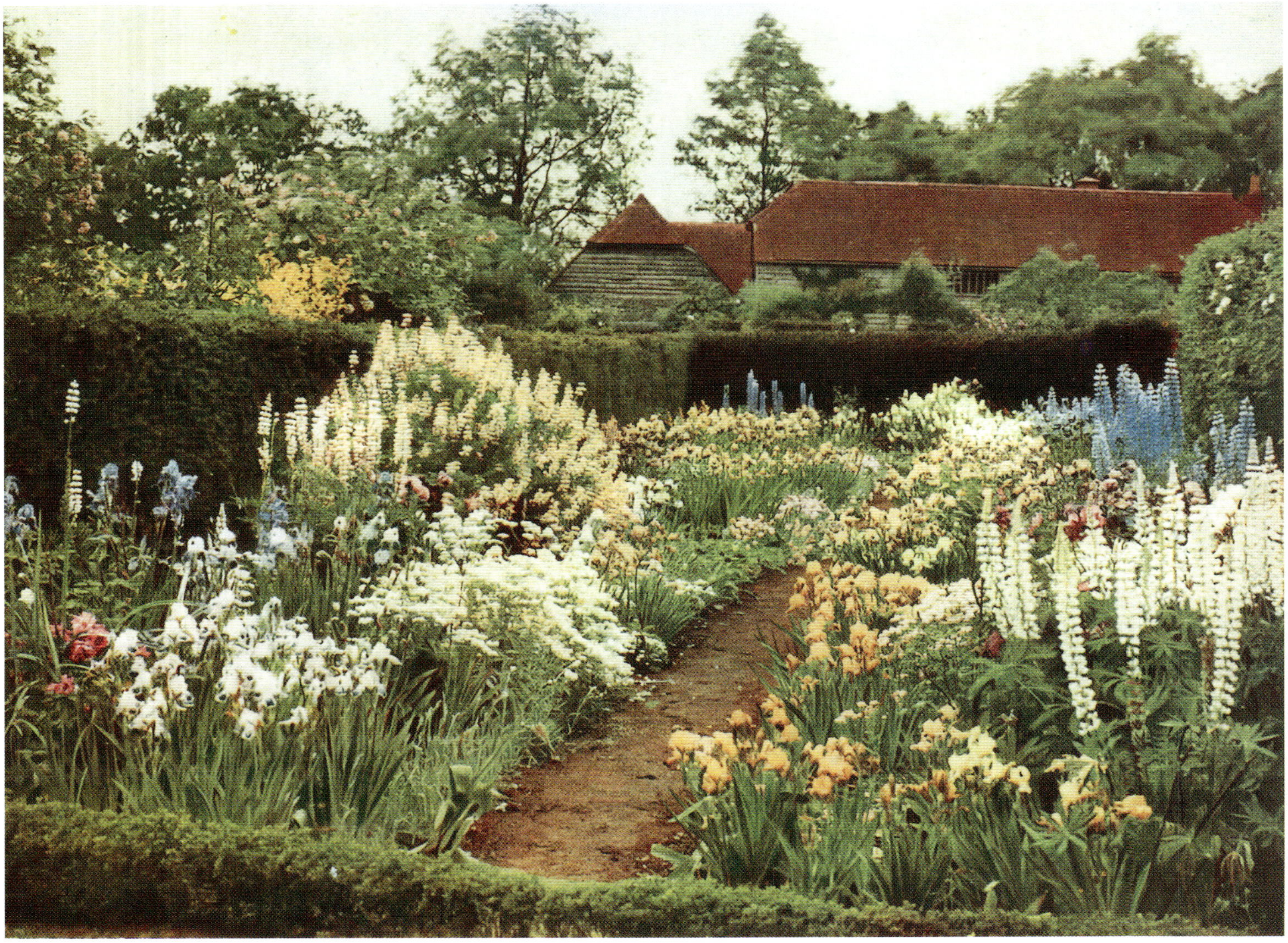

This tinted photograph artistically portrays the way that the key colours of creamy coffee, white and blue weave their drifting colours from the front to the back and across the path in Gertrude Jekyll's 'June Borders at Munstead Wood'. This image was the frontispiece for Gardens for Small Country Houses *which she co-authored with Lawrence Weaver in 1924.*

'The border has a definite colour scheme: at the two ends blue, white and palest yellow, with grey foliage; and purple, white and pink, also with grey foliage, respectively. The colour then advances from both ends by yellow and orange, to the middle glory of strongest reds. Bold groups of yucca are at the ends, and flank a cross path that passes by a doorway through the wall.' If you read this description, omitting the word 'foliage', you might well imagine someone describing the dramatic colours of the dying sun at the core of J.M.W. Turner's The Fighting Temeraire. *The painting was much admired by Jekyll, Monet and McCubbin.*

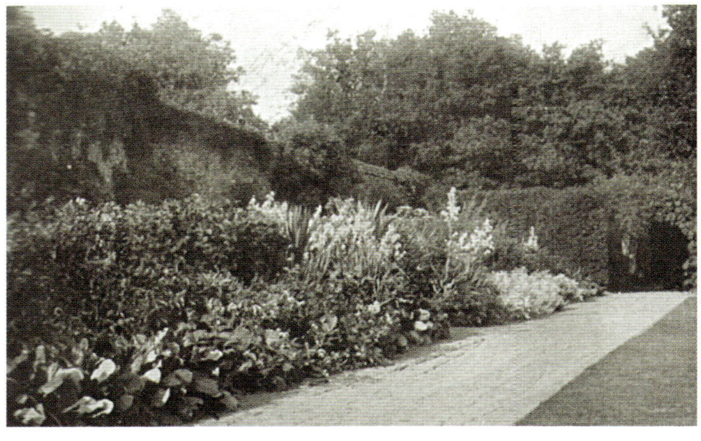

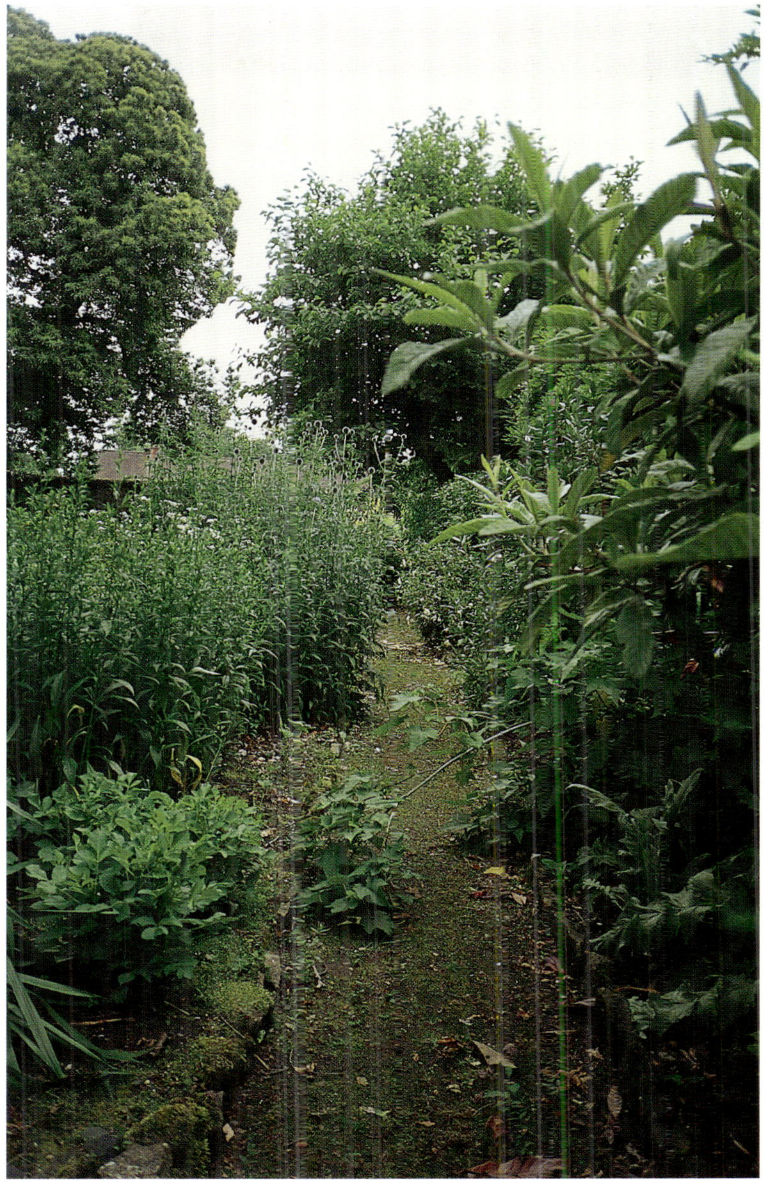

Jekyll's sense of colour and form made a formidable combination with her horticultural insight and knowledge. When writing she berates nurserymen's inaccurate descriptions of plant colour – her sight might have been poor but her vision was fine tuned. Her five primary colour schemes for gardens were orange, grey, gold, blue and green and in order to ensure their effectiveness she advised gardeners that the plant palette should be mixed for artistic effect as follows. 'Orange should offer an effect that is bright and hot, sufficient to visually warm up any grey day, so use oranges that veer towards red not yellow.' The effect for grey was actually grey-green and silver grey foliage with flowers of white, pastel pink and blues. I have noticed that purple flowers seem much more blousy than blue, interestingly Jekyll advises using blue flowers that veer towards white and grey, not purple. 'In order to achieve gold, the leaves and flowers of plants need to veer towards lighter yellows not oranges.' Her most innovative contribution was encouraging a more daring use of green, beyond the usual holly, box and yew. She described the shades, shape and texture of foliage preferably offset with white flowers, her favourites being Funkia and Megasea, now known as Hosta and Bergenia. To create a living lacy screen between colours, especially orange and blue, she advised planting tamarisk that would provide a pink haze.

The writer, architect and garden designer Reginald Blomfield was the first person to apply the word 'formal' when describing the role of architectural gardens in British garden history in his book *The Formal Garden in England*. As an architect he rejoiced in structures of stone or brick providing a geometrical framework for an exuberance of planting. Although he had built both flagged paths and a pergola at Gravetye Manor, his home in Sussex, William Robinson eschewed with vitriol any bourgeois formality such as a clipped yew hedge. Apart from popularizing Latour-Marliac's water lilies, he welcomed hardy plant introductions from North America, Australia and Japan. He appreciated the merits of perennial spring flowers and autumnal tints that could be designed into naturalistic schemes which, in turn, blended into the countryside beyond. Jekyll worked on friendly terms with both Blomfield and Robinson, as well as the exuberant Harold Peto, whilst advancing her ideas for using formal structure as a means of flowing plant colour into all parts of the garden.

On a May afternoon in1889 at Littleworth Cross, near Farnham in Surrey, the rhododendron expert Harry Mangles invited Jekyll to tea to view a new hybrid of rhododendron he had named for her. Mounted on his trusty bicycle, Angelina, the twenty year old Edwin Lutyens also arrived

Like artists' canvases, borders need careful priming and possibly some touching up later. At Munstead Wood Jekyll created a service path between the high Bargate stone wall swathed in climbers and small trees and her famous Long Border. This enabled her (or one of the gardeners) to fine tune the display from behind; there was also a convenient seat from which to think out your planting strategy.

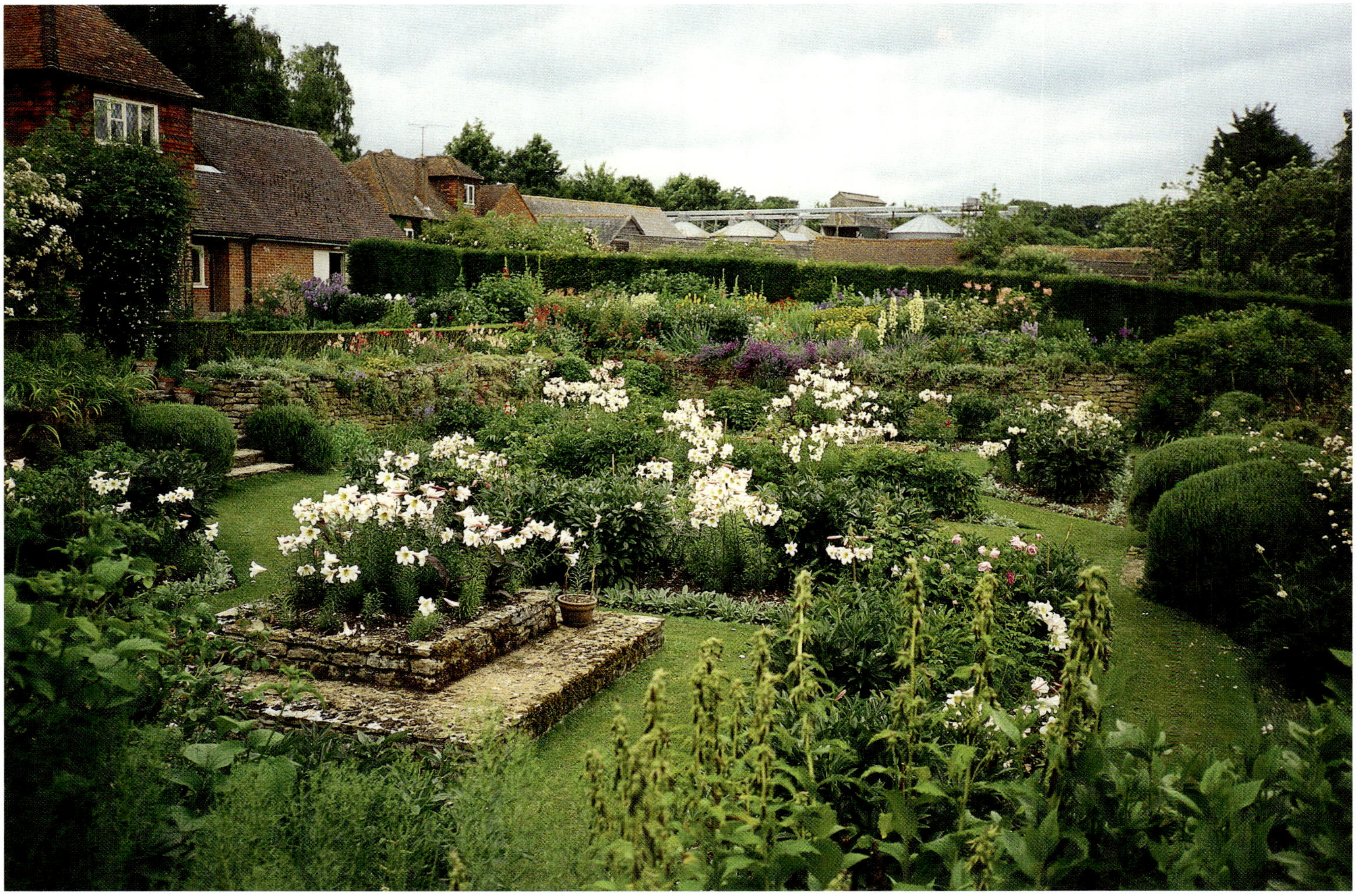

The Lily Garden at the Manor Upton Grey is surrounded by a froth of pastels pinks harmonizing towards palest silver foliage and lavender flowers. The four raised stone beds were designed to show case lilies either planted at the centre or introduced in pots around the stone shelf border. The mass of flowers evoke the sound of bees buzzing and the air filled with summer fragrance from the lilies, roses and pinks.

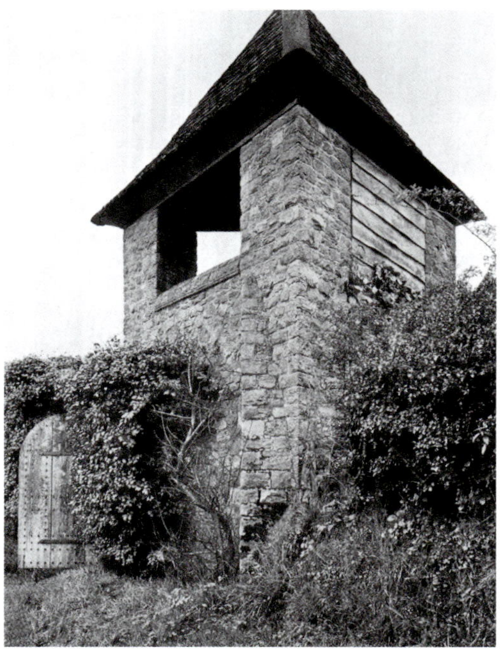

hot and dusty expecting to talk business not take tea. In the event he was bidden to Munstead Wood the following Saturday, and so a patronage blossomed into a professional partnership. Within two years Lutyens had embarked on what Jane Brown in her book *Lutyens and the Edwardians* describes as 'a flurry of Munsteadiana' – a timbered cottage for the Swiss head gardener, a small house for the family butler, and the Thunder House – a little triangular pavilion on the wall in which to both shelter from and watch storms in the Wey Valley. Sandwiched in the middle of these building projects was The Hut, built in 1894, although it was not a hut in the usual sense but a small arts and crafts cottage that gave Jekyll a studio and living space.

Left: *Lutyens designed a range of garden buildings in close co-operation with Jekyll including The Thunder House, a raised gazebo, from which she and her guests could shelter to watch the storms as they advanced from the distant chalk hills over the surrounding fields before soaking her gardens.*

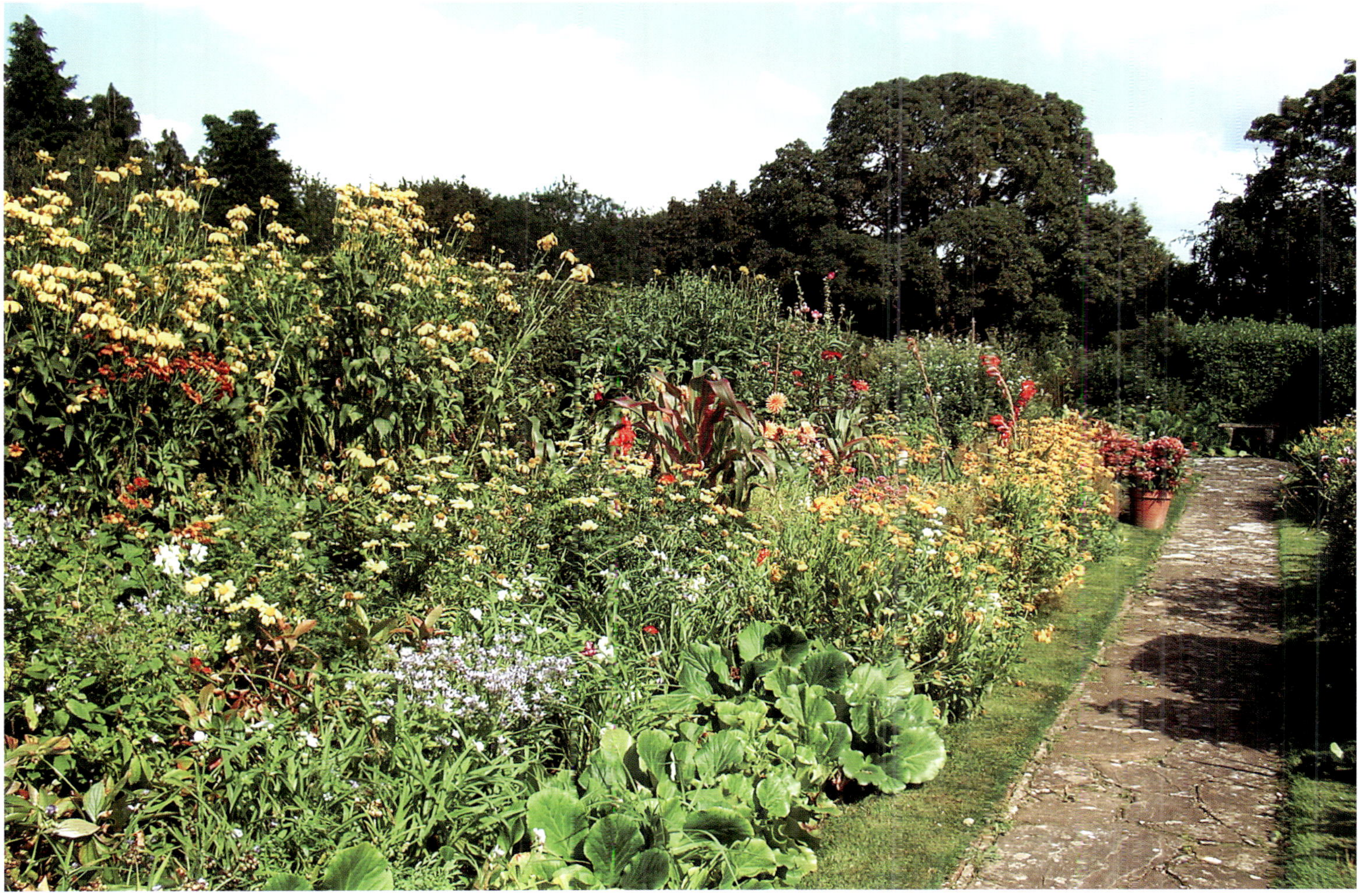

Jekyll and Lutyens trotted around the Surrey courtryside in her pony cart, studying vernacular architecture to the tiniest degree – door locks, window frames and catches, chimneys, porches, etc. Their records of these outings became a 'thorough and honest' storehouse to be raided for the creation of her final house, designed lovingly by Lutyens, which was true to Arts and Crafts principles. Jekyll knew the wood from which the oak timbers were cut, the hard Bargate sandstone that 'grows in our hills' and the red Surrey tiles. She used a local builder, Mr. Thomas Underwood of Dunsfold, and was often on site to oversee the progress. The house was surrounded by flower beds to give the impression of growing out of its own site and the walls were festooned with climbers, the warmth of the chimney breast providing a microclimate against early frosts.

The gardens had been evolving for over thirteen years before the house was finished, and were designed to offer an independent series of seasonal pictures. Eight acres had been set aside for woodland which ran north and west from the house approached by lawns. The gardens to the west and south were screened one from another, accessed by a network of walks and drawn architecturally to the house via The Wedge, which was exactly that – a triangle of ground that marshalled the paths to the north façade, terraces and lily tank. Arguably the most impressive and impressionistic feature was the Long Border, which was backed by an

A hot border of bright yellow heleniums contrasting with the reddish purple striated leaves of maize edged informally with the large shiny round leaves of Bergenia. The plants drifting texture and colour create a painterly effect in one of the herbaceous borders at The Manor Upton Grey.

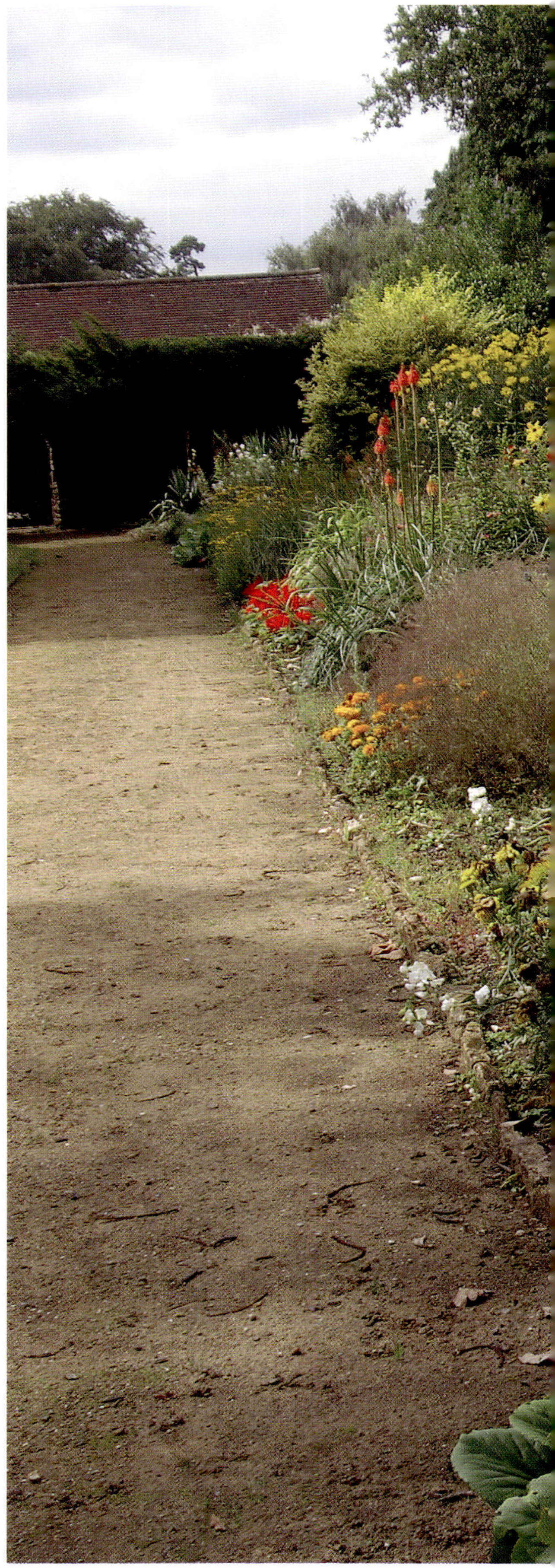

eleven feet high sandstone wall, and was 200 feet long with deep borders in two parts: the first being fourteen feet deep, separated by a narrow service path, from the second, a bed of small trees, climbers and shrubs trained to the wall. The colour scheme started at each end with white flowers amidst grey and silvery foliage, the hues 'warmed up' through warm white, pale pink and grey blue, progressing to strong yellow, orange and mahogany culminating in a dramatic centerpiece of scarlet and crimson against a back drop of the purple leaved vine. Beyond the wall the broad walk took you under the shady canopy of the pergola to the summer house and up to the house by a choice of routes – in spring through the nut walk past the 'Cenotaph of Sigismonda', in late summer through the michaelmas daisy border or, at any time, through the deep shrub borders to the Wedge. Behind the Long Border wall were the Spring and Paeony Gardens, the separate June and July borders and holding beds for plants to fill in any gaps. Striking out to the west took you through a Secret Garden enclosed by evergreens, a Winter Garden, the Rock Garden and up to The Hut.

Approximately 500 garden designs (some just a flowerbed or even a windowbox) are attributed to Jekyll, of which over seventy were in collaboration with Lutyens. In 1897 *Country Life* magazine was founded by Edward Hudson, and Jekyll became both contributor and subject with Lutyens on a regular basis. Two of Hudson's properties showcase their talents: between 1899 and 1901 Lutyens designed The Deanery at Sonning, Berkshire, for which Jekyll designed the gardens. It is a Lutyens frame of terraces, demi lune and circular steps, pergola and pools which she softened with colour schemes and voluptuous plantings.

The second property was Lindisfarne Castle, which Hudson bought as a summer house. It is actually a Tudor fort on Beblowe Crag and often appears lost in the mists that swirl around Holy Island off the coast of Northumberland. A personal favourite of mine, the Lutyens interiors have a 'Whistler meets Vermeer' look of plain colours, polished brass and blue and white china. Jekyll traveled up by train in May 1906 accompanied by Lutyens with her pet raven, Black Jack, and three shillings-worth of bulls eyes. Her initial grand plans for a tennis court or croquet lawn had to be scrapped because of the marshy terrain and the blast of North Sea winds. In the event the tiny walled garden, originally used by the garrison for growing vegetables, was designed into a microcosm of her style – drifts of flowers, clematis on supports, stachys as edgings plus

The Long Border at Munstead today retains the crescendo of oranges and reds at its core. The rounded leaves of one of her other favourite edging plants, bergenia, can be seen in the right hand corner.

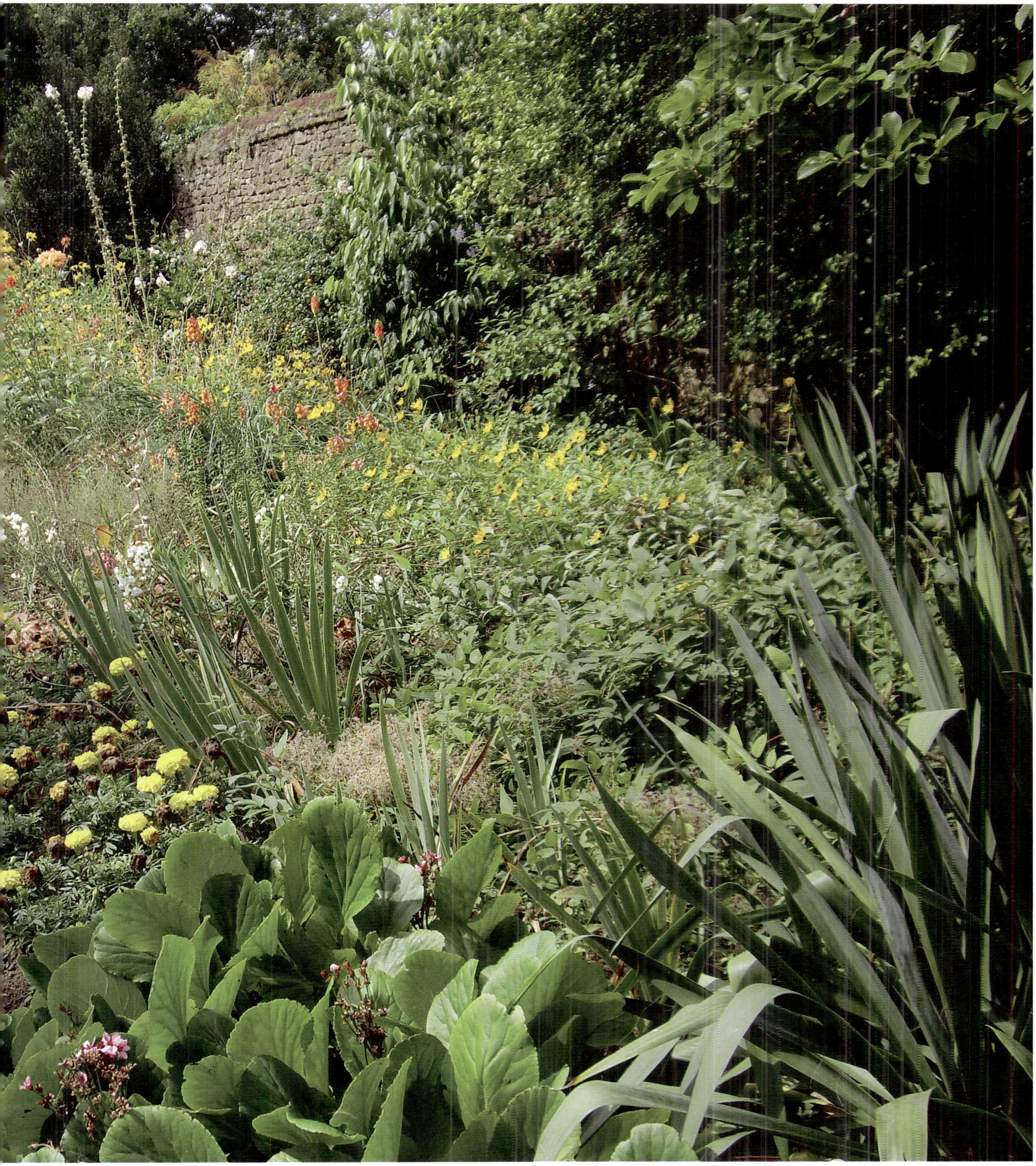

some fruit bushes (see page 137). After her first visit Mrs. Lutyens refused to accompany the children as there was too much scope for mischief, so thereafter they went with their father and roamed free. In 1972 the original plans for the Lindisfarne gardens were discovered in the Reef Point Garden Collection of Drawings in the School of Environmental Design at the University of California Berkeley. These were used as the basis for the recreation and restoration of the gardens in the same year.

In 1926 the wealthy daughter of a founder of Standard Oil, Miss Annie Burr Jennings, came for tea and a tour of the gardens at Munstead Wood. Three years earlier, Miss Jennings had joined a committee to restore Glebe House in Woodbury, Connecticut, the historic birthplace of the Anglican Episcopal Church. On her return to America, Miss Jennings wrote enclosing a plan and photographs requesting designs for an old fashioned garden, to which Jekyll responded with plans for a cottage style garden with drifting herbaceous borders of cool white, blue and pink and hot vibrant yellow, orange and red, as well as flower beds around the clapboard house. In fact it was over fifty years before the gardens were implemented and they are now flourishing.

Jekyll's impressionistic canvases were not limited to gardens, she captured their effects as an able photographer and author. She first wrote for *The Garden* magazine, edited by William Robinson and took over his job for a couple of years. Her first book, *Wood and Garden*, appeared in 1899, and there followed *Home and Garden* (1900), *Lilies for English Gardens* (1901), *Roses for English Gardens* (1902) which inspired Ellen Willmott's magnum opus *The Genus Rosa*. In 1904 *Old West Surrey* and *Some English Gardens* for which she worked with the artist E.S. Elgood, in 1907 *Flower Decoration in the House*, and in 1908 *Colour in the Flower Garden*, that after the third edition in 1914 was retitled *Colour Schemes for the Flower Garden*. Also in 1908 *Children and Gardens*, then she co-authored *Gardens for Small Country Houses* (1912) with Lawrence Weaver and finally in 1918 the weighty, magnificent *Garden Ornament*.

Her manifold artistic gifts and tireless quest for perfection were matched by her warmth as a friend, sister and aunt. Her comments on 'The Mixed Border' act as an apt epitaph: 'There is no day in the blooming life of the late summer border, or indeed of any other, when it does not need close watching and some kind of tending. Many people think that to have a good border of summer flowers is an easy thing; whereas to have it well done so as to show a continual picture of plant beauty, even for three months, is one of the most difficult of horticultural feats.'

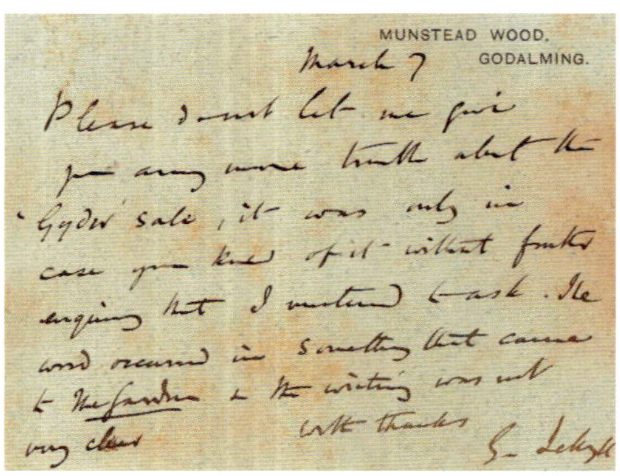
MUNSTEAD WOOD.
GODALMING.
March 7
Please do not let me give you any more trouble about the 'Gyder' sale, it was only in case you knew of it without further enquiry that I ventured to ask. The word occurred in something that came to the Garden & the writing was not very clear
With thanks
G. Jekyll

A correspondence card from Jekyll
This card from Gertrude Jekyll is in the author's personal copy of Old West Surrey. *The book is packed with photographs that are an invaluable record of a rural county that was rapidly disappearing under new development and the arrival of commuters. Like so many impressionist artists, she often included local people, cottage gardens and traditional working scenes in her books and paintings.*

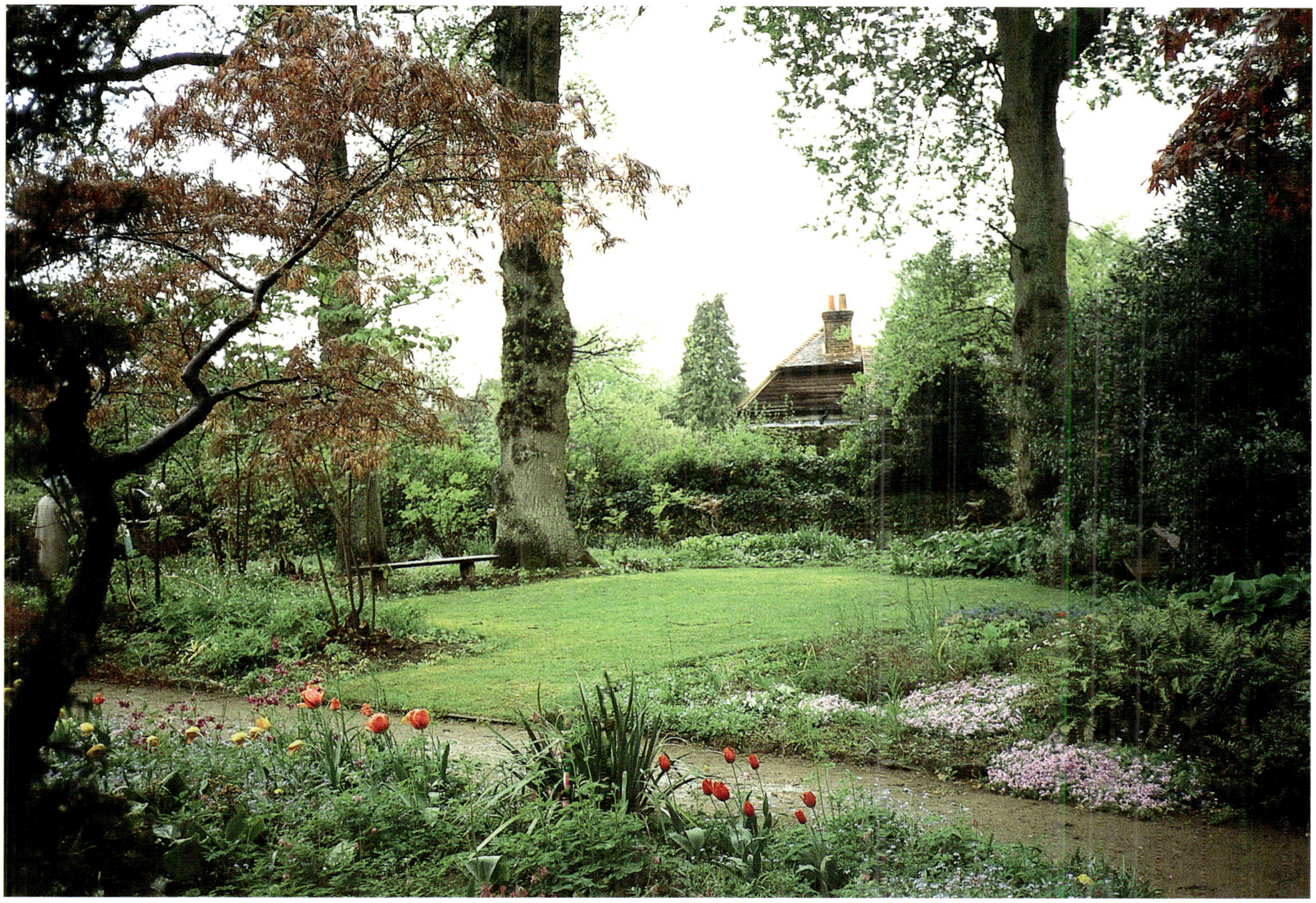

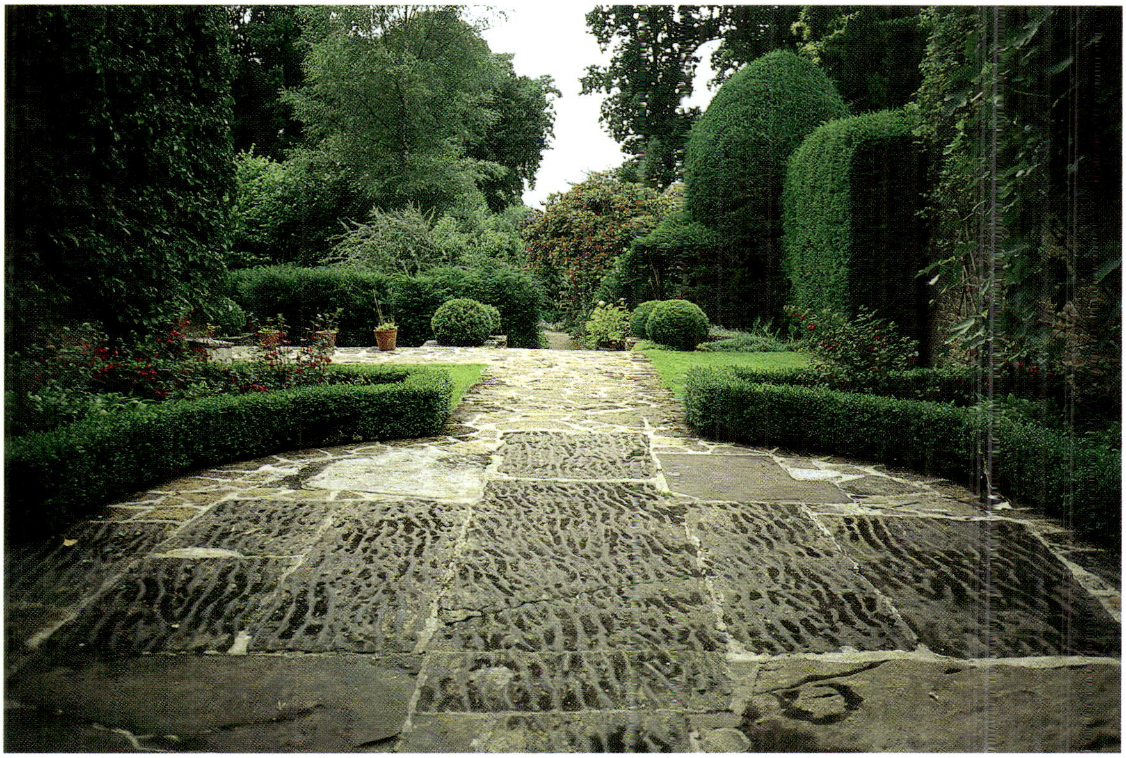

Above: A view today in May from the Long Border through trees to the house. A Surrey garden scene that celebrates the texture of the tree bark and the vivid colours of the foliage and flowers, despite the order it still equates with wilder garden settings painted by the Australian Impressionists.

Left: The jetty is north facing making it an ideal location to grow clipped evergreens such as the low box, Buxus, hedges and yew topiary. The rippled mud effect on the local paving stones provides a brushstroke texture to the foreground as your eye is drawn down into the gardens.

Impressionist Children

When I was still very young – say at the age of three, four or five – instead of deciding on the pose I was to take, he would wait until I found something to occupy me and keep me quiet. That is how 'Jean eating Soup', 'Jean playing with Toy Soldiers', 'Jean with Building Blocks' and 'Jean Looking at a Picture Book' came to be painted. I remember quite clearly all the preparations for the picture now in the Art Institute in Chicago, showing me sewing. It was executed at Magagnosc, near Grasse, where my parents had rented a pretty villa on the side of the mountain. ... We had a pet rabbit, named Jeannot, which we used to take with us when we went for a walk in the wild land on the other side of the road.

Jean Renoir, Renoir, My Father

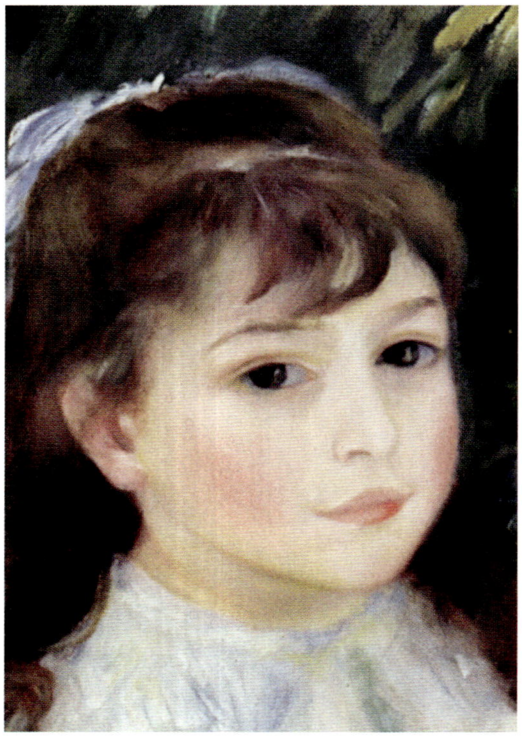

Pierre-Auguste Renoir, **Girl with a Hoop**. *Oil on canvas, 125.7 x 76.6cm (49 ½ x 30 ¼in.), 1885*

A Modern Miss in the making? In 1885, the year of his first son Pierre's birth, Renoir showed a distinct change in style when he painted the nine-year-old Marie Goujon, who seems remarkably self possessed. She appears to only have a moment to spare to glance at the artist, her foot holding the base of the hoop before she sends it spinning across the garden. The colours are far bolder and clearer than his earlier style. In 1881 he had travelled to Italy and studied Raphael, he returned with the intention of making his brushstrokes more aigre – sharp – the effect is a silky smooth focus. This is an early example of Renoir's sharp new approach.

The initial critical reception of the Impressionists was hostile. Their technique was described as 'infantile' and Monet's *L'Impression: soleil levant* was just that: "a mere impression". Far from being disheartened, the artists seized upon this negative damnation as an apt description of capturing fleeting moments, and they defiantly called themselves 'Impressionists'. Infants and children, both their own and those of friends and models, are regularly glimpsed in golden infancy absorbed in almost fairy tale innocence. As Jean Renoir recalls above, his father would only paint children when they were engaged in an activity that ensured they were not posing, such as the gorgeous *Girl with a Watering Can* of 1876.

On the other side of the world, Australian Frederick McCubbin's family life was sparkling. This can be sensed from the jolly picture his student Arthur Streeton paints in a letter of December 1896 to Tom Roberts: 'I walked over to Prof McCubbin's yesterday and had tea with him in his garden. Mrs. Prof in a harmonious yellow gown; all the little Profs buzzing round the garden of fruit trees and the haystack. The Prof is a married man, very happily and securely married.' It is tempting to imagine the McCubbin family reading Beatrix Potter's story of Peter Rabbit who famously squeezed under the gate after eating Mr. McGregor's lettuces and radishes. The story is almost contemporary with the fencing in McCubbin's 1905 *The Wattle Glade (The Boundary of Mr MacGregor's Garden, Mount Macedon)* that was next to his home of Fontainebleau. There is no connection with Beatrix Potter's story, although there is a childlike pleasure in contriving one.

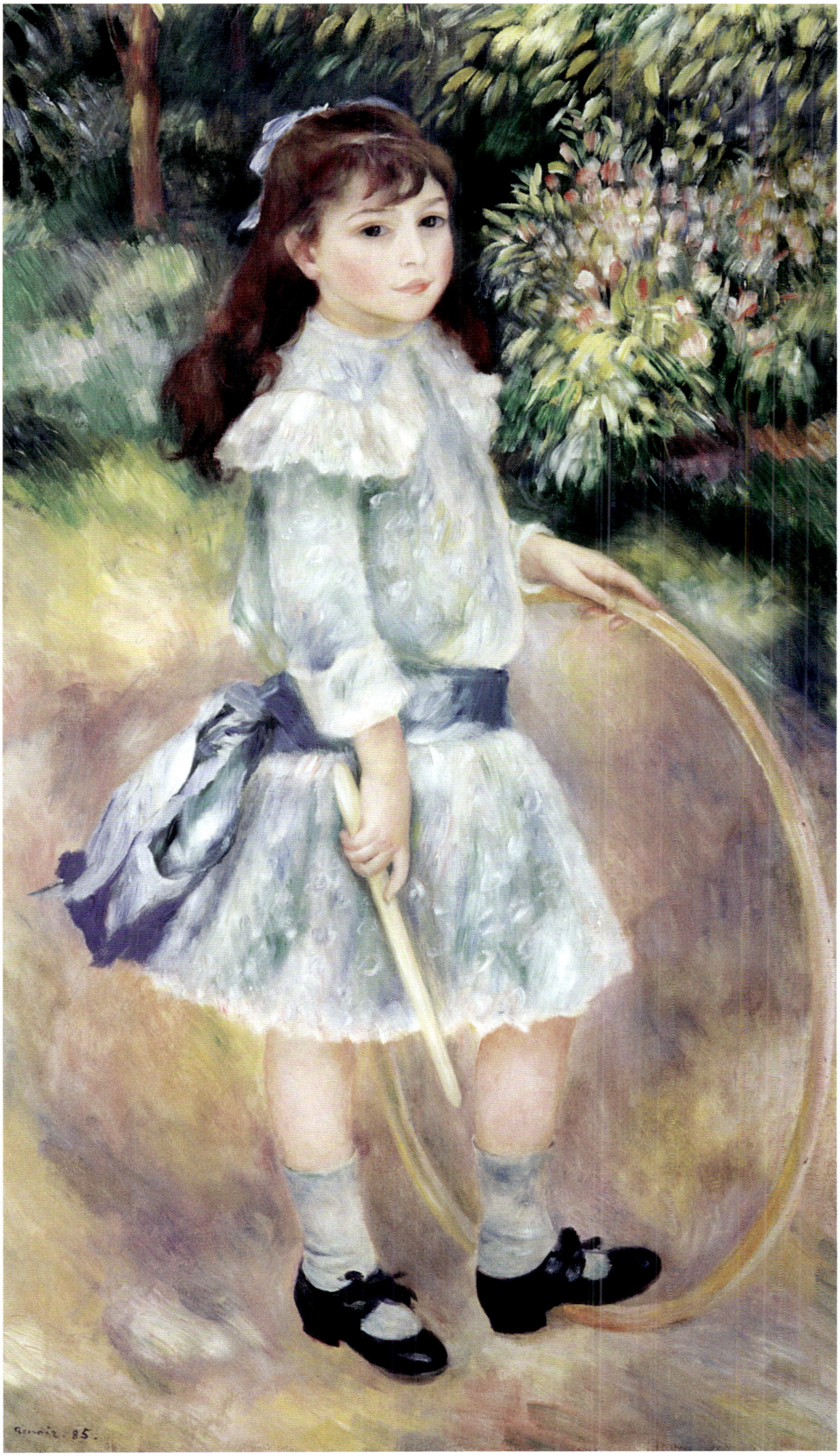
Renoir. 85.

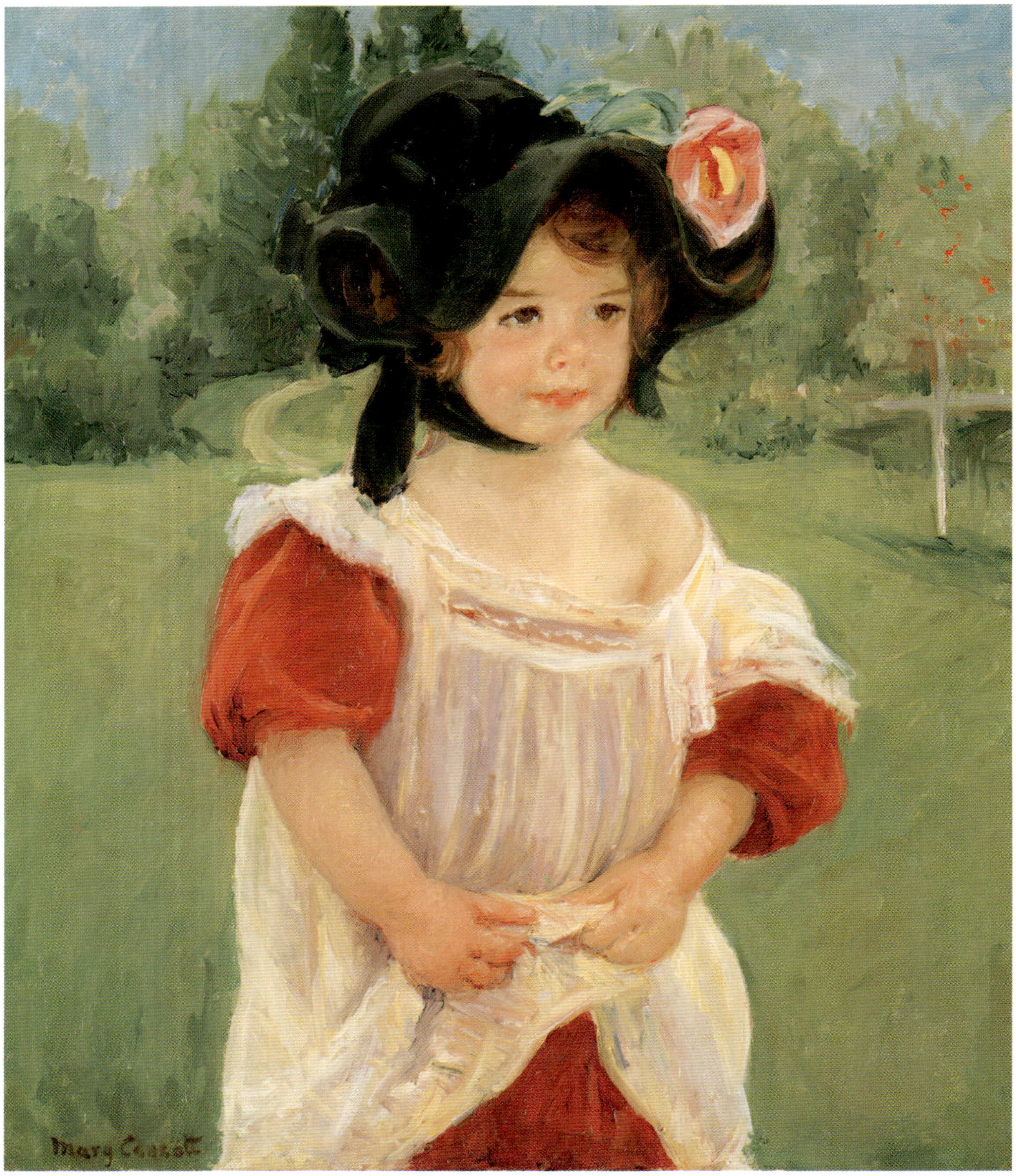

Mary Cassatt, **Spring: Margot Standing in a Garden** *(Fillette dans un jardin). Oil on canvas, 67.9 x 57.8cm (26¾ x 22¾ in.), 1900*

Although she dedicated her life to her art, never marrying nor having children, Mary Cassatt paints children with a maternal sensuality that embodies those moments with children that make parental trials all seem worthwhile. Take the gorgeous Margot Lux, who lived near the Chateau de Beaufresne in Mesnil-Theribus on the River Oise, depicted in the painting Spring: Margot Standing in a Garden. *Included in the Metropolitan Museum of Art's exhibition 'American Impressionists Abroad and At Home' it was described with the words 'unctuous brushwork renders the soft texture of downy flesh, luscious velvet, and flimsy pinafore' – she really is a peach of a child. Cassatt subtly links Margot with the garden, her white pinafore echoed in the white tree trunks and the red of her dress with the cherries: a perfect blossom of childhood, full of future promise. Cassatt has painted her gazing out of the picture – what is she watching as she folds up her pinafore in her hands? The great black hat with its rose looks like she has raided the dressing-up box. A sumptuous Impressionist child.*

Pierre-Auguste Renoir, **Two Sisters (On the Terrace)**. *Oil on canvas, 100.5 x 81cm (39½ x 37⅞ in.), 1881*

The younger of the two sisters looks to have been occupied by having her hat covered in flowers, and is now proudly modelling her beautiful bonnet to her sister with a wary eye on the artist. It was painted in 1881 at Chatou, a suburb of Paris that Renoir considered the most pleasant of all. Whilst enjoying the composition of the demure older sister and her excited younger sibling, you become aware of the exceptional quality of the light glistening on the water, playing on the flowers and foliage. The older girl has been identified as Jeanne Darlot who went on to be an actress, then mistress of a chocolate manufacturer and later of a politician.

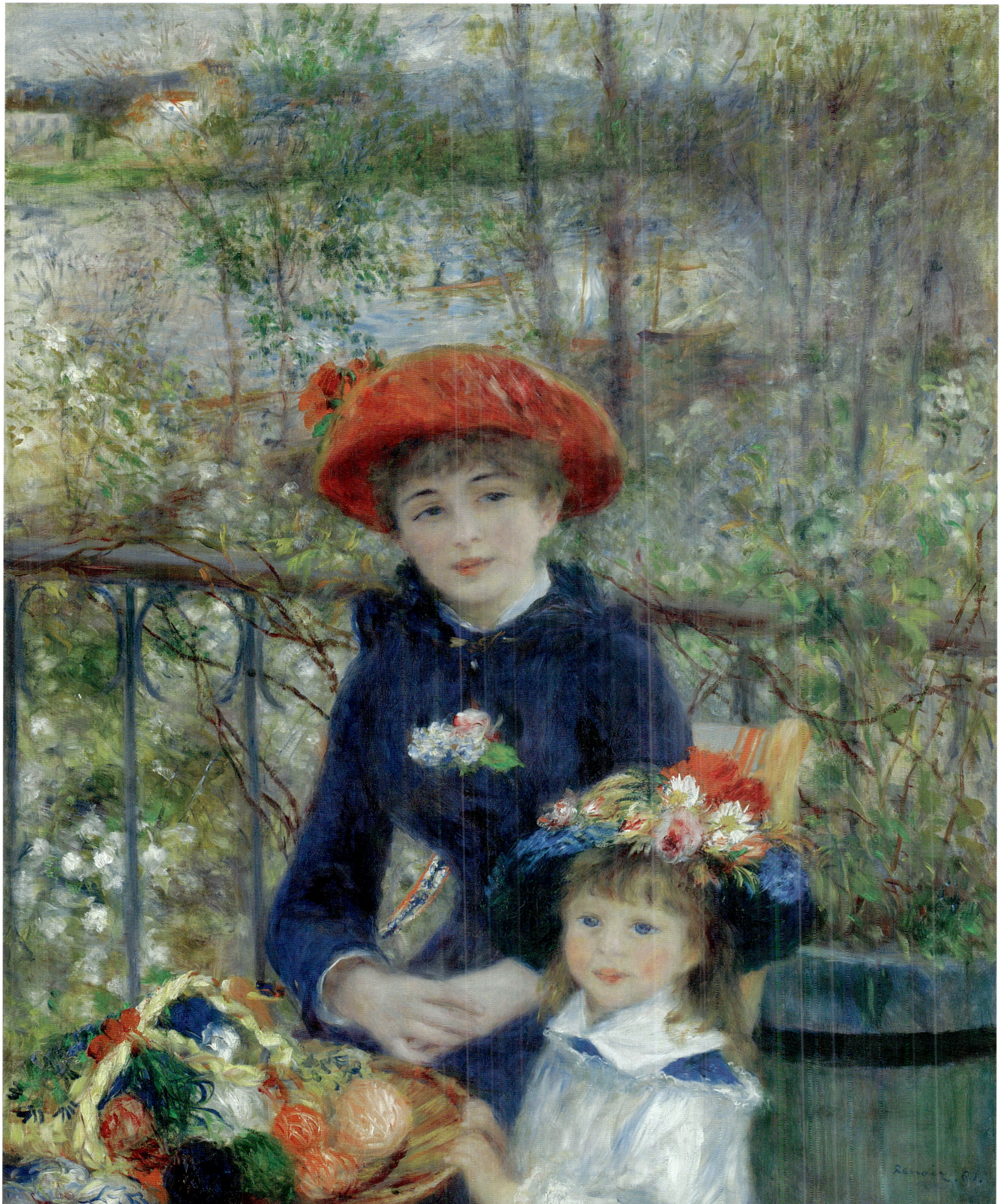

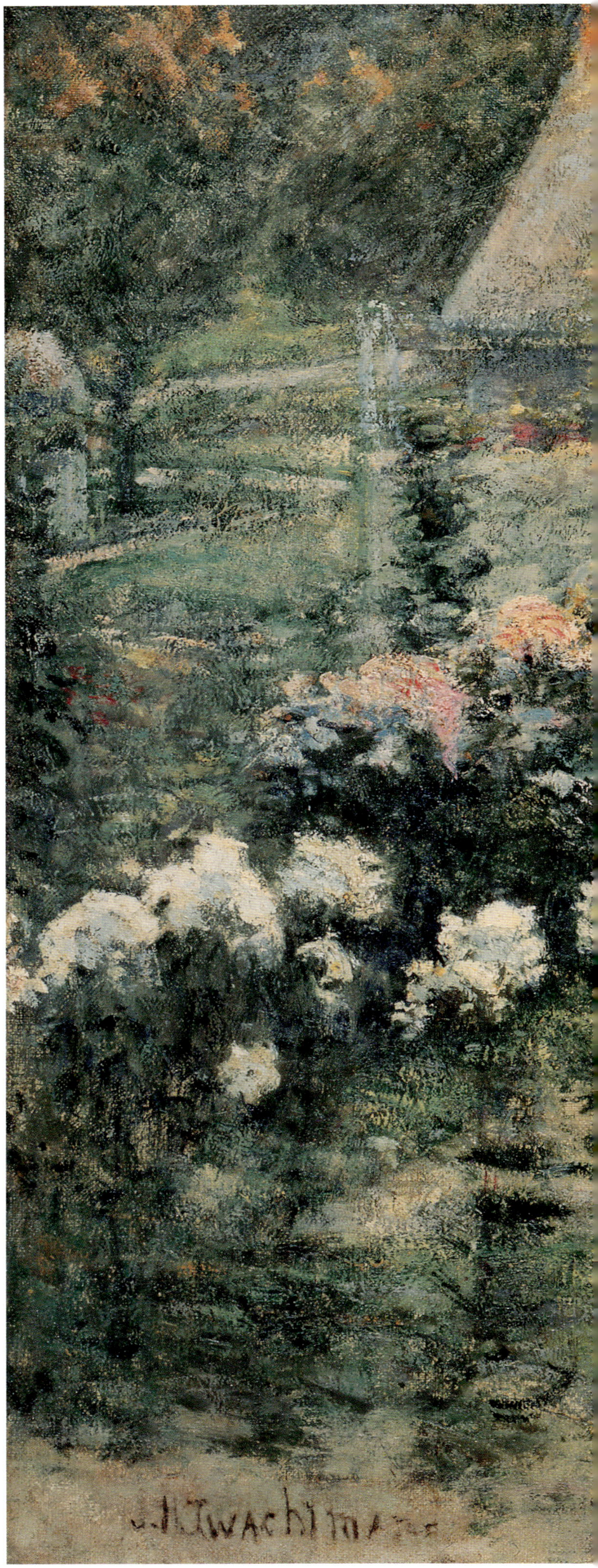

John Henry Twatchman, **On the Terrace**. *Oil on canvas, 64 x 76.5cm (25 ½ x 30 ⅛ in.), c.1890-1900*

The property John Twachtman bought for his family in Greenwich, Connecticut in 1889 was a source of great emotional and spiritual comfort. Like Monet, he suffered mood swings, but unlike him appears to have been far less social. On the Terrace was painted when the lilies were at their zenith and it evokes the freshness, innocence and purity of the flowers. Their massed blooms run all along the pathway and are echoed in the crisp white dresses of his wife and children that form the centrepiece. His wife Martha cradles their newborn son whilst their daughters Marjorie and Elsie quietly play near her, a scene of domestic bliss. The children appear to be clustered like buds in the warm embrace of their flowery mother. Twachtman followed arts and crafts principles by using local stone for walls and paths in his gardens. The lilies appear to become pinker nearer the house, drawing your eye through the arch and out into the rest of the gardens. He took the popular general interest in Japanese prints further by studying zen philosophy and Japanese art, and was among the first to knowingly create a therapeutic landscape. Away from the safety and formality of the terrace, the gardens were crossed by a babbling brook, where he planted willows on the bank and sowed flowers that would naturalise. They feature in his 1890s canvas Meadow Flowers but the captured effect is less naturalistic. Later, with his children in mind, he dammed the stream to create a swimming pool and a boating pond.

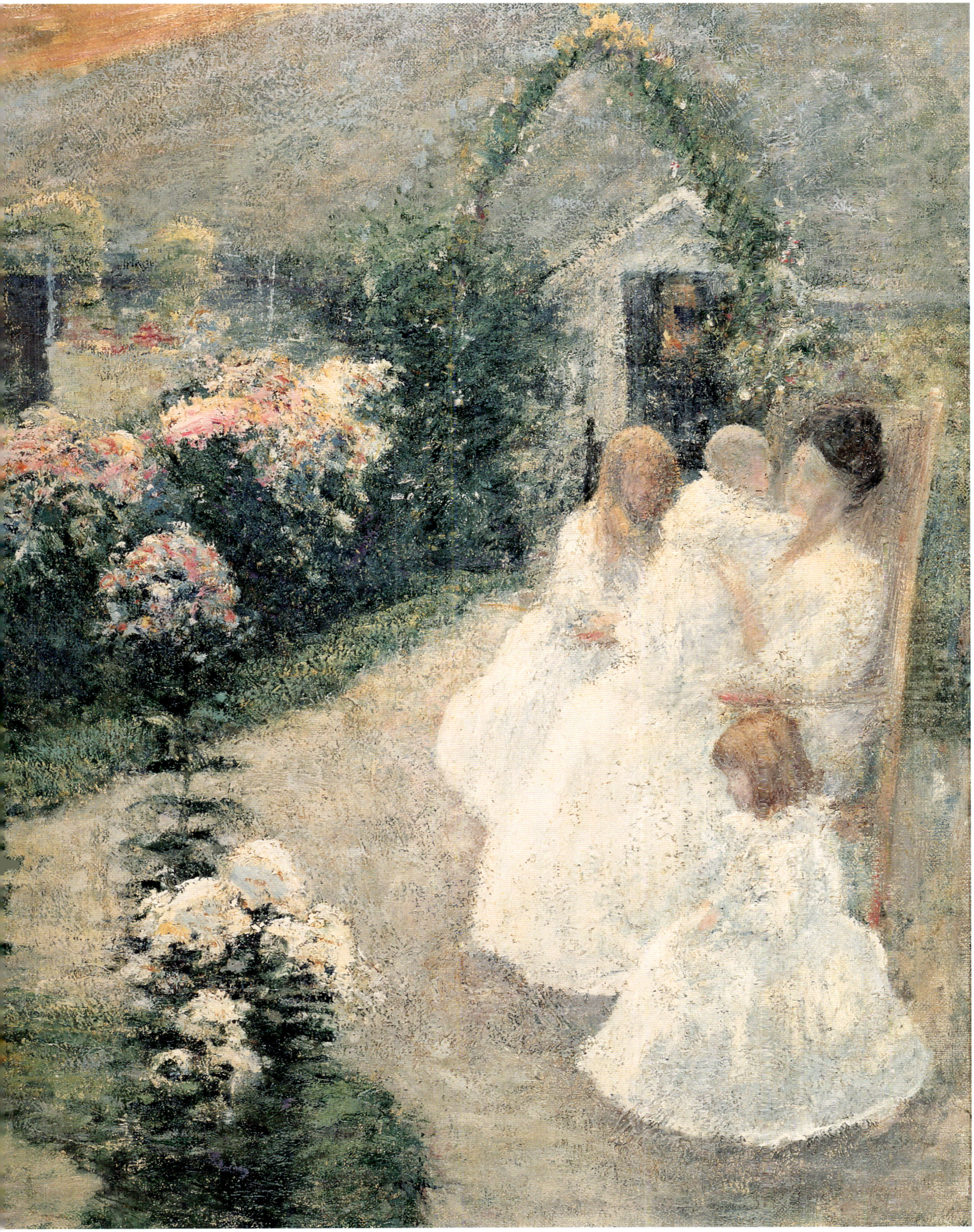

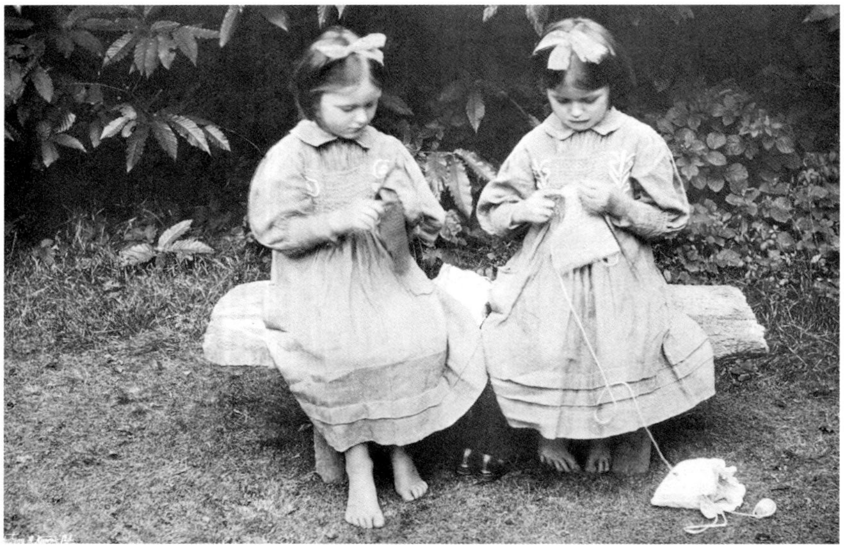

From Children and Gardens. *'Jean and Ann – Ann: "Fraid I've dropped a stitch".'*
Gertrude Jekyll's 1908 book, Children and Gardens, *was full of ideas and activities that children might well want to do. Whether this would extend to knitting is another matter, although sitting outside with the grass between your toes would certainly be pleasant.*

Gertrude Jekyll spent an idyllic childhood in Bramley Park in Surrey. She was surrounded by a loving family and was free to roam and get up to mischief with her brothers in its extensive grounds.This left her with an indelible spark of empathy with children. She used her physical freedom to observe nature closely, and her intellectual freedom to pursue a full education which resulted in the blossoming of myriad artistic skills. She entertained her nieces and nephews with an array of garden tasks and activities from piling up supersized pumpkins, to mixing pot pourri and hosting tea parties for her cats.

It is interesting to observe the difference between the children and the grandchildren of the artist. Childe Hassam painted Celia Thaxter with her grandson in the gardens of Appledore, dwarfed by the tall flowers but safe with his hand held (see page 138). In striking contrast is Monet's painting of his son Michel just after his mother Camille's death; the little boy seems lonely and afraid on the steps of the gardens at Véteuil. There was nearly ten years between Monet's two sons Jean and Michel, and he painted both of them as small children, Jean in the gardens that they had at Argenteuil and Véteuil, elegantly attired and playing in a rather well-behaved way. As can be seen on page 92, his painting of *Madame Monet and a Child in a Garden* would seem to be at Argenteuil. When they arrived at Giverny, apart from his son Jean and step-daughter Suzanne Hoschedé in the orchard, he only painted his younger son Michel and the Hoschedé children (from his extended family) in the surrounding fields and out on boats. He also used the children to carry the many canvases and artists' materials involved in his series of paintings of Poplars and Grainstacks. He never painted his step-grandchildren but there are many photographs of them in the gardens watching him painting, on the Japanese Bridge with visitors, chatting with him on the verandah and one with Alice's grandaughter Sizi Salerou and a peacock.

Imitation is the greatest form of flattery and in the United States there is a miniature 'Monet's garden' in the 4H Children's Garden at Michigan State University. The pond is crossed by a green Japanese bridge and children can swing on the frog scultpures and make them spit across the water lilies.

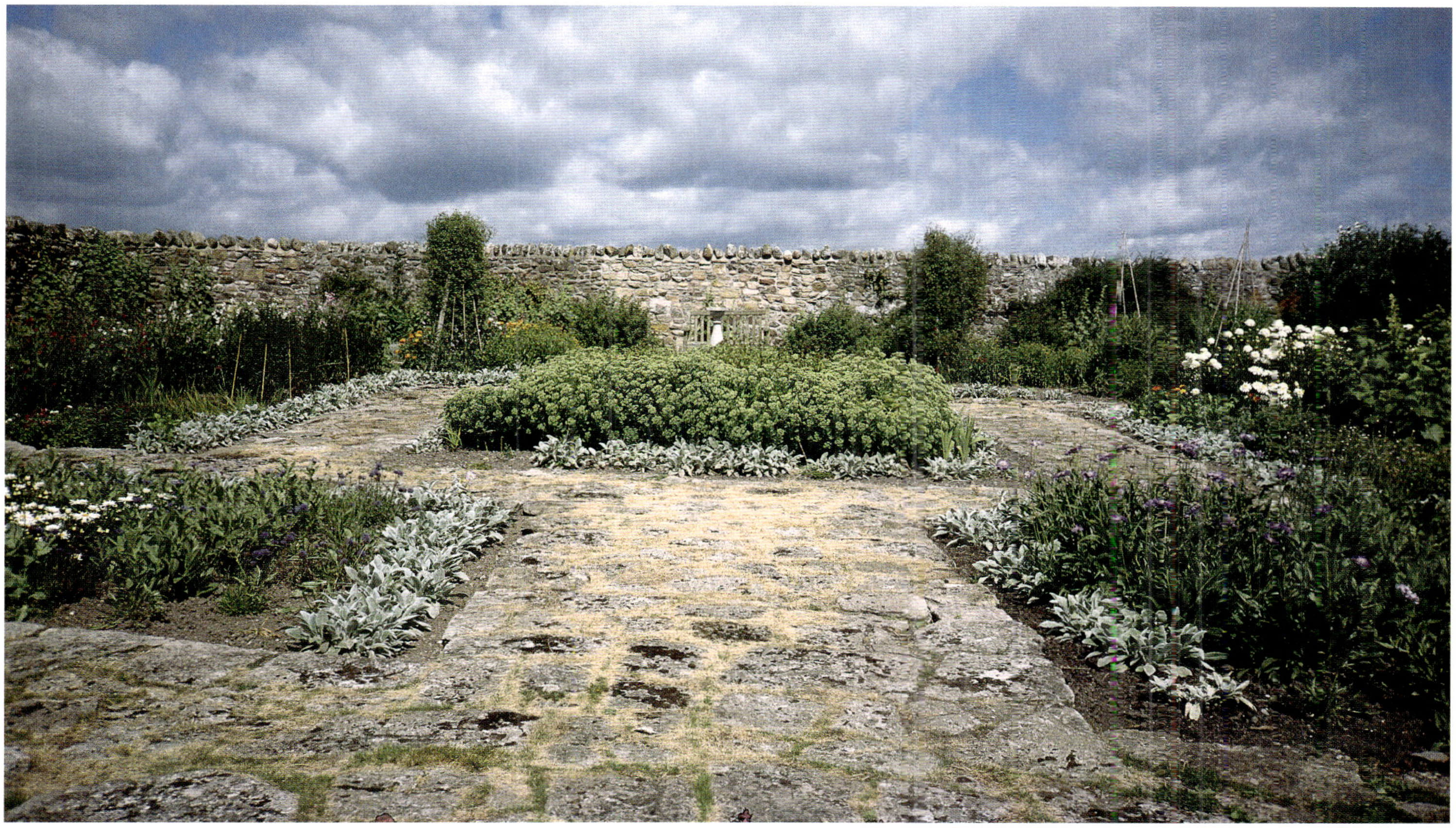

Lindisfarne Castle, Jekyll Garden

Edward Hudson was founder and editor of Country Life magazine. In 1902, having bought Lindisfarne Castle, he commissioned Edwin Lutyens to design what was actually a Tudor Fort into an innovatative holiday home. Lutyens bought his wife, Emily, and children as holiday guests, and wonderful portrait photographs of his children posed within this stony outpost survive. Mary Lutyens, daughter of Edwin, remembered Hudson as a willing co-conspiritor in her games: 'He was good natured. We had a firescreen in the nursery, the bottom part of which could be moved up leaving a gap at the bottom. It was perfect for playing French Revolutions, and Hudson was most obliging in kneeling on the floor and putting his head through the gap so that we could guillotine him.' Gertrude Jekyll designed a rather over-ambitious, extensive garden with croquet lawn and borders, but the unrelenting Northumbrian North Sea wind dictated a more naturalistic approach so that the sole flower borders were within the tiny walled former vegetable garden originally created for the soldiers. A local boy was lowered in a basket from the castle to plant up the crevices on its walls under instruction from Jekyll – he obviously did not have the social status of the Lutyens children. The romance of Lindisfarne Castle is enhanced by its position on a cone of molten dolerite above the coast so that sometimes swirls of mist give the impression that it is floating in the sky.

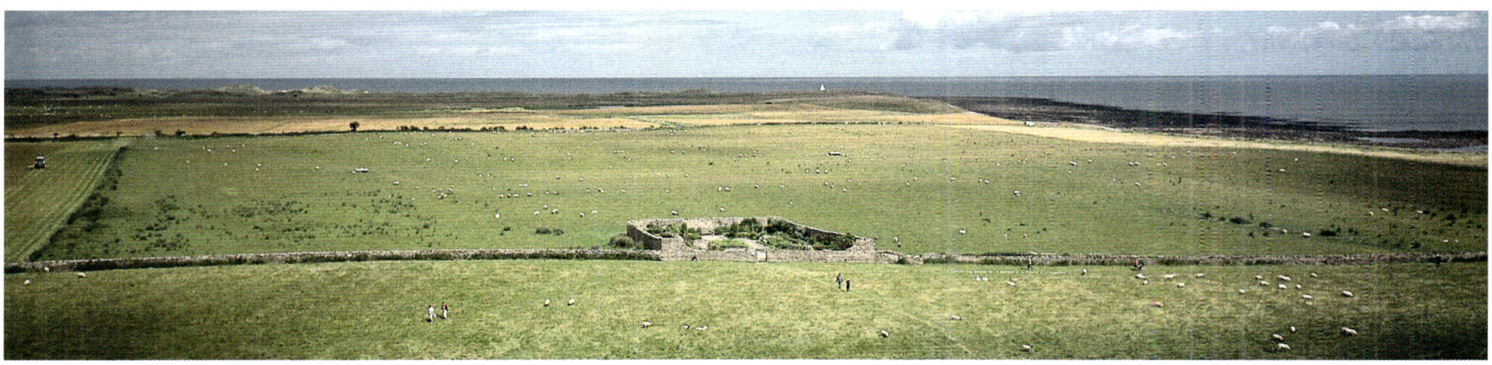

Lindisfarne, the view from the walled garden inside the castle grounds. The North Sea dominates the top right-hand corner.

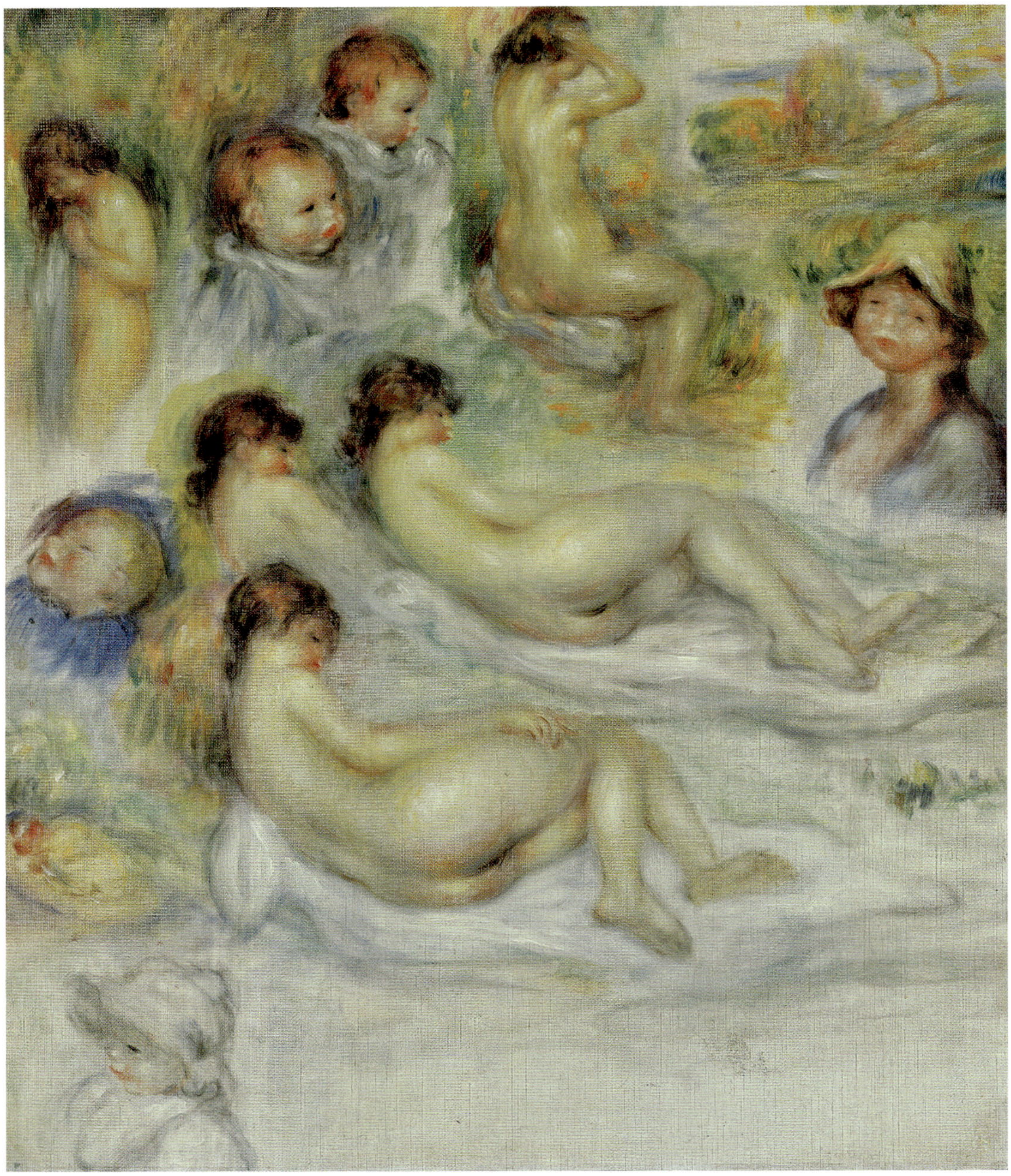

Pierre-Auguste Renoir, **Studies of Pierre Renoir; His mother Aline Charigot; and nudes in landscape**. *Oil on canvas, 46.1 x 39.2cm ($18\frac{1}{8}$ x $15\frac{7}{16}$ in.), 1885/86*

Renoir constantly sketched all three of his children at every stage of their life, at rest and play especially in gardens, as well as their friends and cousins. He did not marry Aline until 1890, formerly she had been one of the models in the Moulin de la Galette. In time her place as his model was taken by her young cousin Gabrielle. Their second son Jean calculated he was about five years old when Jean Renoir, Sewing *was painted in 1888, the backdrop is a simple blue, implying he was painted inside.*

Childe Hassam, **The Garden in its Glory**. *Watercolour on paper sheet, 50.6 x 35.2cm ($19\frac{7}{8}$ x $13\frac{7}{8}$ in.), 1892*

Young Elliott has his hand held lovingly by his grandmother, Celia. Unbeknown to him, his presence that summer raised her spirits from depression and overwork. They are coming out of the cool of the parlour, down the steps under the arches to her flower beds, in her other hand she holds a large bouquet of red flowers. Childe Hassam frames them in a tide of Shirley poppies, asters and sweet peas. A print of The Garden in its Glory *was used as the frontispiece to* An Island Garden, *in which Thaxter's words are wonderfully illumined by Hassam's illustrations. Like the child in the picture, the reader is taken by the hand and guided enthusiastically around the garden. There is a marked parallel but a world of emotional distance in the framing of little Michel Monet in his father's* The Artist's Garden at Vetheuil. *Monet depicts his son dwarfed by the sunflowers that line the step and tower over him. There is a clear sense of abandonment of the four-year-old whose mother has just died, not to mention his father's own grief.*

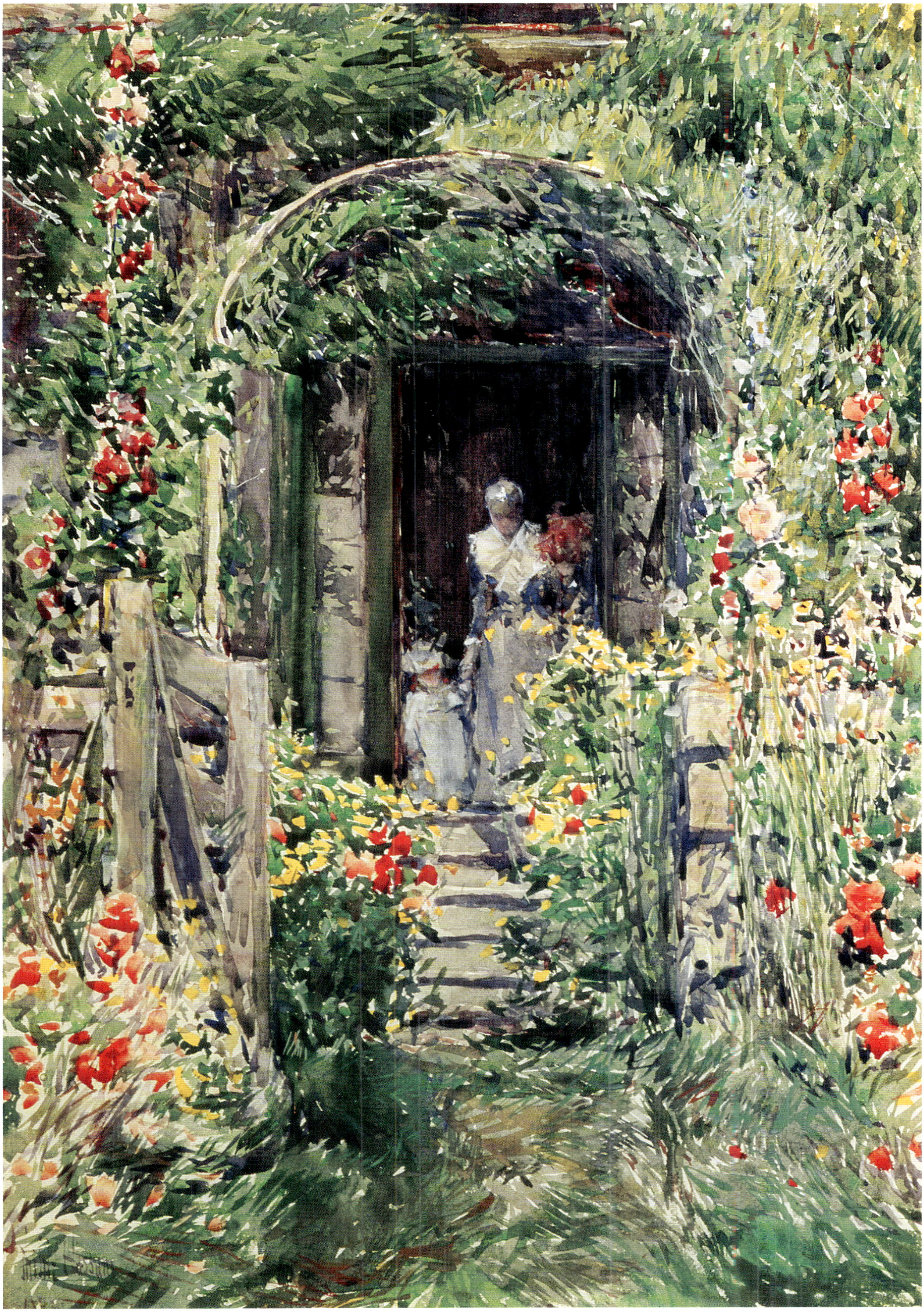

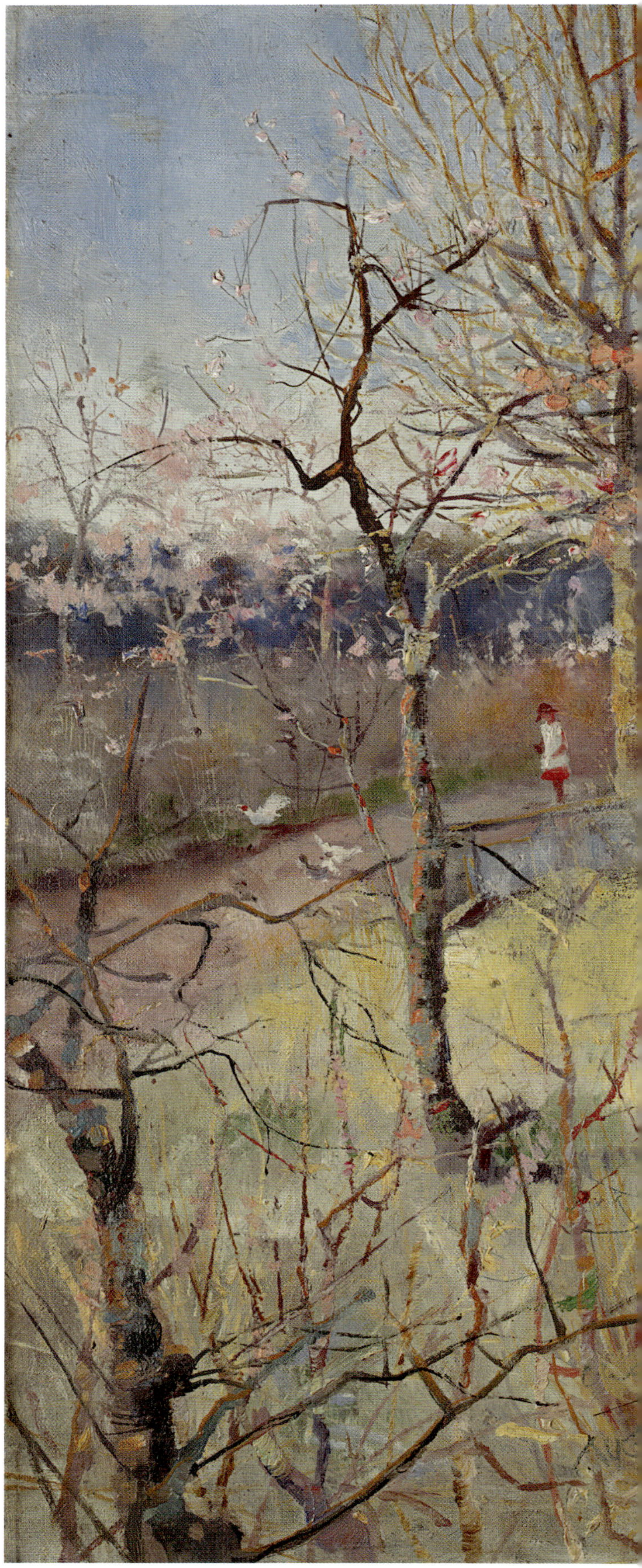

Charles Conder, **Springtime**. *Oil on canvas, 44.3 x 59.1cm (17¾ x 23½ in.), 1888*

Springtime *was painted by Charles Conder in an overgrown orchard at Thomas Griffith's farm on the Richmond side of the Hawkesbury River, a popular landscape for many Sydney artists. Conder gives a subtle narrative of the young nation of Australia, bright, bold and aspirational, that draws the viewer out of the garden and into the radiant light of the bush beyond. The central maternal figure is Griffiths' daughter Abigail Celeste carrying her niece Linda, the helpless baby. Just like tending a young plant in the garden, the baby needs the protection of its mother's arms. The toddler seeks to be picked up (although perfectly able to stand on her own two feet) whilst the older girl, possibly on her way to school and now daringly independent, leaves the garden into a wider world. The bush has been cleared, and in the fields the farmer works the land with horses. On the horizon the lure and riches of the metropolis can be seen. D.H. Souter, a contemporary chronicler of Australian artists and contributor to* Art and Architecture *described the colours of the spring around Hawkesbury as 'pink and green, for English eyes in the pastel form these are hues of apple blossom, new leaves and the promise of things to come.' The delicacy of the blossoms against the branches in Conder's painting is distinctly Japanese as can be seen in prints by Utagawa Hiroshige such as* Plum Orchard at Kameido *(now in the British Museum), and echoed in the works of James MacNeill Whistler, Van Gogh and John Russell. Conder imbibed the sensation of Impressionist colour earlier than Frederick McCubbin who also used the new technique but in a sombre more traditional way (see* The Pioneer, *page 164-165).*

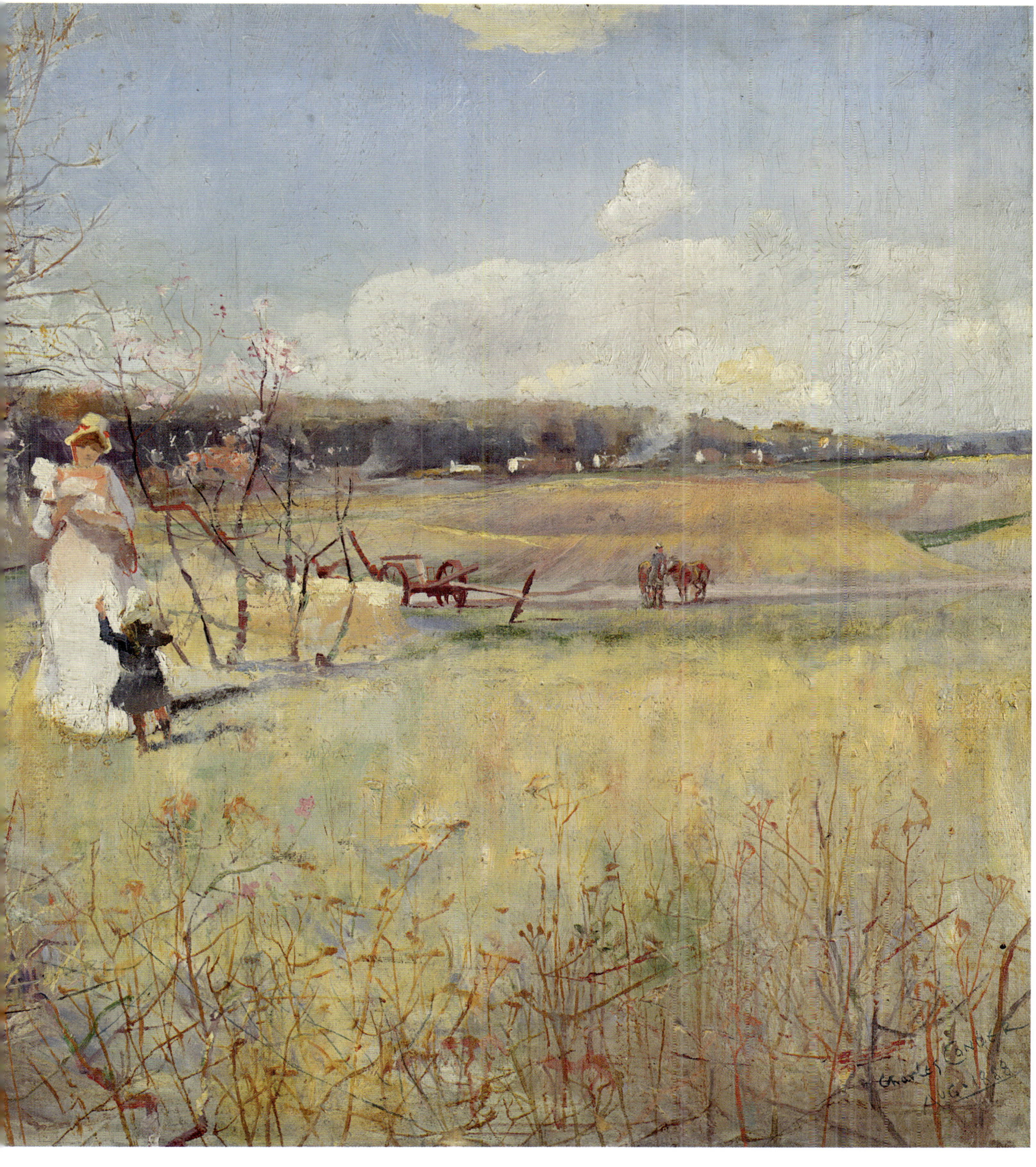

Fur, Fowl and Flutter

Tabby, a fine whole-coloured silver tabby, frequents the nut-walk and pergola, and considers himself the warden of two gates, the hand hanging-gate through the Yew hedge and the five-barred gate that crosses the back road behind the summer-house. Both gates have wire-netting over their lower halves to prevent the passing of rabbits; indeed but for this necessity neither gate would be there …

Gertrude Jekyll, Home and Garden, *1900*

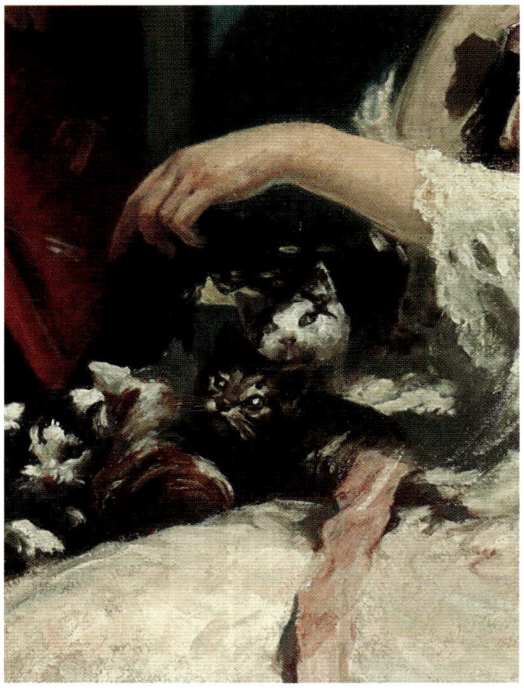

Rupert Bunny, **A Summer Morning** *(Matinée d'été). Oil on canvas, 222 x 181.5cm (88¾ x 72½ in.), 1897*

Rupert Bunny spent most of his life working away from Australia. Living for many years in Paris, he is described as 'an exotic in Australian art'. In A Summer Morning *he portrays a maid pouring milk into a bowl held by a lady for the kittens that are playing on the lap of another, actually Bunny's French wife, Jeanne. The frivolous dresses of the women – all these frills, buttons and bows – seem dated by comparison with the women in Mary Cassatt's paintings, and equates with Monet's canvases of the 1870s. The effect is Belle Époque-meets-Folies Bergeres. The women's languid demeanour exudes the sense of surrounding heat, and the garden outside reflects brightly in the mirror. So how shall we while away an idle morning? How delightful to be playing with these mischievous fluffy feline bundles, especially with a maid in the shadows who is ready to see to your every need.*

One of Renoir's studios in Montmartre was in the rough district around Rue Moncey noted for ruffians, rag-pickers and pimps. When not plying her trade, Angèle modelled for Renoir, and she mentioned to him that there was a little house nearby at a very low rent which would make an ideal studio. Renoir was delighted to see there was a garden with an old apple tree and a child's swing, so he took it. In 1875 the golden-haired Angèle posed for him cuddling a tabby cat, not in the garden but with floral motifs behind her right shoulder. She occasionally helped Renoir out financially, and at times when he was struggling to pay the rent she went out and 'did' one of the boulevards to help him. On one occasion she saved Renoir from a mugging: when returning home late one night, he was about to be robbed by some local heavies; fortunately they recognized him not as the great artist, but as one of Angèle's friends, and so bade him good night.

Monet rose at 4.30am in the summer to start painting to the accompaniment of the dawn chorus. He would listen to birdsong in sun after rain, spring mornings and summer evenings – momentary and seasonal sensations to match the fleeting light. Like Celia Thaxter, watching birds and butterflies delighted Monet, especially the patterns and colours created by kingfishers or swallows. The colourful flutter of butterflies as the zephyrs of summer lift them from flower to flower mirrors the momentary sensations that the Impressionists sought to capture. Monet had a large aviary at Giverny that sheltered parrots and grazing tortoises. Gustave Geffroy described this in his biography of Monet: 'An enclosure shelters birds of many hues, white hens, black ducks, golden pheasants, peacocks displaying their vast fans studded with sapphire and gold, red and ruby pheasants, and in the course of some years, herring gulls, grey-headed gulls, injured animals gathered up by Maurice Hamel in the Somme bay and put into the care of the Monet household.' The hen run near the house became the nursing home for wounded birds, gulls and larks, and a one-legged sparrow took breadcrumbs from the table for over three years.

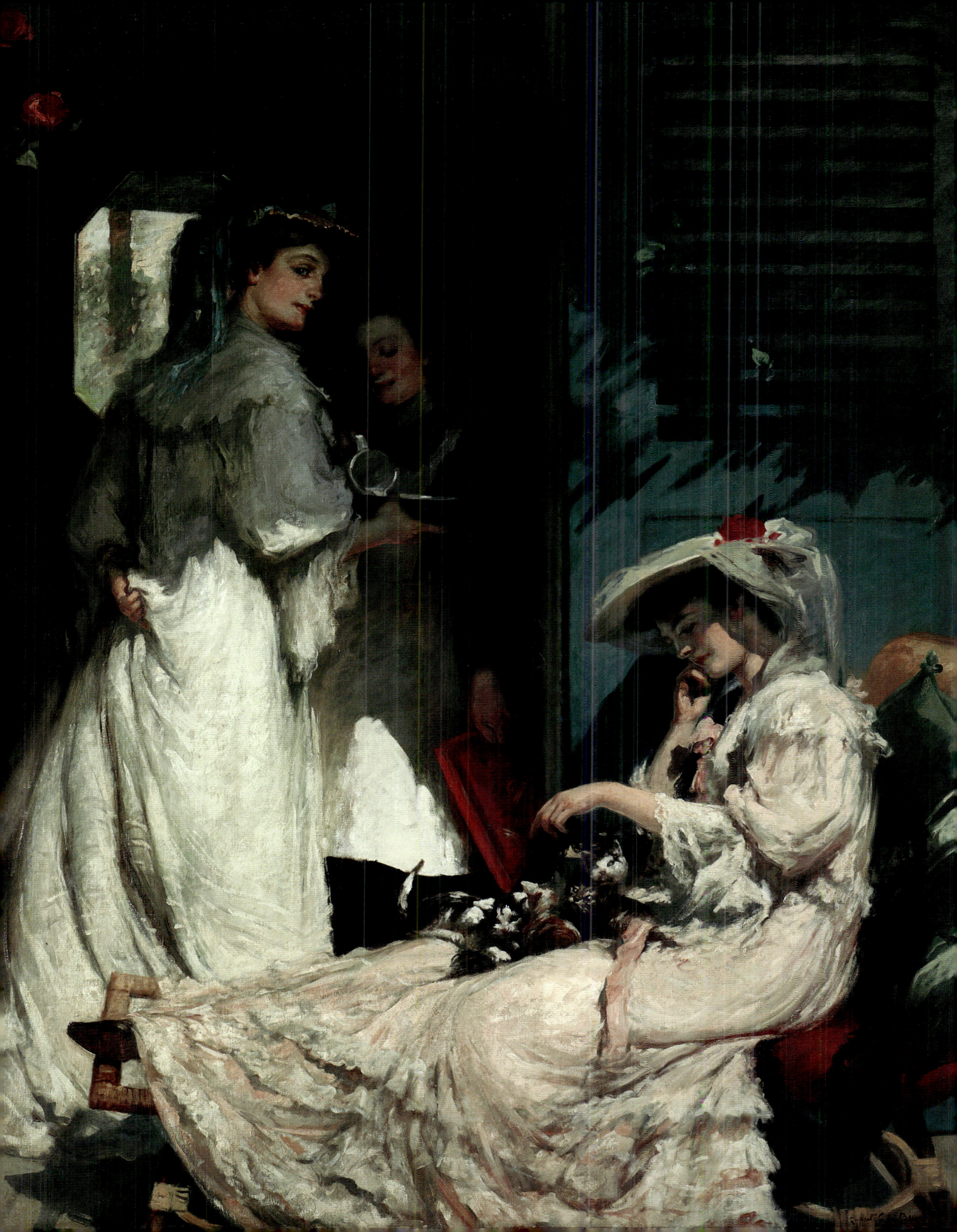

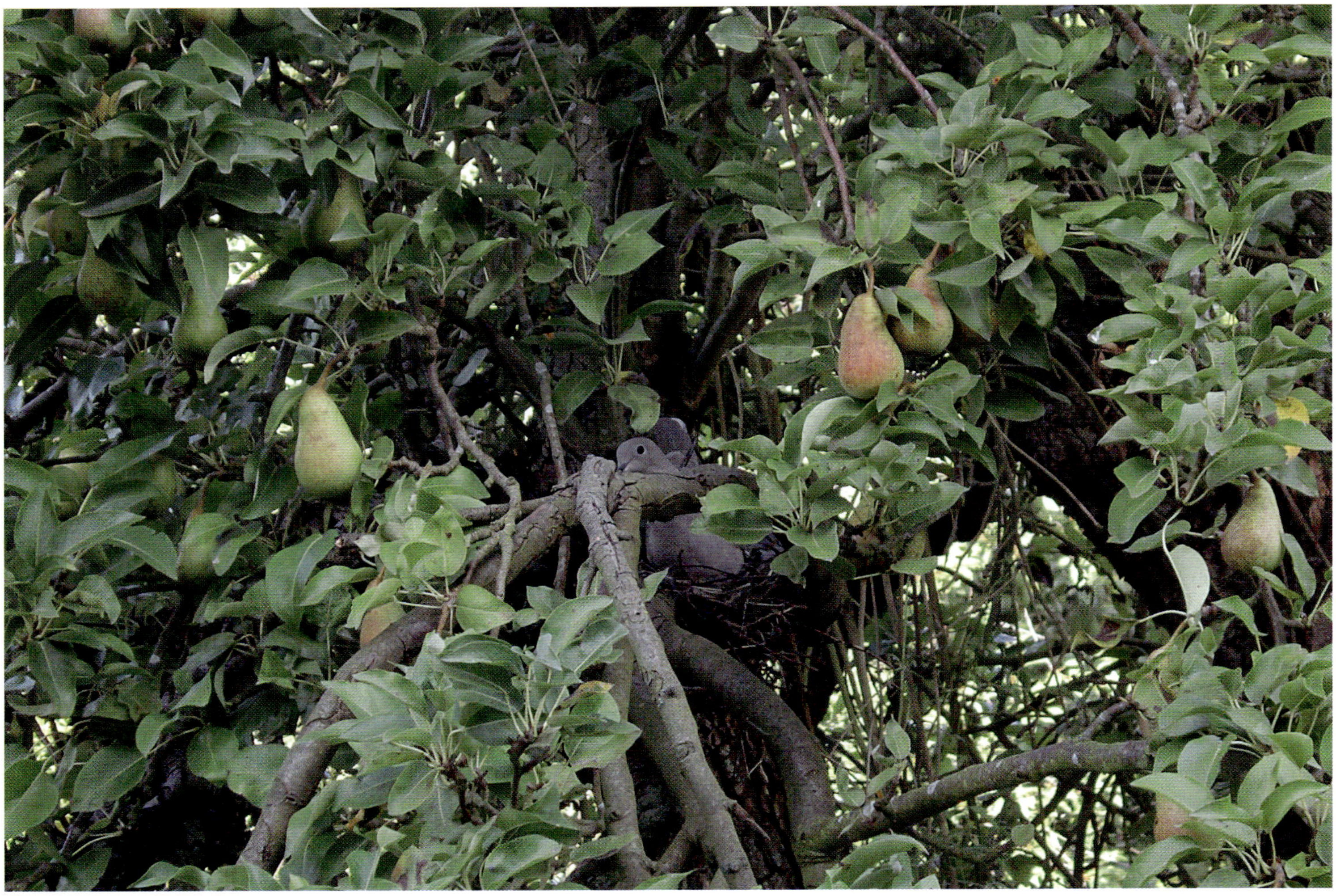

The virtues of olden tyme that inspired the flowers in Celia Thaxter's gardens of Appledore were embodied in the keeping of doves and hens. Not only was there the spiritual symbolism of doves and the romance of their billing and cooing, but their lives are exemplars for family life – they mate for life, share the incubation of the eggs and feeding of the young. Not a partridge in a pear tree but a turtle dove nestled in a Williams pear tree awaiting food from her mate.

Jekyll was much more down to earth when it came to her cats. In Home and Garden *she devotes a chapter to 'The Home Pussies', she was never without four or five cats who had the freedom to roam her fifteen acres and beyond. Rolling in catmint is supposed to have the same effect on cats as cannabis has on humans. Whatever the truth, cats adore catmint and will rapidly flatten any plants in the garden. Jekyll entitled this 'Tabby in the catmint "This smells good"'. The gentle lavender purple of catmint flowers set against their glaucous grey green leaves makes an attractive edging – if it can survive the cats. Her photograph of Tabby perfectly captures the anticipation of a feline high in the catmint, whilst her charming sketch of Blackie the cat depicts his physical weaving in excitement at the preliminary scent of the catmint.*

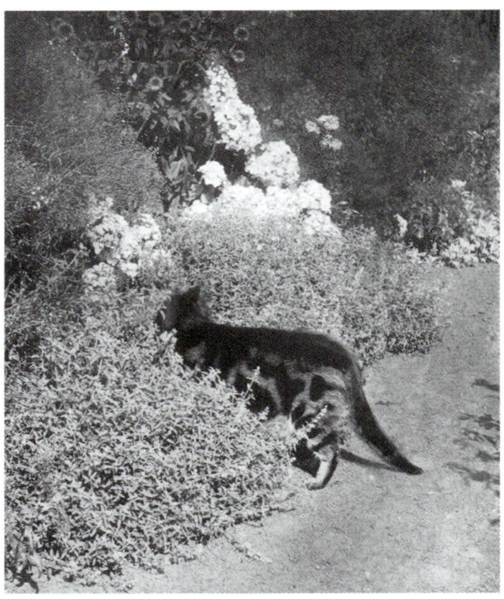

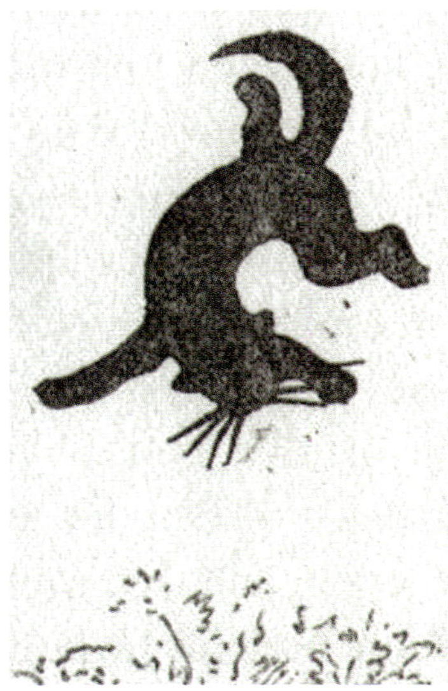

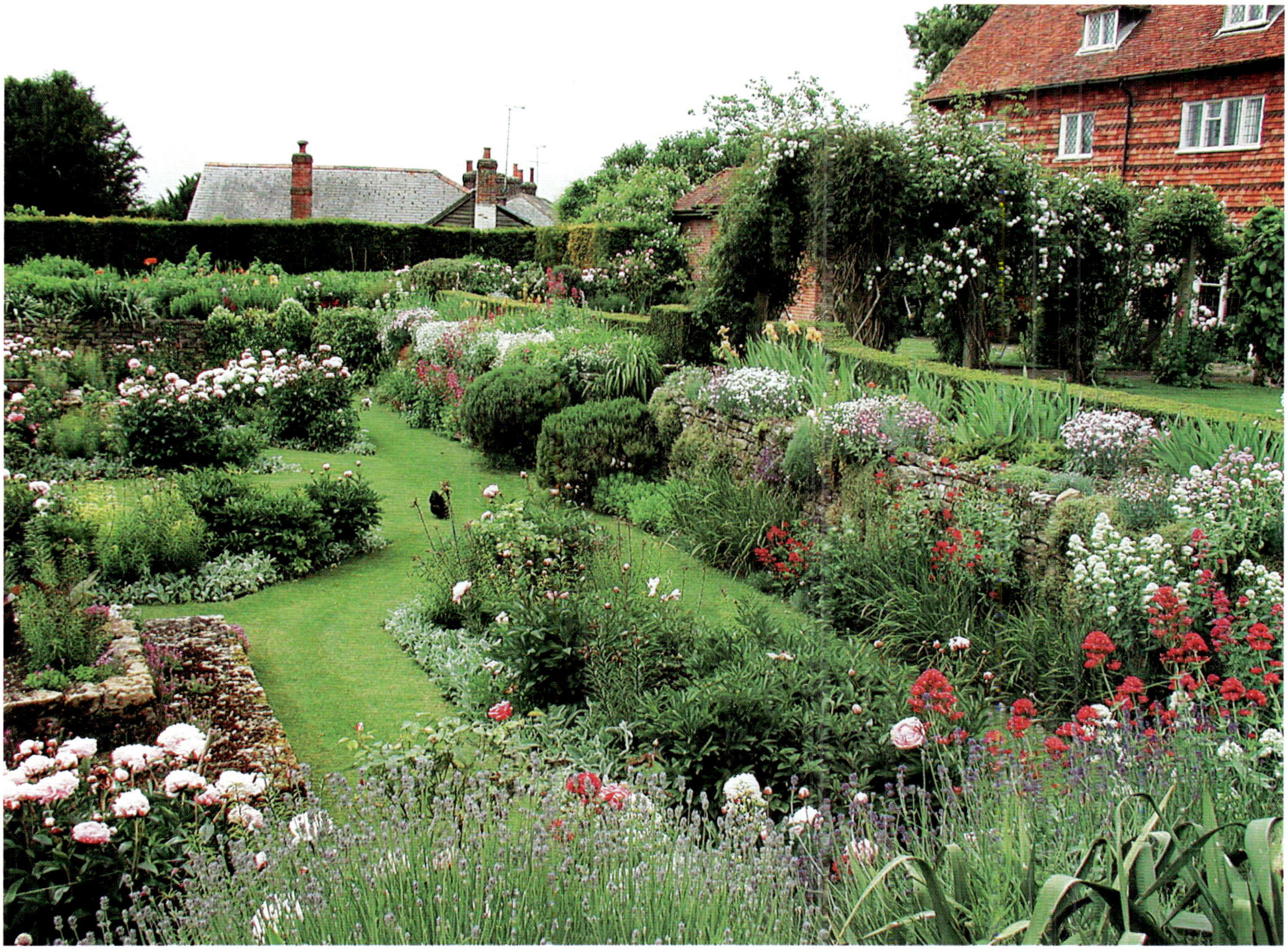

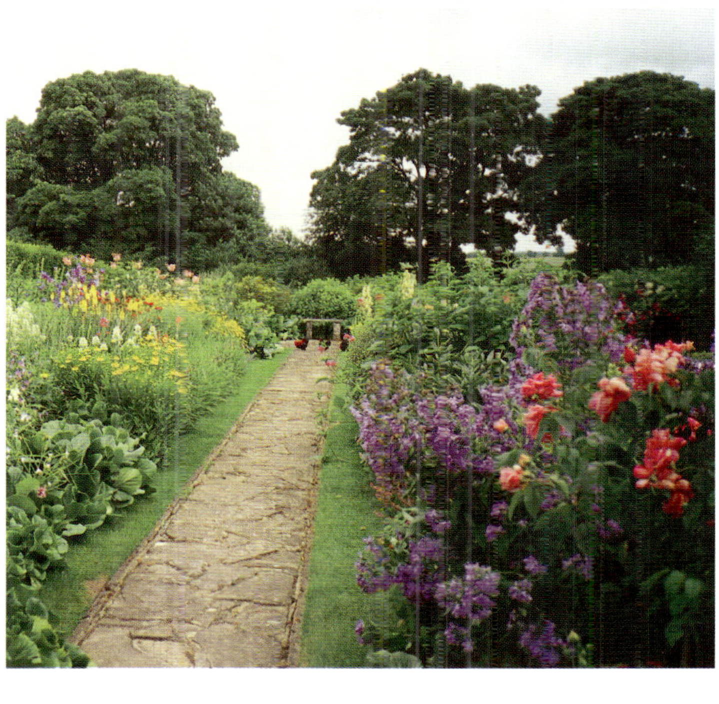

In England, John and Ros Wallinger have perfectly restored the gardens of The Manor Upton Grey which Gertrude Jekyll designed for Charles Holme, the editor and founder of The Studio magazine. Today bantam hens wander freely through the gardens: one can be seen in the Lily Garden above, whilst the others are elegantly strolling down the west facing herbaceous borders – note the drifts of colour. I am sure Jekyll would have been delighted to see the free-range bantams although her cats might have represented a danger. A pergola frames the view as one steps down from the house terrace. The instruction to 'never have a slope where you can have steps and a wall' is perfectly illustrated at The Manor Upton Grey.

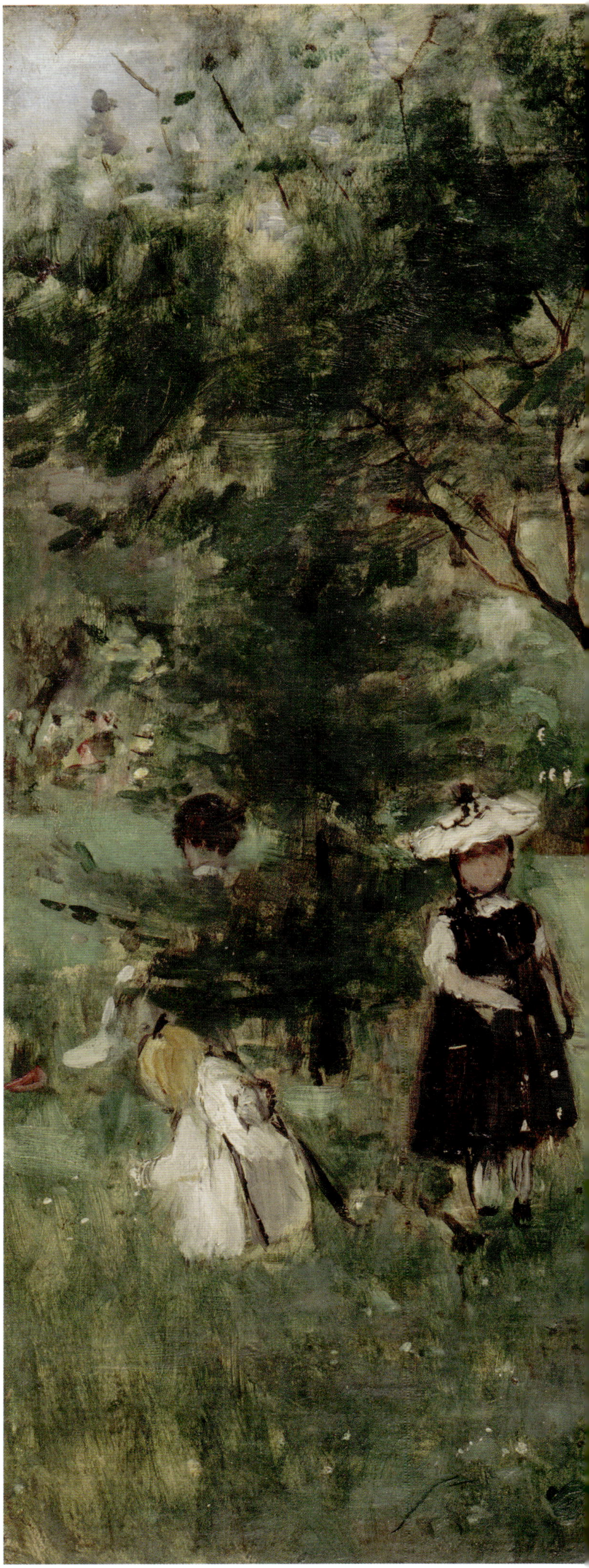

Berthe Morisot, **The Butterfly Hunt** *(La chasse aux papillons).*
Oil on canvas, 46cm x 56cm (18½ x 22½in.), 1874

Executed some fifteen years earlier than Streeton's Butterflies and Blossoms *(see page 152), Berthe Morisot's* The Butterfly Hunt *has a much darker suggestion. The two children watch their rather disengaged mother as they follow the patterns of the butterflies fluttering overhead. Net in hand, you sense that the butterflies represent the freedom sacrificed by the woman caught in the restraining mesh of becoming a mother. The scenario is emphasized by a forked tree that separates the two slightly bewildered children from what ought to be a lighthearted sunny moment with their mother. The models were Morisot's sister Edma, Madame Pontillon, and her two daughters Jeanne and Blanche.*

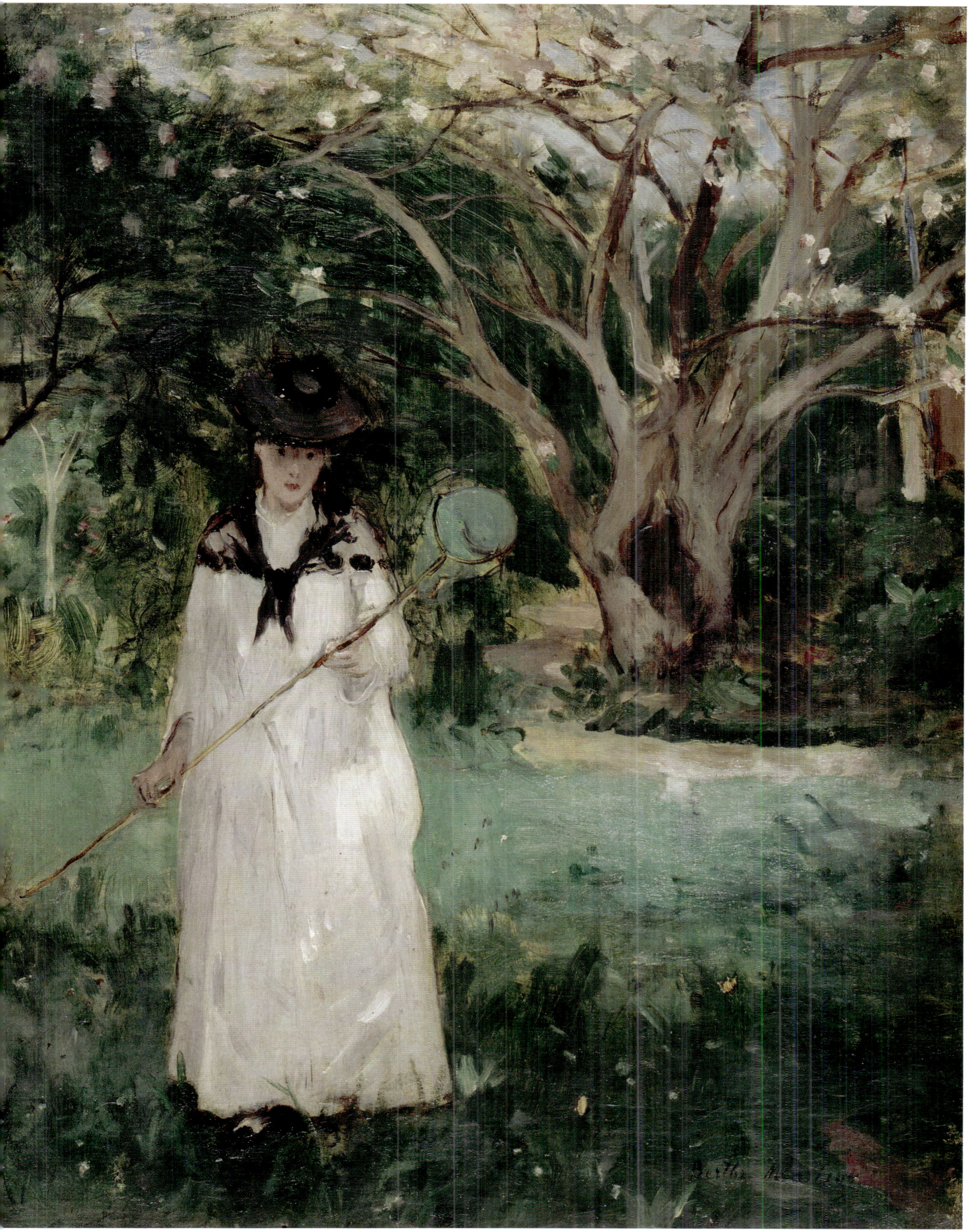

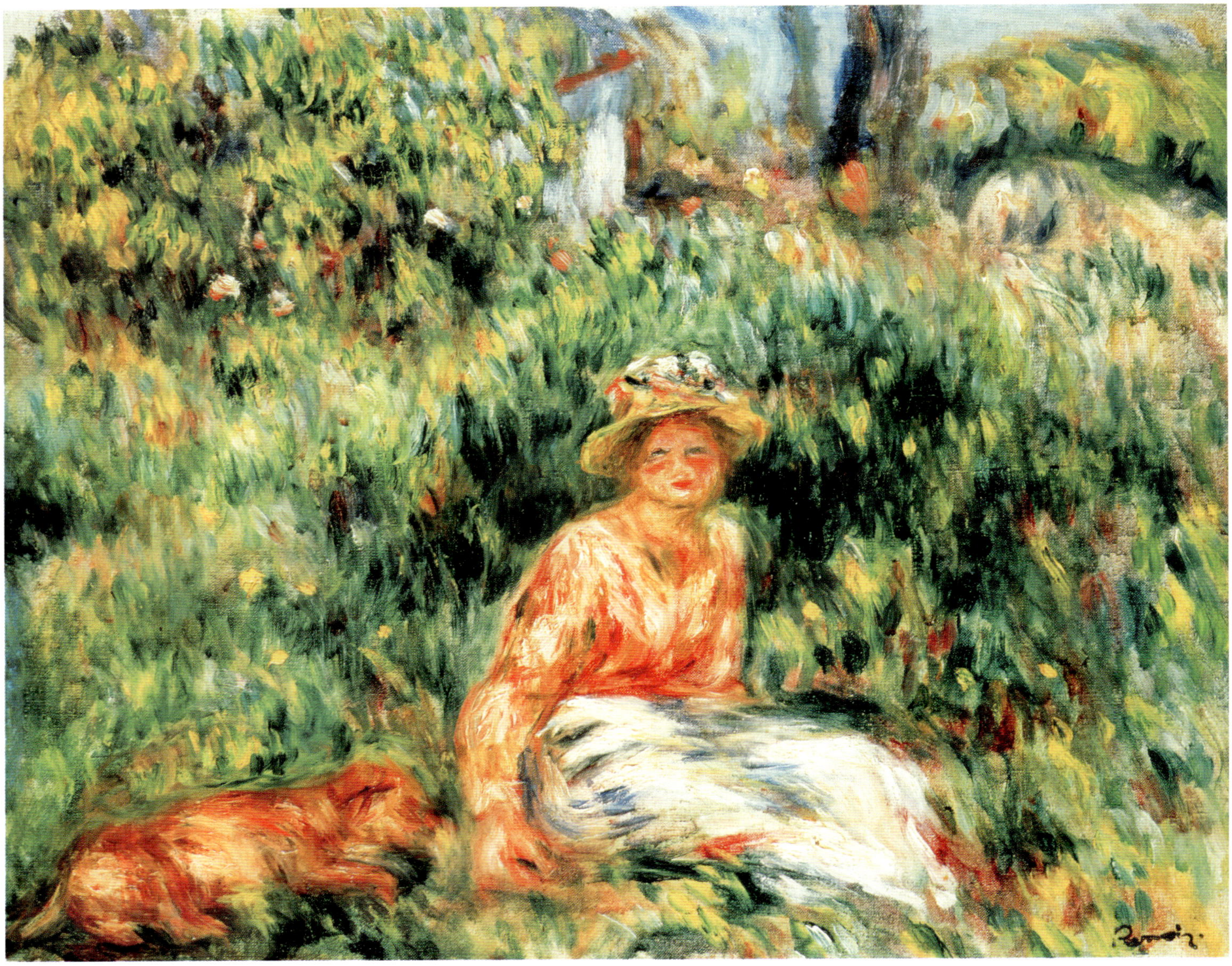

Pierre-Auguste Renoir, **Young Woman in a Garden**. *Oil on canvas, c.1916*

Renoir's youngest son, Coco, was a young boy when they moved to Les Collettes and he had all manner of pets over the years. Aline kept goats, hens and rabbits for the table. One of Renoir's last works was painted in the gardens of Les Collettes on a gloriously sunny day, the auburn-haired model matched by the ginger coat of Renoir's family dog ZaZa, both relaxing in the shade of the trees – you know just how hot it is by looking at the dog flaked out. This is Renoir's last model, the lovely red-haired Andrée Heuschling, known as Dédée, who went on to marry Jean Renoir.

Artists around the globe have incorporated domestic animals and birds into their world, and the Impressionists were no different. In America the painter John Twatchman depicted a small fowl owner in *Barnyard*. Unafraid by the clucking, preening and beating wings of the hens, she scatters corn whilst the doves of peace flutter overhead. The Twachtman family donkey was passed on to the Weir children who had a family farm nearby at Branchville. J. Alden Weir painted his youngest daughter, Cora, stroking the donkey's head in *After the Ride* c.1903.

In Australia, McCubbin's youngest child, Kathleen, probably modelled for the girl feeding the chickens in *The Mountain Cottage* in 1915, with Fontainebleau in the background.

Though technically dogs have coats rather than fur, they do make occasional appearances: Pierre Bonnard included one in his 1892 *The Croquet Game*. Knowing what a vicious game this can be, one can only hope that it was keeping a watchful eye on the balls. And in one of his final paintings (above) Renoir captures the 'dog days' of summer as both model and dog languish under the trees.

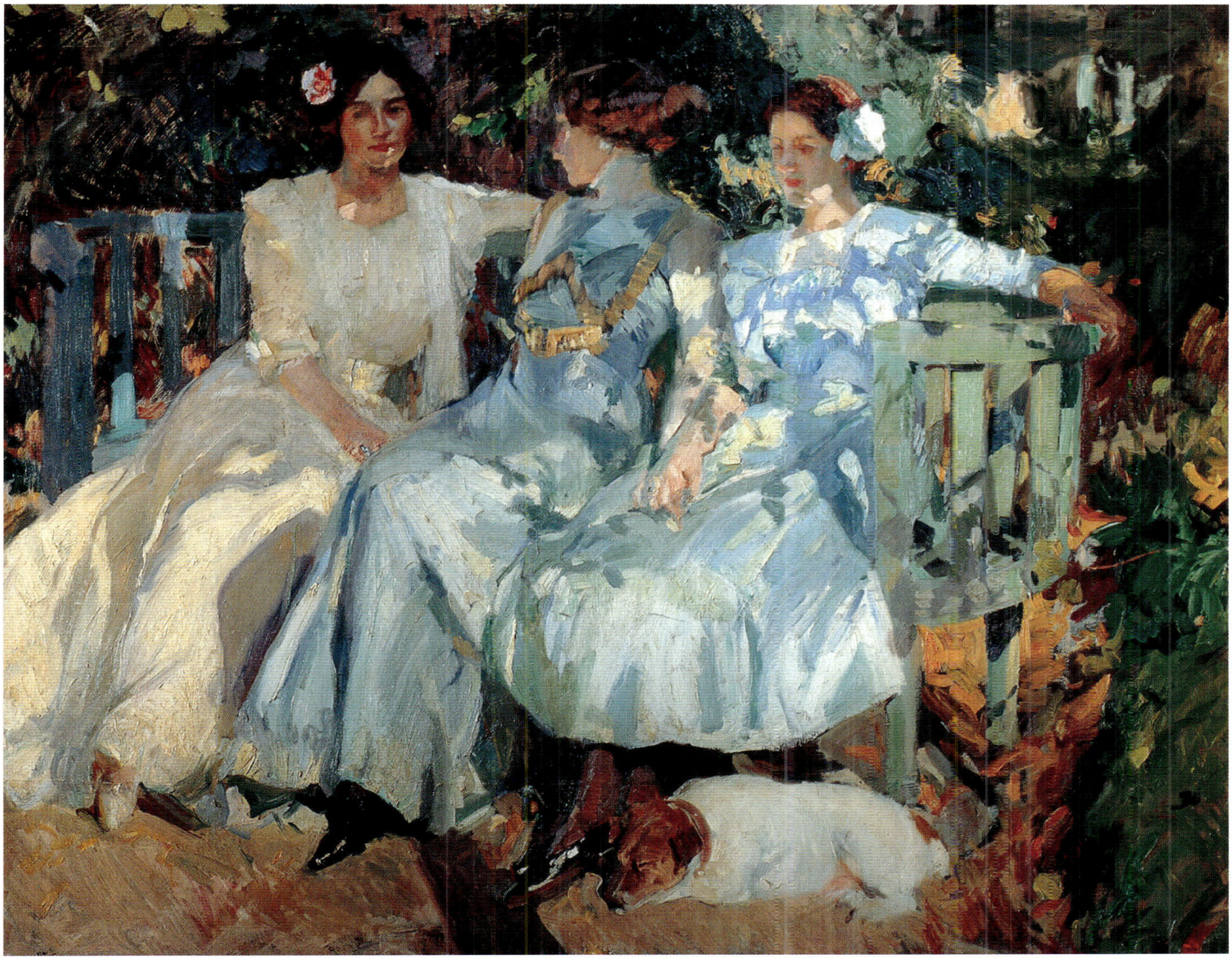

Joaquin Sorolla y Bastida, **My Wife and Daughters in the Garden**. *Oil on canvas, 166 x 206cm (66½ x 82½ in.), 1910*

Sorolla rarely painted portraits, but the warmth of the sun and his love for his family fill this canvas with light and colour. He admired and rivalled Sargent to sensational effect here. The three elegant women in his life are in modern, more relaxed dresses and obviously engaged in pleasant conversation. At their feet lies the family dog, whose separate portrait Sorolla also painted, sun-soaked and snoozing – the picture of canine contentment. Compare how very twentieth century this painting is set alongside Renoir's Young Woman in a Garden, which was, in fact, painted six years later.

Overleaf. *Edouard Manet,* **The Monet Family in Their Garden at Argenteuil**. *Oil on canvas, 61 x 99.7cm (24 x 39¼ in.), 1874*

Though children and fowl can have a deleterious effect on a showcase garden, both can be accommodated to create a scene of contented domesticity. Hens feature in many Impressionist paintings: starting with Camille and Jean sharing the garden at Argenteuil with Monet hard at work gardening and a few hens scratching around. In the 1870s Manet and Renoir both painted Monet in his delightful gardens at 2, Rue Pierre Gienne in Argenteuil. Monet had made new friendships and received several commisions through the patronage of the wealthy industrialist Ernest Hoschedé and his wife, Alice, at Chateau de Rottembourg at Montgeron. The Rottembourg gardens were extensive and formal, and Monet painted the family, the house and the gardens, including their free-range turkeys, in a park-like setting. Manet painted this happy domestic scene during 1874, the year that he and his fellow artists adopted the name Impressionists. Monet is gardening, whilst Camille has Jean sprawled against her. In the background is the rose and dahlia bed that features in so many of Monet's own paintings, whilst in the foreground two hens wander about contentedly.

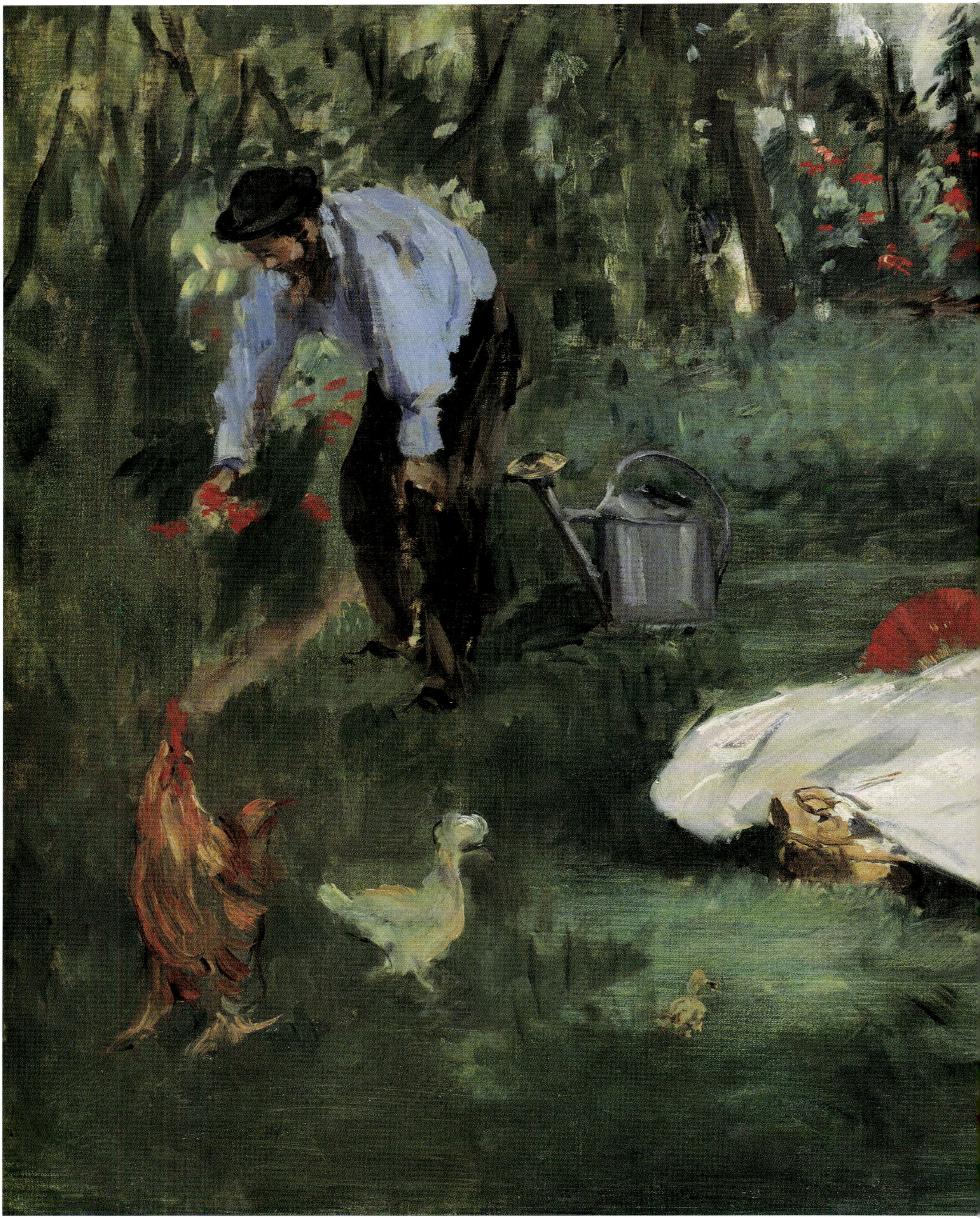

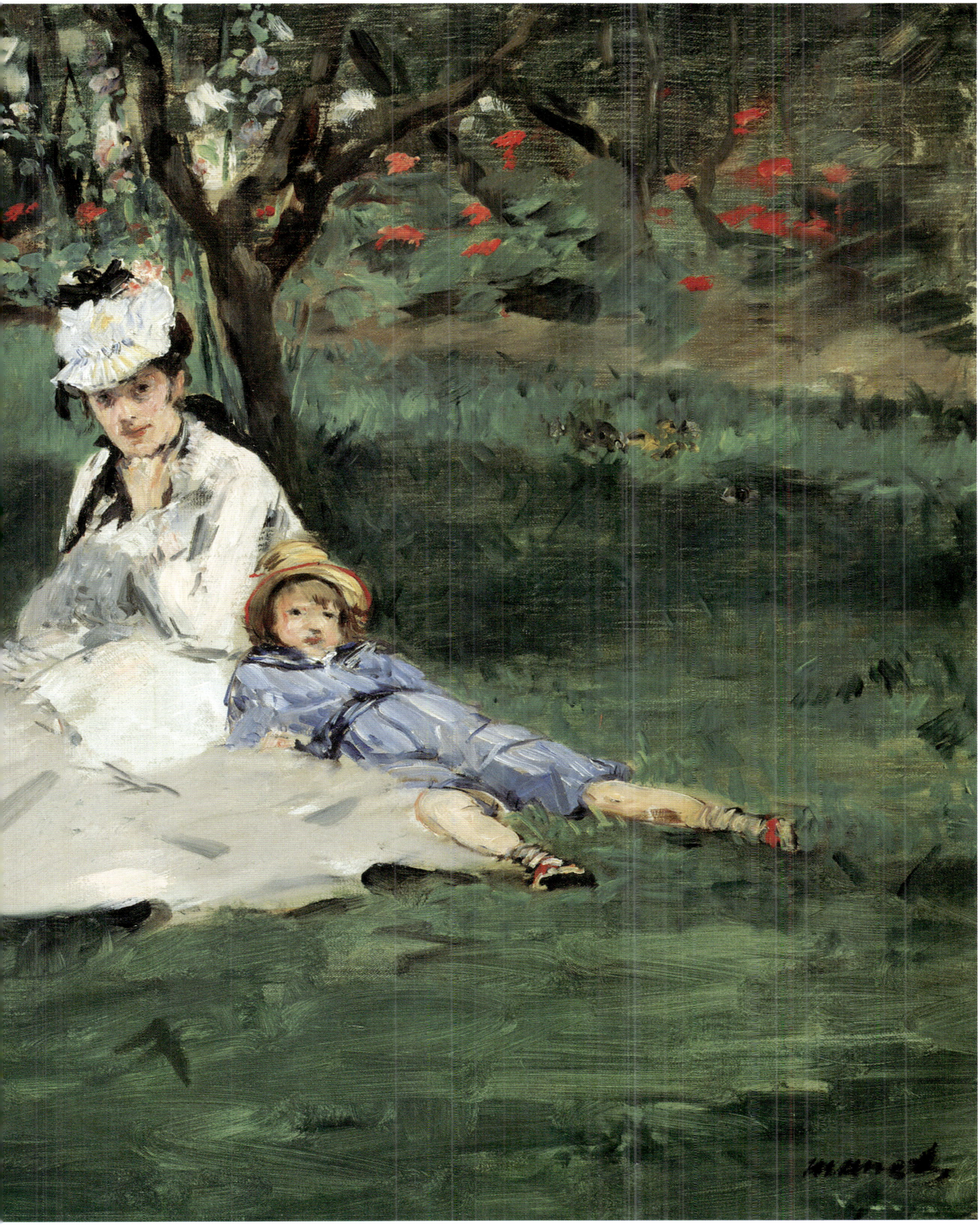
manet

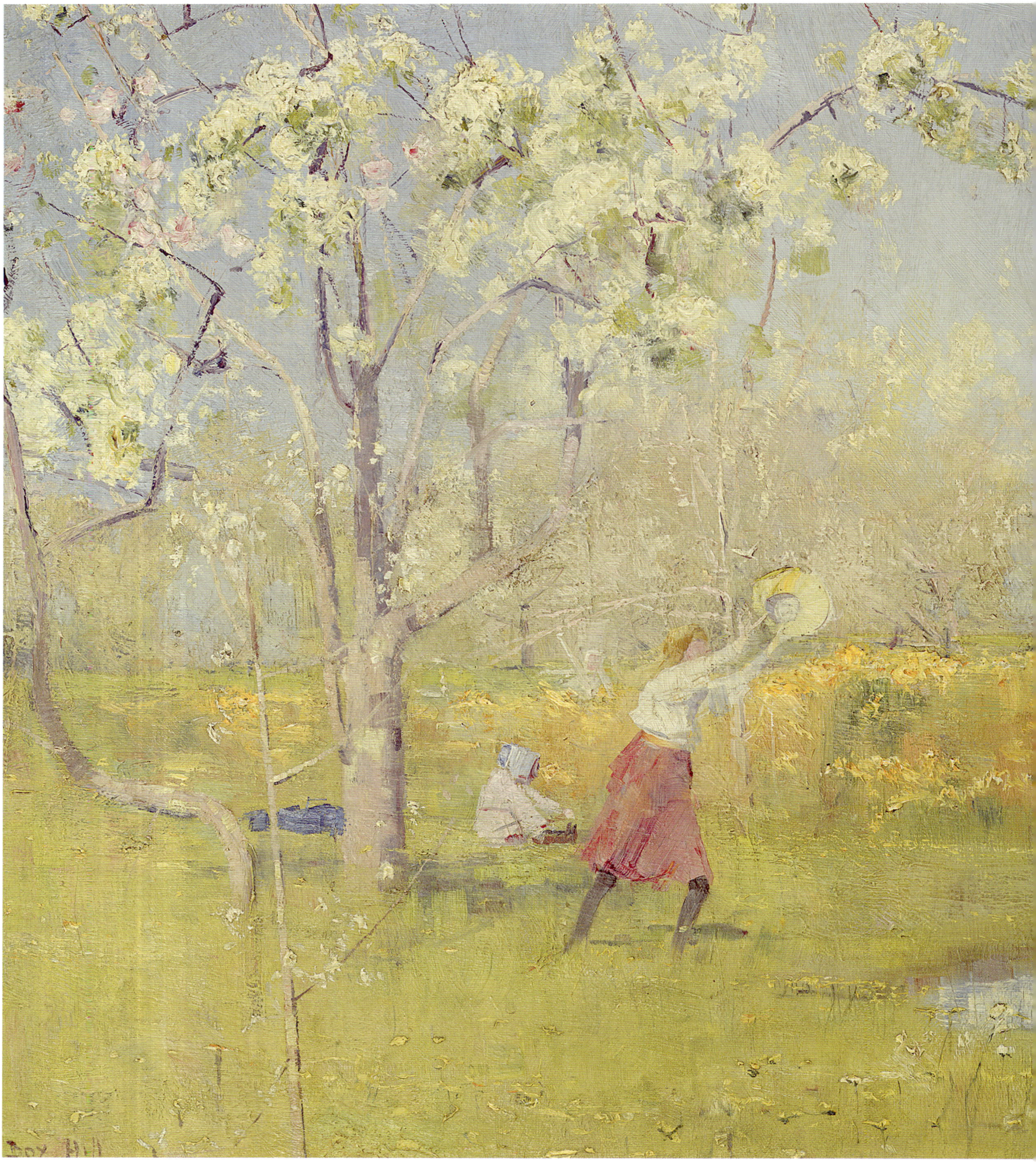

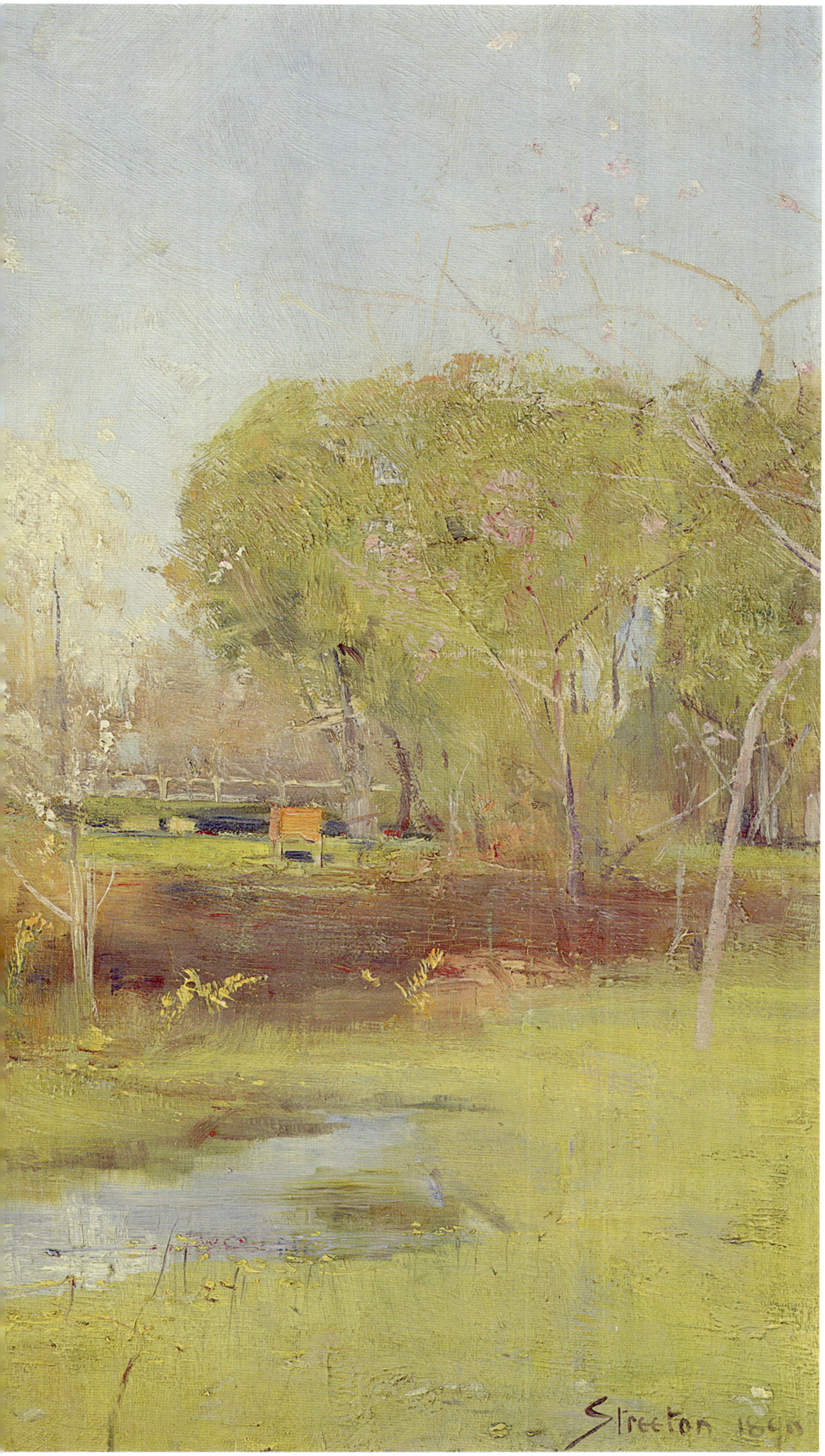

Arthur Streeton, **Butterflies and Blossoms**. *Oil on canvas on composition board, 45.5 x 56cm (18¼ x 26½ in.), 1889 (dated 1890)*

The delicate fluttering of butterflies encapsulates the essence of Impressionist fleeting sensations in their colourful movements. The light is gloriously bright and warm in Arthur Streeton's Butterflies and Blossoms *as the children scamper under the trees and the blossoms are scattered by the breeze. The nearby pond must have given succour to the richly blossoming tree, and spring is in the air in every sense as the young girl leaps about, waving her hat after butterflies. Streeton 'Smike' painted this in 1889 and it encapsulates John McDonald's comments in his magisterial* Art of Australia*: 'impressionable and energetic ... dazzling views of Australian countryside ... displays a joie de vivre that has never been equalled in Australian Art.'*

CHAPTER SIX

Australian Impressions

Frederick McCubbin and Fontainebleau, Mount Macedon

How could he, or I, or anyone, from glances snatched in a fleeting passage, hope to divine what is real, what is fundamental in the character of this young nation? I have caught impressions – mere impressions – just as a bird would skimming over a forest – but what could that bird learn of the life and spirit underneath?

Mark Twain, 1896

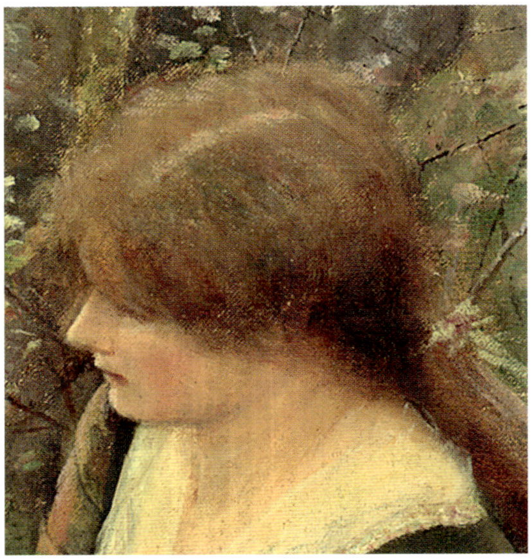

Frederick McCubbin, **Autumn Memories**. *Oil on canvas, 123 x 153.3cm (49¼ x 61⅜in.), 1899*

Frederick McCubbin's Irish wife Annie modelled for Autumn Memories, *her auburn hair and heavy green mantle echoing both her ancestry and the season. Fred and Annie's parents were first generation immigrants to Australia and the misty, mellow fruitfulness of the painting echoes childhood reminiscences of the 'old country'. The gulf between the perception of 'home' between parents and their Australian-born children is encapsulated in the opening lines of Dorothy McKellar's 'My Country' written in 1904:*

The love of field and coppice,
Of green and shaded lanes,
Of ordered woods and gardens
Is running in your veins.
Strong love of grey-blue distance,
Brown streams and soft, dim skies -
I know but cannot share it,
My love is otherwise.

Botany Bay was named by Captain Cook and Joseph Banks in delighted recognition of the rich flora they found on the east coast of Australia in April 1770. Until his death in 1820, the great botanist Banks, acting as first (unpaid) Director of Kew Gardens, established an international clearing house and repository for botanical knowledge, plants and seeds which superseded the physic garden. After a twenty year decline, William Hooker, was appointed (paid) Director and the Royal Botanical Gardens, Kew was once more at the forefront of a worldwide network of botanic gardens. Banks had returned with 30,000 plant specimens aptly pressed between proof sheets of Addison's commentary on *Paradise Lost*. They included 2,000 species of which 1,400 were previously unknown. A young Quaker, Sydney Parkinson, was one of the expedition artists who had to draw through the night in order to record all that was found. His first impression of Australia was that '... the country looked very pleasant and fertile; and the trees, quite free from underwood, appeared like plantations in a gentleman's park'. His naturalistic accompanying landscapes predate the French artists of the École 1830 who painted in the forest of Fontainebleau around Barbizon and had such a profound influence on Impressionism, and also in the naming of Frederick McCubbin's home on Mount Macedon as Fontainebleau in 1901.

Although there was much celebration during Australia's Centenary of Settlement in 1888, there was also a dawning realization that British and European influence also held dominion over art and garden. The gardeners at Kew might grow Australian plants with enthusiasm, but in general the British Empire expressed itself with the English rose garden and the Victorian bedding scheme wherever the globe was painted pink.

What a contrast to the intimiste paintings of dappled light and gnarled bark in the French forests around Barbizon and Fontainebleau by Jean-Baptiste Camille Corot and Jean Francois Millet which were exhibited at the Centennial Exhibition.

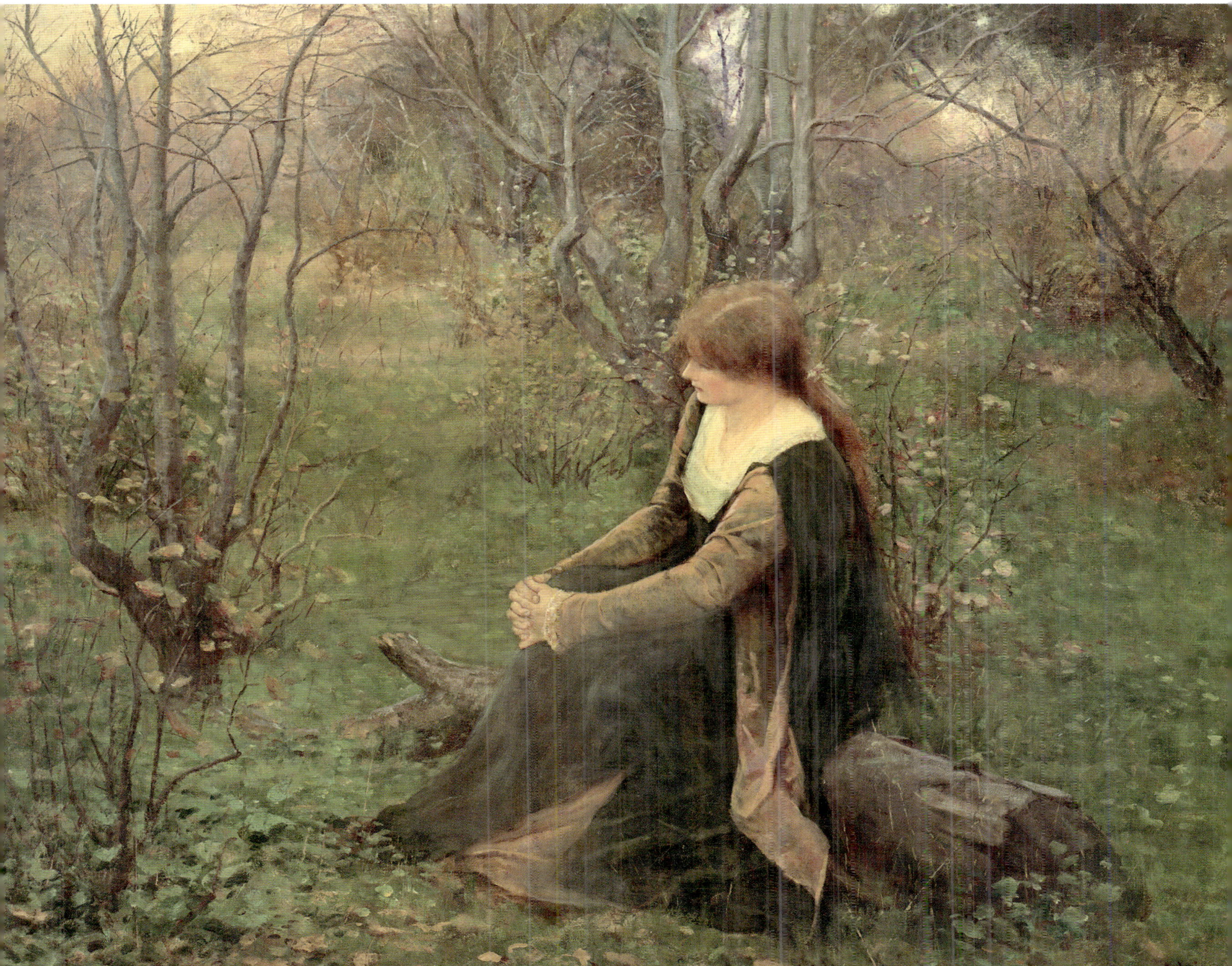

Australia's indigenous forest still survives, in the late nineteenth century it started where towns petered out. The Heidelberg School could access it by train, followed by a short walk, they were the first to revel in it as an artistic expression of their national identity. In the early twentieth century McCubbin bought a car so that he could track the wilderness as it retreated from the increasing urban and industrial sprawl. At a glance the silver foliage could be that of the Mediterranean's ancient olives.

In and around Melbourne a small group of artists started to develop a form of impressionism that was informal, evocative and naturalistic evolving into a nationalistic style, revelling in the searing colours of the Australian landscape. They colonized the still untamed districts of Box Hill, Templestowe, and Heidelberg, the seaside suburbs of Mentone and Sandringham giving rise to their name the Heidelberg School. Their key members were Tom Roberts, Arthur Streeton, Frederick McCubbin and Charles Conder and their art evolved into sundrenched and bold impressionist narratives. The enclosure of a wall, hedge or picket fence naturally suggests a garden, but at Box Hill the group enclosed their landscape vision by building up a familiarity with nature and concentrating on close-focus views so that they could appreciate the transition of tones on plants. Australian plants such as blue gum, wattle and the extraordinary almost metallic gleam of drought-hardened grasses such as the gum sapling became the motif for the Heidelberg School.

Another important member of the Melbourne group of artists was Portuguese-born Arthur Loureiro. He had studied in Lisbon, Madrid, Florence and Rome, painted and exhibited in Paris, he then moved with his wife and son to live at Brolles on the edge of the Fontainebleau Forest before deciding to chose the bright sky, the warm sun and the pure Australian air 'in which we breathe champagne.' He arrived in Melbourne in 1885, and in 1886 was a founder member of the Australian Artists' Association and exhibited at the Centennial Exhibition.

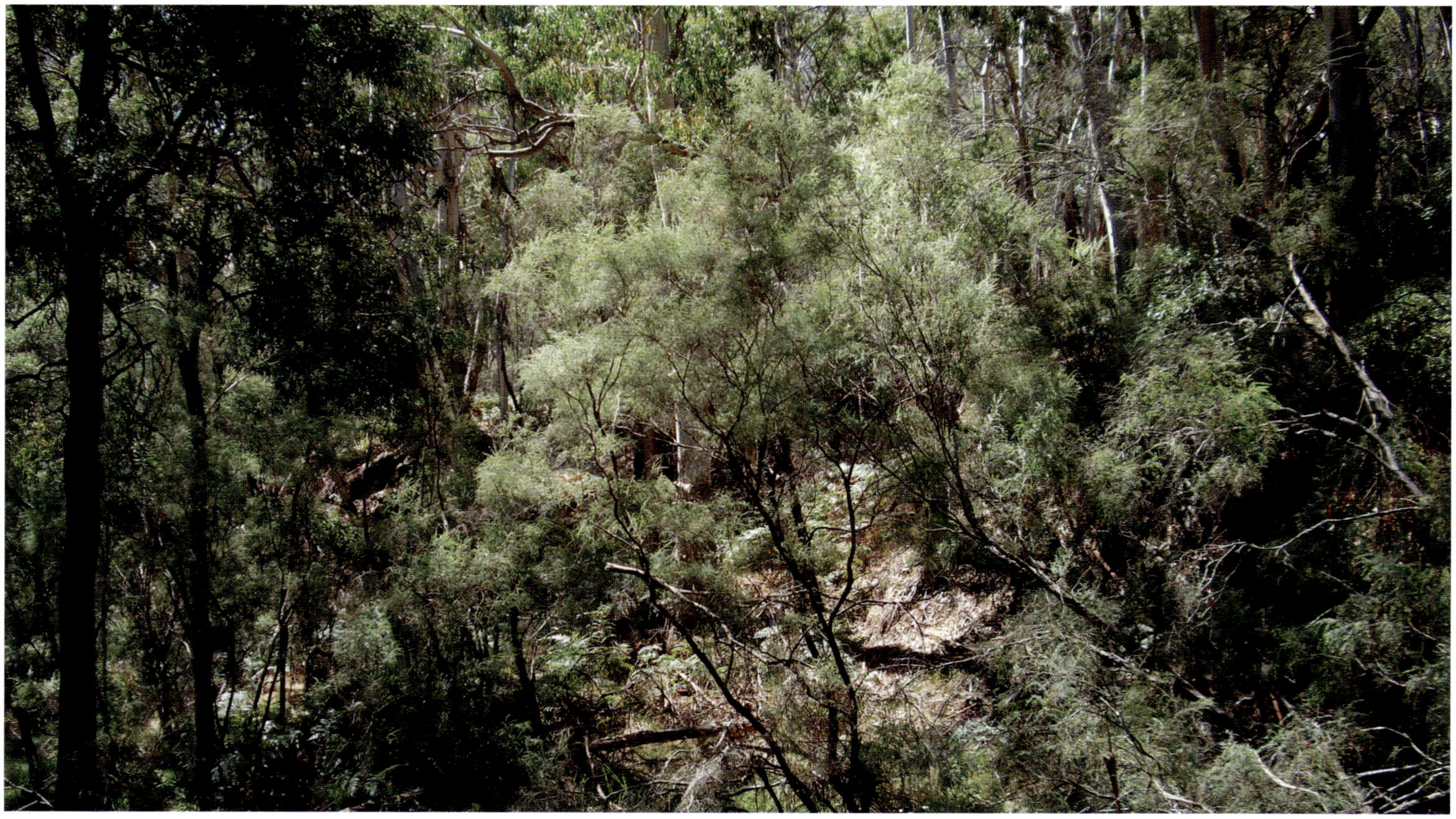

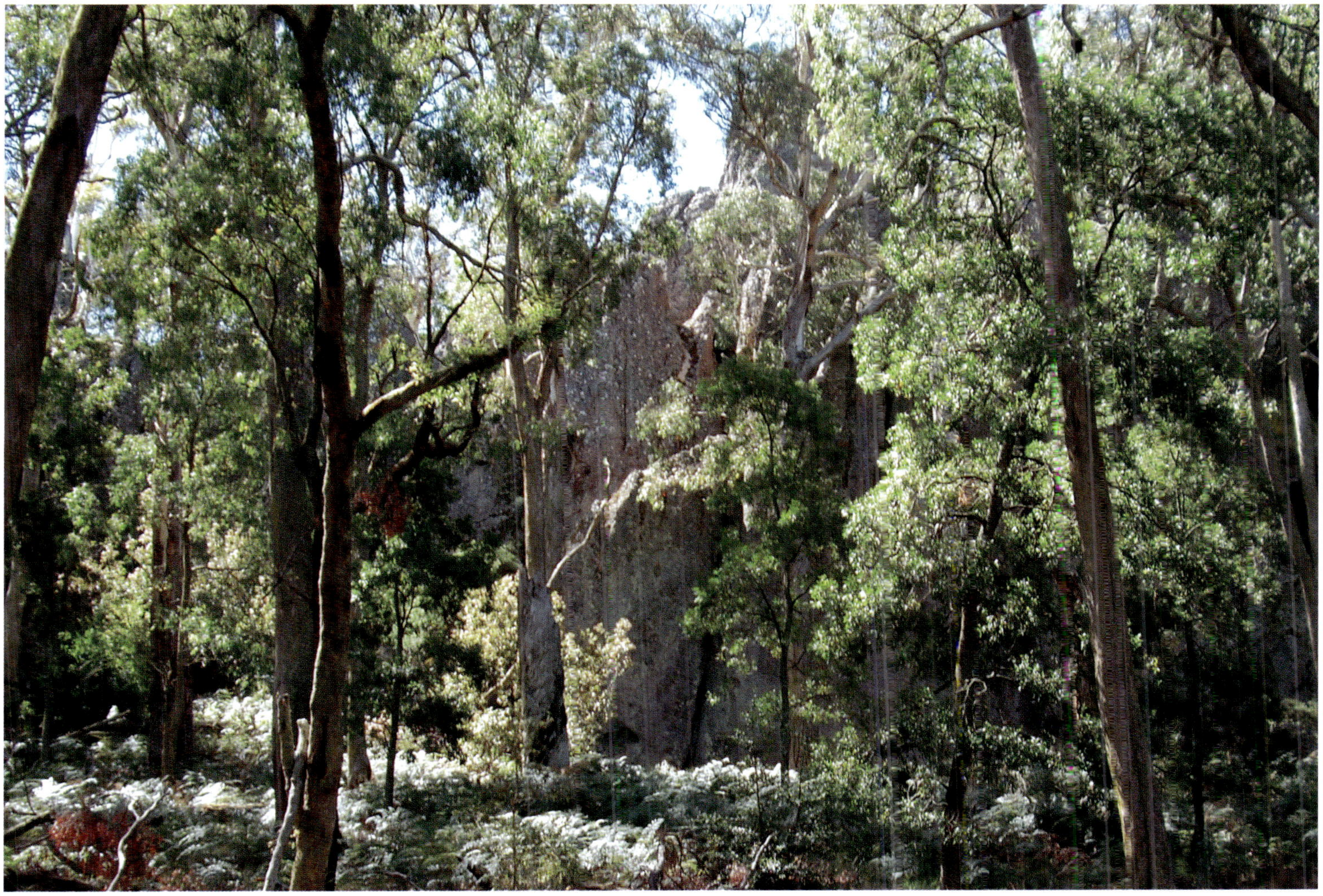

The painterly sensations of shimmering golds in the light, and in the flowers and leaves of gardens followed the less artistic dash for real gold around Melbourne in the mid-nineteenth century. By 1888 entrepreneurship and sheer hard work had created this vibrant city and its smartly landscaped hill station of nearby Mount Macedon, but some of its citizens sought a more nationalistic expression of Australia's Centenary of Settlement. In the next decade this opinion gathered momentum as the Federation of States was established in 1901.

Australian artists looked to Swiss-born Louis Buvelot who had painted in Paris and Brazil before arriving in Melbourne in February 1865. He had been awarded a silver medal at The World's Fair Centennial International Exhibition of 1876 in Philadelphia. Buvelot taught several members of the Heidelberg School, who were heavily influenced by his French-like naturalism that also expressed a romantic vision of God in nature. In reality his depictions of the sublime untamed wilderness and rural idyll could still be found a mere train ride from the city.

Frederick McCubbin was always known to his students as 'Prof'. His father was a baker and in 1855 Fred went into the family business, but knowing he liked painting his father apprenticed him to a coach painter. Although repetitious and boring, like Renoir's early experience as a ceramic painter, McCubbin came to admire the skill required.

The eponymous Hanging Rock is only a few miles from Fontainebleau and was painted by McCubbin starkly jutting out from the bush. Joan Lindsay was one of McCubbin's talented pupils who, nearly sixty years later, stirred up an impressionistic stew of fact and fiction in 1967 when she wrote the novel Picnic at Hanging Rock. *Lindsay also wrote '… most of the interesting and intelligent people in Melbourne came to partake of Mrs McCubbin's delicious soups and unconventional salads… Mr McCubbin was a magnet who drew towards him the finest and the best.'*

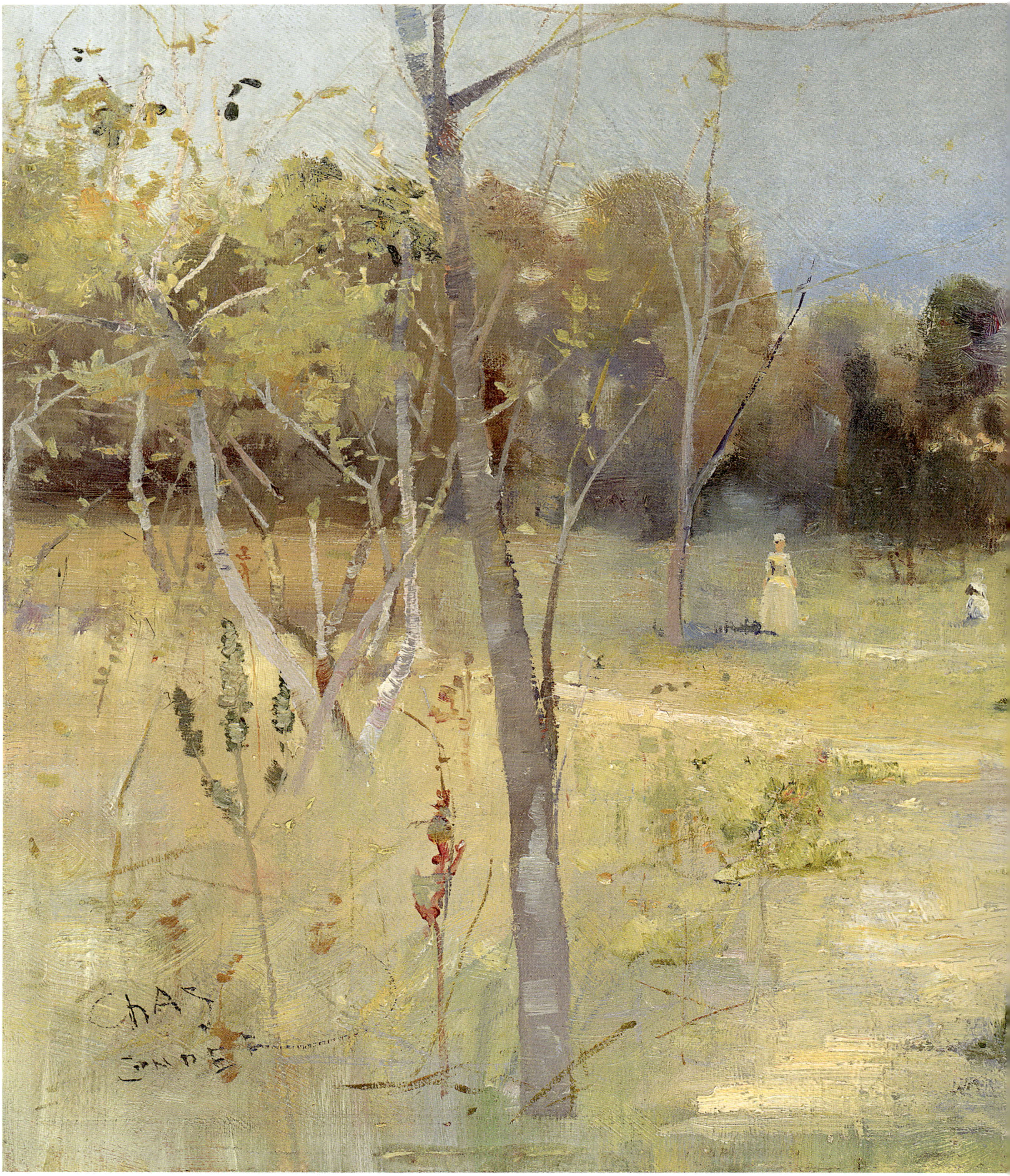

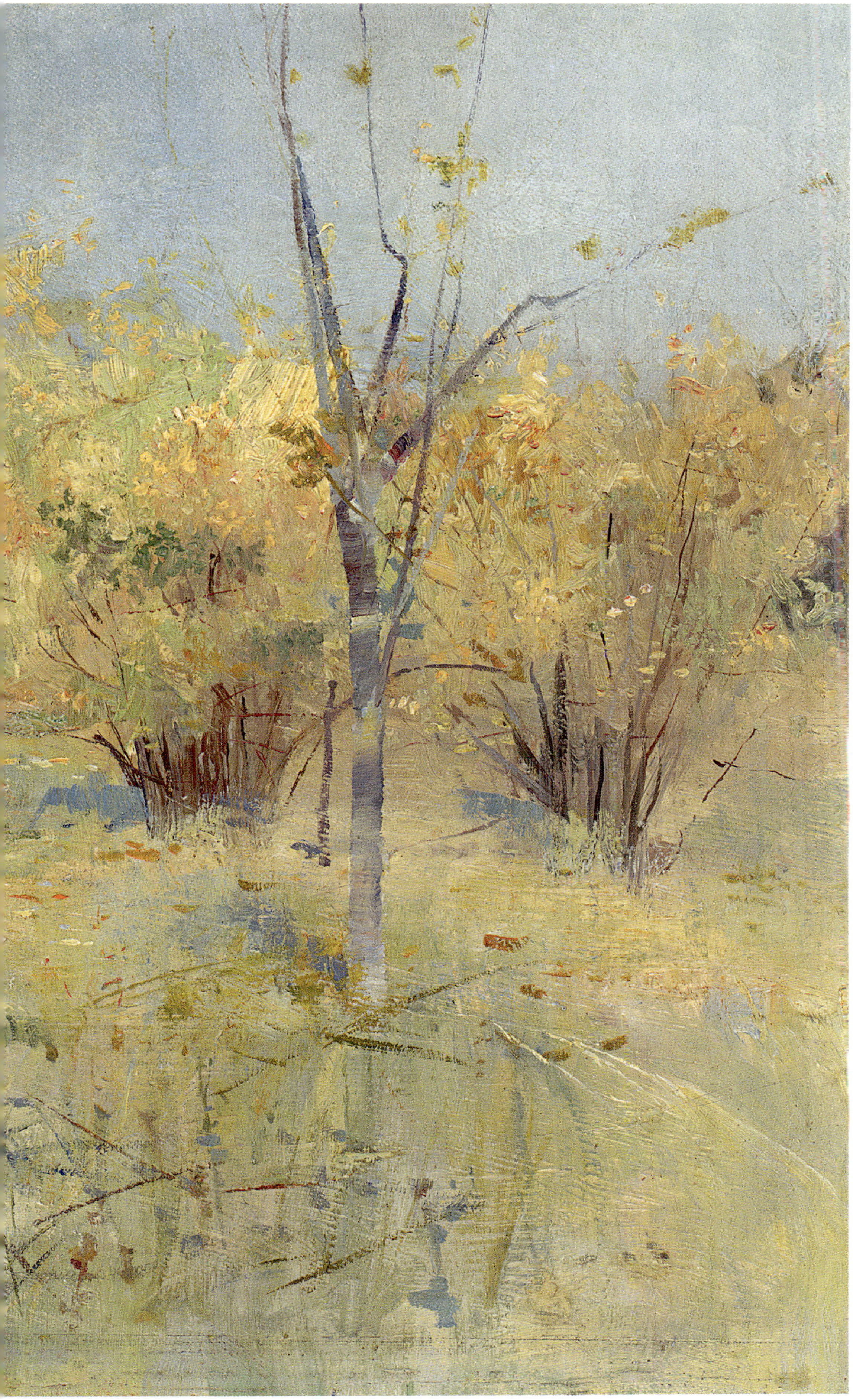

Charles Conder, **Summer Idyll***.*
Oil on canvas, 30.6 x 45.6cm
(12⅛ x 18⅛in.), 1889

The bone-dry orchard at Box Hill, near Melbourne, painted in 1889. Although most of his painting life was spent in France, Conder retained golden memories of his time with McCubbin, Roberts and Streeton from 1884-90. The searing colours echo in the verses in Dorothea McKellar's My Country.

I love a sunburnt country,
A land of sweeping plains,
Of rugged mountain ranges,
Of droughts and flooding rains.
I love her far horizons,
I love her jewel-sea,
Her beauty and her terror –
The wide brown land for me!

The stark white ring-barked forests,
All tragic to the moon,
The sapphire-misted mountains,
The hot gold hush of noon,
Green tangle of the brushes
Where lithe lianas coil,
And orchids deck the tree-tops,
And ferns the warm dark soil.

Core of my heart, my country!
Her pitiless blue sky,
When, sick at heart, around us
We see the cattle die –
But then the grey clouds gather,
And we can bless again
The drumming of an army,
The steady soaking rain.

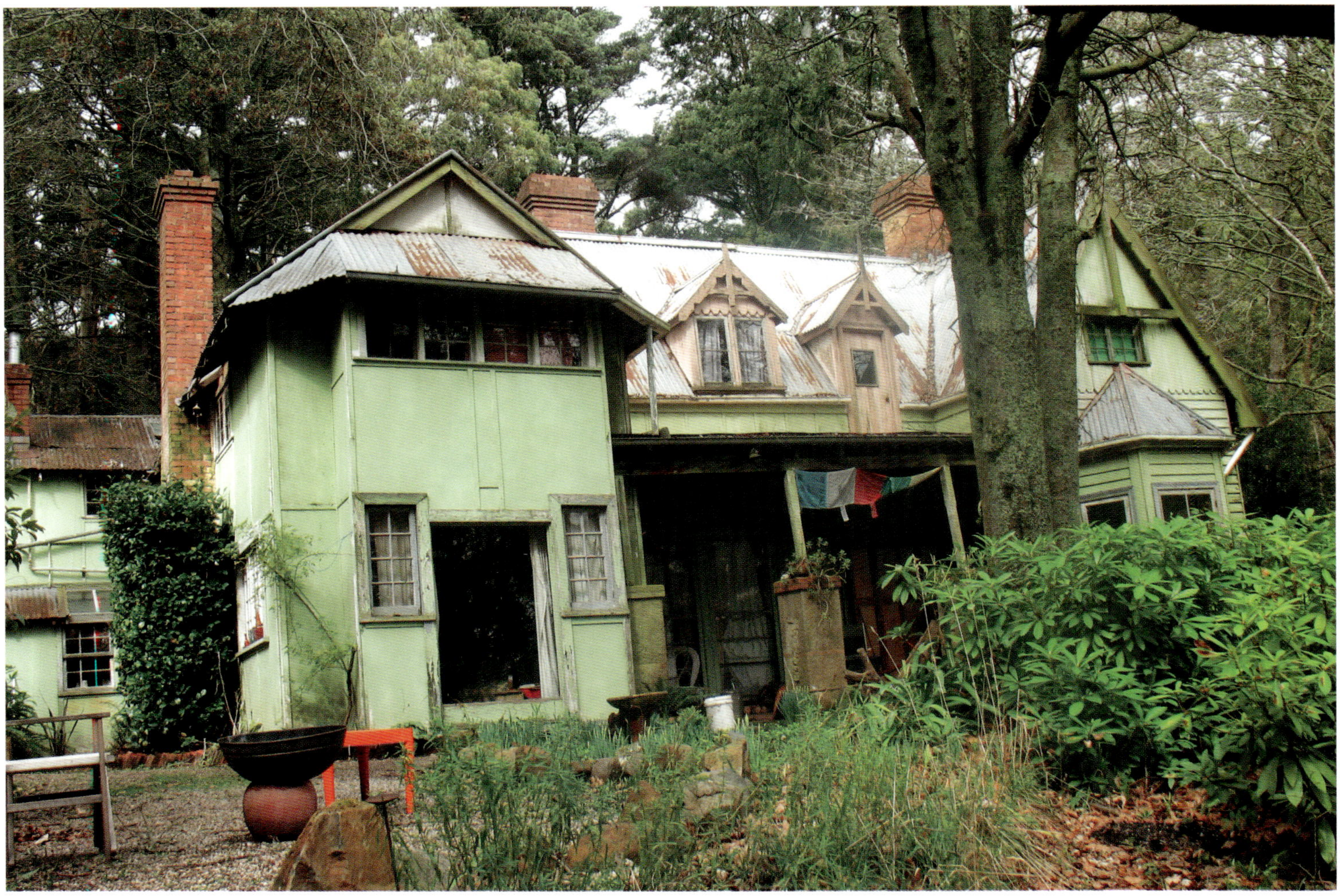

Fontainebleau in 2009. The McCubbin's house may look dilapidated but it is a miraculous survivor of early twentieth-century Edwardian Australian architecture, as Mount Macedon was razed by bush fires that destroyed many properties. In its heyday great names such as Nellie Melba and Ellen Terry were entertained here, the former being a frightening presence. Rupert Bunny painted her dramatic portrait whilst they were both in London.

He studied art in the evening, from 1867-70 attending the Artisan's School of Design in Carlton where he met Louis Abrahams and Charles Douglas Richardson. In 1871 he enrolled at the National Gallery Art School as a student for the following fifteen years until he became one of its masters. He worked there until his death in 1917. Inspired by the intimate sense of landscape in the work of Buvelot, Tom Roberts and McCubbin undertook *plein air* painting. McCubbin recorded: 'Roberts and I had an immense reverence for the work he [Buvelot] did but we had not a chance of knowing him, he perhaps being the only man at that time who could give us a hint of all the beauties that were under our very eyes ... But most of us owe it to him that slowly we were able to see the paintable qualities of that which lay immediately around us. The exquisite beauty of our lovely skies, the glorious colour and form of our green trees.' McCubbin later stated: 'I painted I think the first picture that was ever painted in this part of the world entirely out-of-doors.'

In 1885 he took the train with Roberts 'Bulldog' and Abrahams 'Don' just fourteen kilometres out of Melbourne to Box Hill, on the first of many excursions to paint the sensation of Australian light in its natural surroundings. Later they were joined by Streeton 'Smike' who reported that he had worked 'in a kind of intoxication with Shelley in his mind' as he completed *The Purple Noon's Transparent Might* during a heat wave

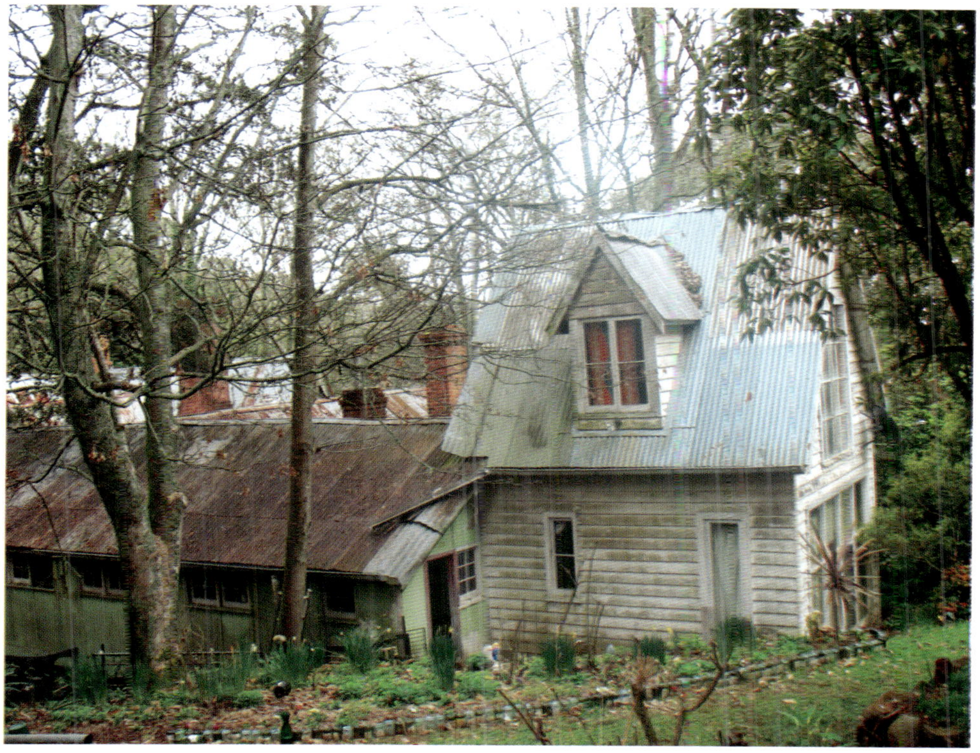

The chalet additions to Fontainebleau and tents in the gardens were used by the Prof's numerous students for whom the property provided food, shelter, guidance, inspiration and a generally good time. Unlike Giverny and Les Collettes the gardens were not a source of subjects, but a setting for sociability. McCubbin and visiting artists painted in the surrounding bush or the old trout hatchery at Lake Strathmore on the adjoining property of 'Ard Choiile' that was the setting for his painting Afterglow *(see page 24).*

in just two days. Heading back from a painting expedition at Templestowe en route for Heidelberg station in 1888 Streeton met Miss Janet Davies, a friend from the Gallery School, and her husband-to-be David Davies who co-owned the nearby Mount Eagle Estate. Apparently then and there Davies offered Streeton 'artistic possession' of the semi-derelict property with extensive grounds and a pine plantation. The estate had been developed thirty years earlier by the Member of Parliament John Henry Brooke who had planned to build a mansion on the summit of the hill and had landscaped the grounds and planted an English-style garden. His fortunes proved to be rather more modest so he built a weatherboard house of eight rooms which had declined into dilapidation. Streeton renamed it Eaglemont and Roberts and Conder rapidly joined him there, but McCubbin declined.

During the 1890's the combination of teaching commitments and an ever increasing family of little Profs kept McCubbin in the Blackburn suburb of Melbourne, however, he was able to borrow Arthur Loureiro's large house and studio in Stawell Street, Kew. In 1895 the McCubbin family moved twelve kilometres south east of Melbourne to bayside Brighton, where their weatherboard house hosted artists such as Roberts and Streeton on their trips from Sydney. McCubbin's painting *Autumn Memories* (see page 155) romantically depicts his wife Annie seated on a log in their orchard with no sign of the little Profs. The fruits and sunshine of December are long since past, but the browns and greens retain a warm earthy hue. Other *plein air* artists regularly came to stay such as Walter Withers, nicknamed The Colonel for his efficient and organized ways, Australian-born David Davies (co-owner of the Mount Eagle estate where Streeton resided) and John Longstaff.

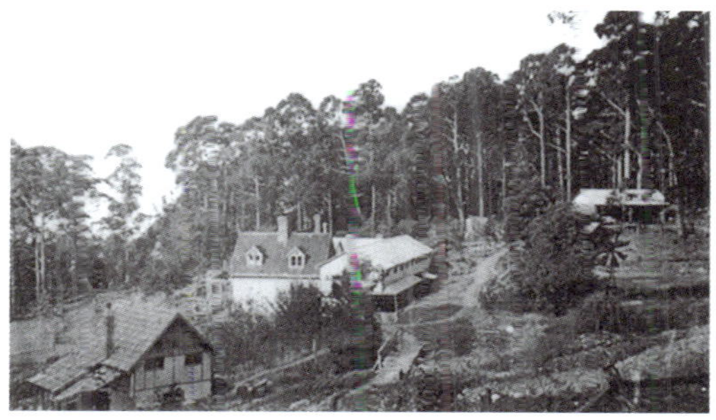

Fontainebleau, Mount Macedon, Victoria, Australia, c.1905.
On 24th September 1901 'Dillons Summer Residence' with 4 acres was bought for £500, it became the McCubbin family residence, renamed 'Fontainebleau'. The site had been carved out of the bush on the north side of Mount Macedon, the 'gardens' included these areas of untamed nature that provided perfect settings for many of his paintings, most famously the triptych The Pioneer.

Photograph, Kathleen Mangan Collection, courtesy Andrew Mackenzie

In 1900 the McCubbin family moved from Brighton to Carlton. Annie McCubbin had contracted bronchitis which led to pneumonia, so in the hope that clean mountain air would assist her recovery, they moved to a small cottage in Woodend on Mount Macedon. On the north side of the Mount, in a valley beneath Camels Hump, they discovered an old fashioned red-roofed English cottage with traditional attic windows, which was known as 'Dillon's Summer Residence' and which had been brought from Melbourne by bullock wagon. McCubbin was by now in a position to actually buy the cottage with four acres, the purchase for £500 was made in Annie's name, and the Transfer of Land document is dated 24 September 1901. The surrounding bushland became the inspiration for some of his best-known works, and the family named the property 'Fontainebleau'. It was too far for McCubbin to commute into Melbourne so he would stay with his sisters who managed *The Rose of Australia* hotel. Fontainebleau soon became a popular campsite with the Prof's students, who put up tents close to his cottage so that they could join him to discuss their art and put the world to rights.

There are parallels with Renoir's garden at Les Collettes in that Fontainebleau sits very naturalistically in the Australian bushland, but this is frontier country, so the plantings made at Fountainebleau were the first. The triptych of *The Pioneer* was painted nearby and depicts the reality of their surroundings. The narrative is essentially that of Australia: a free selector and his wife (modelled by Annie in the first and second panels) are shown on their small acreage of land in three stages. Firstly their arrival into virgin bushland; secondly, the landscape has been settled in that it is cleared, useable and utilitarian with a small cottage (actually one on the neighbouring property) – in many respects the point at which *The Pioneer* and the McCubbin family at Fontainebleau meld; the third panel shows a settler's grave and the vibrant distant city of Melbourne so well-known to them, but it leaves the conclusion open to speculation.

The model for the man in the first and third panel was a local gardener, Patrick Watson, and the child in the second panel his nephew; the man in the second panel was a professional house painter and swagman, James Edward.

The small cottage was part of the neighbouring estate called 'Ard Choille', gaelic for 'Height of the Woods', and belonged to William Peter McGregor who modelled it on a Scottish estate complete with lakes, trout hatchery, a resident piper and cottages for each of his keepers of highland cattle, deer, pigs and angora goats McCubbin painted as much within this estate as his own grounds. The play of light through the tangled undergrowth and native blue wattles were frequent motifs in his work. He was increasingly influenced by J.M.W. Turner and gained further knowledge and insight through the 1903 publication of *The Genius of J.M.W. Turner RA*. He wrote to Roberts delightedly reporting 'We have all Turner's skys up here – divine.'

In 1907 the Trustees of the National Gallery of Victoria granted McCubbin six months paid leave to visit Europe. He met up with Tom

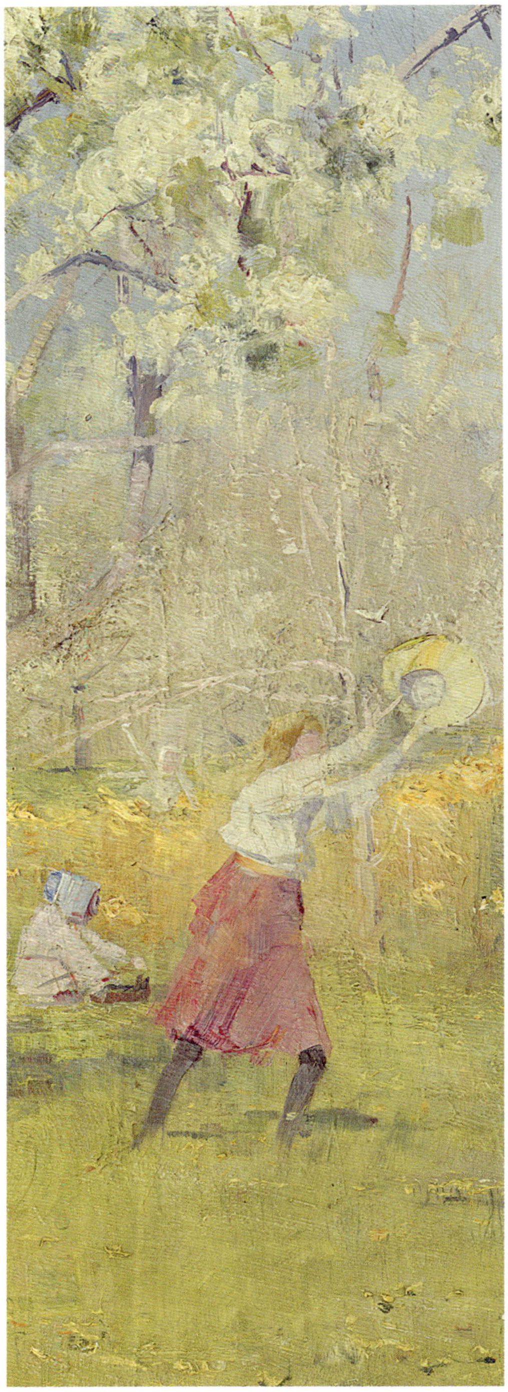

Arthur Streeton, **Butterflies and Blossoms** *(detail, see pages 52-53). Oil on canvas on composition board, 45.6 x 66cm (18¼ x 20½in.), 1889 (dated 1890)*

Roberts in London where he had the opportunity to see several of J.M.W. Turner's paintings first hand. He would have known Turner's *Dunstanborough Castle*, gifted by the Duke of Westminster to the National Gallery of Victoria in 1888.

Of all the Heidelberg artists, McCubbin is the truest Australian, his life rooted in Melbourne and Victoria. Europe inspired him, but he desperately missed Annie and his family, and the legacy of this long-awaited trip can be seen in his paintings. Gone was the nostalgic view of the 'Old Country'. The truth was it had never existed for them as born-and-bred Australians. They epitomize Dorothea McKellar's contemporary poem 'My Country' which is quoted liberally in the captions. Moving away from traditional folk tales, McCubbin's post-1907 paintings shimmer with his Australian-born sensations. On his return from Europe he rented a colonial-style stone house at 42, Kensington Road, South Yarra with three acres of gardens which ran down to the River Yarra on the outskirts of Melbourne. He renamed it 'The Studio', and the view from the verandah looked out through old lime trees across the river to the Burnley Quarries and Richmond. It became the subject of his final painting *Yarra River from Kensington Road* known by the family as *The Lime Tree*. The neighbouring mansion had a well-planned garden whose almond grove and gardener's cottage features in *Rain and Sunshine* and *The Old Cottage, South Yarra*. McCubbin continued to travel up to Fontainebleau on a regular basis until his death on 20 December 1917 at The Studio. His wife Annie then ran the property as a guest house for which she built additional wings, and it continued to be a guest house until the 1960's.

When researching Fontainebleau I was told by John Jones, former Curator of the National Gallery of Victoria, that its seven hectare garden was currently in a sorry state but mercifully that it had been spared a modern make-over (and bush fire destruction). In 1979 it had been bought and set up as a not-for-profit trust by brothers Mark and Paul Cutler for $75,000 (currently valued between $1-1.5 million). Paul's intention was to create a place of education, contemplation and creativity, without knowing at the time that this had belonged to McCubbin. In the event he used it as a family home for 21 years. In 2000 he left Mount Macedon to move to Tasmania, leaving the property to a decade of slow decline.

The turning point was heralded by 'Last Impressions 1907-17', a major National Gallery of Australia travelling exhibition of McCubbins' late work. It concentrated on the last eleven years of his life when he produced his most vibrant works, ones which express his sense of delight and comfort within the Australian landscape. From August to November 2009 the exhibition ran at the National Gallery of Australia, Canberra, before touring to the Art Gallery of Western Australia, Perth and finally into McCubbins' home state of Victoria at the Bendigo Art Gallery. As the exhibition opened, Jones took a group of curators to see the property, and in April 2010 Fontainebleau was officially placed on the Victorian Heritage Register. It is hoped that it will soon be restored to its former glory as a place of living light and colour with a sense of delight and comfort.

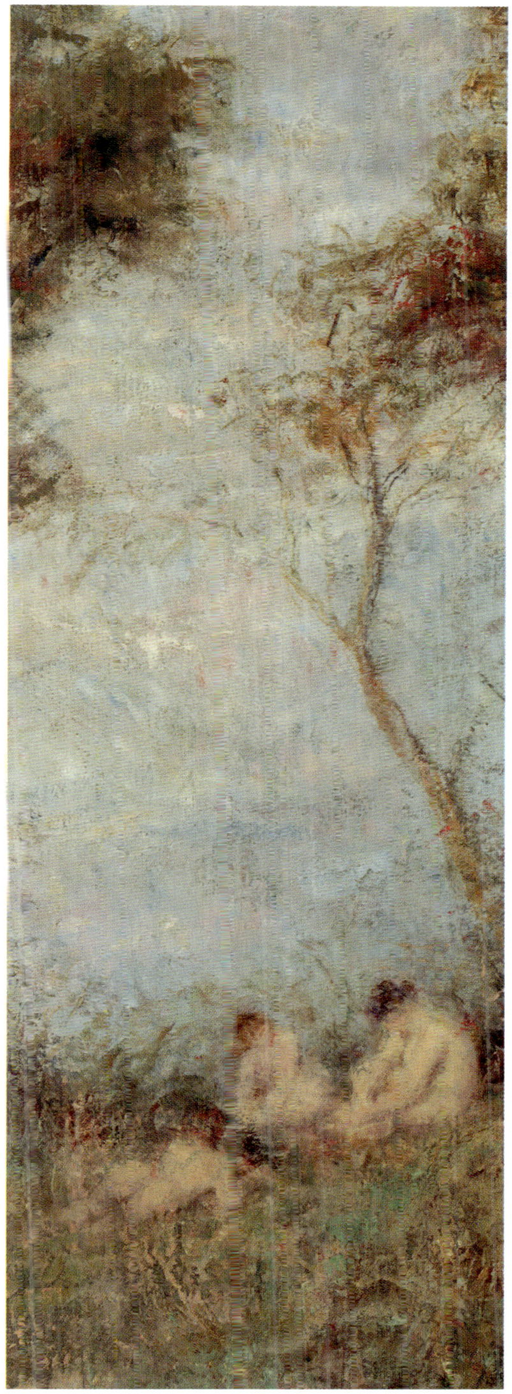

Frederick McCubbin, **Afterglow** *(Summer evening) (detail, see pages 24-25). Oil on canvas, 91.5 x 117cm (36 x 46in.), 1912*

Frederick McCubbin, **The Pioneer**. *Oil on canvas, 225 x 295.7cm (88 x 116in.), 1904*

For the pioneer, trying to control the relentless harshness of the bush in order to create a subsistence garden was a priority. Sadly, garden enclosure could not prevent drought. This is a typical narrative of Australia's first settlers but we do not know the whole story, for example: who is being buried in the final scene? Natural beauty lies in the bark of the eucalyptus and the dappled shade of the trees. In the far distance is 'Marvellous' Melbourne representing relentless urban and suburban spread. McCubbin painted The Pioneer *three years before his only trip to Europe; it illustrates a wider narrative of immigrant families creating a life and livelihood out of the indigenous landscape, traditional in its story line and presentation. In contrast his rendition on his return of* Hauling the Rails for a Fence, Mount Macedon *shows how he has shaken off the poignant but conventional narrative into an altogether brighter Australian scene of activity and optimism. It was painted in the same year that Dorothea McKellar wrote the poem* My Country.

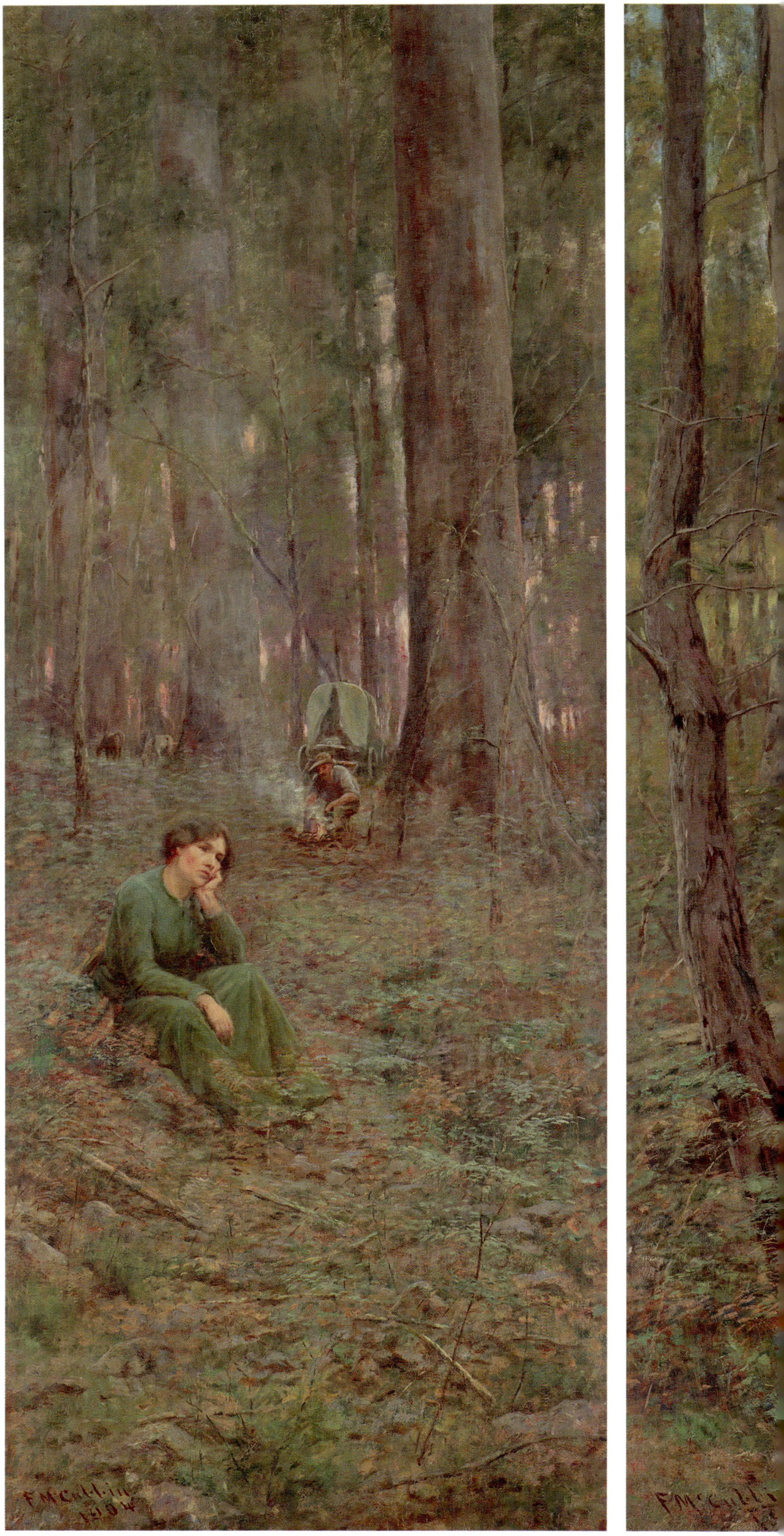

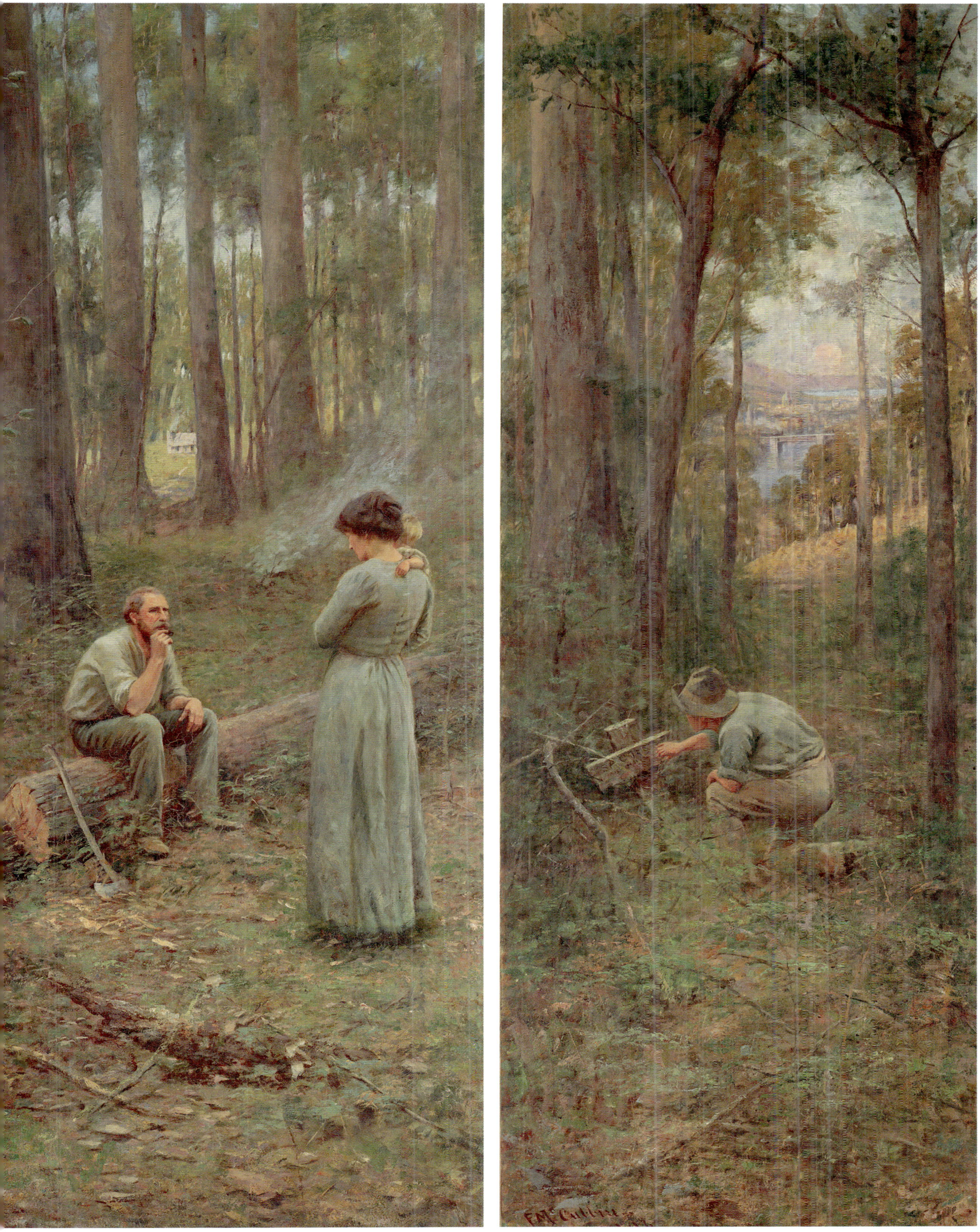

Capturing the Light

They loved the zenith landscape with the baking sun at high noon and a luminescent moment of moonrise. Above all they believed that the task for the Australian artist was to paint Australian realities. After the grave and splendid vision of colonial masters, painters of the Heidelberg School turned for inspiration to the grit of daily Australian experience. They won for themselves, their contemporaries and for future generations a rich and stirring poetry from the spectacle of a landscape being transformed into a country which bore its own distinctive identity.

Patrick McCaughey, 1985

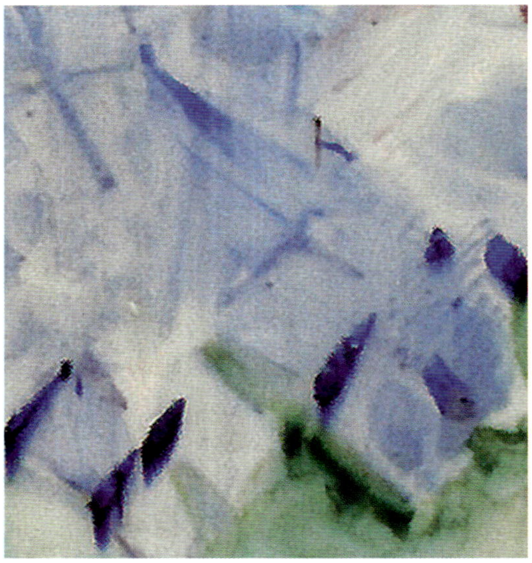

Ceramic plaque by Théodore Deck, painted by Paul-César Helleu, 67 x 36.5 x 2cm (27 x 14½ x 1in.), c1887

The vivid almost evergreen leaves and lavish flower heads made the new varieties of hydrangea – arriving from China and Japan at the end of the nineteenth century – very popular in gardens and in pots. The language of flowers today suggests the hydrangea represents vanity and boastfulness, but in late nineteenth century France the choice was between symbols of isolation, difference or coquetry – vanity and boastfulness under another guise perhaps? In 1896 the symbolist poet, Robert de Montesquiou published Les Hortensias Bleus. *The cover was designed by Paul-César Helleu who about ten years earlier had painted a quietly superior portrait of a modern Parisienne wearing a hydrangea, on a ceramic plaque, for Théodore Deck, shown here. Her manner exudes the same air as Gertrude Jekyll, Mary Cassatt and Berthe Morisot who each in their own way represent a new breed of independent woman. Helleu signed as one of the witnesses to Monet's marriage to Alice Hoschedé.*

Above all, the Impressionists sought to capture the light – often in their own gardens – onto canvases. Monet painted in all weathers, famously inspired by the snow patterns on the local grainstacks at Giverny and the ice blocks flowing in the river that relate so closely to his later depictions of the water lily leaves on his pond. There are reports that icicles would hang from his beard, however, it was never that cold within his garden and towards the end of his life he used his third atelier for painting in the winter as well as finishing other canvases. He was so wrapped up against the weather when painting on Belle Ile in 1886 that the art critic Gustave Geffroy mistook him for a local fisherman. This was the start of a long and dear friendship.

There are gardening parallels between the American artist John Twachtman and Monet, one of which was their fascination with the contrasts between ceaselessly moving and mirror-still water. Twachtman's garden bridge leads over the Horseneck Brook whose contour and flow were radically reshaped by winter freezes and snow, as can be seen in *Icebound* (see page 110) which he painted around 1889. The scene is more pastoral in Frederick McCubbin's *A Winter's Evening, Hawthorn* (1897). It is chilly but there is no snow or ice as the ducks come to dabble in the stream. In the blue hazy distance lies Melbourne, of which Hawthorn is still a rural suburb. The picket fence just defines the garden from the bush and the worker trudging home evokes the tradition of Jean Francois Millet whose work was exhibited at Australia's Centennial Exhibition in 1888.

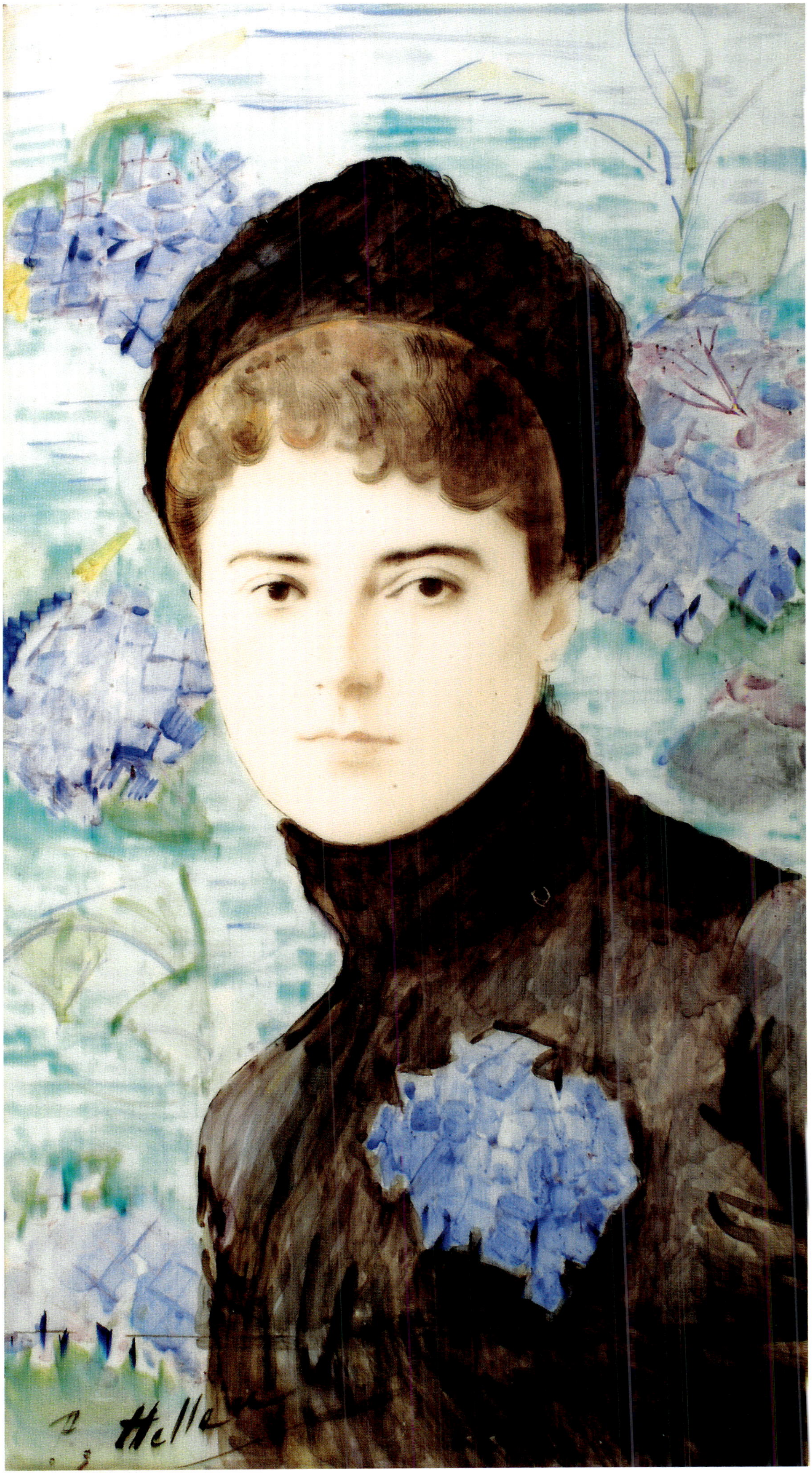

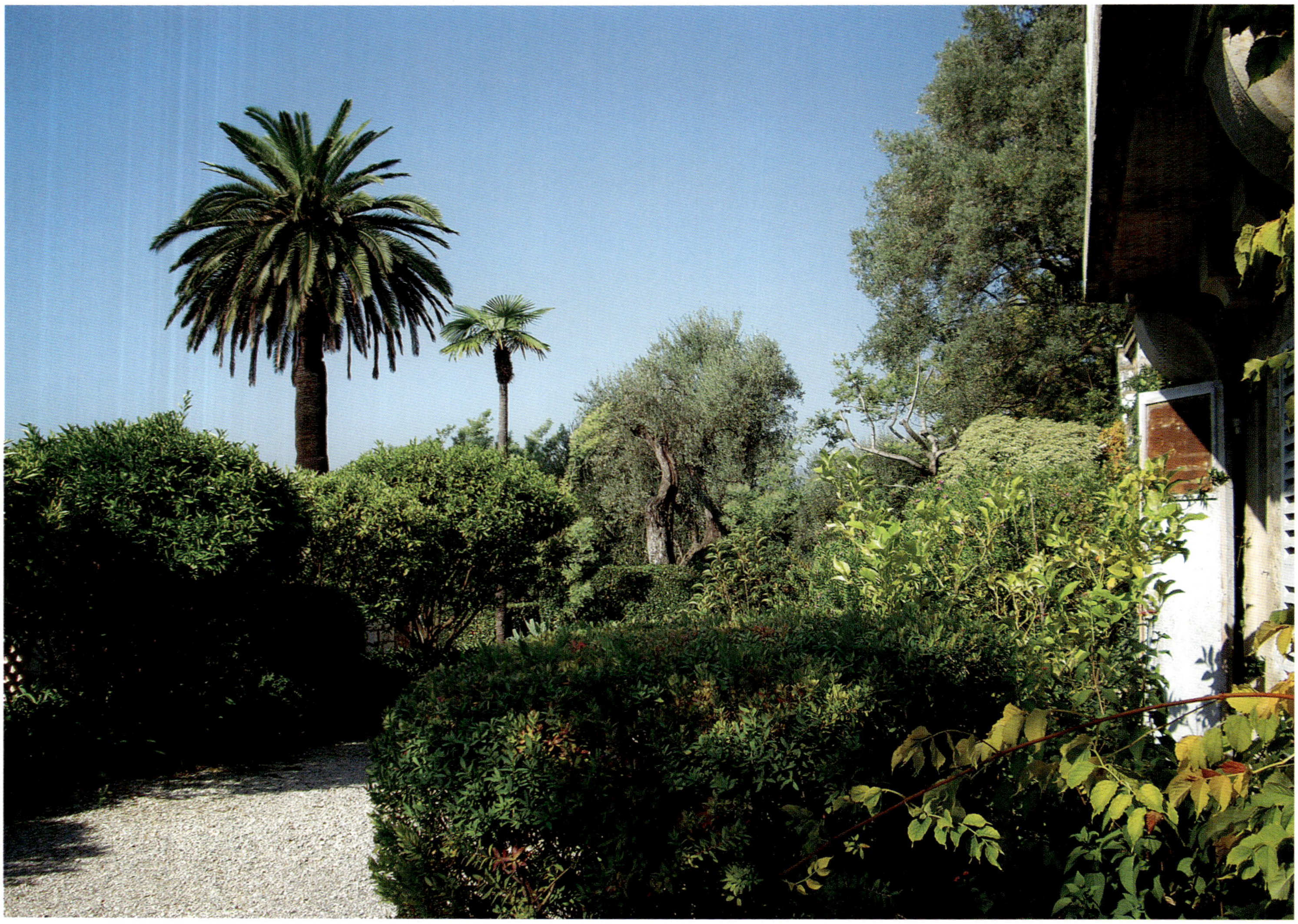

Above: *The canopy of palm trees and olives sculpted against the sky at Renoir's final home, Les Collettes. Renoir and Monet had toured this region in 1883 on a painting expedition that included meeting up with Cézanne. Monet returned the following year and painted the palm trees in M. Moreno's garden about fifty miles up the coast, which was said to be the finest in the region at that time.*

Opposite: An *agave plant in the Jardins Exotique in Eze, close to Bordighera. In December 1883 Renoir and Monet travelled to the Mediterranean from Marseilles, via Saint-Raphaël and Monte Carlo to Bordighera. On their return trip they visited Cézanne in L'Estaque. The next year Monet returned alone and rented accommodation in Bordighera in Italy and in France close to the Italian border at Menton. Monsieur Moreno invited Monet to paint in his garden which reputedly had the best palm trees in the vicinity. Monet captured them in a haze of blues, greens and golds against the backdrop of the coastal mountains. In contrast,* Villas at Bordighera *radiates heat as the flowers and foliage burn in reds and oranges cooling down to white and blue leaves. The flowers of the agave – which can reach up to four metres high – tower out of the painting taller than the palms in the mid distance. Monet used the sword-shaped cluster of leaves that provide the base of the plant to fill the centre of the canvas, then the straight stem shoots up in glowing oranges and red to the tall cloud shaped flowers and thence out of sight.*

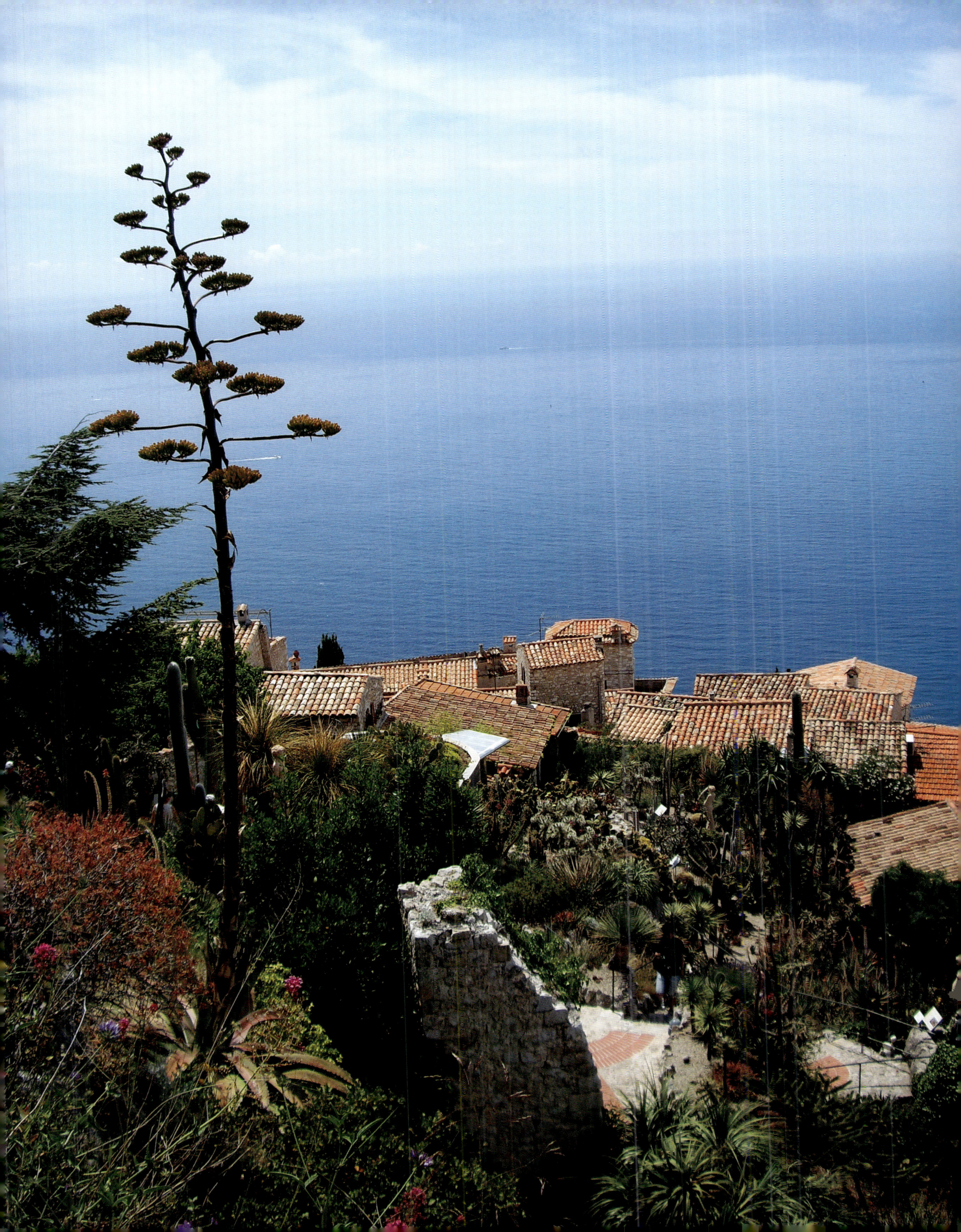

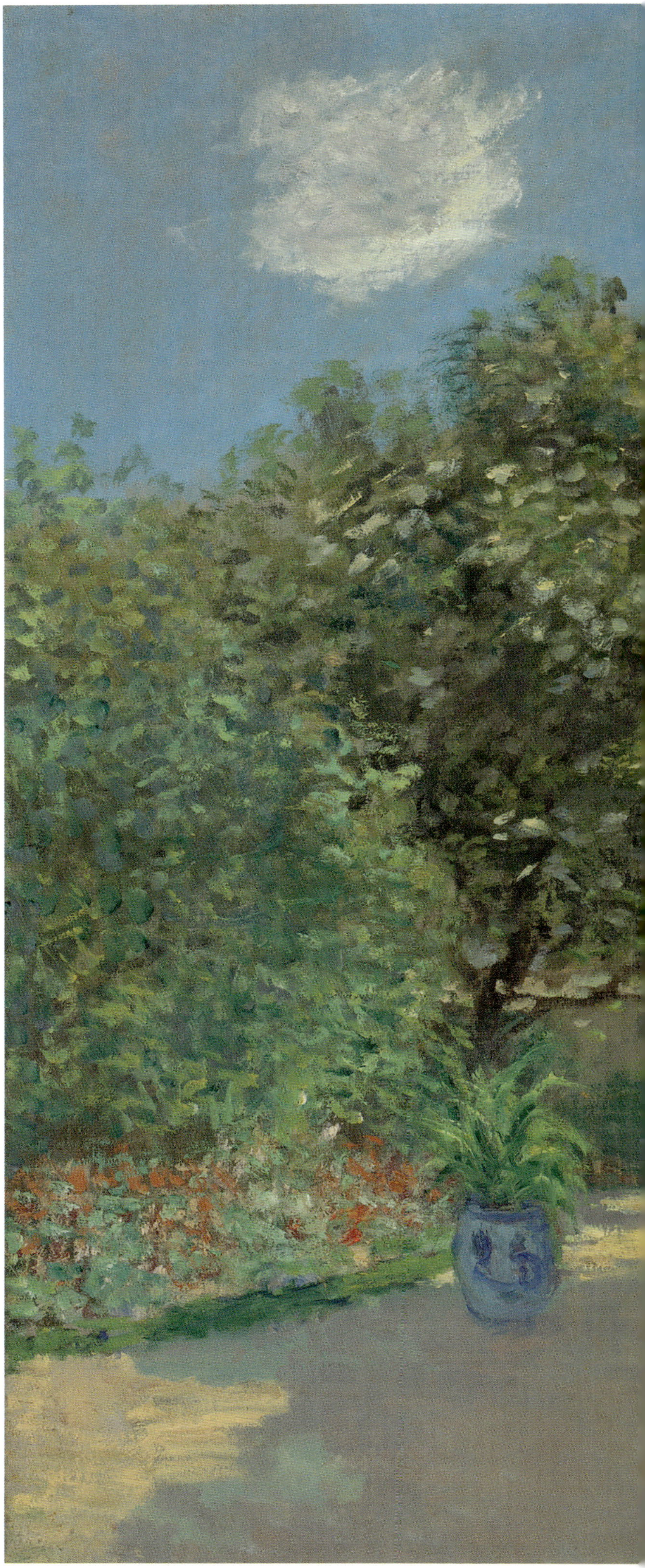

Claude Monet, **The Artist's House in Argenteuil**. *Oil on canvas, 60.2 x 73.3cm (23¾ x 29in.), 1873*

The elegant blue and white ceramic pots that line the façade were transported to Véteuil and finally to Giverny. In many respects, the design approach at Argenteuil was very similar to the upper garden at Giverny. Here Monet depicts a large blossoming fruit tree whose leaves are tinted gold by the sunshine pouring round the side of the house, the house itself appears afloat on drifts of flowers, its façade softened by what seems to be a climbing rose. The fruit tree catches the warmth of the sunshine and a path invites the viewer to go further into the garden. Elegantly hatted, Camille watches Jean Monet preparing to roll his hoop, seemingly not with the same confidence shown by the older Marie Goujon in Renoir's painting (see page 130). Small boys all wore dresses until they were about five years old.

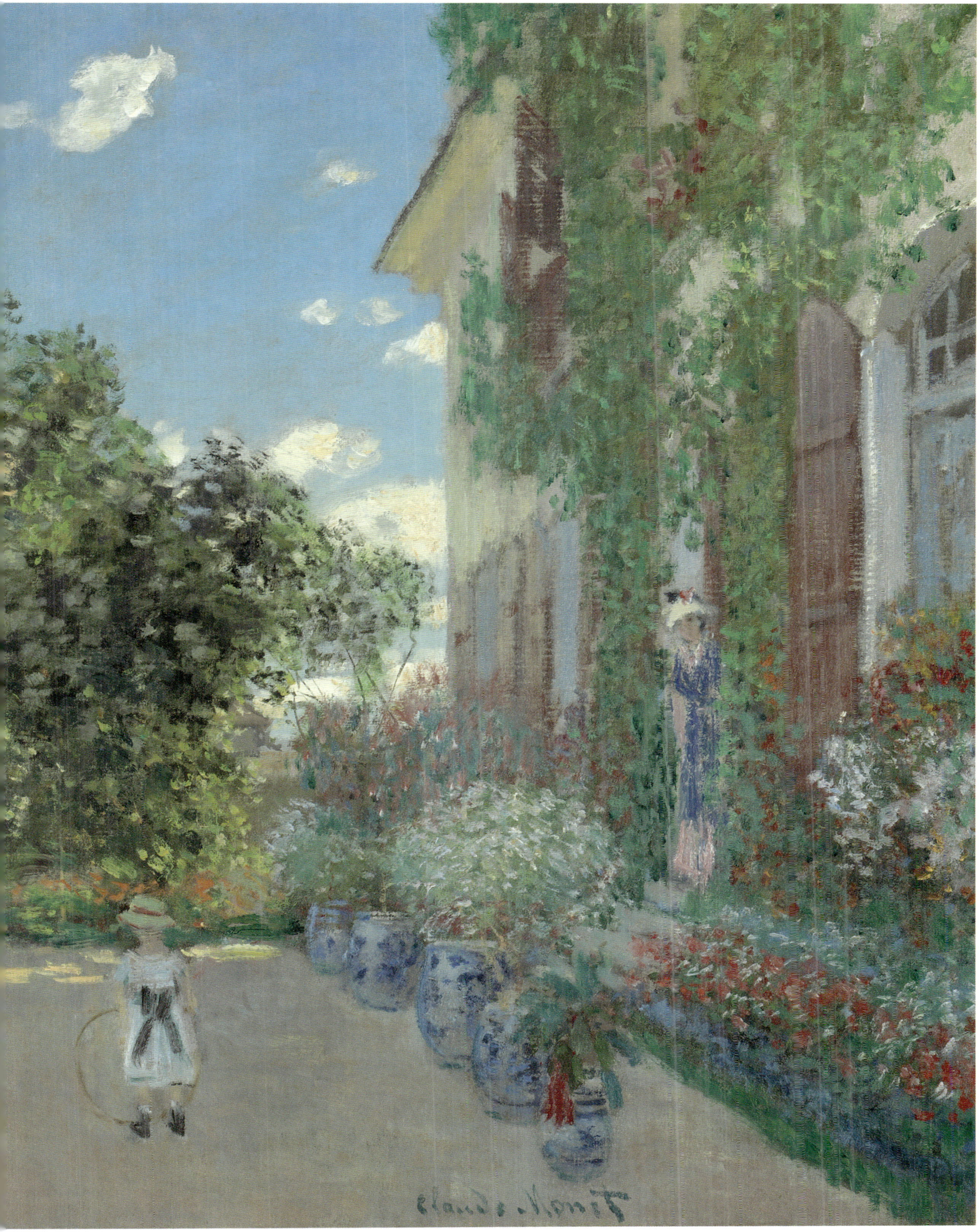
Claude Monet

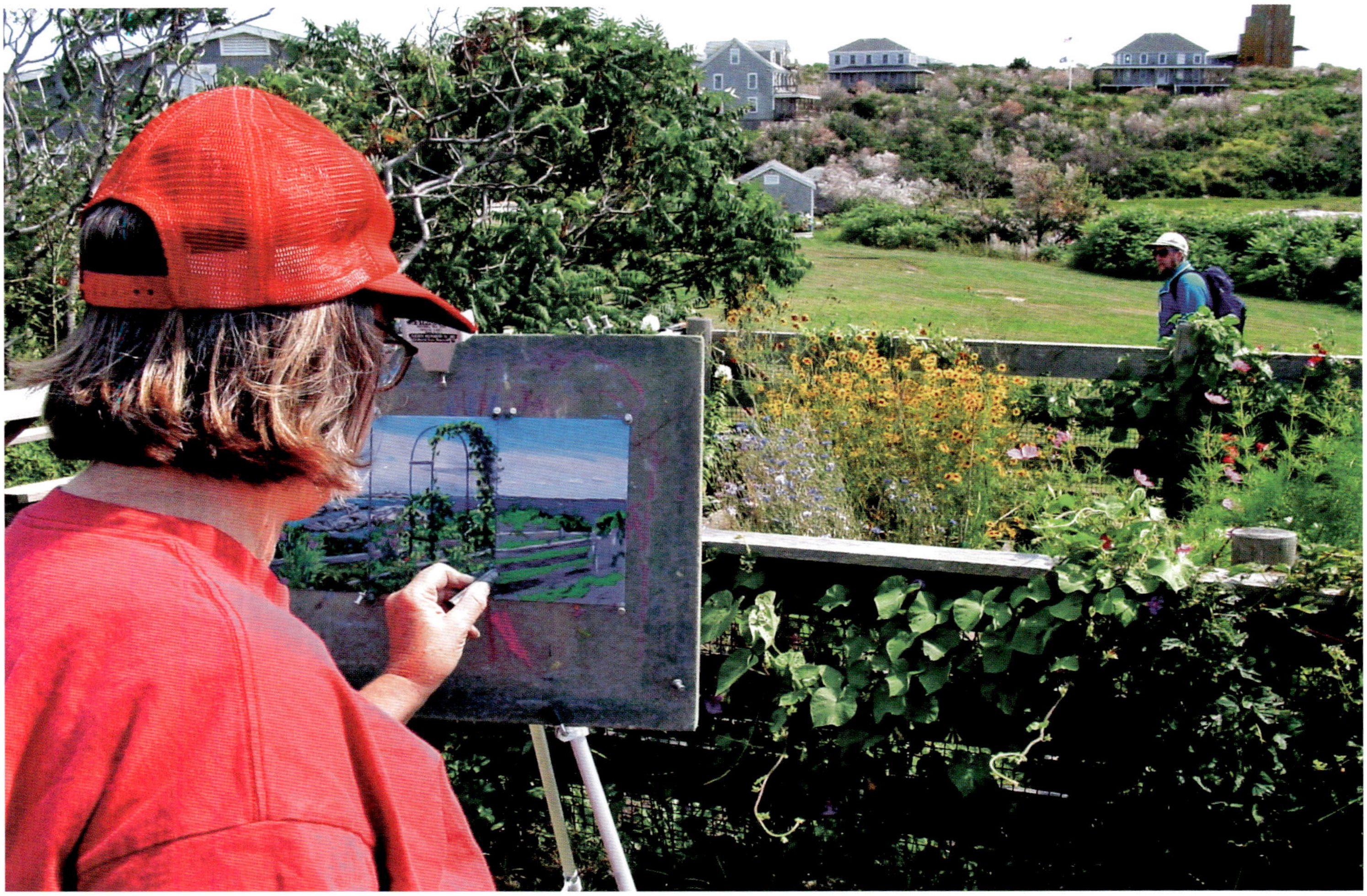

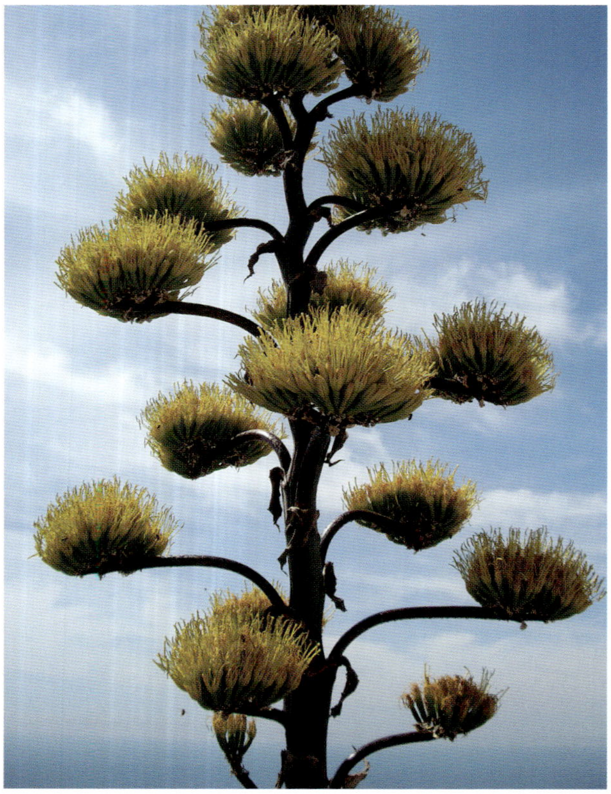

Above: *'Manipulating the space' at Appledore. In art historians' definitions, one of the key Impressionist principles was that the dominance of light and colour required a new manipulation of space. This comprised of a 'grille' intimation of faint forms seen through the scintillating surface pattern of light; or oblique angles of vision that suggested movement through an implied contiguous space. Gardens and gardening unpack these words into simple effects that illustrate the concepts. The grid pattern of Monet's upper garden perfectly provides the faint form that manipulates his flowers as did Celia Thaxter at Appledore. Today, budding artists also try to rekindle the spirit of the past by painting in the footsteps of great artists at Les Collettes, Giverny and here at Appledore where easels are still put up to capture the moment and perhaps to evoke the spirit of Childe Hassam who created twenty two watercolours here to illustrate and illumine Celia Thaxter's* An Island Garden.

Left: *The spectacular flowers of the agave actually spell out its death sentence echoed in its basal leaves, which twist upwards and outwards to reveal shades of muddy pink and green. Introduced from Central America, it is also known as the sisal plant because of its fibrous leaves, and the leaf tips are so sharp that they were used in the past as needles. It flowers in late June and literally drips with nectar, although only agave tequilana is used to make tequila. This image was taken in the Jardins Exotique in Eze.*

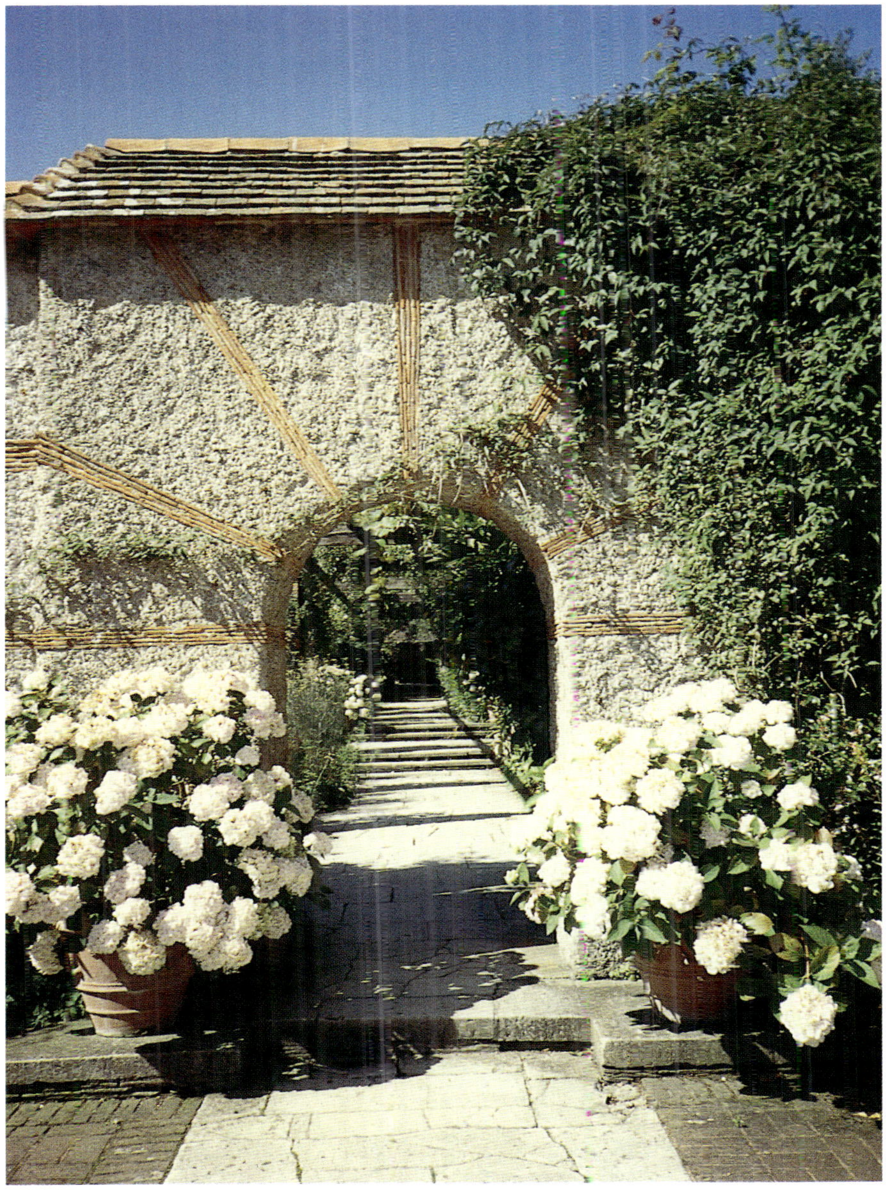

Jekyll recommended hydrangeas in borders but more especially in pots where she would encourage full blooms of pale pink. When perfect, she would drop them amongst grey foliage in her borders at Munstead Wood. In 1898 Edwin Lutyens was commissioned by Guillaume Mallet to design the house and gardens of Le Bois des Moutiers at Varengeville-sur-mer. Lutyens provided details of the site and aspect to Jekyll who designed a series of gardens around the house. The sunburst arch and potted hydrangeas at Le Bois des Moutiers capture the essence of their individual design geniuses. Today the gardens and park hold the world's largest collection of over 1,000 varieties of hydrangeas monitored by the Conservatoire français des collections végétales spécialisées.

The earlier chapter 'Plants as Paint' examined how planting became living proof of Impressionist principles and how the plants form an integral part of the composition. Take tulips, for example, standing aloof in a froth of forget-me-nots; the sound and grey-green sway of poplars evoking the sea; the clouds nuzzling up to water lilies in the mirror of the water; the light playing through the lanceolate olive or eucalyptus leaves; and the green tunnel of Monet's Grand Allée. Paintings and photographs can create optical illusions, masterminded by Monet in his bid to lose the horizon or have wisteria appearing to cascade from the sky. Deceiving the eye meant removing or disguising eyesores, as when Childe Hassam omitted the unattractive plant supports and netting in the rectangular flowerbeds in the garden at Appledore. Gertrude Jekyll took this possibly a step too far in her recommendation to plant bindweed around unsightly woodpiles to disguise them – planting that might well survive long after burning the wood.

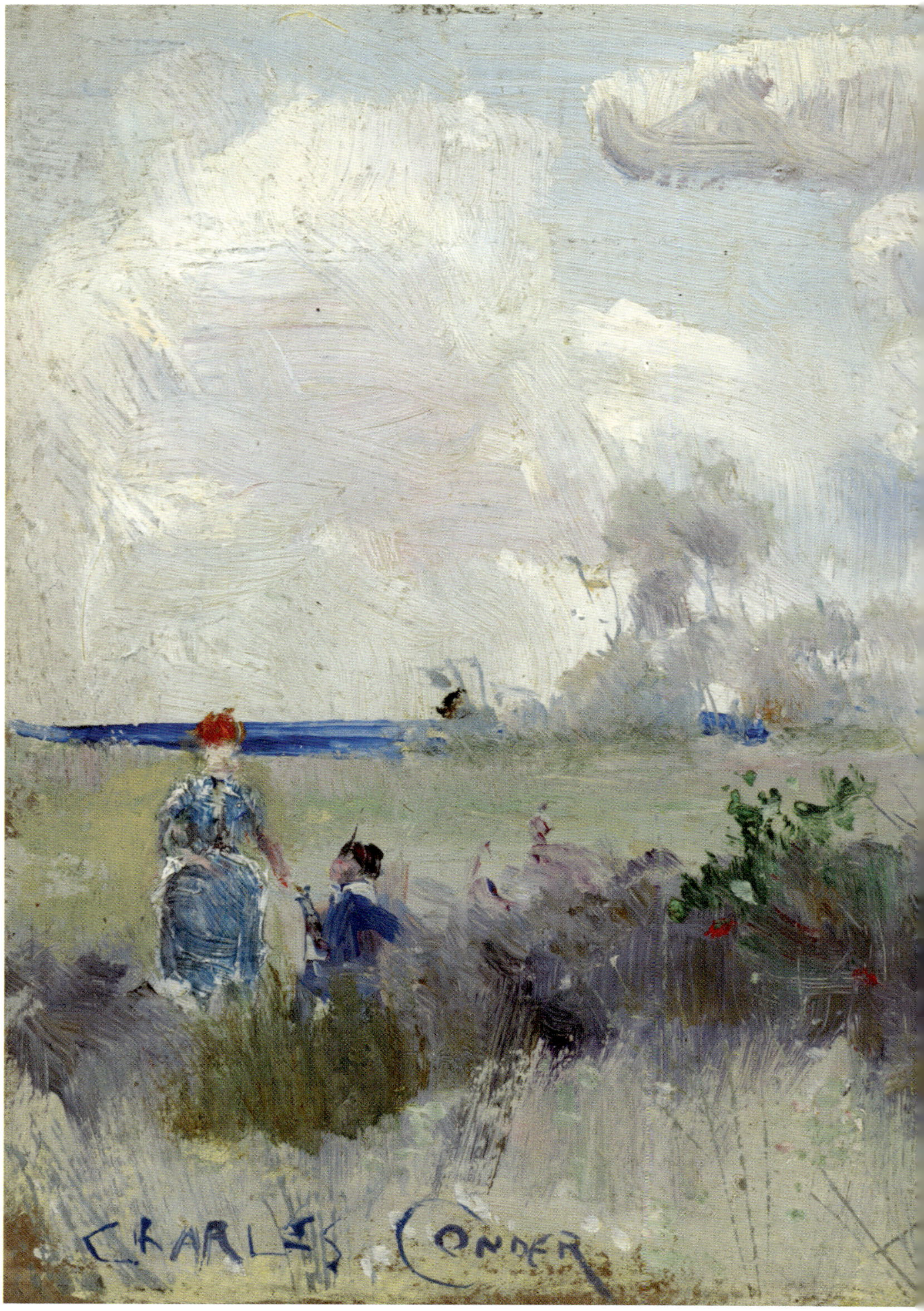

Charles Conder, **Herrick's Blossoms**. *Oil on cardboard, 13.1 x 24cm (5¼ x 9½ in.), c.1888*

To paint the glaring Australian light, pervasive grey-green of the bush or the glowing yellow burn of summer was, according to James Gleeson – a revolution and a swansong. Aged sixteen, Charles Conder had arrived in Sydney in 1884, and spent his first two years as a surveyor before turning to art. Australia inspired in him a lyrical impressionist style, expressed in the delicate way he used colour. The large canvas of The Farm, Richmond, New South Wales *was painted in 1888 in an old neglected orchard, the fragile blossoms on the gnarled trees presage* Herrick's Blossoms *and echo the use of blossom in Japanese prints. The '9 x 5 Impression Exhibition' (most of the impressions were painted on cedar cigar-box lids) was held in Melbourne in 1889 at which Conder exhibited this painting:* Herrick's Blossoms. *The state of Victoria had suffered an appalling drought during 1888 and 1889 which one can sense in the bleached grasses; and yet life goes on, as portrayed by the two hazy figures balanced by the ephemeral deep pink blossoms. Conder's lyrical style, like so many of the Heidelberg School, was inspired by poetry.* Herrick's Blossoms *derives from 'To Blossoms' by the English poet Robert Herrick (1591-1674):*

Fair pledges of a fruitful tree
Why do ye fall so fast?
Your date is not so past;
But you may yet stay here a while,
To blush and gently smile;
And go at last.

What, were ye born to be
An hour or half's delight;
And so bid good-night?
'Twas pity Nature brought ye forth,
Merely to show your worth,
And lose you quite.

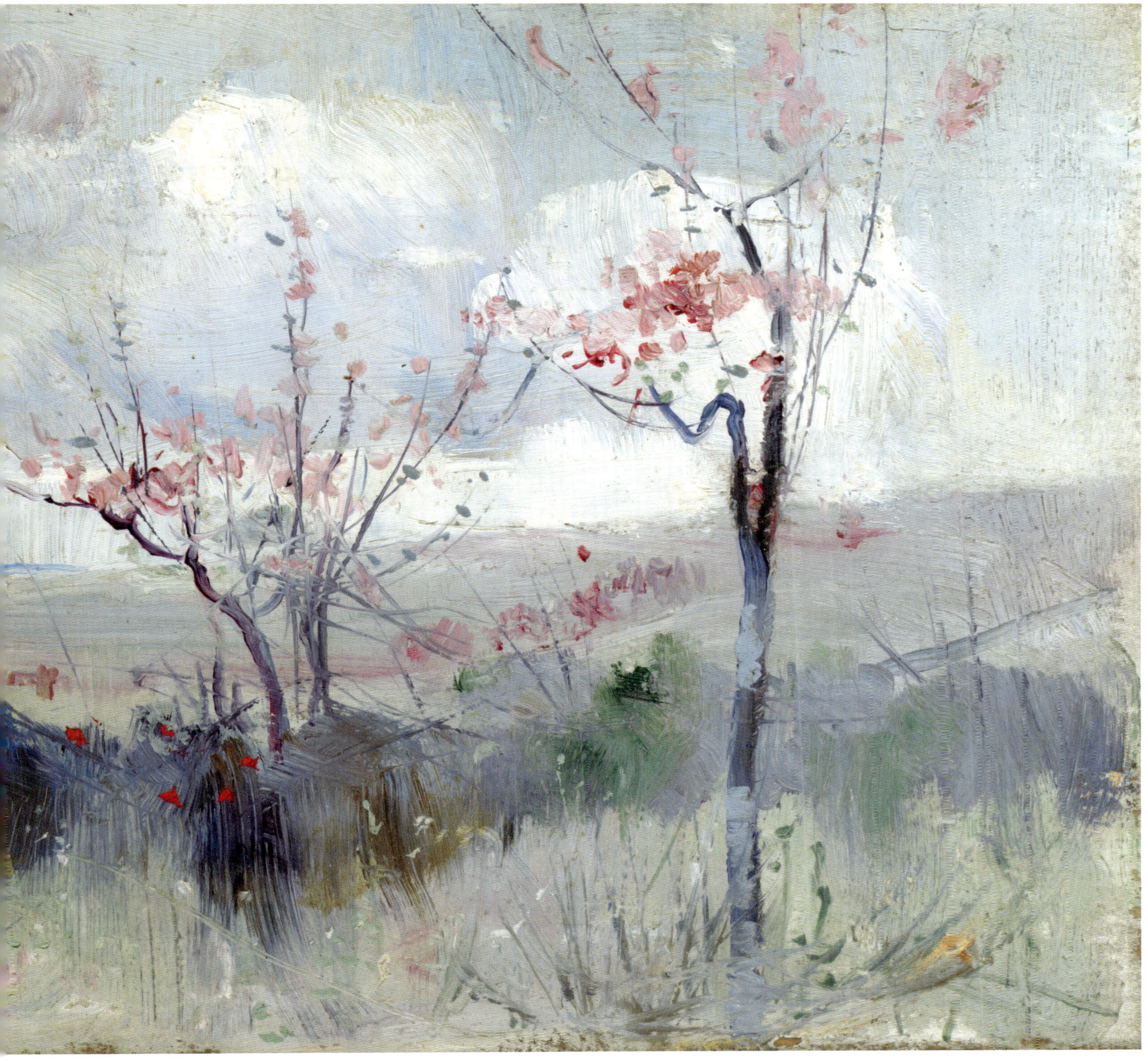

CHAPTER SEVEN

French Impressions under Mediterranean Skies

Renoir at Les Collettes

In this intimate paradise enlightened by sunbeams, scintillating and glowing, he consecrated his art to all the goddesses that had made the cult of his existence: the fecund earth enriched with summer foliage, the dying riches of autumn, the renewal of spring; flowers throughout the seasons whose buds juggle singular faces, curious looks, magical perfumes, mysterious graces; ... finally, the woman who reigns in this painterly kingdom as one of its own, she too springs from the nourishing soil, from the flourishing garden, from the shining water of the sun.

Gustave Geffroy, Memories of Monet (Monet, Sa Vie, Son Oeuvre), *1924*
Chapter Four 'Memories of Renoir'

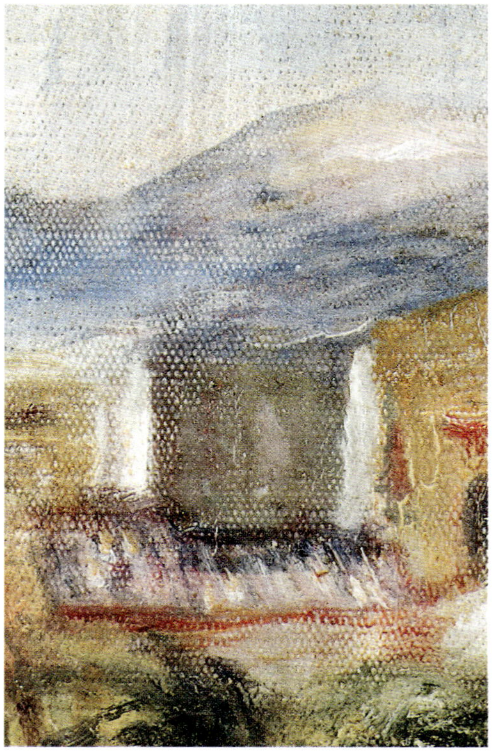

Pierre-Auguste Renoir, **The Post Office, Cagnes**. *Oil on canvas, c.1907*

From 1904 the Renoirs wintered at Cagnes, finally renting rooms overlooking the garden at The Old Post Office. The red pantiled roofs and pinky orange wash of the houses echo the warmth of the climate, even in winter. The grey canopies of the olive trees planted in terraces give a certain softening formality to the composition. Renoir found painting olives very difficult, he said that the colour was not on the leaves but between them.

So finally to the artist for whom the garden was a canvas primed for a thousand years by traditional methods, understood by him, but tended by others, especially his wife Aline. Aline Victorine Charigot was of rural family stock from Essoyes near the Champagne Burgundy border. She became one of Renoir's models, appearing in the *Luncheon of the Boating Party* in 1881, mother of his first child Pierre in 1885 and then his wife in 1890. The unpretentious family life that she created with their children, Pierre, Jean and Claude, with her cousin Gabrielle acting as both nurse and model were central to Renoir's philosophy and artistic output. Readers looking for a bigger picture should consult *Renoir, My Father* written by his son Jean, whose consummate skills as a film director provide a scenic narrative of Renoir's life landscape and domestic domain.

Monet, the plant collector and gardener, artfully designed his gardens with trees, shrubs and flowers in order to harness the light to sensational effect, increasingly with no human reference. Renoir, the collector of artists' models and lover of the unpretentious, placed people in paintings where nature took the upper hand. Like Monet (and Alfred Sisley and Frédéric Bazille) he had studied art under Charles Gleyre in Paris in the 1860's, then during the Franco-Prussian War 1870/71 Renoir had quietly carried on painting whilst Monet moved to London. Renoir had also travelled extensively to Algeria, Spain, Italy and the Channel Island of Guernsey, both painting and viewing the works of great masters. He and Monet visited Cézanne in Provence in 1883 before painting along the Cote d'Azur and into Italy.

From the age of three, Renoir's childhood had been spent in Paris. As a young artist he had stayed frequently in the forest of Fontainebleau, but his first studios were around Montmartre. At this time Montmartre was still a village outside the boundary of Paris to the northwest, but the arrival of the railways meant it was easily accessible to working class Parisians who transformed its daytime tranquility into boisterous nightlife. At the centre was La Butte where the *guingettes* – restaurants with dance gardens – could be found, notably the Moulin de la Galette, later painted by Vincent

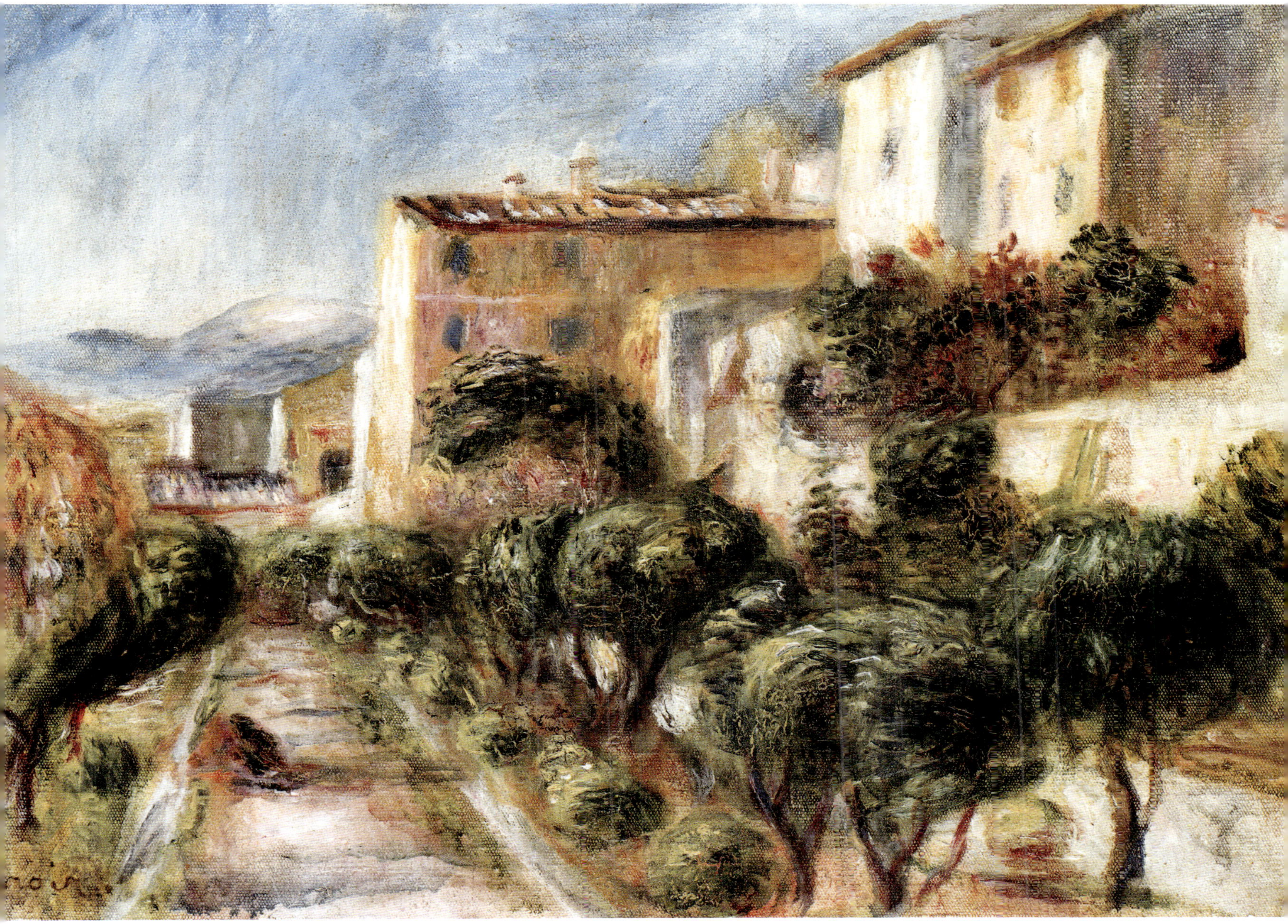

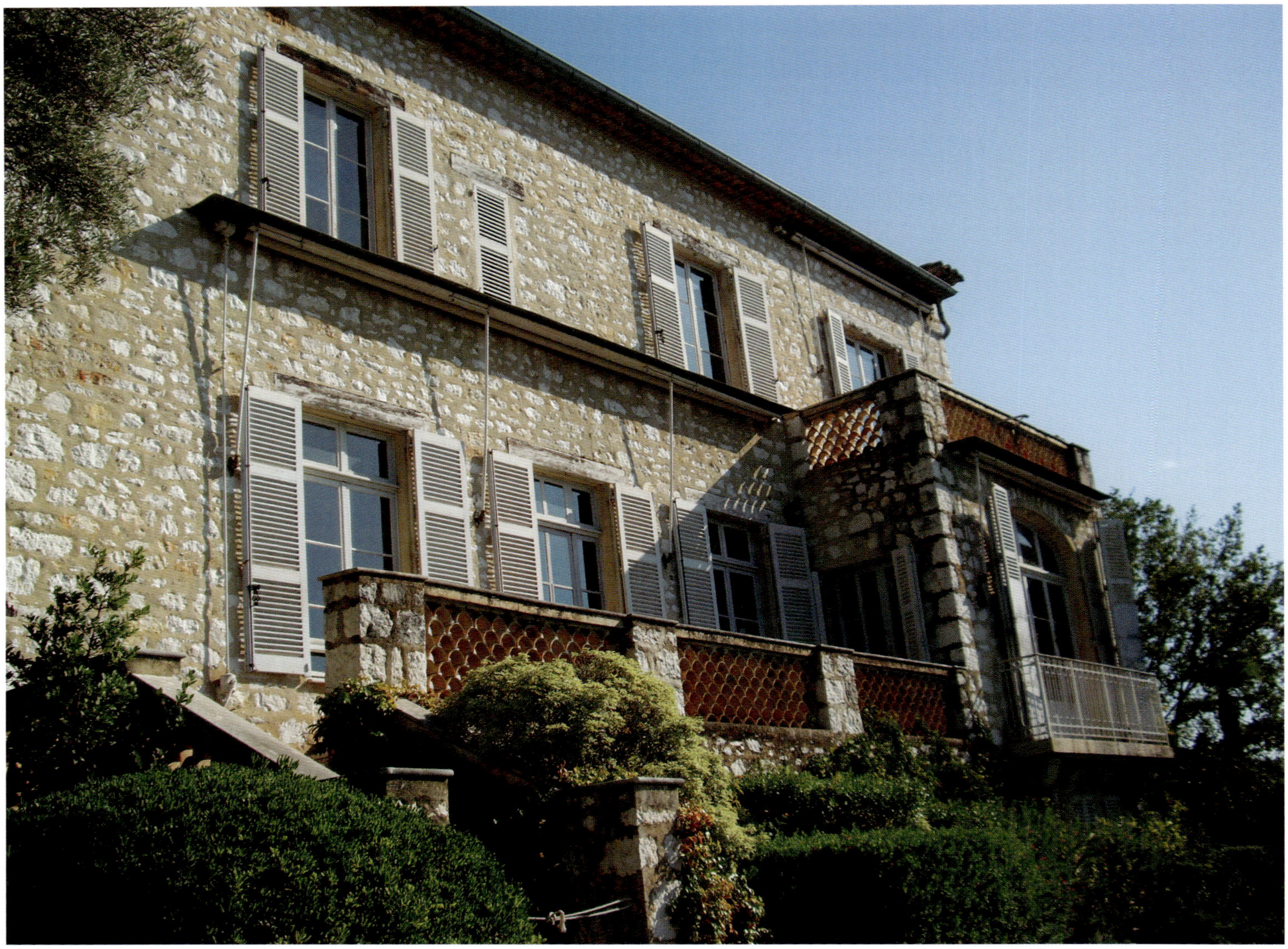

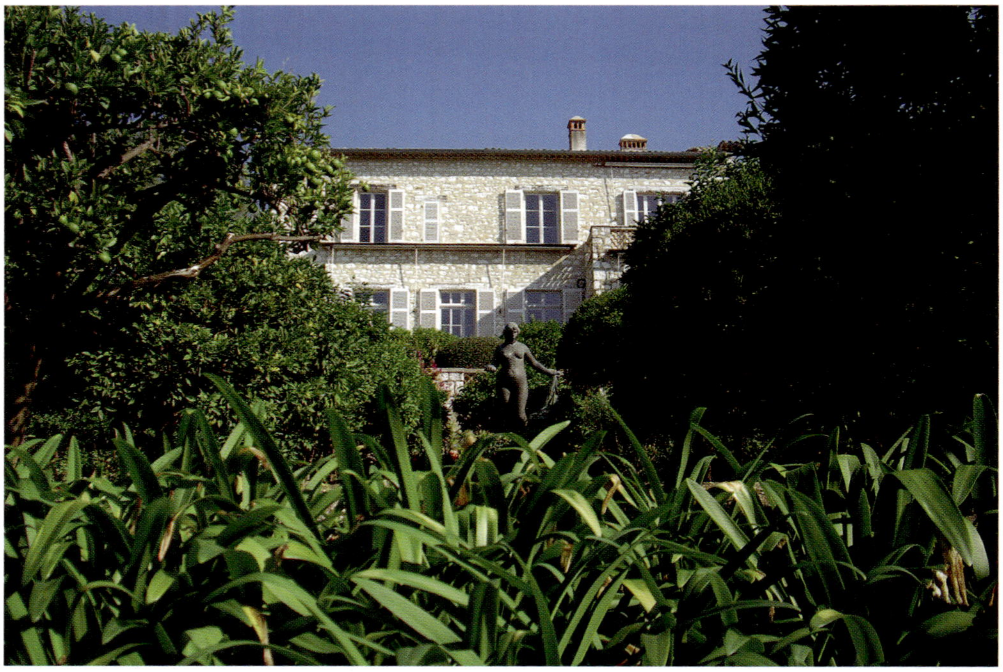

Above: The nine acre domain of Les Collettes lies above the upper village of Cagnes which gives the house spectacular views down to the Mediterranean. The terrace was often used for eating with the scent of the roses and orange trees below wafting abroad on the air.

Left: The house from the garden. Visitors made their way down the slope to the front door on the opposite side of the house. Today this is your first view. The agapanthus leaves frame Renoir's sculpture of Venus Victorix, whilst the trees have a heavy crop of oranges that are still green. Originally it was planned that the house would be swathed in wisteria and this would be a more formal garden.

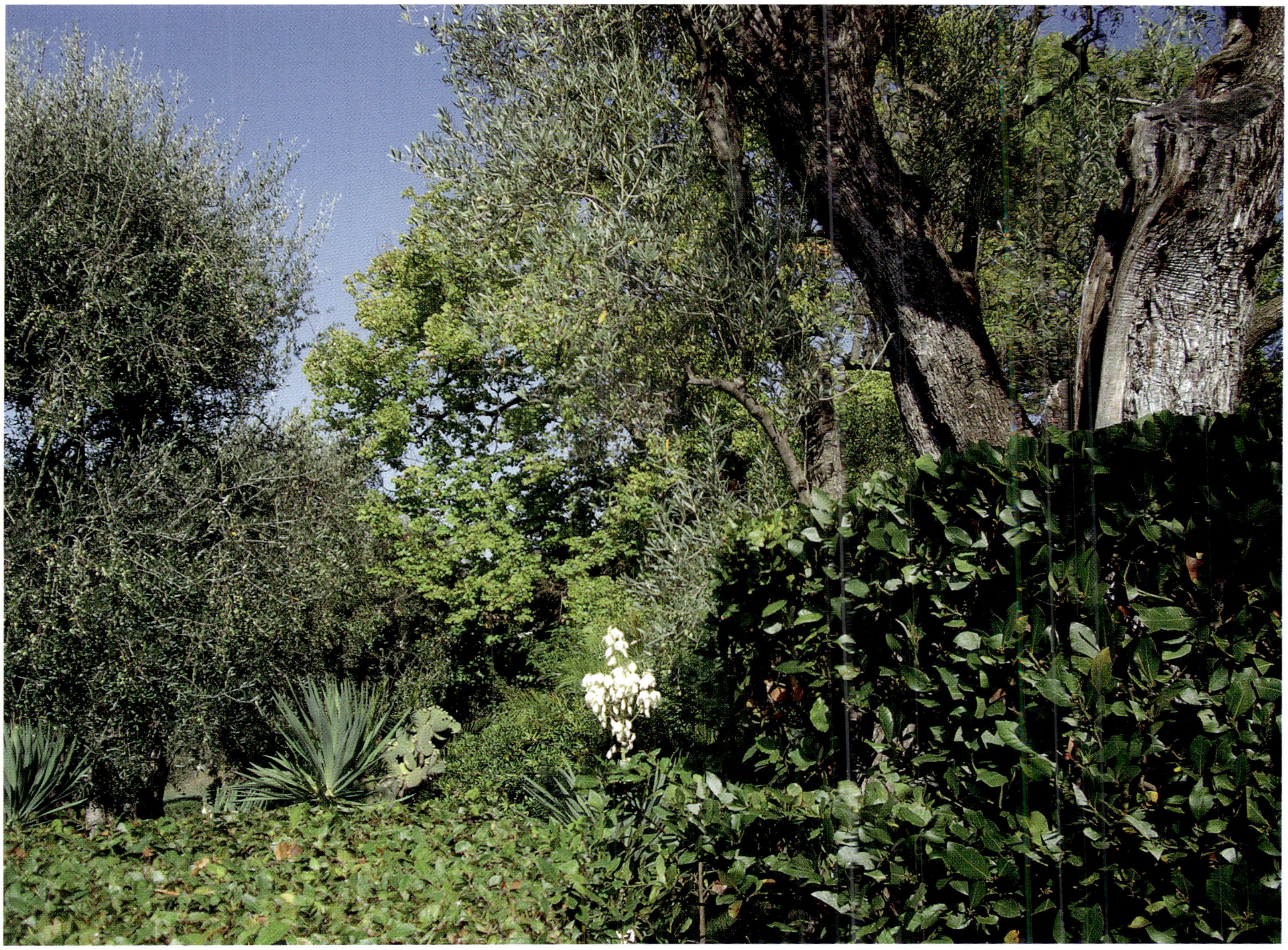

Van Gogh and Pablo Picasso, or the gardens of Maison Rose where *La Balançoire* was painted. Over the years Renoir rented several rundown properties as studios, preferably with a patch of garden about which he did nothing except to delight in the way nature took them over. One such was 12 Rue Cortot, described earlier, which overlooked overgrown gardens of faded glory with roses in the summer, replaced by dahlias.

After their marriage the Renoir family home was at Château des Brouillards, in Paris, set in an wild garden of rambling roses, uncut grass and mature stands of deciduous trees. If home is where the heart is, for the Renoirs this was at their next house at Essoyes, beautifully evoked by Jean Renoir: 'There is no other place like it. There I spent the best years of my childhood. My enchantment used to begin as soon as I got within ten miles of the village, when the train from Paris had passed the flat plain of Champagne and entered the hilly region covered with vineyards near the hamlet of Bourguignons. One can still see the big stone post set up by the kings to indicate the boundary-line between Champagne and Burgundy. And the countryside has the same aspect as all regions that produce good wine: a river at the bottom of a valley. In

Tones of green against the blue sky, can be seen in the olive, orange and bay trees with the white flowers of a yucca shooting skywards. Many of the ancient olive trees growing along the Cote d'Azur were planted in the sixteenth century on the orders of Francois I, however, the cultivation of terraces dates back to the Romans. Some of the olives at Les Collettes are reckoned to a thousand years old. Too venerable to be turned into napkin rings.

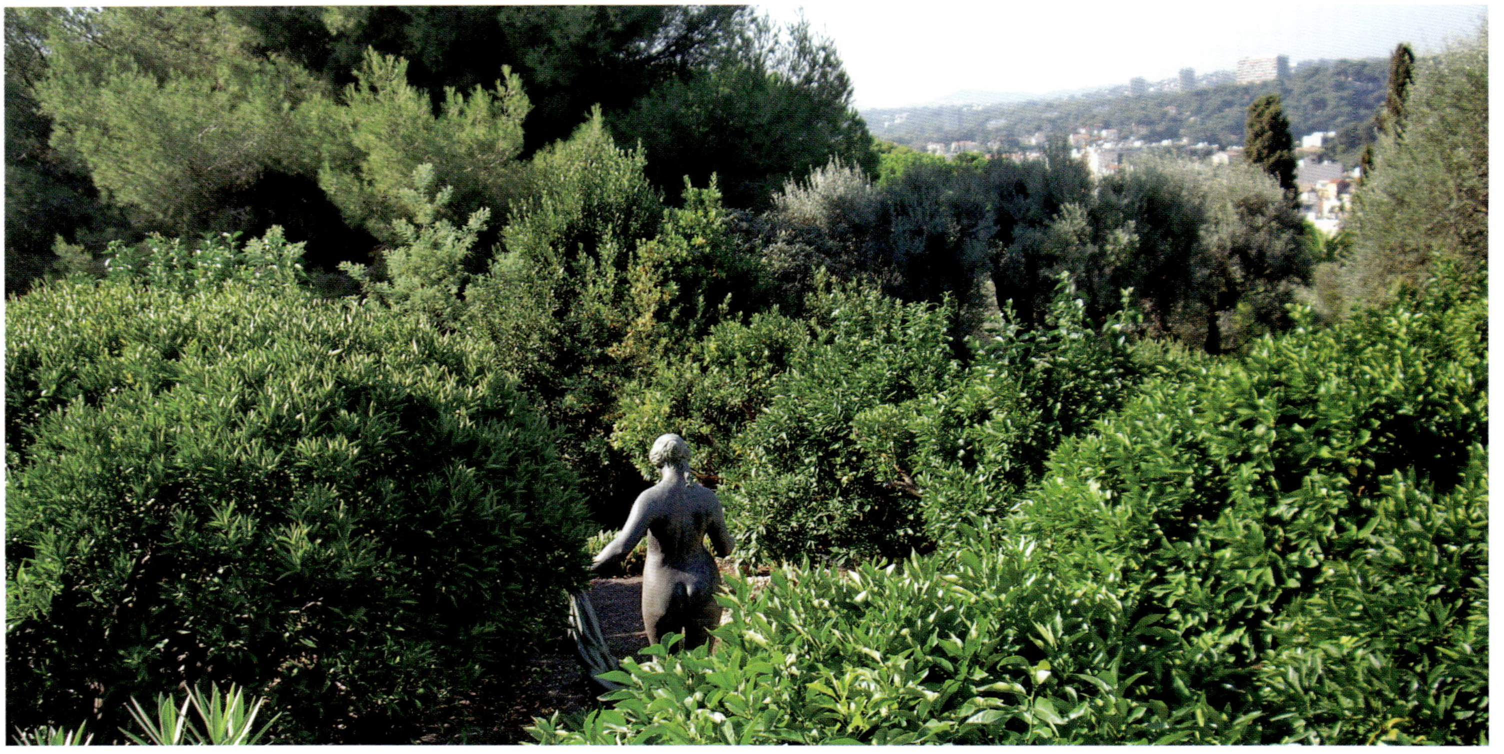

The soft grey voluptuous contours of Venus Victorix can be glimpsed in the orange grove near the house. Nestling in the evergreen shiny leaves of the oranges with the silver grey foliage of olives beyond, she is unaware of the building development in the far distance. Renoir sculpted with the aid of two sculptors, first Richard Guino, then Marcel Gimond.

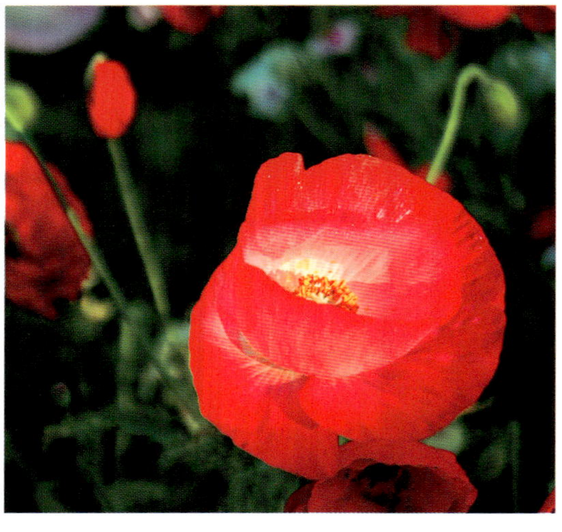

These poppies were photographed in Celia Thaxter's garden on Appledore. Both during her lifetime and through to the present day they continue to self-seed across the island. Renoir also loved poppies and insisted that the grass at Les Collettes should not be cut without his permission to encourage the poppies to naturalise.

this case it is the Seine. Down below there are meadows with cows, while along the slopes are woods or vineyards. At the top, the land flattens out into long plateaus, more or less arid. ... By 1897 my mother had installed us in a part of our own house at Essoyes. The studio... was not built until a little later ...' It was not until 1905 that she planned another studio at the far end of the garden near the saw-mill belonging to M. Decesse. Renoir thought it the ideal location. It was there that he tried out a bit of sculpture – 'a notion I had running around in my head' – with the sculptor Morel, a native of Essoyes, who was then quite young. The garden contained a vineyard and fruit trees, which made it very pleasant.'

As far as the locals were concerned (just as when Monet had arrived at Giverny), Renoir's painting activities in Essoyes were viewed as unusual to say the least. In his early days there he painted canvases that he sometimes left behind when the family returned to Paris, and were recycled as roofs for rabbit hutches or put to other practical purposes. Decades later in Cagnes when asked by his gardener/chauffeur, Baptistin, for some extra money for Christmas, Renoir gave him two paintings. Baptistin was flabbergasted – how could *paintings* possibly be used to buy what he needed for Christmas?

In winter the Renoir family moved south; the warmth of the south of France was hugely beneficial to Renoir's rheumatoid arthritis. He refused to stay in Menton, then a popular health resort near to the Italian border, because it was frequented by sufferers of tuberculosis and he was convinced that the mountains immediately behind stopped the contagious air from being blown away. The smart international set wintered all along the coast from Menton to Cannes and into Provence, staying in fabulous villas with extensive gardens oozing wealth from every pore. The Renoir family found the rural split village of Cagnes more to their

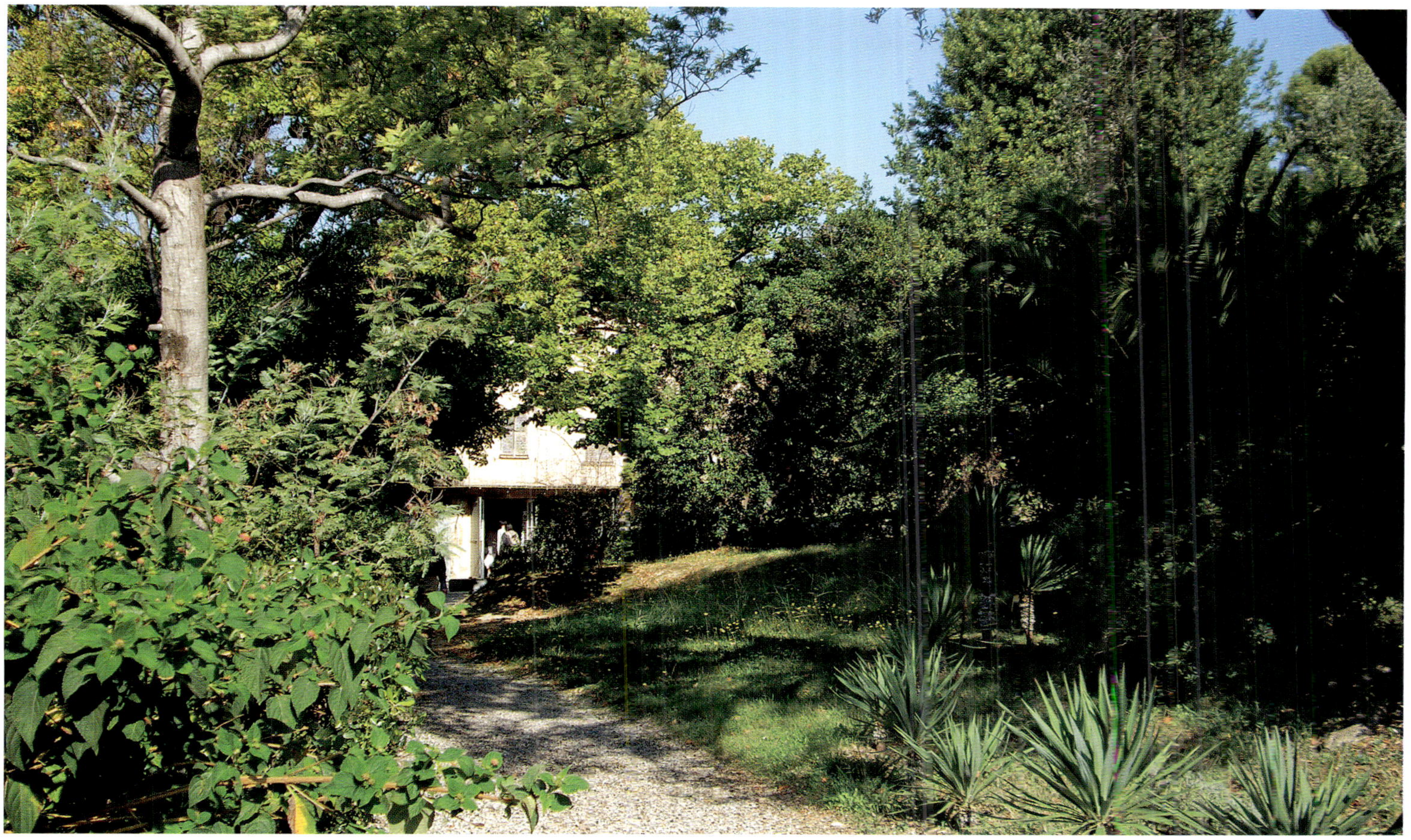

taste, its lower streets on the coast devoted to fishing, especially sardines, and upper part of the village devoted to terraces – orange and olive groves, vegetables as well as rabbits and hens. From 1904 the Renoir family started to winter in Cagnes, renting one third of The Old Post Office which overlooked a large grove of orange trees. One of Renoir's favourite haunts was a little farm with beautiful olive trees – Les Collettes – occupied by Catherine Canova, her son Paul and a little mule called Litchou. Legend said that the olive trees had been planted by Francois I's soldiers to keep them occupied, back in the sixteenth century. In 1907, to the Canova's utter consternation they were informed that an estate agent was selling their property to a horticulturist who specialized in carnation growing, so the ancient olives would have to be sacrificed.

With visions of olive wood napkin rings sporting 'Souvenir de Nice', Renoir acted swiftly and bought the terrain to safeguard the status quo. He had no intention of living there permanently, however to appease Aline he agreed to build a house so that the family could live on site. The new house never really interested Renoir, what he loved was the ancient terrain, his own worn physique echoing the bark of the gnarled olives, their fruits a living testament to centuries of summer drought and winter cold. Renoir said he could taste the difference between the first pressing of his own olives known as 'the flower' and that of his neighbour – of course the ones from Les Collettes were better! In 1909 Monet and Alice came on a prolonged stay, and a photograph of Monet amongst the olives has survived.

Aline did not consider that the original Farmhouse at Les Collettes was good enough for someone of Renoir's status. Renoir never included their new house in his paintings, preferring the weather-beaten old farmhouse or its associated buildings. This is the view from their new house, the grassy slope is blanketed with irises in the spring. When Renoir heard of Van Gogh's suicide, he questioned how a man who painted and loved irises could not be happy.

Although new, the house was designed to grow organically from its own site. Built in local stone which can look a little stark, it was originally designed to be swathed in wisteria and vines. In fact Renoir only ever included the Canova's old farmhouse in his paintings of Les Collettes. The 'formal' gardens were on the south-facing terrace, they were filled with roses and orange trees into which Renoir placed his Venus Victorix sculpture for, as he said, 'Under this sun you have a desire to see marble or bronze Venuses among the foliage.'

Crippled with rheumatoid arthritis towards the end of his life, he was unable to sculpt, so he would stand back and instruct, first the sculptor Richard Guino, then Marcel Gimond, as to what he wanted, and the result was his painted models translated into three dimensiona form.

The garden landscape was formed of ancient terraces that were cultivated, some devoted to producing flowers such as De Caen anemones and dahlias, to cut for the house and for Renoir's studio that was built in the gardens. In addition, Les Collettes had vines along the terraces, which were tended by Aline for grape production rather than for wine. Shades of Australia also filtered through the gardens in the form of eucalyptus and Banksian roses as well as Jekyll's preferred edging plant, Bergenia and the Impressionist stalwart, irises, which naturalized along banks.

The non-productive grassy areas were left as meadow with self-sown poppies running through them. Renoir insisted that anyone working in the gardens asked his permission before scything; you have only to think of the many late paintings of young nudes to see how the soft long grasses provided a perfect foil for their voluptuous bodies. The youngest son Claude (or Coco) Renoir was only six when they moved to Les Collettes so the gardens were also home to his various pets, including ZaZa the family sheep dog who barked a warning when unexpected guests arrived, as well as the usual array of domestic fowl and rabbits.

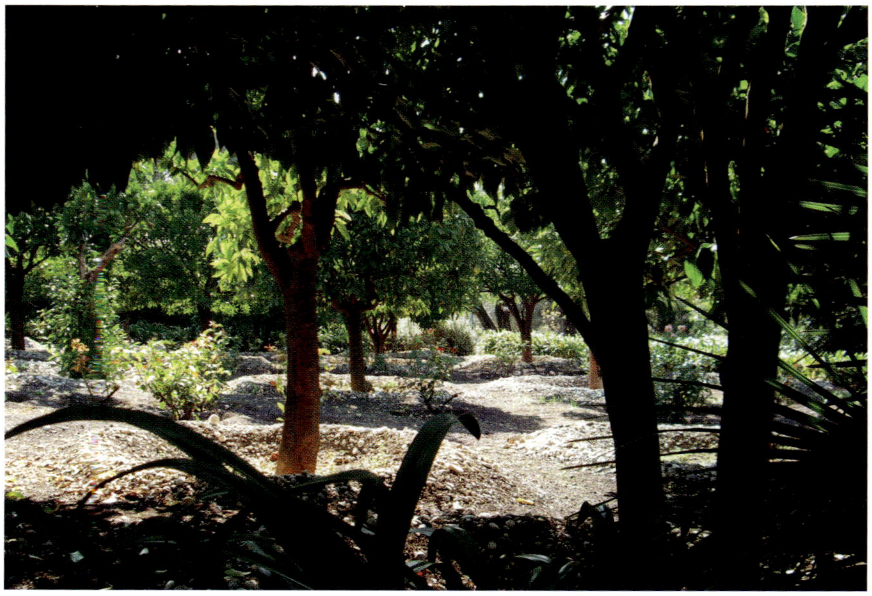

The first orange trees planted below the house were a sweet variety, but after the entire crop was scrumped by Renoir's sons, he planted a sour variety so that crop remained untouched. Aline was a good market gardener and guests enjoyed the fruits of her labours. Note the way that the soil is built up around the base of the orange trees to retain water. Blossom from the larger orange grove was harvested and sent by donkey cart to nearby Grasse.

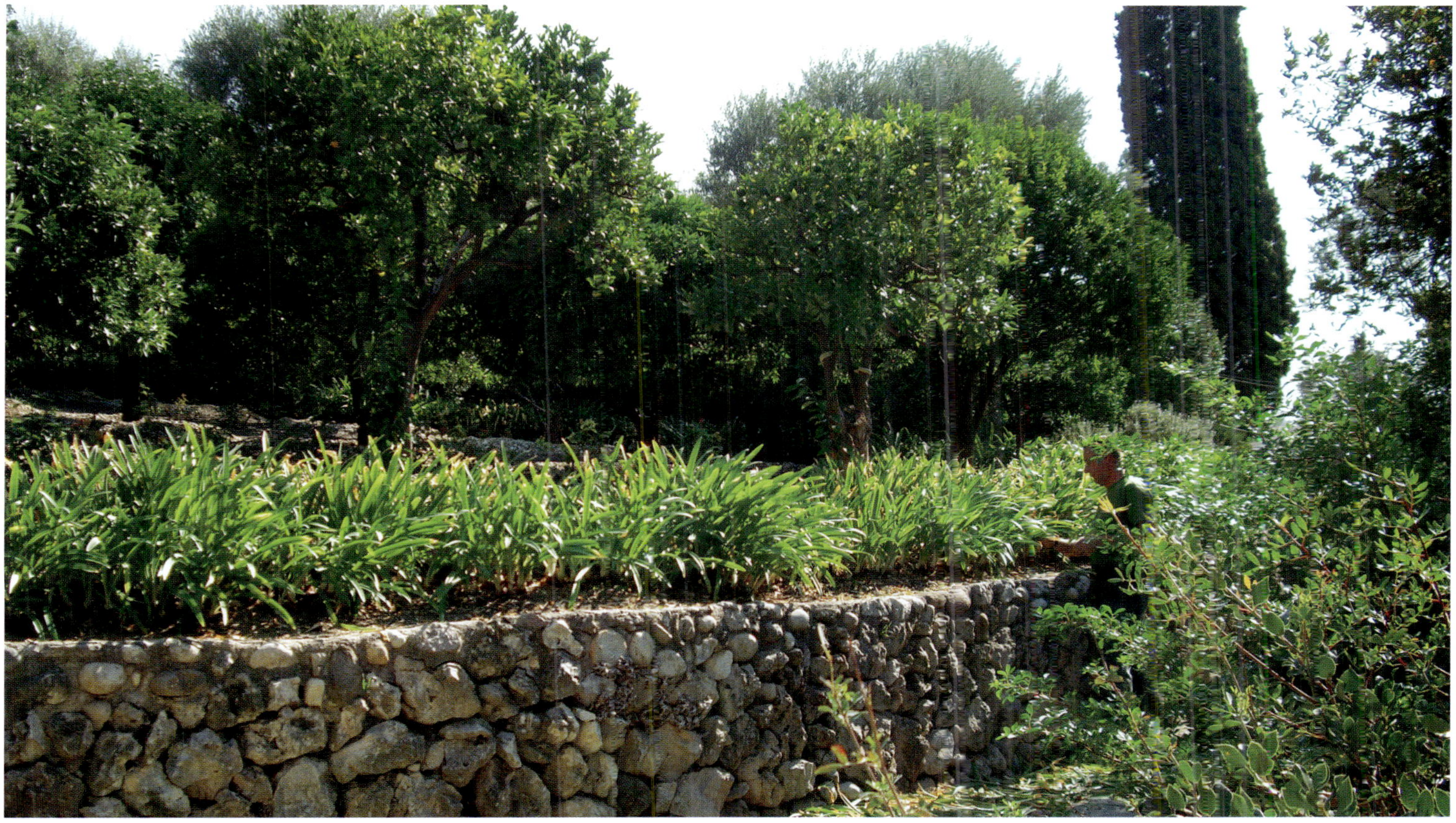

Les Collettes became a pilgrimage site for budding artists from around the globe who came to stand on hallowed ground and watch the master at work. Language was no barrier, and generous hospitality, much harvested from the gardens and from the sea, was extended to both artists of his own generation and up-and-coming stars such as Matisse and Modigliani. But the Renoirs were not immune from events in the wider world. The tragedies of World War I were experienced first hand when Pierre and Jean were both wounded, and the toll of two injured sons proved too great for Aline. Having visited both and ensured life saving treatment for Jean, she died in June 1915. The following year Jean was back in action on the battlefield, he received a letter from his father simply saying 'To you. Renoir' and enclosing a violet picked by the wash house. Jean described the gardens as going into mourning for his mother; the pruning and productivity effectively ceased, the orange trees and vines became wild, and he wrote of being shocked by an all-pervading sinister atmosphere.

However, through pain and misery Renoir rekindled his love for the joys of nature, spending his last four and a half years painting and painting, whether it was the flowers that were brought to him, or his new red-haired model whose skin took the light – later to be Mme. Jean Renoir. Even on his last day he was carried to his studio in the gardens where, as his son wrote: 'The landscape was a microcosm of all the riches in the world… He now dominated Nature, which all his life he had served as a worshipper. In return she had finally taught him to see beyond surface appearances and, like herself, to create a world out of almost nothing.'

The lower part of the terrace at Les Collettes is lined with agapanthus, a popular motif with Monet, to the right you can just see the gardener tidying them up. Renoir might have allowed such manicuring work as it is at the base of the ornamental orange grove and rose garden. Jekyll would have been able to provide a list of plants that would thrive in this dry south facing wall and softened its effect.

CONCLUSION

In Memorium

The great painter of Montmartre has died at Cagnes, a village on the Mediterranean coast. His life and work were prolonged in this land of azure blue and sunshine. There he could both breathe and paint again, contemplating the verdure, the flowers, the sky and the water. Renoir could own all the beauties and joys of nature from the doorstep of his house, by voyaging along the paths of his garden. Despite year by year the worsening state of his health, he was able to live outside, to hold his brush in his deformed hand, to transcribe once more on to a canvas the coloured visions that his eyes admired, and which in turn were recoloured by that marvellous crucible of living forms and luminescent harmonies, his brain.

Gustave Geffroy, Memories of Monet (Monet, Sa Vie, Son Oeuvre), *1924*
Chapter Four 'Memories of Renoir'

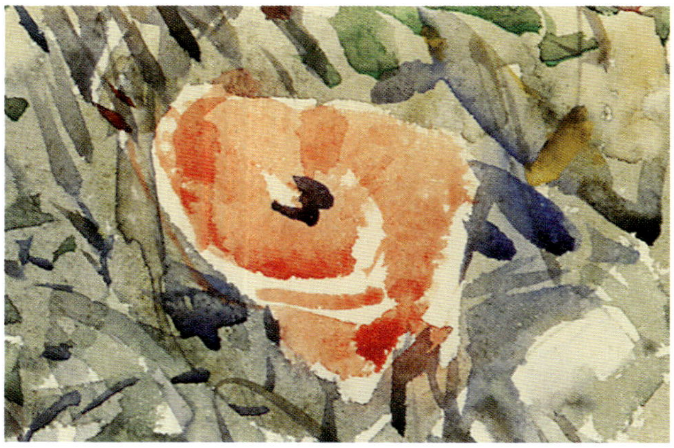

Childe Hassam, **The Island Garden**. *Watercolour on paper, Sheet: 44.4 x 35.5cm (17 x 14in.), 1892*

When in 1919 poppies sprang up all over the World War One battlefields, a journalist appropriately named Newman Flower collected their seeds and those of the other wild flowers. Through his newspaper column he offered to send seeds from a battlefield where anyone had lost a loved one. His seeds went out to Australia, America and around the world to grow and give comfort. Celia Thaxter had died before the war, but during her lifetime she encouraged poppies to naturalise beyond her garden borders. One of her verses in An Island Garden *is as unanswerable as the questions that must have been in the minds of relatives who sowed Flower's seeds:*

How should the poppy steal sleep from the very source
That grants to the grapevine juice that can madden or cheer?
How does the weed find food for its fabric coarse
Where the lilies proud their blossoms pure uprear?

Who shall compass or fathom God's thought profound?
We can but praise, for we may not understand;
But there's no more beautiful riddle the whole world round
Than is hid in this heap of dust I hold in my hand.

The death toll and aftermath of the Franco Prussian War of 1870/71 took many forms. Politically the wounds inflicted on the French by the exacting terms demanded by the Prussians remained unhealed. The Prussians had directed operations from the Palace of Versailles where they made the Proclamation of the German Empire in the Hall of Mirrors on 18th January 1871 and later accepted the French surrender. Versailles, once the potent symbol of France in its heroic age, was now witness to its ignominious defeat.

Following the end of the First World War in 1918, Monet's great friend Georges Clemenceau, much to Winston Churchill's disgust, insisted on retribution at the Treaty of Versailles which, as the age of Impressionism was closing, set the seeds for the rise of Fascism. These two wars frame the dissemination of Impressionism from Paris in the 1870s to its blossoming across the world and the flower of its youth from all three continents coming to die on the battlefields of the second. The Impressionists lost one of their founder members, Frédéric Bazille, in the first conflict, but thankfully their revolutionary drive to celebrate their naturalistic roots in sensations of colour and light remained. Their gardens were outside studios, planted to reflect their painterly tastes where people could play within landscapes drenched in light and colour.

After the 1871 surrender, the humiliated French nation looked back for an example of their former greatness, and where better than the masterpieces of Andre le Nôtre during the reign of The Sun King, Louis XIV. These gardens were tightly controlled Baroque designs of formal architecture, where clipped

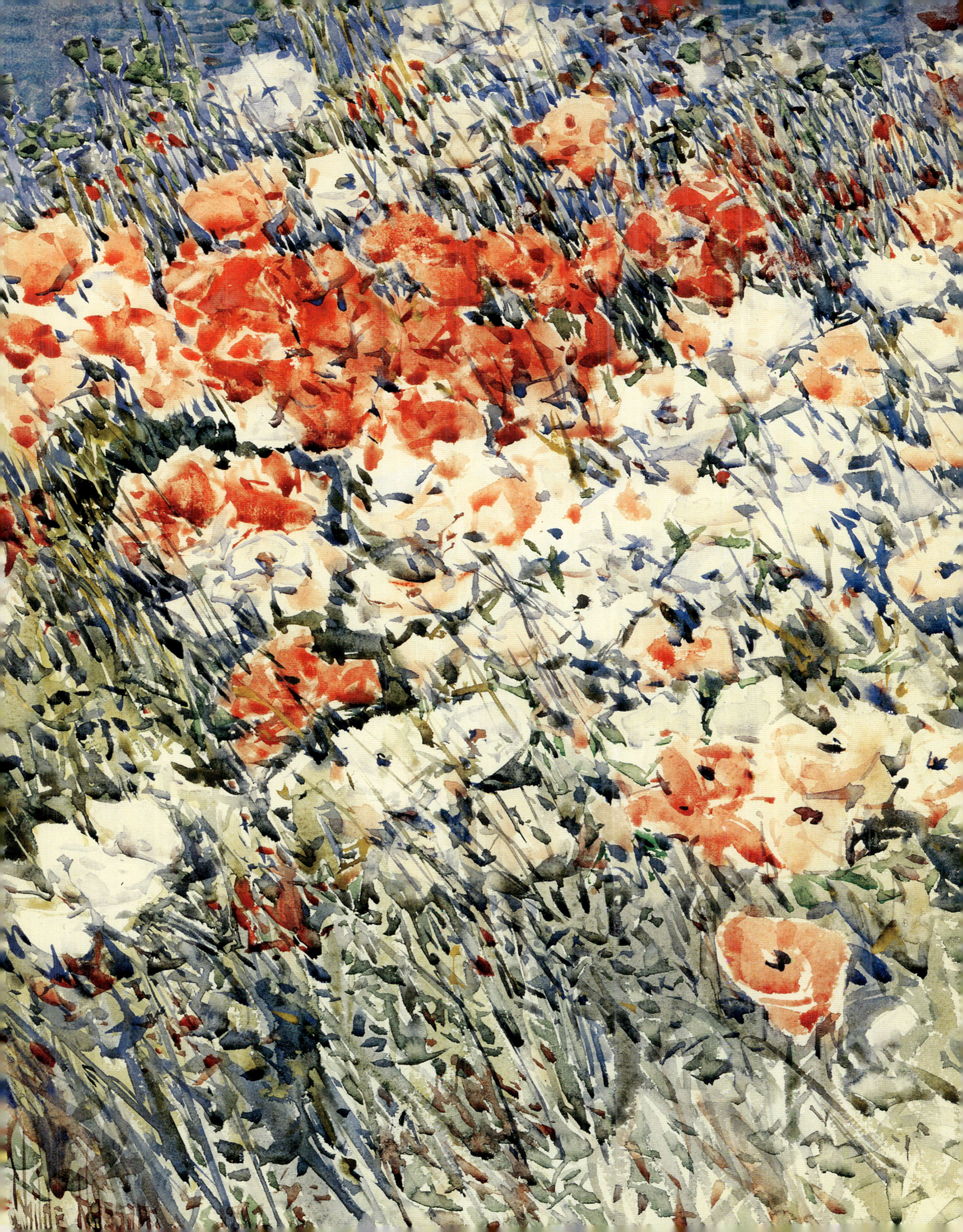

box hedges swirled into patterned parterres filled with coloured gravel, and stone-edged mirrors of water. Grand restorations and recreations of the French Garden were masterminded in no less than 6,000 gardens worldwide by Achille Duchene. The sheer scale and grandeur of these designs was copied around the world in the gardens of the seriously wealthy, and manifested in floral clocks and bedding in a multitude of municipal parks. What a contrast to Monet and Renoir. Monet, whose first task had been to uproot the neat box hedging that patterned his gardens at Giverny, looked forward with a choice palette of trees, shrubs and flowers and a sinuous watery mirror, elaborated with flowering nymphs in the form of waterlilies. Renoir safeguarded a Mediterranean working garden whose olives dated back a thousand years or terraces some of which were created by the Romans.

Essentially the English garden takes two forms – the cottage garden with roses round the door and a mass of flowers such as delphiniums and hollyhocks, a fruit orchard and supersized vegetables that thrive in the English maritime climate. On the other hand the English landscape garden, a beautiful and sublime classical landscape of pasture, trees and serpentine lakes sporting architectural gems, has been translated into 'le jardin anglais'. Gloriously hot summers and cold freezing winters make it difficult to translate European gardens to American soil, just as unrelenting drought has shaped the individualistic development of the Australian garden.

At the start of World War One, Fred McCubbin's three sons volunteered for active service. Hugh (who was wounded at Gallipolli) and Louis were enlisted, but Alexander was not accepted. Tragically, Fred's brother James was Chief Purser on the liner *The Lusitania* and was one of the 1195 fatalities when it was torpedoed off the coast of Ireland by a German U-boat in May 1915. 'Avenge the Lusitania' became a recruiting slogan on British posters, and as 123 American passengers were amongst the dead, the tragic sinking was the first step in bringing the Americans into the war. McCubbin joined Mrs. Alfred Deakin, the former Australian prime minister's wife, in organising volunteers to serve tea and buns to wounded servicemen on the lawns at the military base hospital in St Kilda Road, Melbourne. At the start of the war, the actress Ellen Terry came to Melbourne and Fontainebleau and McCubbin wrote: 'her visits make us forget our sad hearts.'

In 1915 Australian Arthur Streeton joined the Royal Army Medical Corps, and worked at the third London General Hospital in Wandsworth but his distress became so great that by 1917 he was discharged with the rank of corporal and deemed medically unfit. He recovered and Australia appointed him as an Official War Artist in the Australian Imperial Force. He travelled to France in 1918, where his paintings concentrated on the times away from the battlefield, vignettes of war-weary men making the best of their bleak surroundings. Back in Australia, two canvases by Rupert Bunny painted during 1915 and 1916, depict two women, firstly in leisured conversation on a garden bench, and then sitting at a table imbibing every last detail in a letter from the Front.

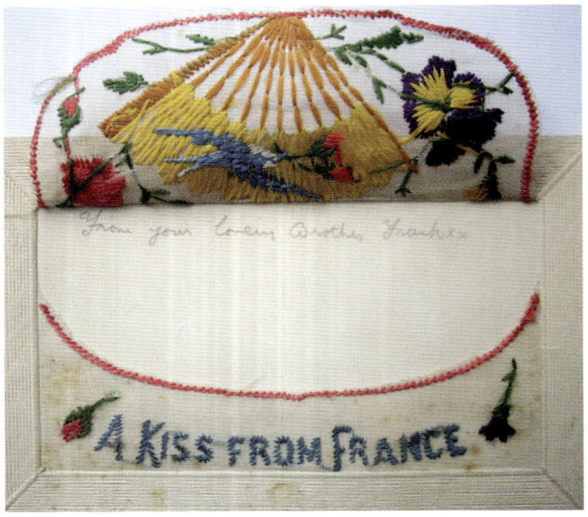

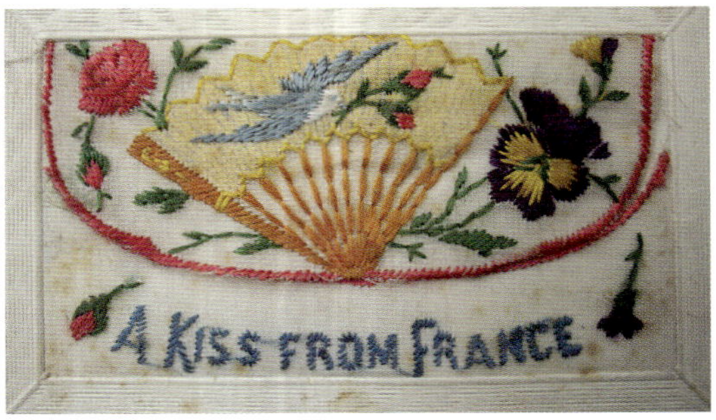

Young men from across the globe were called up to fight, leaving their loved ones left at home anxiously awaiting any news from the Front. This English Valentine was sent 'From your loveing brother Frank xx' embroidered with pansies for thoughts, roses for love and the dove that might bring peace. It was an ephemeral and poignant echo of the receipt of a violet which Renoir had picked near the wash-house at Les Collettes in 1916 and sent to his son Jean with a simple note 'To you. Renoir'. Outside the Stock Exchange in Melbourne Annie McCubbin and others set up stalls to raise money for the Anzac Appeal, selling hand-painted fans, some painted by Fred in watercolour and oil on cardboard and gum leaves, onto which they tied red, white and blue ribbons.

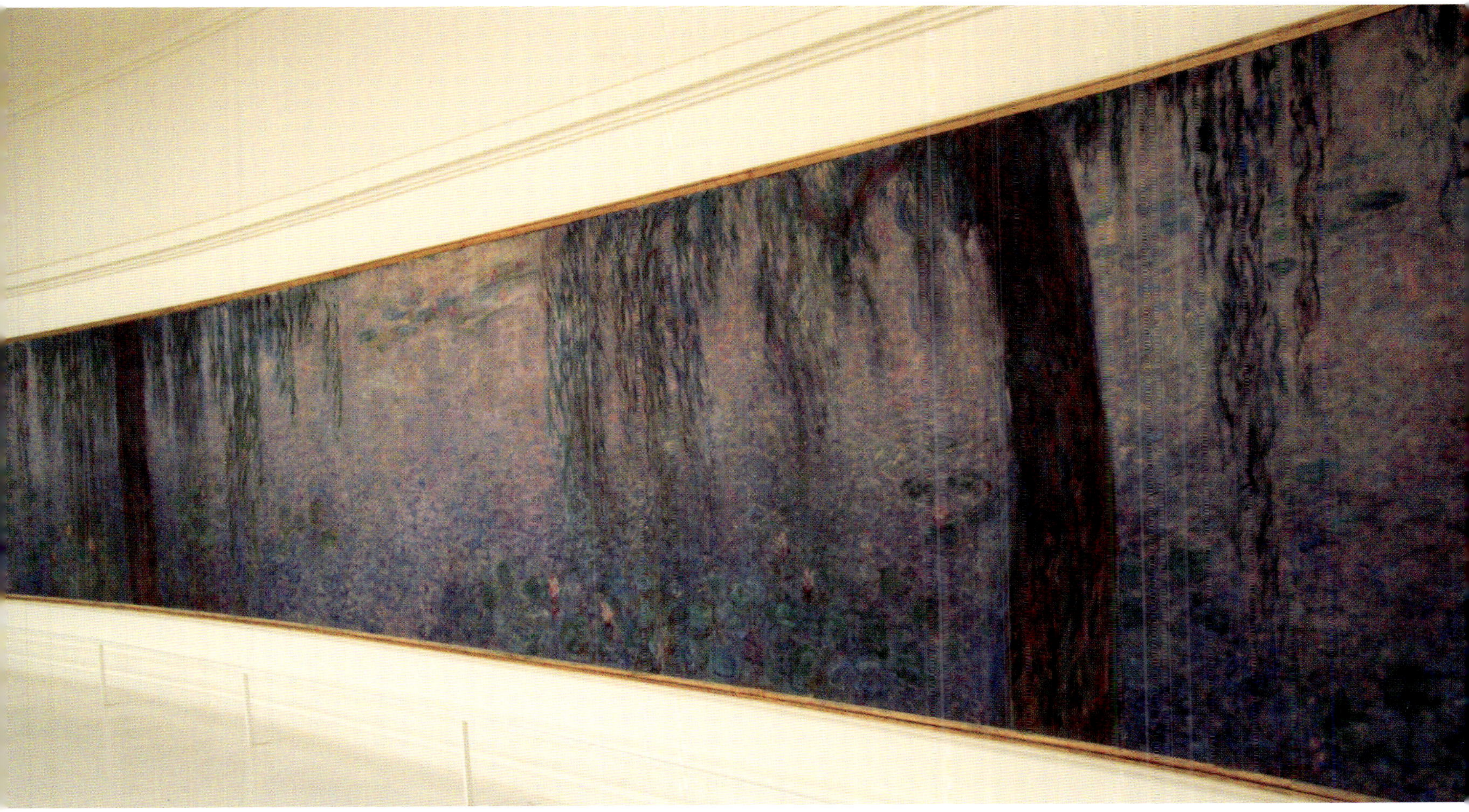

After John Russell's wife Marianna had died in 1908 he temporarily deserted Belle Ile, living in Paris and travelling with his only daughter. In 1912 he married an American singer, Caroline de Witt Merrill in Paris, but the outbreak of war drew them to England in 1915. His five sons, Sandro, Cédric, Alain, Lionel and Siward, all enlisted with the Allied Forces.

Pierre and Jean Renoir fought and were wounded, their mother Aline went to their rescue, she insisted on moving Jean and finding proper treatment thus saving his life. The emotional and physical toll led to her premature death.

The Giverny Art Colony disbanded with the exception of the Friesekes who stayed on throughout the war. Monet's stepson-in-law, Theodore Butler, took Marthe with the children, Lily and Jim, from Giverny to the safety of the United States. Monet stayed behind and was close enough to hear the battle sounds, he even sent fruit and vegetables from his gardens to the field hospitals. He refused to leave his beloved gardens and focused his energy into creating a series of works that could bear testament to the terrible human sacrifice. A third atelier was built to house the vast canvases that captured the course of the light reflected in his water gardens. He continued working on them until his death on 5th December 1926.

In England, Edwin Lutyens worked with the Imperial War Graves Commission to design suitable burial and memorial gardens for the many who had perished. On 19th July 1919 Prime Minister Lloyd George asked

Claude Monet, **Morning with Willows**. *Oil on canvas, three sections each 200 x 425cm (80 x 170in.), 1916-1926*

Monet refused to leave his house and gardens at Giverny during World War I despite being able to hear gunfire from the nearby battlefields. Too old to fight, he focused his patriotism and support into building his third atelier in 1916. Between this and the contemplation of his pond, the last ten years of his life were poured into the vast canvases that captured the course of light reflected second by second in the waters of his lower garden. After much discussion with his close friend Clemenceau he donated these Grandes Décorations as his memorial to the dead, but only after his own death. They were transferred to their final resting place in the oval basements of the Musée de l'Orangerie in Paris where you can experience the sensation of immersion amongst his trees and waterlilies.

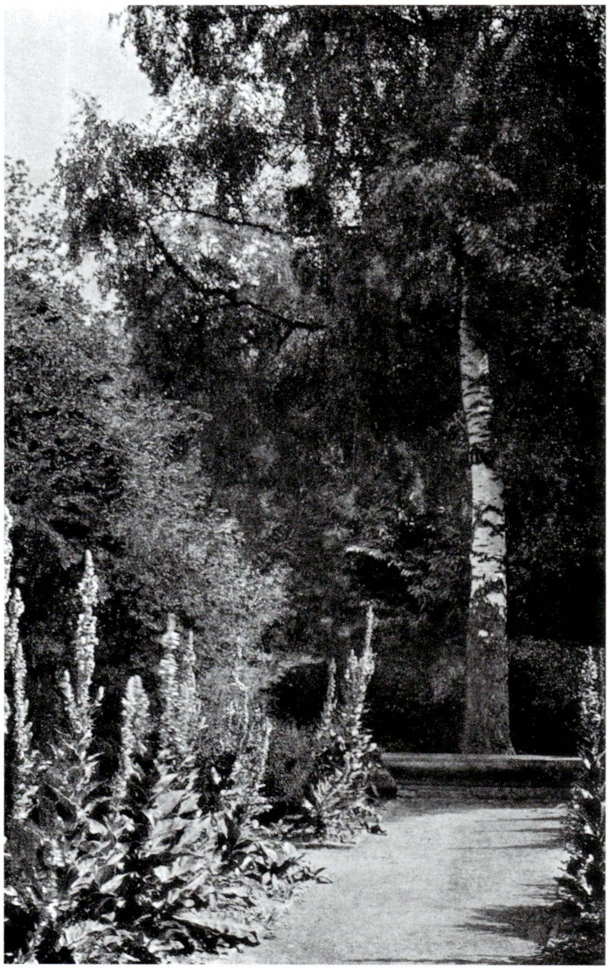

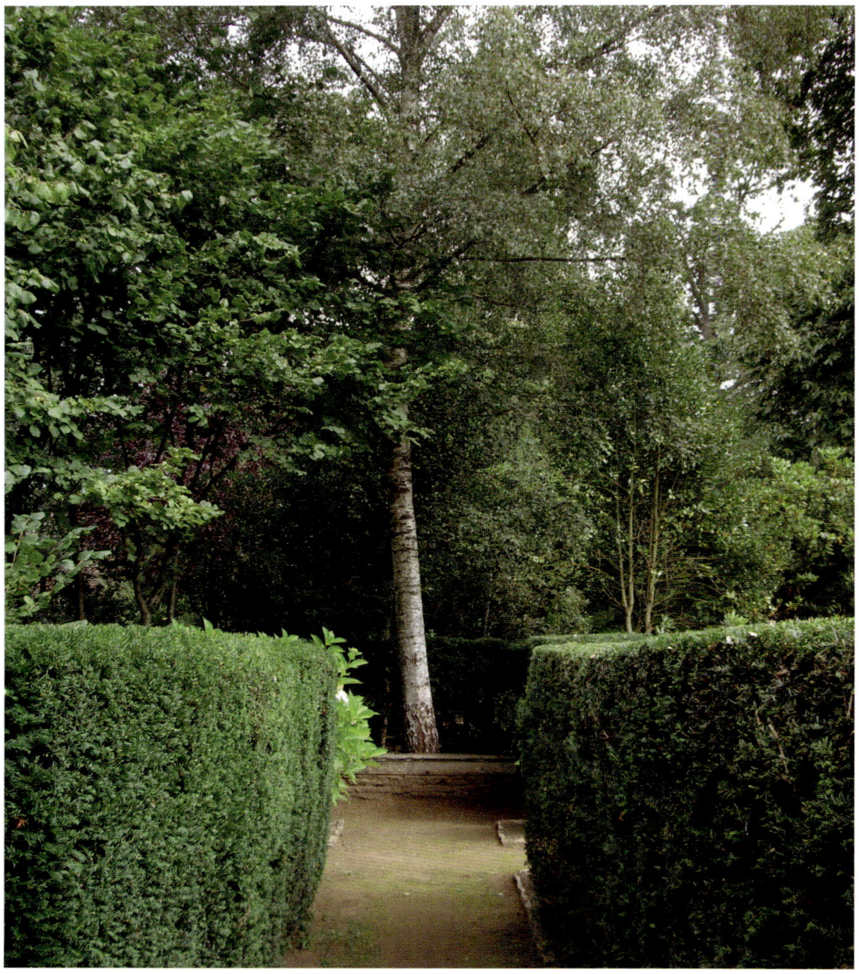

Above: *Gertrude Jekyll's photograph of the Cenotaph of Sigismunda. Named by a friend of Jekyll's, which she found 'so undoubtedly suitable to the monumental mass of Elm and to its somewhat funereal environment of weeping Birch and spire-like Mullein.' Its setting and name inspired Edwin Lutyens when he was called up to design a 'catafalque' for the war dead by Prime Minister Lloyd George on 19th July 1919.*

Right: *The Cenotaph of Sigismunda today, the elms long gone and the spires of the mullein replaced by clipped hedges but retaining a sense of tranquility.*

him to design a catafalque to stand in Whitehall. Lutyens knew he wanted a memorial that would resonate with all faiths and nations, and he recalled a quiet corner at Munstead Wood where there was a shaped stone seat under a birch tree. A friend of Jekyll's had called it the Cenotaph of Sigismunda, and thus inspired, Lutyens embarked on what Jane Brown describes in *Lutyens and the Edwardians* as his 'mathematical pilgrimage in the quest of the sublime', the powerful yet neutral Cenotaph.

Travelling to Whitehall or to the many war grave sites was an impossibility for the bereaved across the world, however, Newman Flower, a journalist visiting the battlefields in 1919 was moved by the drifts of poppies and other wild flowers that blanketed the ground. Later that year, he returned to the site to collect their seed heads. Flower planted his own 'War Garden' about which he wrote: 'I keep the patch very carefully weeded so that no vagrant wild flowers shall come in and assume a glory they have never earned. I take the poppy seed each year at the end of the Summer and sow it again in the patch at Springtime, lest the old parent poppies should not have cast the ground as heavily as I would like with their seed. I am not taking any chances of this War Garden dying out. And every poppy – every flower drew its ancestry from the trenches.' Through his newspaper columns he invited people to write to him for seeds to sow in his own war garden in remembrance of where their loved ones had died. The seeds were despatched to the four corners of the world.

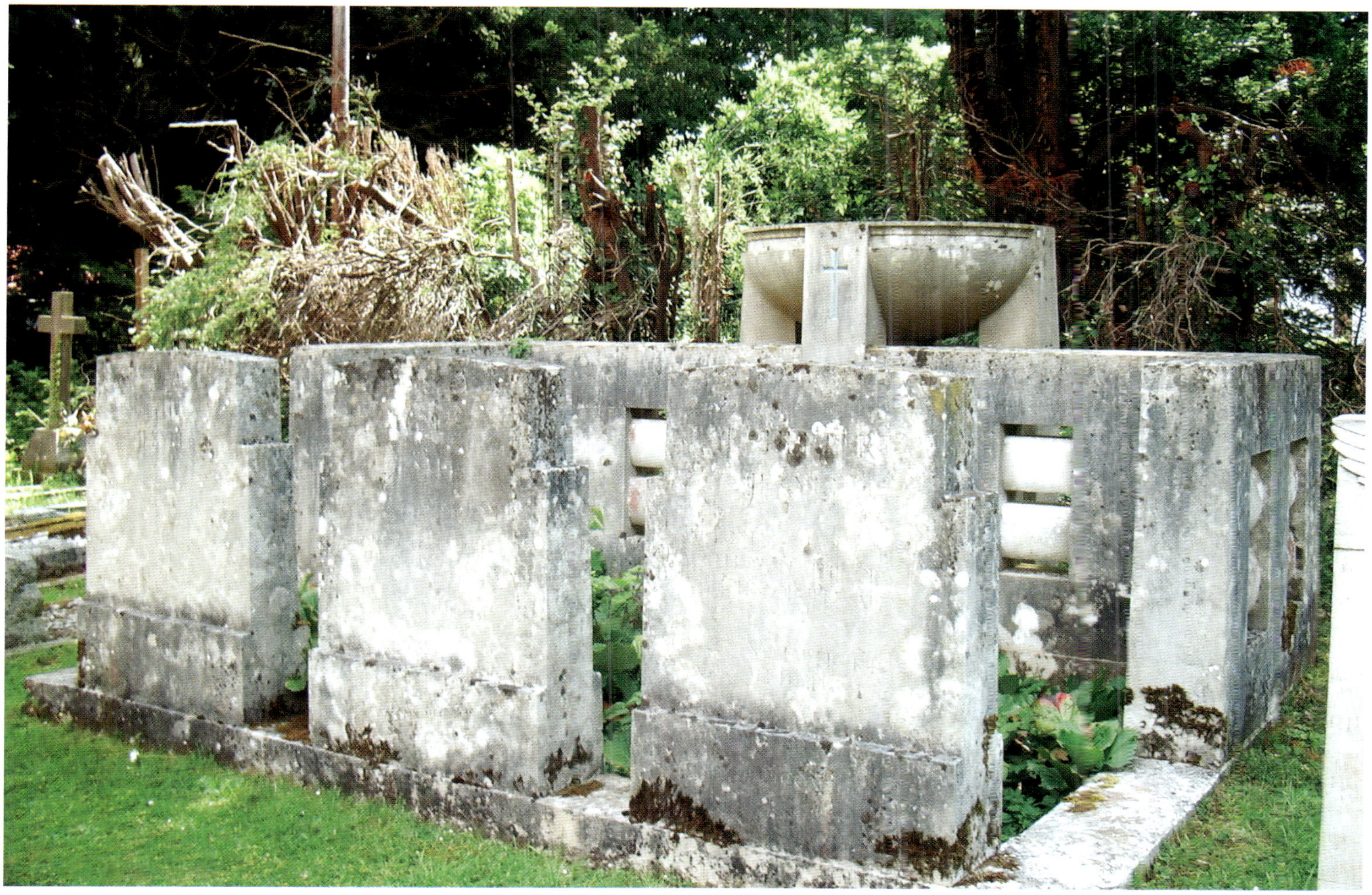

For Monet, his gardens had protected him from the realities of both the war and post-war France. He continued to paint frenetically, battling with increasingly poor sight, and to destroy work that displeased him. Nonetheless the water lilies and willows, the rising and dying sun, and the passage of clouds, continued to cover the vast stretched canvases under the watchful, loving eyes of Clemenceau and Blanche Monet. Weeks after Monet's death the *Grandes Décorations* were transferred from his third atelier to their final resting place in the oval basement of the Orangerie in Paris. Monet once said: 'To me the motif itself is an insignificant factor; what I want to reproduce is what lies between the motif and me.' The *Grandes Décorations,* more popularly known as *Les Nymphéas* allow you to submerge yourself between Monet and his motifs.

An opal-hearted country,
A wilful, lavish land –
All you who have not loved her,
You will not understand –
Though earth holds many splendours,
Wherever I may die,
I know to what brown country
My homing thoughts will fly.

Dorothea McKellar *My Country*

Gertrude Jekyll's grave at her local church, St John the Baptist, Busbridge, Surrey, designed by Edwin Lutyens and planted with her favourite flowers. It carries the simple words

GERTRUDE JEKYLL
29TH NOVEMBER 1843
8TH DECEMBER 1932
ARTIST
GARDENER
CRAFTSWOMAN

INDEX OF PLANT NAMES

GENERAL INDEX

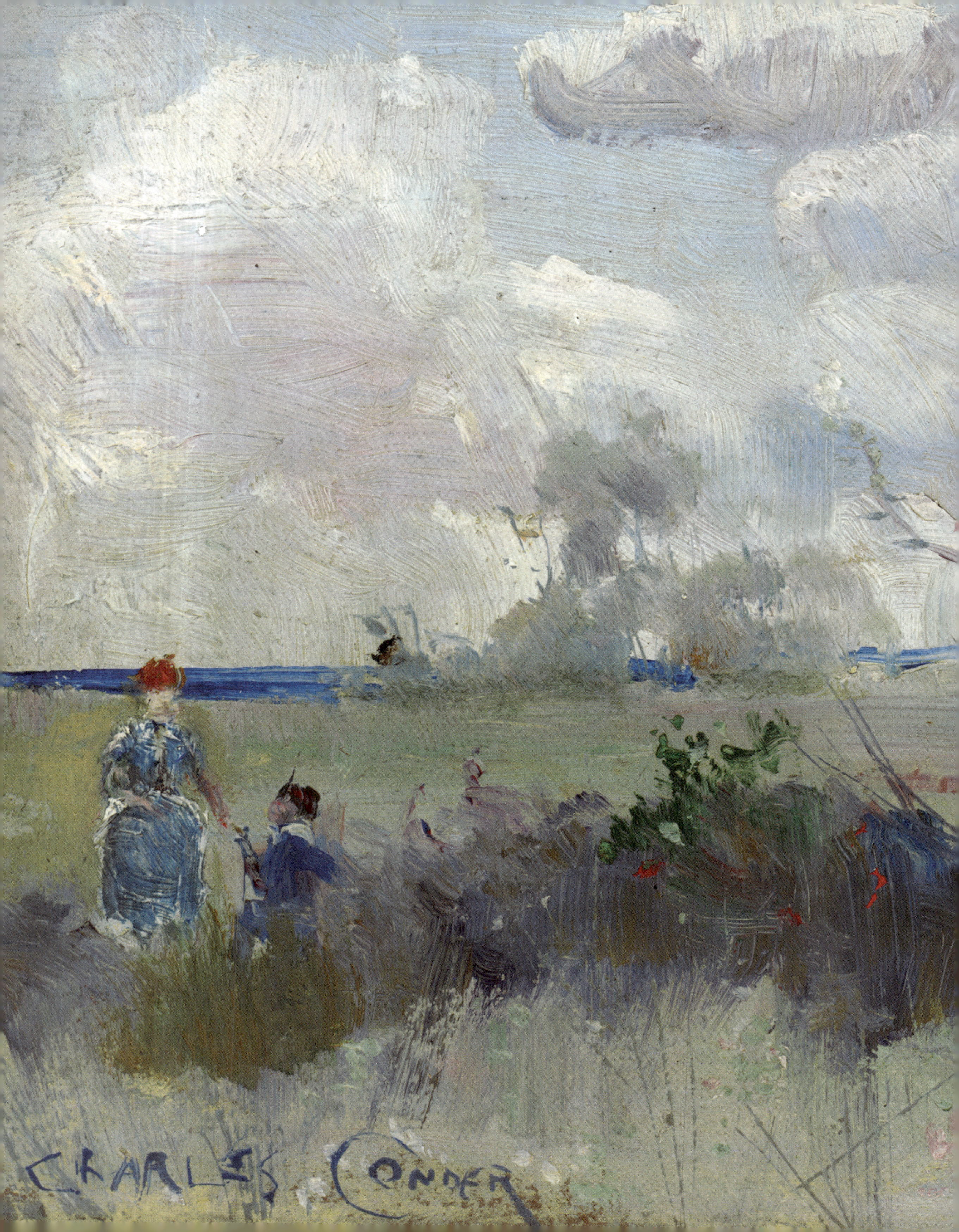
CHARLES CONDER